LL 8/97

THE MISSING PIECE

THE
MISSING PIECE

Solving the Puzzle of Self

CLAUDIA BLACK, Ph.D.
LESLIE DROZD, Ph.D.

BALLANTINE BOOKS
New York

Copyright © 1995 by Claudia Black and Leslie Drozd
Illustrations copyright © 1995 by Judith S. Cummins

Grateful acknowledgment is made to the following for permission
to reprint material:
Harcourt Brace & Company and Faber and Faber Ltd.: Excerpt from "East Coker" in FOUR QUARTETS by T.S. Eliot. Copyright 1943 by T.S. Eliot and renewed 1971 by Esme Valerie Eliot. "East Coker" is published in Great Britain in COLLECTED POEMS 1909–1962 by T.S. Eliot. Reprinted by permission of Harcourt Brace & Company and Faber and Faber Ltd.
Cathy Joseph: "Mommy Me" by Cathy Joseph. Copyright © 1995 by Cathy Joseph.
Libby Roderick: Excerpt from the lyrics of "How Could Anyone" words and music by Libby Roderick. © 1988 Libby Roderick Music. From the recording IF YOU SEE A DREAM. Available through Turtle Island Records, P.O. Box 203294, Anchorage, AK 99520, (907) 278-6817.

Library of Congress Cataloging-in-Publication Data
Black, Claudia.
The missing piece : solving the puzzle of self / Claudia Black, Leslie Drozd.
p. cm.
Includes bibliographical references.
ISBN 0-345-37668-4
1. Self-perception. 2. Self-management (Psychology) 3. Self-psychology.
I. Drozd, Leslie. II. Title.
BF697.5.S43B57 1995
158'.1—dc20
95-23080
CIP

Book design by Ruth Kolbert

Manufactured in the United States of America

First Edition: August 1995

10 9 8 7 6 5 4 3 2

THIS BOOK IS LOVINGLY DEDICATED

T O

my many mothers:
Mom, for her stability and strength;
Charlotte, for a place of safety and acceptance;
Lois, for her quiet love.

—CLAUDIA BLACK

T O

Dan and Jaime
for their love and patience
for asking "Why?"
for their dedication to speaking up for what they believe in,
and for being not only my children, but my teachers.

—LESLIE DROZD

CONTENTS

ACKNOWLEDGMENTS

The Missing Piece would not be what it is today without the participants in Missing Piece groups,[1] which were originated by Leslie in 1984. It is with much appreciation that we also dedicate this book to each and every one of you. We couldn't have done this without you!

Many thanks to Cheryl D. Woodruff, executive editor, for her challenging questions and dedication to perfection — both have made this book what it is today. Thanks to Barbara Shor for her thoughtful line editing and to Leah Odze, assistant editor, for her outstanding coordination of the many pieces of this book. Much appreciation as well goes to Amy Morris for her endless hours of typing and retyping the text in the face of demanding deadlines.

The research that this book is based upon was done with the assistance of Connie Dalenberg of the California School of Professional Psychology, San Diego. Larry Hedges of the Newport Psychoanalytic Institute provided encouragement and support in the initial conceptual stages of this book. Betty Bosdell of Vista, California has mentored both of us in learning about parts of self and Voice Dialogue.

Along our own individual paths to find our own "missing pieces," we have both had many teachers who have sometimes directly and sometimes indirectly influenced this book. We have each individually thanked our individual and joint circles of mentors and friends in the Notes section in the back of this book.[2]

Claudia and Leslie would like to offer a mutual thank-you to each other — to Leslie for continuing to speak her truth and daring to live it, and to Claudia for helping to strengthen the bond of friendship throughout the journey shared in writing *The Missing Piece.*

Introduction

Are there many selves inside you competing to be heard? Do these selves leave you feeling fragmented and disjointed, or integrated and whole? Do you know who you *really* are? Or do you just fake it and show a finely crafted mask to the world? If so, this book is for you.

In *The Missing Piece: Solving the Puzzle of Self*, we take you on a journey to the depths of self, a journey to get to know yourself better. Your sense of self is made up of all that you are and all that you do. And like a puzzle your self has many parts.

You are not just one characteristic. There are in fact many aspects of you. Some that you own or know something about and have learned to live with. Some that you disown and keep hidden even though you know something about them. And still other parts of you remain unknown—even to you! Parts of you are indeed missing, buried deep within the recesses of your unconscious.

The parts of you that you own, like, and use every day are easy to identify. Although your disowned parts take some courage to face and integrate, they, too, can be put to good use. Then there are the unknown parts. These seem by definition undiscoverable at this point in time. However, we've found a way for you to get to know all of you—the owned parts, the disowned parts, and even the unknown parts of you.

In this book we take you on a journey to get to know yourself better. The journey is an active process that calls for you to do exercises in which you learn to look at yourself over and over again in the many mirrors you hold up to yourself. Throughout the book we challenge you to move deeper and deeper into the puzzle called Self.

There are many, many kinds, shapes, and sizes of puzzles. But no matter whether it's a thousand-piece jigsaw, a crossword, or a three-dimensional puzzle, by participating actively in this book, you'll learn how to assemble yourself into wholeness.

The Missing Piece grew out of Claudia's work as an educator and nationally known lecturer teamed with Leslie's work as a clinical psychologist and professor. Whether in an audience of a thousand, in a classroom, or in a session with an individual client, as people spoke about their personal lives, we kept hearing the same message over and over: "My life is like a play. It doesn't seem real. Inside there's an emptiness, a hollowness. It feels like something's missing. It feels like there's a missing piece."

Although this book is rooted in both developmental and self psychology and Leslie's research into sense of self, it has been written for the general reader, to help you clearly and easily understand what may appear to be complex psychological phenomena.

This book is not another way of shining the armor of the "Me! Me! Me!" generation. It will not lead you to be more selfish. Rather it will lead you to be more self-caring. Good mental health is about connecting with others as well as with self. This book provides the tools you need to achieve this. It offers solutions that will help you better connect with and get along with others *outside* of you as you get to know all the parts *inside* of you. Along the way we will guide you through a spiral process into the depths of self to discover unknown treasures, unknown parts of yourself. Slowly but surely you will learn how to hold those parts up to the light of day, to name them, to get to know them, and to help each and every part of you to work together.

The Missing Piece will move you along a path from questions to answers and then from answers to action. It's about achieving a sense of balance between your inner and outer worlds. It's about forging lasting bonds between all the aspects of you. It's about getting unstuck in your life in the here and now. It's about learning from the past and moving on. It's about integration and wholeness.

WHAT YOU WILL FIND HERE

In the first chapter of *The Missing Piece* we invite you to take your first steps on the Spiral Path of Healing. We provide you with "Tools for the Journey." We help you get to know your strengths, your resiliency, and your defenses. These are your inner allies, and it's helpful to be able to call on them when you need them.

Next we help you figure out what to do when your self-exploration leaves you feeling stuck or overwhelmed. We teach you how to get some distance from your problems. We help you gain better control over the process of stretching your awareness a little bit at a time so that you can build stronger muscles for dealing with your feelings. This book is a workout, but it's doable. We don't want you to strain or tear your muscles. We simply want you to stretch and strengthen them so that you can begin to move and act in new and more healthful ways. It took you many years to develop the patterns that govern your life today, and it will take a while to undo the ones you choose to work with. But we promise that you will see progress— movement toward wholeness.

In chapter 2, "How Pieces End Up Missing," we help you take a brief look at the past to see how you originally lost those pieces of self. We then ask you to move back into the present and look into the mirror of Self. It is our philosophy that it does no good to look at the past unless you're specifically trying to change something that's not working for you today. Otherwise looking at the past is fruitless and may even be harmful. But with your feet firmly planted in the here and now, and your pack of tools for the journey on your back, you should find this trip into your past a healing adventure.

In chapter 3, "Naming the Pieces," we take you on a journey to name all the parts of you through a series of exercises, one stepping-stone at a time. By the end of the chapter you will have discovered the key to this whole process—how to look inside, not outside, for your answers. You will have begun to sense the richness inside of you, in the depths of your puzzle of Self.

In chapter 4, "Your Family Portrait," we have you look at what we call your external family, the context in which you were raised as a child that still affects the way you live today. Through a series of gentle exercises we take you back to the times when some of the pieces of your puzzle of Self may have first been missing. We place you in a time capsule and send you back into your past, where we help you look at some of your woundedness. Not to worry. We all have wounds, some of us more than others. No one had a perfect childhood. If yours was much less perfect than others, this section of the book may very well open up some old wounds. But this is why we provide you with a bag of tools for healing at the beginning of the book. Now is when you need to remember to use them. You know how the pieces ended up missing, and in naming all the parts of you, you see clearly who you are today.

In chapter 5 we offer you a road map for healing. We call it "The Spiral Path" because we believe that no healing process is linear. Healing is a lifelong journey of initiation—sometimes more intense, sometimes less so. On this journey we find ourselves passing by the same places again and again, moving round and round the spiral but each time at a different level with the benefit of a new and elevated perspective. There are definable signposts along the Spiral Path that will help you identify which stage of the healing process you're in and encourage you to keep on moving.

With your map of the Spiral Path firmly in hand, chapter 6, "A First Look Inside," gives you an initial introduction to some of the most common parts of self: the protector, the nurturer, the wounded child, the innocent child, the victim, the critic, and so on. You may find that you don't have all of these parts. This is perfectly okay. What's important here is that you get to know what's going on inside you—not us, you! *You know you best.* Never forget that your missing pieces are found within you, not outside you.

As we spiral into chapter 7, "Getting to Know You," you will begin to meet all your parts on a more intimate level. Here we ask you to hold each part up to the light and to discover what a gem each part is—so many facets, so many angles, so much depth and richness of hue.

Interestingly enough, as you get to know each part separately, you will come to feel more and more whole. And as you do, in chapter 8, "Coming Full Circle," we introduce you to the idea of holding frequent internal-family meetings and dialogues between parts of you and the whole of you. After all, you probably talk to yourself anyhow—we're just giving you an excuse to do so. In fact we're encouraging you to do it, because as you do, you will come to feel more and more whole, more and more integrated, more and more as though you've found the missing pieces of your puzzle of Self.

Chapter 9, "Making It Happen," offers practical examples of how and when to access the various parts of yourself in order to feel more empowered as you move through your day.

In chapter 10, "The Empowered Self," we ask you to feel what it's like to operate from a place of integration, to have an empowered self. If you follow the process in this book—if you work it—it will work for you.

But please don't think that this process has to be all work. We hope you have fun with it as well. After all, isn't life just one big "parts party," in which a part of me is interacting with a part of you? Our whole thesis is based on our belief that if you don't know all of the parts of your self—the Beauty and the Beast within you—you might experience life not as a "parts party" but as a "parts war." That's why we want you to get to know all of you, one part at a time.

We want the parts of you that have been repressed or exiled to emerge, slowly and carefully, one at a time, until you see and get to know them in the light of day. Have you ever tried to tell a teenage boy, for example, not to do something and to be quiet? Our hunch is that he did exactly the opposite. He rebelled. The same process goes on with the various parts of you. If you tell them to be quiet and drive them underground, they will run your life from the deep crevices of your being.

The best thing to do with both teenagers and unruly parts of one-self is to invite them out—slowly, one at a time. Set proper limits on them. Set boundaries. Listen to them. Your parts may simply want to see the light of day, to have a voice in your life. You don't have to do everything they say. After all, they're only parts of you, not the whole. We don't want them to take over. We simply want you to treat them with the respect you'd offer any other part of you. They may have something useful to say.

As you bring each of the parts of you out into the open, you will discover that you have choices in your life. Free the enslaved parts of you. Let them see the light. Then and only then will they be able to work for you instead of against you.

In chapter 11 we explore "The Spiritual Peace." We believe that it is not until you assemble all the missing pieces of your Self puzzle that you will indeed find the spiritual piece—a sense of inner peace—a feeling of wholeness, a sense of connectedness within self and with others. Is it possible that external peace is the step that follows after finding and integrating one's internal pieces? Is it possible that world peace has eluded us so often in our history because we've been looking outside ourselves to find it while all along the real answers have been waiting within each and every one of us?

By the time you come to the end of *The Missing Piece: Solving the Puzzle of Self*, it is our hope that you will already be living in harmony with others and with your selves. It is our hope that you will be relying less on others to define who you are. That you will have become more authentic and have more choice over which part is out when. That you will have found a better ability to be in relationship and in solitude. And, above all, that you will have discovered unsuspected resources and wisdom inside yourself.

We hope, too, that you will be better able to hold the energy of opposites. That you will be able to see and function effectively in the gray areas of your life. That you will have found room for differences. Lastly it is our hope that you will now experience yourself as lighter, more energetic, with more color, intensity, and depth to your life. These are the gifts that you will give yourself as you examine and get to know all the parts of your Self puzzle.

PART ONE

GETTING READY

CHAPTER 1

Tools for the Journey

Many of us at some time in our lives have felt as though something is missing. Sometimes this emptiness comes and goes in waves. Sometimes it feels as though we've fallen into a never-ending hole. Most of us go searching outside of ourselves for something to fill this emptiness. Our society promotes that. Just look at the ads on TV or on billboards. If you wear this, smoke this, drink this, associate with this group, you'll feel better. Guaranteed. If only our family was like the Brady Bunch or the Cosby family, then we'd be okay; then it wouldn't feel like something was missing.

We tell ourselves, *Maybe if I find the right partner, my life will be better. Or If only I can get out of this marriage, my life will be better. Or If only I had a better job . . . Or If only I had a job. Maybe that's what's missing. Maybe that's the cause of the emptiness I feel deep inside.*

Have you ever wondered where this sense of emptiness came from and why you didn't feel whole? So many of us wonder who or what to blame as we look for answers, look for the missing piece. We wonder, *What is it that'll make me feel whole?*

Let's begin by imagining a crowded room with everyone speaking at once. The volume increases steadily. A gavel sounds futilely. A shrill voice rises above the din: "Can somebody please bring this meeting to order?"

Have you ever felt as though there were a meeting like this going on inside your head? As though there were many, many parts of you, and each of them had an opinion about everything. And worse yet, they were all speaking up at once. We're not talking about hearing voices. We're talking about people like you and me who have many parts of self that talk to us and vie for attention inside our heads.

Shelly recently told us about a time when she was driving home from work feeling that she'd had a good day. "I felt calm and relaxed. I was even singing in the car. But once I got home, all it took was fifteen seconds before I found myself acting like a crazy person. I was screaming about the toys that were all over the place, angry because I'd stumbled over my oldest child's shoes, which were left in the middle of the sidewalk. I nearly ran over the bicycle that was lying on the driveway. How could my calmness have been undone so quickly? What happened to me? Which one is the real me—the calm one or this other 'crazy person'? What's going on inside of me?"

For quite a while Alyce had been dating a man who was "the love of her life." At work, everyone admired Tom. The consensus among Alyce's friends was that he was the star of any social gathering. But in the privacy of the bedroom "another Tom" appeared. *Where did Mr. Take Charge—I Can Handle Anything go?* Alyce often wondered. "Tom is pure rocket fuel at work. But that's not the man I sleep with. In the bedroom I always have to take the initiative. It's as though he's two different people. I want the part that shines in the world to come into the bedroom, at least some of the time, or this just isn't going to last."

As Michael, a fast-track entrepreneur, headed home for the holidays, he found himself musing over how well things had gone in the past few months. He'd acquired a mid-sized computer company, and earnings for the last quarter were up. He'd been able to give a year-end bonus to his employees for the first time ever. *What an achievement! Things are going well, and I feel great,* he thought.

But within minutes of climbing into his parents' car at the airport, Michael no longer felt accomplished. His mother had begun by asking him why he never called his sister. Then his father had taken over with, "Put on quite a few extra pounds, there, eh, son? And jeez, what happened to all your hair?" Both parents were critical of Michael's attire. He'd worn sweats on the airplane. After all, his parents were both turned out in their Sunday best, although it was only seven A.M.

Michael found himself retreating into himself just the way he'd done as an adolescent. He began to ask himself, *How can I be so competent at work—someone that everyone envies—but when I come home, my opinions never count and I feel as if I'm always wrong?*

Michael's co-workers would never have imagined their leader's terrifying inner battle with his frightened secret self—the self that was guaranteed to receive his parents' disapproval without question.

Most of us can identify to one degree or another with Michael or Shelly or Alyce. We all know that deep inside us there is a core self. But there are times when we wonder, *Who made me do that?* or *Who said that?* Most of us know we each have one self—There's one you, one Claudia, one Leslie. Yet we also have multiple selves. This doesn't mean that we're schizophrenics or multiple personalities. Most of us are simply whole people who contain within our one sense of self multiple parts that take over from time to time, depending on the circumstances.

Sometimes there are competing parts of self, and sometimes parts that work together in unison. We know some of these parts better than we know others. Some we show to the world; others we keep hidden inside.

Let's approach this from another angle. How about using your imagination for a few minutes? Make yourself comfortable before you can do the following:

THE "IN AND OUT" BOX

Imagine that you have an old shoe box, or any box with a lid. Now imagine that you have a stack of magazines. In your mind's eye visualize yourself going through those magazines and cutting out the pictures and words that best describe the you the world is able to see. Paste these on the outside of the box. The images and words on the outside of the box represent the you that you show to the world.

Now stop for a few moments and pretend that you're looking inside the box. Does it appear to be empty? If the outside of the box represents the outside part of you, then the inside of the box represents the inside of you. We're willing to bet that the emptiness is only an illusion, that there are some things you keep hidden deep inside you—parts of you that you don't show to the world, certainly not to the clerk at the market. Perhaps not even to your best friend or partner.

Ask yourself, *What belongs inside the box—the box called "me"? What do I keep hidden from those around me?*

For example, do you show your anger to others? Do you

show your fear or sadness? Do you show your insecurities, your vulnerabilities? Do you show your playful side, your competent side, your sensuous side, your creative side? Do you let your jealous part out often?

Once again, visualize cutting out pictures or words from your magazines. This time they represent the parts of you that you keep hidden from the world. You can draw things, too, and write down words that come to mind, especially if you can't find them in the magazines. All of these things go inside the box. Place them there in your mind's eye.

When you're done, stand back for just a moment to get a new perspective. Look at the box—the inside and the outside. It's you—the parts that you show to the world *and* the parts that you keep hidden inside the box.

All of the words and all of the pictures you've used to describe your inside and your outside represent the many parts of you.

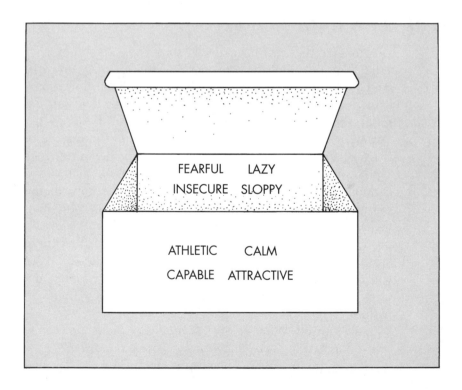

The journey to find the missing pieces is rather like the Greek myth about the nymph Pandora.[1] Hidden inside the box were all the parts of Pandora that she was trying to avoid, the parts of her that she had disowned. It was those hidden and buried parts that were giving Pandora trouble. When she first opened the box, all of the hidden parts came storming out.

This is the part of the story that most of us know, but there's more. As those parts were exposed to the light, as she explored the hidden pieces, she made her way to the bottom of the box, where she found that which had been missing in her life—hope. As she explored all of the hidden pieces, she found her key to wholeness. When you open the Pandora's box within you, you will find many, many rich and wonderful parts of you—parts that hold the key to your wholeness. And we believe you will find hope at the bottom of the box just like Pandora did.

It's the thesis of this book that you can't be whole until you have learned about yourself, about all of your selves—the parts that live outside and the parts that live inside the box. We're expanding another ancient Greek piece of psychological wisdom, "Know thyself," to "Know thy selves." We want you to take each piece of the Self puzzle and examine it in the light. We want you to get to know you better.

THE CHALLENGE OF THE JOURNEY

It's so easy to move through life simply reacting to outside forces, to fall into alignment with the circumscribed roles our family, culture, and gender have cast us into—even though we each have our unique personal variations on these themes. All this has led us to develop both strengths and hidden fears. Yet if we can simply slow down long enough to be still and listen to our inner self, most of us come to realize that our lives seem to have become an act, a role-play. At such times we feel separate and apart from the rest of the world. We aren't clear about who we are or what we want. Everything seems up for grabs. However, it's during these times of greatest confusion that we encounter our greatest opportunities for change and growth. But to take advantage of these times, we need a special set of tools with which to explore the many aspects of self and our true desires.

So at this point we'd like to take you on a journey to get to know the many parts of you, and through this exploration to come to get to know the whole of you. On this inner journey you'll spend some time looking in the mirror of Self. There you'll discover that the mirror reflects both the you others see as well as those hidden parts of you way deep down inside. As you look in the mirror, please try to develop a sense of compassion for yourself—to recognize your real strengths in those places where you've only seen weaknesses up to now. It's our hope that during this inner journey you'll become a better friend to yourself—to all of your selves—rather than continuing to be your own best critic or worst enemy.

Before we hit the road, we first have to get ready for the journey.

How do you go about preparing for a trip? Do you gather information from others who have been there, or do you prefer to fly blind? Do you acquire maps and consider various routes, or do you spontaneously jump in the car and take off?

While it can be a lot of fun to just jump in the car and not even know which direction you're heading in, this particular journey into the depths of self requires a bit of thoughtful preparation. For many of us life has not been safe. As you embark on your healing process, we want you to feel grounded and a deep sense of security.

Doing the Exercises

Throughout this book we will be offering you a smorgasbord of exercises. But we'd like you to remember that the true value of the exercises lies in doing them, not just reading about them. This is the time to grab a notebook, diary, or journal. Many exercises require reflection. Some require writing. So please keep your journal nearby to record your questions, answers, and reflections.

We realize the process of doing exercises may be new for many of you. We simply ask that you keep an open mind and a sense of adventure. We not only believe you're going to learn a lot about your selves, we're convinced that you'll have fun doing it as well. You can approach these exercises in many different ways. Some people read a chapter first and then go back and do each one of the exercises. Others do the exercises as they go through the chapter. Still others pick some exercises to do and skip others. Ideally we'd like you at least to try each exercise. It's your choice as to how you go about it, but whichever way you choose, please remember that this process doesn't offer any magical quick fixes. It has been our experience that this book will work best for you if you work it.

Because we want this journey to be a safe one for you, we have gathered together nine tools for you to put in your tool bag to help you on your journey:

1. Motivation
2. Commitment
3. Strengths
4. Healthy defenses
5. Firm, not rigid, boundaries
6. Creating a safe space
7. Being present, grounded, and balanced
8. Gaining distance and perspective
9. Be-ing

Now let's look at each of the tools one by one.

1. MOTIVATION

Most of us approach the challenge of the growth process with some ambivalence. It's perfectly normal for part of you to want to have things change in your life while part of you feels too scared to let change happen. For example part of you probably wants to show up at a therapist's office for your first appointment, while part of you doesn't. This is called resistance. It's quite normal, but you need to be motivated to get past it.

The motivation that you feel at first may be external, for example your partner may no longer be able to tolerate your workaholism, your short temper, your excessive drinking, or your avoidance of emotional intimacy. The fact is that she's had it, and this may be the motivation you need to look at yourself in the mirror. Money can also be a motivator for change. The promise of a job promotion, or the threat of being fired, may motivate you. A physical illness can be a motivator. Love can be a motivator. Children can motivate you. A birthday can motivate you.

For many of us the most effective motivator is often pain. Most of us resist changing our way of doing things unless it simply becomes too painful to keep on in the same old way. Realistically would you be reading this book if you didn't feel as though something was missing inside? Sometimes the pain that motivates you may be minimal, and sometimes it takes a real knock on the head to get you to move from your stuck place.

At some point in your journey, though, the source of your motivation needs to shift from external to internal. You, not someone or something outside of you, needs to become your motivating energy.

Joni came into therapy angry and scared. Her boss had told her she'd lose her job if she didn't change certain behaviors. He'd said that she was unrealistic in her expectations for her staff, that she was much too critical of them, and that she wasn't delegating work as she should. Her staff members were leaving their positions or asking to be transferred because they disliked her so much. However, because she had tenure, her boss was giving her one last opportunity to change—she had to go into therapy. Joni only agreed to this to save her job, but she felt as if she'd been sentenced to prison at hard labor.

As a result Joni spent her first six weeks in therapy being very hostile and closemouthed. But then a subtle change began to come over her. Gradually she heard some things from her therapist that made sense to her, that helped her to understand why she was the way she was. These understandings planted a seed of hope, and it became easier for her to communicate her feelings and to listen. In time she was able to make changes that translated into much more effective supervisory skills.

Initially Joni's motivation was external—pressure from work. But then it changed from her desire just to save her job to a real attempt to learn how to be more patient, less fearful, and more trusting of others. In time she grew to like herself better, and she knew that she was better liked.

Think of something you'd like to change in your life. It may be as simple as changing the furniture in your room, cleaning out your closets or the garage, or planting flowers. Then again it could be as complex as realizing it's time to change the way you relate to women, to men, to children, or to authority figures. Or maybe it's time to do something about that critical and penetrating inner voice that constantly nags at you. Could it be that you've finally seen how you get yourself into a position where your husband verbally abuses you over and over again? Or is it time for you to take a look at how you repeatedly get into situations where you lose control of your temper?

For just a moment go inside yourself to that place of *knowing* deep within you. Ask yourself what you would like to have change. Do you feel that you have some control over what you want to change? If it's a person, place, or thing outside you, you may have little, if any, control. And yet, if you're motivated, you can change your own behavior and attitudes toward whatever the issue may be. It might be hard to pull off, but it's doable so long as you stay motivated, and so long as you have support. So ask yourself, *What motivates me? What supports me?*

MOTIVATING YOURSELF FOR CHANGE

Identify five areas of change or risk taking that you've participated in over the past five years about which you feel proud—for example entering marriage counseling, making a job change, buying a home, enrolling in a class, exercising regularly, stopping smoking, and so on.

What motivators helped to fuel your willingness to take these risks?

Was it fear? Anger? Threat of job loss? Threat of relationship loss? Threat by an authority figure, such as a judge? Positive attraction? Desire for new skills?

Remind yourself that, whether the motivator was outside yourself or within yourself, whether it was based on positive self-esteem or on a more hurtful feeling, you still took a risk. And now you feel much better about yourself for having done so.

2. COMMITMENT

A second tool for your inner journey is a sense of commitment. We all make commitments to things that are important. A commitment is a pledge, a promise, an obligation, or an agreement to be involved in something, to follow through on something. We tend to pledge ourselves to a position on issues that are dear to our hearts.

It's important to understand that any exploration of self involves a confrontation with emotional pain to some degree. Before you venture forward, you need to be committed to walking through, not around and not away from, the pain. This is the only way to get past it once and for all. And to be able to do this, you need to be committed to finding the missing piece of your Self puzzle.

Many of the people we've worked with have problems making committments in the first place, and even more problems sticking with them. If you come from a troubled family where commitments were simply empty promises, then you may have difficulty with commitments as an adult. You may take one of two extreme positions on commitment. On the one hand you may rarely make and/or rarely keep commitments. On the other hand you may keep commitments no matter what, even after the circumstances under which the commitment was made have changed. You may even overcommit to things that are not humanly possible to achieve.

The commitment we're asking you to make to your integration is serious, but one that's realistic. We're asking you to make a promise, an internal commitment, between you and you. We're asking you to commit your time and your energy to work on healing the most important person in your life. We're asking you to entrust yourself with yourself.

Ask yourself, under what conditions do you work best? Do you work better doing a little something every day of the week—or at least five out of the seven days? Or do you work best working in blocks of time, say an hour or so once a week? The nature of the pattern that you establish in doing this work is not so important as long as it fits you, and as long as you stick with it consistently. It would be better to consistently spend ten minutes a day on this five days a week rather than an hour here or there, hit or miss. Consistency is what counts.

When you make a commitment—even if it's with yourself—it's helpful to put it in writing. It may also be helpful to share that commitment with another person. Sometimes it even helps to make the commitment part of a ritual. When we pledge ourselves to making a commitment "to love and to cherish someone till death do us part," we usually do that in writing, with others present, as part of a ritual.

Commitments also need to be renewed over and over again to keep them current. We once worked with a couple, Belle and John, who had been married for fifty years. Considering their age, their notion of commitment was quite progressive. Realizing that any marriage takes hard work and would have difficult times, Belle and John made a commitment that they would not abandon each other or a problem because they were scared or because they couldn't find a suitable answer right away. They pledged themselves to stay with each other for six months after one of them became aware of a problem in their partnership. They were committed to speaking up about the problem, to working with their partner to resolve it, and to seeking outside assistance if they were stuck. They had renewed their commitment to each other many times over the fifty years.

We recommend that you commit yourself to a similar philosophy before you set out to do work with your "internal family." We encourage you to renew your pledge to yourself from time to time, and even to alter the terms of your commitment if appropriate. We want you to be so committed to your healing process that you can stick with it when the going gets rough or when the process seems boring. As in any intimate relationship there will be times during this journey to the self when you feel a tender closeness with yourself as well as times when you feel a distance. There will be times of peace and times of great intensity. Sometimes you won't be working on yourself at all, and sometimes you'll be working very hard. This kind of fluctuation is normal. But this is also why a solid yet flexible commitment to yourself is an important tool to have in your bag.

3. STRENGTHS

Each one of your parts of self is valuable, although you may find that some of the pieces of the puzzle are more positive than others. Before looking at your internal family of selves in any depth, it's important that you first ground yourself in your strengths. Each of us is good at something. What are your specialties?

Resiliency[2]

One of the strengths that all human beings have is resiliency. Over the past decade or so psychologists have become interested in the characteristics of people who are particularly resilient to stress. They have discovered that there are sixteen threads that seem to wind through the stories of resilient children from troubled families. Cultivating these qualities can be of great help as we do the work on our internal family. Read through the following list and think about which of these characteristics describe you now or at any other point in your life:

THREADS OF RESILIENCY
- Ability to take an active stance
- Can-do attitude

- Sense of hope
- Persistence
- Sense of control
- Sense of accomplishment
- Problem-resolving skills
- Wide range of interests
- Flexibility and adaptability
- Curiosity
- External resources
- Consistency
- Ability to put boundaries around problems
- Ability to delay gratification and endure frustrations
- Ability to get some distance from things
- Ability to see problems as a challenge

People who are resilient take an active, not passive, stance when approaching the events of their lives. They see most problems as workable, changeable, and resolvable. They have a can-do attitude. They persist in continuing to find a way of improving things. They have some sense of control over the choices they make. And they've experienced a sense of accomplishment in some area of their lives.

Such people develop strategies and skills to help resolve problems. They possess a wide scope or range of interests and goals. They are flexible and adaptable and are able to discriminate which strategy to use when. They have a curiosity about people, places, things, and ideas. And they have external resources for support—friends and family they can call, support groups, or perhaps professional assistance.

They are consistent in at least some areas of their lives over some period of time. They have the capacity to put boundaries around situational problems and not allow them to spread to other areas of their lives. They have the ability to delay gratification, to endure frustrations, and they have a general sense of hope that things will get better even when they're not looking good. They have the ability to see things from someone else's perspective, and to get distance from them. And they tend to see problems in life as challenges, not burdens.

Few of us have access to all these resiliency factors all the time. Hopefully most of us have some of them some of the time. The goal is that with some work on ourselves, and with some support, we can rekindle these abilities when we need them the most.

We want you to have access to your own inner resiliency as you move into your inner-family work. Go back now and take another look at the sixteen resiliency factors. Ask yourself:

- *How can I rekindle these qualities in myself?*
- *How can I commit myself to employing these factors in my daily life?*

Recognizing Strengths

For some of us the strength pieces of the Self puzzle are more deeply buried than they are for others. If you were raised with criticism, there may be a tendency for you to be self-critical. If you were raised with perfectionism, there will be a tendency for you to perceive yourself as forever insufficient, as never enough. In general you may feel bad about yourself. For these reasons recognizing one's strengths may be a difficult process.

And yet there is much courage and wisdom within every one of us. We all have strengths. We're all resilient to one degree or another. You're here today; you survived. It was your strength that helped you make it through the rough times. Your task now, which we know is a difficult one, is to uncover and discover these strengths so that you can come to count on them.

Here is an exercise that might help you get in touch with some of these strength pieces in your puzzle:

UNCOVERING YOUR STRENGTHS

For a moment dig deep inside. Ask yourself what you're good at. Ask again. And again. Let the answers float to the surface. These are your strengths. Write your strengths down in your journal.

As you pull out the strength pieces of this puzzle called Self, lay them out on the table and examine them. Ask yourself:

- *What do my strengths look like?*
- *When do I use them?*
- *How do I use them?*
- *How can I find them again when I need them?*

Save this list. You will use it to remind yourself of your strengths during your journey.

Joyce, who was raised with a sick mother, took on the mothering role for her three siblings. By the time she herself was the mother of five children, she was burned out. She realized in doing this exercise that for over thirty years she had become expert at taking care of everyone but herself. She was depressed and angry. She was self-critical and confused. She discovered that she was doing the only thing she knew—caring for others—but that in the process she had lost sight of her own needs, which were clearly not getting met.

As she began to gather her tools for her journey into the depths of self, she found that her primary task was to figure out just how she went about taking care of others. In doing so, she would be able to move from feeling burdened and overwhelmed to identifying her strengths.

Step by step Joyce began to discover just how she went about taking care of others. *Observe.* First of all, she would look at a person's expression to figure out whether or not they needed to be taken care of. *Check it out.* Next she would ask whether or not that person needed something. She was so sensitive that it was easy for her to tell when *yes* meant *yes* and *no* meant *no,* as well as when *no* really meant *yes. Action.* Then, if care was indicated, she went about administering the best of care to her partner, child, or friend. *Feedback.* Lastly she asked for feedback after the fact in order to determine how to improve her services next time. She realized that she had become able to do all of this in the blink of an eye, without a moment's thought.

Like so many women in our society, Joyce was an expert at caring for others at her own expense. After doing the Strengths exercise, she began to see that these same steps could apply to taking care of herself. *Observe.* She paid close attention to all sorts of clues from her body, from her feelings, and from her thoughts as to whether or not she needed to take better care of herself. *Check it out.* Next she asked herself, *Do I need something? Do I need to take care of myself? Do I need to get some nurturance from myself or from a friend in this situation? Action.* If the answer was *Yes, I do need something,* then she'd ask herself, *What would make me feel taken care of here? Do I need a bubble bath? Would a cup of tea do? Do I need a few hours to myself? Do I have a creative project I want to work on? What would I do for someone else who was in the same situation? How would I nurture them?* In that way she discovered what she needed to do for herself. Finally, she'd check in with herself for feedback. *Feedback. Okay, how'd that feel? How am I now? Do I need more?*

Joyce transformed what could be a problem into a strength by using it to care for herself as well as she did others.

Jim was a very hard worker on his job. He was very driven and highly motivated, the "perfect employee." Often his boss had to tell him to stop working—to relax. At home, though, Jim's drivenness did not serve him well. His partner couldn't stand it when he got tunnel vision about projects around their apartment. She felt ignored, unimportant, left out, and abandoned by Jim when he got wound up in that kind of energy.

Yet Jim relaxed when he gardened. He just puttered around their small yard. Sometimes he'd stop and smell the flowers. Sometimes he'd spend hours just watching the birds that flew to their bird feeder. In this arena he had ultimate patience. He was able to just "be" with nature in a way he wasn't able to on the job or while doing projects at home.

The goal for Jim is similar to the goal for Joyce. He needed to turn his strength—relaxing with nature—into a strength that he could use in other areas of his life, such as relaxing with his wife. Like Joyce, Jim analyzed what he did in the yard. He found that when he spent time outdoors, he was able to stay focused on the process rather than the end product. It was just the reverse at work and with his home projects.

Jim had learned that it's supposed to take twenty-eight days to break a pattern. So for the next twenty-eight days at home and at work Jim concentrated on staying with the process of a project as opposed to going for the end result. He slowed down. He enjoyed his time with both his partner and his co-workers. He did something as simple as take a lunch break. He tried working in fifty-minute time blocks and resting for ten minutes every hour. This ten-minute break gave him time to just be, to relax, not to get more work done. Jim soon found that he was not only good at getting things done, he was equally good at relaxing and enjoying himself along the way.

Owning Strengths

Sometimes it's hard to "own" your strengths. For example some of us have trouble taking compliments, especially if we don't feel good about ourselves. A very practical way to begin to do this is to make sure that each time you hear a compliment, you take a deep breath and count to ten as you let the compliment sink in. This allows it to get rooted deep within you and to continue to give you inner support. Then you simply say, "Thank you," and keep breathing deeply.

If you're working a Twelve Step program (AA, Al-Anon, OA, ACA, etc.),[3] you might want to take a look at the Fourth Step, the one in which you wrote out a list of your character defects. Or, if you're not in such a program, make a list of the characteristics about yourself that you see as particularly negative and that you would like to change.

Now stretch your imagination for just a moment. Can you find the positive side to these apparently negative characteristics of yours? Do you see the glass as half empty or half full? What assets are hidden within your defects? For example, when Sue was addressing these issues, she first listed the following character defects and then she found the accompanying assets within them:

Sue's Character Defects	Character Assets Within the Defects
Controlling	The more I recognize how well I can get back in control, the more I can let go of some of that control.
Obsessive and driven	I get things done. Others look up to me and say, "How can you ever do as much as you do?"
Spaces out	This offers me a way of taking a break mentally. It enhances relaxation and meditation.
Procrastination	Once I accept this, it allows me to set goals, limits, and deadlines, which I then meet.
Self-deception	As I accept this and work with this, I am becoming more and more honest with myself and with others. In turn I expect honesty more and more from partners in relationships.
Demanding—wants it all and wants it now	What I want is usually clear, and accepting this has helped me learn patience.

Sue's Character Defects	Character Assets Within the Defects
Needy	This part of myself allows me to get in touch with my needs. This allows me to figure out ways to meet them myself or to put people in my life who will help me meet them.
Intense	As the root of this is my creativity and it also teaches me that I need to relax and to just let things be.
Hypersensitive	The positive side of this is that it keeps me in touch with my feelings. It lets me be sensitive to others' wants and needs, so long as I don't personalize everything.
Selfish, self-centered	I can turn this into knowing my needs and into being self-caring. I can also use these same skills to nurture others.
Blunt, candid	I have learned to be honest and to speak with integrity and with a deep respect and compassion for how the person I am confronting is feeling. Candor without compassion is cruelty.

When you look deep inside you, what do you see? What are some of your assets within your negative characteristics?

In identifying their character defects people often judge themselves harshly for who they've become. So often in a growth process we do just that—analyze, criticize, and critique ourselves and others—and we forget to give ourselves a pat on the back for a job well done. Don't forget your character assets. Use the information that you've discovered about yourself to guide you toward what you'd like to do differently. Use it to help you change patterns in your life. As you look at what you do that has been hurtful, be equally diligent in identifying what your strengths have been. For every part of you that you analyze, criticize, and critique, promise yourself that you will give as much time and energy to embracing your strengths.

4. HEALTHY DEFENSES

When you're feeling hurt and vulnerable, how do you get the pain to stop? How do you get back in control? This is when you call on your defenses. We all have defenses. We all need them. Being defensive is not always bad.

When we're feeling vulnerable, we may rationalize things or we may intellectualize. We may choose to ignore, suppress, or minimize things. We may box off or isolate our feelings. We may use humor. We may space out and daydream. Most of us don't like pain, so we defend against it, and that's normal.

Healthy Denial

When something strikes way too close to home, we sometimes deny the seriousness of the situation because it is just too much to fathom all at once. It is as if we're wearing blinders and refuse to see what's really happening. In the short term, though, this can in fact be helpful.

Take the parent of a child with a terminal illness who denies the seriousness of the situation to make it more tolerable. It's normal to deny things when they become overwhelming or when current circumstances are so demanding, we don't have the time and energy to deal with them emotionally. In such a situation a parent with healthy defenses will not rely solely on denial; he or she will use other defenses as well. For example the parent may sublimate the pain after a time, perhaps by working harder at making every moment with the child a special one. Or the parent may intellectualize that this is all happening to this child for a reason—such as bringing the family closer together. The parent may read books about the child's illness, or use humor to get some distance. These can all be helpful and constructive defenses, ones that help fend off the pain of losing a child.

Unhealthy Denial

Everyone uses defenses. They aren't bad per se. We need them. However, if we come from a background with a lot of pain, we may use these defenses to an extreme. We are also more likely to use primitive defenses, such as denial and projection at the expense of others. Denial only becomes a problem when it goes on so long that it blinds us to other choices and prevents us from getting on with life. In the example of the parent of the terminally ill child, denial becomes problematic if it's the only defense the parent uses over a long period of time, or if it gets in the way of making rational and informed decisions about the child's medical care.

Denial may also become problematic for an adult woman who was molested as a child when she uses it to blind herself to the abuse she's taking from her current partner. Denial may have served her very well as a defense when she was a child; it helped her defend against overwhelming pain. Yet today her denial may limit how she functions as an adult.

Sandy was molested by both her father and her uncle as a child. She was told directly by her uncle, "If you tell your mom about our little secret, she'll die." Her father had implied the same thing. So Sandy chose not to talk. But to do this, she needed to deny to herself what her uncle and father were doing. And in fact she denied the abuse so well that it wasn't until she was in her forties that she began to remember what had happened to her as a child.

It was when her own daughter turned the age Sandy was when the worst abuse occurred that Sandy began to have flashbacks. Meanwhile she was married to a man who verbally abused her on a daily basis. She soon realized that her tactics with him were the same ones she'd used with her father and uncle. Just to survive, just to make it from day to day, she found that she had needed to deny even the verbal abuse. But the result was that her self-esteem had plummeted to a lifetime low. The denial that had allowed Sandy to stay in an abusive situation as a child was now so immobilizing her as an adult that she was unable to stop the ongoing current abuse. Denial had become a way of life. Helpful denial had become hurtful denial.

Projection

Some adults, especially those from troubled families, deal with their vulnerabilities by projecting them, like a movie, onto others. The woman who is angry, for example, sees her friend as the one who is angry. The friend who feels guilty for breaking a date with you at the last moment on New Year's Eve reassures you that she still likes you, when what she really wonders is whether you still like her. The husband who is having an affair blames his wife for not being trustworthy. The woman who is emotionally not there for her children sees the children as abandoning her. In all of these examples people are clearly confusing the boundaries between "what is mine and what is yours." Projection is the ultimate way to deny responsibility for something.

Defense Inventory

In nonnurturing families children create defenses that provide protection against whatever doesn't feel safe. It's often a form of self-care. Unfortunately the same defenses that we used as children and that protected us can often be hurtful to us today as adults. Some of these defenses that we used as kids might have been fantasizing, people-pleasing, intellectualizing, daydreaming, keeping busy, and becoming pseudomature.

We may have used our defenses to numb out the pain. However, today, as we begin to heal the wounds from our past, we're going to need to face that pain—small pieces at a time. This means that our defenses may need to change as well. For example, at first we may use food as a source of nurturance but then it may become our primary defense against pain. Reading or watching television may also become a way to escape.

Even reading one self-help book after another may become a defense. After all, it's not just in the reading, or even through the subsequent insights, that things change. It happens by actually allowing yourself to feel the old feelings, work through them, let go of them, and move on. In a similar manner addictions can become defenses, or ways of assuaging pain. Although these ways may work in the short term, they eventually become life-threatening and can no longer serve you as you try to heal yourself.

Defenses created as a form of self-protection may in time separate us from ourselves, others, and from reality. For the most part our defenses exist below the level of our conscious awareness. However, as we heal, we want to be able to actively choose our defenses rather than having our defenses choose us.

Do you have a favorite way of getting back in control when you get too vulnerable, when you're hurting too much, or when you feel totally overwhelmed? This is one of your defenses. It's okay to use defenses. We all need defenses. Take a few moments now to inventory your defenses.

DEFENSES—PRO AND CON

What are your surefire, totally dependable defenses? Here's a list of some common defenses that people in our Missing Piece groups have used. Circle the ones that fit you.

Anger	Tears
Busyness	Sarcasm
Humor	Daydreaming
Intellectualizing	Isolating
Focusing on another	Shutting down
Analyzing	People-pleasing
Spacing out	Food
Reading	Television
Telephoning	Workaholism

- What are the circumstances under which you usually use each one of these defenses? For example Samantha used to use isolation when her husband criticized her about doing the dishes. Bruce used sarcasm when he was angry at his girlfriend.
- Identify both the value and the problems associated with *each* defense. For example the value of John's caretaking was that it allowed him to get some distance from his own pain as he watched his life partner slowly die of AIDS. And yet the constant caretaking impeded John's own process of grieving and letting go.
- Imagine for a moment how you'd react if someone you trust a great deal began to criticize you nonstop. What defenses would you use to defend against the hurt and the pain?

Watch yourself over the next few days to see how your defenses work and which ones you use the most. We believe that before doing any intensive work on your inner family, it is important to know how to pull up your defenses when you feel it necessary. Think for just a moment about what you do to get back in control when you feel overwhelmed. Then come up with a plan and write it down so that you can refer to it when you find yourself in that space in the future:

OVERWHELM PLAN

Here's what I do, step by step, to get back in control when I feel overwhelmed and when everything feels just too much:

First I, _____

and second I _____

and third I _____

and then fourth I _____

and then fifth I _____

and so on. After you've outlined this game plan, put it in your journal or somewhere you'll remember to look the next time you feel overwhelmed.

Dan said that when he feels that he's in over his head, his first move is to get away from the situation he's in and take some deep breaths. If he doesn't feel better after that, he calls a friend (whose name and number he keeps listed on his Overwhelm Plan) to talk about what's going on. Then he asks himself how he feels about what's happening—other than overwhelmed. Next Dan writes down all of the possible solutions to the problems at hand—even ridiculous ones. Then he sets this brainstorming list of solutions aside for a period of time. Later, when he's feeling clearer and more in control, he goes back to it. Dan told us that sometimes he can tackle whatever makes him feel overwhelmed by himself, and sometimes he needs to ask a friend for help.

Getting Unstuck

We've also found that it helps people to have a plan for when they get stuck. After all it's highly likely that at some point you will get stuck some in your own healing process. We all do. So here's a small exercise to help you with that:

PLAN FOR GETTING UNSTUCK

Think about the last time you got stuck on something, whether it was at work or at home.

• What was it about that situation that made you feel stuck?
• What did you do to get yourself unstuck? List the things that worked, and even the ones that didn't work.
• Think of at least two other situations at home, or at work, or with friends when you got stuck, and answer the previous two questions about those situations.
• Now come up with a game plan that will work for you the next time you get stuck. You may actually need several game plans—one for when you get stuck dealing with something at work and another for when you get stuck dealing with something in a relationship.

Make sure that your Plan for Getting Unstuck includes what you have done or plan to do when you get stuck in your healing process. For example, what do you plan to do when you get stuck in doing some of the work in this book?

Put your plan in your journal or some other safe and accessible place so that you know where to go the next time you get stuck.

Marlene found that she had several strategies when she got stuck. One was just to set aside whatever it was that she was doing, whether it was an engineering project at work or a big disagreement with her partner at home. Then, with some time and perspective under her belt, she would go back to the stuckness. At other times she found that when she got stuck on a project, it was helpful to run the situation past a friend. At other times she just broke the project down into small pieces and tackled one piece at a time. Whenever she'd make little steps toward her end goal, she'd reward herself by going for a walk with a friend. All of these strategies became part of her Plan for Getting Unstuck.

Your defenses have gotten you to where you are. They're not all good. They're not all bad. They just are. They're yours to choose among. The goal is for you to choose them, not for them to choose you. Choice is the cornerstone of this healing work.

5. FIRM, NOT RIGID, BOUNDARIES

Boundaries are an edge, limit, or dividing line between one place or one thing or one person and another. They allow us to establish guidelines for who is responsible for what. Boundaries also allow us to set limits on what we can and cannot do, what is safe and unsafe for us. In the psychological world there are both physical and emotional boundaries. Physical boundaries are the dividing line between the physical you and the physical me. Emotional boundaries are the line between my emotions and yours, between my side of the street and yours.

Jean's mother had poor physical boundaries. She would tell Jean to wear a sweater when it was she who was cold. Jean said, "My whole locker was full of sweaters that I simply wore to the bus in the morning and then stuffed away. I'm warm-blooded. Mom thinks I'm cold when she is. That's ridiculous."

Tom's father had poor emotional boundaries. The father frequently accused his teenage son of being angry at him when in fact it was he, the father, who was angry at the son.

Melinda, a forty-seven-year-old social worker, has poor internal boundaries. She prides herself on how many people she helps on a daily basis. But she's so tired when she arrives home at ten o'clock each night after a fourteen-hour day that she just falls into bed. Melinda has difficulty knowing what her own limits and boundaries are. She has difficulty taking care of herself. She has difficulty saying no.

We learn about setting boundaries from those around us. Children learn to be intrusive from their parents. They learn to trample over other people's feelings from their parents. Similarly they learn to keep people away by putting rigid wall-like boundaries around themselves. They learn to have malleable boundaries from those in their environment.

Children who come from more nurturing families learn to distinguish between how they themselves are feeling and thinking and whatever mom or dad is feeling or thinking. They rarely project their feelings onto others. They learn to identify and express their feelings in appropriate ways. Parents of these children consciously work at making the distinction between a thought of their own versus one that is their child's.

In some troubled families, however, there are few boundaries.

Privacy is not respected. Sharon grew up not being allowed to have doors to her bedroom, and her parents constantly went through her drawers. Sharon said, "My sister always took my clothes without asking. It drove me crazy. I knew it was wrong because it didn't happen to my friends, but no one in my family would listen to me about this."

When you don't have healthy boundaries as a child, you may become extremely intrusive with friends and partners as an adult, and you may tend to have difficulty respecting the boundaries of others. At the other extreme your boundaries may be so rigid and brittle that they are problematic for those around you. Or perhaps your boundaries are so malleable that you bend like a seedling in the wind.

In college Sheri would eat her roommate's food without asking. "I couldn't see why my roommate was upset. In my family you took what you wanted. You didn't stop to think about others." Jerry's friends would complain about him, saying, "When you are with Jerry everything is on his timetable. We eat where he wants to eat; we see the movie he wants to see. He never bends on an issue." Terry's boundaries were of the malleable variety. When her friends ask her what she wants to do, they invariably hear, "What would you like me to do? Just tell me what you want."

Becoming conscious of your boundaries will help you set healthy limits for yourself. Boundaries allow you to be true to yourself. They allow you not to just acquiesce when others tell you what to do. Part of establishing healthy boundaries is ascertaining what feels safe and what doesn't feel safe—that distinction is vital. The ability to make a distinction between "what is mine" and "what is yours" is crucially important, especially as you read this book. We want you to look at the examples we have provided for you with your boundaries in place. We want you to be able to take only what fits and leave the rest behind.

All of us have some sense of boundaries, some sense of where I begin and you end. Some of our boundaries are rigid and impenetrable. Some of our boundaries are malleable. In some instances it may seem as though we have no boundaries at all, for example, when we say yes to our children's every demand for toys. There may be circumstances in which our boundaries are very clear, and there may be instances when they are very unclear, perhaps even nonexistent. The goal is to have boundaries that are clear and firm but not rigid.

Let's take a look at your boundaries. Consider the following questions and write out your responses:

THE ROOTS AND NATURE OF YOUR BOUNDARIES—WHERE DID YOUR BOUNDARIES COME FROM?

- What did you learn about boundaries as a child? As an adult?
- What were your mother's boundaries like?
- What were your father's boundaries like?

THE NATURE OF YOUR BOUNDARIES
- Can you picture what your boundaries look like?
- Are they made of flexible steel? Are they like a brick wall? Are they made of see-through plastic or an opaque material? Are they made of a marshmallow-like substance? Are they porous?
- Under what circumstances are your boundaries clear? Unclear?
- Are there times when it seems as though you have virtually no boundaries? How does this feel physically? How does it feel emotionally? Does it feel good? Does it feel safe or not so safe?
- Are there times when your boundaries are rigid like a wall of brick and mortar? How does this feel?
- Are there times when your boundaries are brittle like crumbling plaster? How does this feel?
- Are there circumstances where your boundaries are flexible? Permeable? Malleable? How do these different states feel?

CHANGING BOUNDARIES
- How and when do your boundaries change? Are they the same with all sorts of people? Are they the same with men, with women, with children, with authority figures, with strangers, with family, with friends or co-workers?

CONTROL OVER BOUNDARIES
- Who or what has control over what gets in and out of your boundaries and what doesn't?

The issue of boundaries is very complex. We don't expect you to have resolved all of your many boundary issues, particularly if you come from a troubled family. However, it is extremely important that you develop great clarity about what is yours and what is another's. About what feels good and not so good. About what feels safe and not so safe. A sense of boundaries is an important tool for you to take along in your satchel as you travel into the depths of Self.

6. CREATING A SAFE SPACE

One of the most important tools for your journey is the ability to create a safe environment, to make a safe place for yourself in both your outer and your inner worlds.[4] It's also important to find a safe person or persons to support you as you do this work on yourself. Your environment is really important. If you're in a toxic space, you inevitably pick up that toxicity. If you have no one or a limited support system around you as you do this work, you may not feel safe enough to allow yourself to heal.

The goal is not necessarily to create the perfect environment or the perfect support system. What's important is to create an environment around you that's safe enough and supportive enough for you to be able to heal your wounds.

It is possible to heal oneself in a toxic environment, but it's a lot harder. We've found that there are nine characteristics of an environment that can help make it safer for you:

A SAFE ENVIRONMENT WOULD INCLUDE ...
- A solid support system
- A reduction of chaos in your life
- Consistency and predictability
- Flexibility and room for spontaneity
- Trust and the ability to speak from the heart
- The freedom to identify and express feelings
- Physical safety
- Ground rules that protect people's privacy
- The setting of clear limits and a recognition of boundaries

A safe environment is one that is stable and supportive enough for you to do some very important work. Your goal in finding your missing piece seems to be the creation of an inner family system that is

- Nurturing
- Healing
- Sustainable

In order to embody these three features, your environment needs to become more nurturing and less destructive. It needs to be able to promote healing, and it needs to be enduring and sustainable.

You also need to have a *safe* support system, both *within* you and *around* you as you heal. When you feel old pain, it's time to be gentle with yourself, to nurture and take care of yourself. Can you do that for yourself? Do you have friends who will do that for you? Think of someone in your life who has said something or done something that offered you support or validation. If you can't think of someone, imagine what would feel supportive or validating, and come up with an imaginary adult friend who could do those things for you—someone who could become your "safe person."

A SAFE PERSON WOULD ...
- Be with you in your pain, your rage, and your fear
- Be able to listen to you without projecting her or his own stuff on you, without judgment, and without trying to fix you
- Mirror back your feelings and thoughts

If your safe person knew that you were hurting or that you were trying one more time to run from, avoid, or bury the pain, what would he or she do for you? Are you able to ask for this support? Can you ask for what it is that you specifically want or need at any given time? Can you practice doing this with your safe person?

Safe places and safe people are important tools for your journey. Whatever this supportive nurturing person would suggest to you is what you now need to do for yourself. Growing out of the pain caused by childhood wounds means finding the balance between turning to safe people outside yourself and turning within yourself in order to nurture and "hold" yourself.

7. Being Present, Grounded and Balanced

As you begin to find and work with your missing pieces, it's quite important that you know how to be present, grounded, and balanced.

The healing process works best when one is open and receptive to change and when one is present in the moment and not distracted. It also works best when you stay in your body in the here and now and don't space out. When you can do this, you will find that the past and the future impinge upon the present less and less. And it is through this work on the Self that you will become more and more present.

For example Jim was preoccupied with a million-dollar business deal. He was worried about whether the buyers he'd found would qualify for the loan. "My wife keeps complaining," he told us. "She says that she can't get through to me, that it's like no one's home. She's right. My mind's on this deal."

Samantha, a working mother, does ten things at once. "My kids always have to repeat things to me. It's like I'm physically there, but I'm always focused on what needs to happen next. Lists of things to do in my head. So I guess I'm really not there."

Robbie dissociated almost every time she got angry. When this happened, she spaced out and was not able to attend to the task at hand. "I'm just not here all of the time. It's getting better the more I'm able to release the old rage, but I'm still not always present. I'm trying, but I'm not there yet."

People who are grounded, who have their feet firmly planted on the ground, do better as they heal from childhood wounds. Most of us float around in fantasy at least some of the time, but it's also important to have a clear sense of "ground control" in order to help you deal with reality. You can still dream and fantasize, but healing from childhood trauma is reality-based work.

For example, when the going got rough, Karen went shopping. Shopping temporarily took the pain away. It was fun to shop. It was fun to have new things. It was fun to have people deluge her with compliments on her new outfit. But because Karen wasn't grounded when she ran into pain in her healing process, she went into fantasy and bought more clothes than she could afford. Shopping was only a short-term fix. And when the bill came, she not only still had the original pain she was running away from, now she also had the pain of a large bill to deal with as well.

Scott, on the other hand, lost his "ground control" when he fell in love. He would find himself running to "the most perfect woman in the world—a ten on all counts." He'd become irresponsible at work while the bills piled up at home from wining and dining her. Until the day when reality would hit. "I can't believe I didn't see how much I was neglecting my work, my friends, my exercise. Love is most certainly blind. I thought my life was falling together, but now I see I have to work to keep it from falling apart."

When you're grounded, you're better able to see things from another perspective. You're able to accept the paradoxes and the gray area in your life. Jonathan decided he wanted to live off of his student loan money while at college. His parents felt he should get a job. Jonathan just knew he was right. The more he argued with his parents, the more rigid his position became. Finally one morning, after several weeks of not talking to his parents, he found himself looking through the job ads. When he quit reacting to his parents, he became more grounded. Time offered him a different perspective.

When Sharon felt grounded, she was able to grasp how letting go of an old lover might be an act of courage and strength rather than an act of weakness. Ground control helped her to understand the paradox and to be able to take appropriate action.

Anne had been severely wounded as a child. However once she was able to ground herself in reality, life was no longer black or white, right or wrong to her. She began to perceive the gray areas of life. "Tim couldn't be all wrong about our relationship. I have a hard time asking for what I want, and I keep waiting for him to read my mind. But rather than taking all the cues from him, I could initiate. We both have areas to work on."

On many of the paths on this journey into the depths of self you will run into pain. Many of us will do anything to avoid pain. Yet pain is a natural part of any healing process. When we try to avoid it, we end up off center, out of balance. Balance is defined as being in a place that is steady and stable. It's about being centered, being in touch with our core, our essence.

We can get out of balance when we ignore one part of our being for the sake of another part. Often people who read books like this one get out of balance. They read and read, looking for the answers in their heads, all the while ignoring their bodies and their feelings. But when we maintain our balance, we're able to keep all of these channels for healing open—our minds, hearts, bodies, souls. This is some of the most important work we do in the ongoing process of healing, for it's when all the parts of us are in balance that we actually do begin to heal.

Serena found that she was out of balance when she got stuck in her head. "If only I could just figure out why I act this way, I'd be happy. Maybe if I just keep reading and doing these exercises, something will click. I can just ignore the fact that I'm physically exhausted because, after all, the answers are in my head. My body is just the thing that carries my head." Needless to say, it wasn't until Serena began to listen to and act on her body's messages that she noticed major growth spurts.

Here are a few questions that might help you see whether you have this tool ready for your journey.

GETTING PRESENT, GROUNDED, AND BALANCED

- Am I present today? Am I functioning in the here and now, with my eyes fully open?
- Am I able to see things from another perspective?
- How do I get grounded without deadening myself? Without becoming fearful? Without closing down?
- Can I accept the paradoxes in my life?
- Can I see the gray areas in my life?
- Is my life on track and in balance today?
- What are some early warning signs that I'm about to be out of balance or that I'm already out of balance?
- What's blocking me from doing any of the things listed above?
- What's my plan for getting unblocked, for getting centered and back in balance?

To take this shield with you as you proceed on this journey, take a moment to remember a time when you felt present, grounded, and balanced. As you remember, notice how you feel. What are your thoughts? What are you feeling in your body? Come up with a picture, an image, or a symbol that will help you get back to this at another time. Practice getting in touch with this once a day—even more often when the going gets rough.

The goal here is progress, not perfection—progress toward being present, grounded, and balanced.

8. GAINING DISTANCE AND PERSPECTIVE

One key ability we discussed earlier is that resilient children have the ability to distance themselves from any trouble brewing in their families. As adults, whether we came from troubled families or not, we can still benefit from this broader perspective.

The children who are the most resilient in divorced families, for example, are those who are able to make something other than their parents' divorce the central organizing feature of their lives. They are able to create a nonreactive position, an external buffer between themselves and the stress. They are able to go on with normal life tasks with friends and with school and to create and maintain a support system with some sense of give-and-take between themselves and others. They have things to do that provide some breathing room for repair work. In addition they develop an internal strategy for dealing with their own anxiety and negative feelings—a functional way to self-soothe.

The Observer Self

Resilient children seem to have an "observer self."[5] It's as if they're able to rise above the chaos, to separate themselves from the stress, and to get distance from the problem. They can step back from a situation to observe things. They are in what some call a witness state. They are able to have an outsider's perspective.

In fact they can see things from several different perspectives. They seem to have the ability to be both self-reflective and autonomous. This observer we're asking you to get in touch with is like a scientist objectively collecting data. It's not a critical parent, and it's not judgmental. It doesn't tell you what to do. It allows you to see yourself and others the way they truly are rather than the way you want them to be. The observer sees things as clearly as humanly possible.

For example Joan, the mother of nineteen-year-old Allison, found her observer to be very useful to her interactions with her daughter, who had just come home for the summer after her first year at college. Mother and daughter had begun to have power struggles and "turf wars." But when Joan stepped into her observer self, she was able to get enough distance from the hassles to break the pattern. She was able to reframe the adjustment problems so that they shifted from being a burden on her to being a challenge.

Allison flew off the handle when Joan told her she could not drink alcohol or smoke at home even though she had done so in her apartment at school. But by staying with her more detached observer self Joan was able to see the hook her daughter had thrown out. As a result, instead of becoming hooked, Mom remained detached and didn't have knots in her stomach as she stuck to the rules she'd set in her own environment.

Jack was able to use his observer during a meeting at work. He was one of several salespeople trying to get a big corporation to buy his product. Everyone had presented their proposal. When they all went into overkill to try to swing the buyer in their direction, Jack pulled back and observed the whole situation. Like a scientist he began to collect data. And after some thought and some introspection he made a well-balanced, realistic offer that was accepted on the spot without any further negotiations. His competitors sat there dumbfounded.

Many people from troubled backgrounds already have this capacity to do adaptive distancing, to step into the shoes of the observer self. They already have the ability to space out, to rise above the situation and see things from a wide-angled view. They get perspective.

However, when we speak of the observer self, we're not talking about dissociating. This observer is much more grounded than when someone is in a state of dissociation. Part of the observer self keeps its feet on the ground and simply gets distance from the situation. Those who dissociate often don't remember the circumstances from which they have separated themselves mentally or emotionally. However, the observer self sees and remembers everything. It has a wide-angled view of what's going on. It has perspective and distance.

We believe that all of us have this capacity to observe things, to put on the scientist's hat, to practice adaptive distancing, to step out of a situation and see things from a different perspective. Sometimes we lose touch with this capacity. Here are some things that will help you step into the shoes of this observer:

FINDING THE OBSERVER SELF

- Can you think of a time when you were able to get distance from a tense situation?

- Can you see the situation with more clarity from a distance? Specifically, step by step, what do you do to get distance?
- Watch yourself over the next few days. Watch how you get distance. Write down in your journal how you do this. Sometimes this distancing may or may not be by choice. The goal for this skill is to be able to step into the shoes of the observer self when and only when you choose to.
- For twenty-eight days, at least once a day, practice stepping in and out of the shoes of the observer self. (Remember that a part of you always needs to keep its feet on the ground.)
- Finally, teach someone else how to identify the observer self and how to step into its shoes. We often learn best what we teach others.

Finding and getting to know the observer is a tool on the journey. You are not any one of the parts of your internal family. You are a combination of all these parts. The observer self helps you get to know, observe, and embrace all of the parts of you without acting out and without becoming stuck in any one of these parts.

Using the Observer Self

The best example of someone acting from a part rather than simply being aware of it via the observer involves the inner child. Some people working with their inner child actually become that child for a while. You can spot it easily. For instance when adult men and women set their teddy bears next to them in a corporate board meeting, they're literally acting childish.

On the other hand, when your observer is in place, it gives you the ability to be aware of your inner child without literally needing to act childish—or at least you have a choice about when you want to act childish. All of us have the right to act childish at times. It's just nice to choose when and where.

Robin, a Missing Piece group member, told us about a time she knew she was using her observer self. She was working in a group, trying to figure out the patterns in her life that led to her bingeing on food. For a week she had written down the foods she had eaten and the feelings and thoughts she had had before and after eating.

This was a big accomplishment, and she was really pleased with herself.

But for some reason another group member was unusually critical that day. She wanted to know why Robin had eaten chocolate chip cookies when "you know you shouldn't do that." Robin felt shamed. She began to feel childish. But rather than staying with that part of herself, she pulled back into her observer and tried to see what was happening. Robin decided that this woman had been behaving like her mother. She had shamed her. She had been critical of her in an area of her life where she was hypersensitive. Robin drew all of these conclusions from being in her observer self without having actually to act out being childish. Later on, in the privacy of her own home, she cried hard as she allowed the child to feel the shame and despair.

Then, the following week, from a very strong place, she was able to approach the group member with what she thought and felt had happened. The two were able to work through the situation and let go of it. If Robin had responded as a child in the group and had not stepped into the observer's shoes, she might have escalated the situation and gotten more shaming messages if the member hadn't been able to step out of her "critical mother" shoes. One of the two of them needed to step into the observer self, and in this instance it was Robin.

When your observer is present, it can call for a nurturing or protective part within you to help care for your inner child. This observer can be with you without becoming part of you. Having access to this observer at will is one of the final tools that you need before doing internal-family work.

9. BE-ING

People find that there are times in the midst of their healing process when the circumstances of their lives make it necessary to pause for a while. The energies of revolution and evolution involved in deep change are intense, demanding, and quite complex. Just as it takes energy to heal from the flu, from a broken bone, or from cancer surgery, it takes energy to heal from a wounded self.

The process of continually seeking change can become addictive. Sometimes the next step in the growth process may simply be to take time out, to just let things be, not to dig up anything more for a while, and just let things integrate. Too much change too fast can be problematic in and of itself. After all, even while just sitting still, you are in a kind of dynamic motion. For example, when a person is in a deep state of meditation, it might look to an outsider as though the person is no longer breathing. Yet the heart is still beating, the blood is circulating, and the lungs are expanding and contracting as the person's inner self is rejuvenating. It is this same paradoxical process—of action within nonaction—that we believe needs to go on in the healing process.

Some people evolve into this sabbatical more gradually, and some make a conscious decision to let things be. Joe's time-out period was pretty much forced on him. He suddenly lost his job in the aerospace industry because of budget cuts during recessionary times. Until that point he'd been spending some of his free time working on getting to know different parts of himself. But now he needed to take time out, to spend his extra time and energy looking for a new job. He needed to change his commitment to his personal growth. Later, when the external stress of being unemployed ends, he may be able to go back to his internal-family work.

It's nice when we can choose to take time out. Penny chose to take a vacation from finding her missing pieces after she'd worked through a lot of pain from her adolescence. She knew she'd come back to the work. But for now she simply set *The Missing Piece* aside for a few weeks and read junk novels. Meanwhile the work she'd been doing sorted itself out internally and began to become integrated into her life. She just needed to take care of herself and to let things be.

It's as if the changes within her were like little seeds that needed sun, food, and water. Penny provided these for herself, and then she just let nature take its course. After a while she found that she had stopped taking everything in her life quite so personally. She found she was less jealous of others. She even began to take better care of herself. Then, just as she promised herself, she brought her time-out to a close and picked up *The Missing Piece* again. But now she realized that she had more energy and a better sense of herself. Some seeds had germinated, and she was ready to move on. The time-out had really helped.

ALL OF THE TOOLS ARE IN THE BAG

We firmly believe that you need to be involved in the process of gathering tools for the journey before you go any farther in this book. You need to be motivated to do this kind of intense work. You need to be committed to continuing your growth process even when the going gets rough.

Do you remember your strengths and how to get in touch with them in the hard times? What are your surefire defenses? Remind yourself of what you need to do when someone verbally attacks you or what you do when someone is passive-aggressive with you. It's helpful to have clear and firm, not rigid, boundaries. Do you know how to create a safe space and support system for yourself? How do you tell if you are grounded, present in your body, and balanced? And what can you do if you're not? Can you gain distance from a difficult situation? Do you take time to just be?

When you have the capacity to do these things—even when you're in the process of developing this capacity—you're ready to journey farther into your depths and you're ready to begin internal-family work. Are you ready now? Then read on and get to know your true self. If you're not ready quite yet, that's okay too. Simply stop and let things be for a while. Wallow in your strengths before you venture into some of the more vulnerable spaces that lie ahead.

For just a moment picture yourself with a bag of tools—the ones that you've collected in this chapter—slung over your shoulder as you set out on your journey. These tools are your friends. They're instruments of healing. You may even choose to check back with each of them from time to time along the way. You may want to reread this chapter if the going gets rough. Your trusty bag of tools will get you through most anything. Happy trails to you!

CHAPTER 2

How Pieces End Up Missing

We all have a sense of self.[1] It's how we describe ourselves. It's what we do. It's what we feel. It's what we believe. In this book we refer to the self as if it were a three-dimensional puzzle. One that is constantly in motion and constantly changing, a puzzle that is greatly influenced by the environment and the context in which it exists.

Pieces of this "Self puzzle" are formed by powerful interactions with the significant others in our lives. The environment, the culture, and the society in which we were raised all affect the development of our sense of self. Because these interactions differ, and our perceptions of these interactions differ, some of us have a stronger sense of self than others and some of us have more missing pieces in our puzzles than others. Some of us have pieces missing on the outer rim of this three-dimensional puzzle, and others of us have pieces missing close to the core of the puzzle. The nature and the location of our missing pieces is dependent upon how and when we were hurt.

In this chapter we are going to look at four different areas of our sense of self:

- The creation and formation of our sense of self
- Factors that create missing pieces
- The dimensions of our sense of self
- How missing pieces affect us today

THE CREATION AND FORMATION OF THE SELF

Many psychologists believe that the self forms over time in clearly identifiable stages. We all pass through these stages, although some of us walk through them more successfully than others.

Developmental Stages

Renowned psychologist Erik Erikson defined these stages in a linear fashion as follows.[2]

ERIKSON'S STAGES OF DEVELOPMENT

age 0–1	1–2	2–5	5–12+	12–20	20–40+	40+–60+	60+
trust v. mistrust	autonomy v. shame	initiative v. guilt	industry v. inferiority	identity v. role confusion	intimacy v. isolation	generativity v. stagnation	integrity v. despair

Stage	Age	Task	Issues
1.	First year	**trust v. mistrust**	Through basic attachment to mother or caretaker, a child develops a sense of trust or mistrust and comes to respond in that way to other people.
2.	Second year	**autonomy v. shame**	A conflict develops between the child's need to explore, to be independent, and the child's remaining basic dependency on parents. Ideally a child gains a sense of competence and self-control. A poor outcome occurs when the child feels shame and doubt and when she/he does not feel in control of self.
3.	Third through fifth years	**initiative v. guilt**	During this stage a child develops the ability to initiate activities and to see them through. Whether a parent encourages or discourages such attempts affects the child's sense of ability, purpose, and direction in life.

Stage	Age	Task	Issues
4.	Sixth year through puberty	**industry v. inferiority**	The child constantly tests peers at school and in the neighborhood. In so doing, the child gains feelings of competence and industry or the lack of it and inferiority.
5.	Adolescence	**identity v. role confusion**	In this stage the person attempts to integrate various roles (son/daughter, sibling, friend, peer, etc.) into one identity. If unsuccessful, the person ends up with role confusion—trying to live out one role after another, trying to be all things to all people.
6.	Early adulthood	**intimacy v. isolation**	During this stage, the person directs energy to developing close interpersonal relationships and to career. Problems here lead to isolation from other people.
7.	Middle age	**generativity v. stagnation**	This is when people need to feel that they are somehow perpetuating themselves—through work and through family. Resolution of this crisis can mean the difference between a sense of fulfillment and of life being worthwhile, and a sense of boredom and of feeling that there is a missing piece in their lives.
8.	Old age	**integrity v. despair**	This is the time in life when people try to make sense of what their lives have been about, what life has meant, and what death means in that context. Those who do not make it through this stage tend to sink into the depths of despair and wonder if it's all been worth it.

We are proposing that these stages can also be looked at in a circular sort of process as well. Imagine a spiral that begins at the core of an onion and that winds around and around, layer after layer, out to the surface. The first layers, the ones closest to the core, have to do with trust. At a very early age we learn the answer to the questions Do I trust you? Do I trust me? Do I trust the world? The next layer out involves the issues of autonomy versus shame: Do I have a sense of mastery over my world, or am I to be ashamed of who I am and what I do? These issues are on the table when we are toddlers.

Then, when we're in elementary school, the issues involve our ability to try new things, to take the initiative, versus feeling guilty if we fail to do the right things perfectly. The next ring of self that is

Tasks that Transcend Developmental Steps

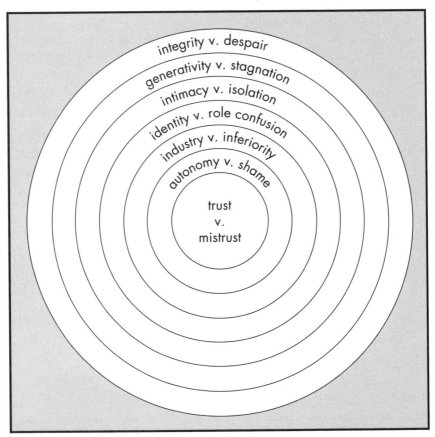

formed deals specifically with identity. Those who trip up on this part of the spiral end up confused about who they are and their roles in life. A problem in this layer leaves one feeling ambivalent about what is important to him or her. Much of this layer is worked on when we are teenagers.

Then we reach adulthood. If there haven't been too many holes in our self-development, we spiral into a new stage—a stage of intimacy, that is, the process of being able to feel whole and to be emotionally vulnerable in relationships with others. A wound due to problems in earlier stages and/or in this stage itself can lead one to feel isolated.

As the clock ticks and the years pass, the next layer of self is formed. Those who walk through this stage feel as though they have something to offer future generations. If not, they feel stagnant as they age. Finally the outer layer of the process of the formation of Self spirals to a feeling of integrity and wholeness, or, if wounds predominate, to a feeling of despair.

Picture a toy with a series of toys inside it like the one shown above. The core of the innermost toy is formed in childhood as we interact with those in our external family. Then, as the years go by, other layers of toys are put in place from the inside out as we interact with new people in our environment. The development of self is an ongoing process—layer by layer, toy by toy, year by year. The goal of the development is to complete each toy before moving on to the next.

Tasks That Transcend Developmental Stages

Children have two primary jobs as they are growing up, jobs that transcend all the layers of the onion: They try to stay connected with their caretakers and they search for the answer to the question Who am I? These two jobs spiral throughout each layer of the onion, from the core to the surface. The tasks are interrelated. In order for children to develop a strong sense of Self, they need to have a sense of belonging and connection with members of their family and in their community. When children are consistently validated for who they are, they will feel connected both externally and internally.[3]

Being Connected

Before and while the first layer of the onion, the trust layer, is being developed, infants attempt to stay connected to their primary caretaker. Their lives literally depend upon it. Throughout their lives children will continue to go to great lengths to stay attached to their parents. Children need parents for food, shelter, nurturance, and guidance, and most importantly to help them establish a sense of value. When the physical and emotional needs of children are not genuinely met, they will develop alternate strategies that help them feel better about themselves: They will distort reality; they will deny their perceptions; they will bury their feelings—all to stay connected.

Jeremy said the way for him to get validated or to feel valued was by bringing home straight A's.

> My dad didn't have a high-school diploma. He was smart, but he had to quit school early to support his mom and two sisters. He always felt others were better than him because of this. He wanted to make sure I was someone, and that meant a high-school diploma, a college degree, and a career. But the problem was he only cared about my grades. It was so important to him that I was smarter than everyone else and that they knew it. I loved my dad and wanted him to be proud of me. Every A I got seemed to lessen his pain!

Jeremy developed a strong "scholar" part of his self to protect himself against criticism from his father and in order to stay connected to him.

Pauline said she got her father's attention by stealing.

> My dad was never around the house. He didn't even know we existed. But the first time I was caught stealing, he showed up and acted all angry. It was a game. I even realized how much I liked disrupting whatever was so much more important to him than us kids. So it was like my dad and I had dates—court dates! At least I got his attention then!

Pauline had developed a "rebel" self to protect herself from her father's anger and to stay connected to him.

For some children, getting in trouble may be the only way they can get attention. Some attention, even if negative, is experienced by the child as being better than no attention at all. Being totally ignored tells children that they have no worth to that parent. Connection seems to be the goal, whether that connection is positive, fulfilling, validating, and/or secure—or negative, anxious, and/or painful.

As a child struggles for attention—vying with siblings, with a parent's work, or with a parent's depression or addiction—the child develops masks to defend against the pain of how devastating it is to feel alone, abandoned, and disconnected. To fend off that pain, children bury their vulnerabilities. They create shields and barriers to protect themselves. Some grow up fast. They become children who act like adults—pseudoadults—a five-year-old going on thirty years of age, a twelve-year-old going on forty. Yet if you were able to look behind the protective mask, you would find that they're actually still children. They've simply developed very effective protector selves that make them appear grown up to the world. Because it hasn't felt safe, they've needed to hide their childlike vulnerabilities behind such a protective shield.

However, they remain fragile because they are so well protected. And when they grow up, they're adults with the vulnerabilities of a child. They're thirty still feeling the vulnerabilities of a five-year-old, or forty feeling the vulnerabilities of a twelve-year-old. Literally what seems to happen is that when they get into an intimate relationship as an adult, when it is appropriate to be vulnerable, they reach inside to find their vulnerable selves. But they discover that these selves, which have been locked up for five, ten, fifteen, or twenty years, remain the age at which they were locked up. These vulnerable parts have not been allowed to experience the emotions and challenges of different ages along the way.

The protective selves continue to protect the vulnerable selves behind the locked doors. Some people become angry and hostile to keep hurtful people at bay. Others use their humor to distract and keep unsafe people at a distance. They become the family clowns. Many busy themselves with activities. Later we take these same masks that our protector selves began to wear in childhood with us into adulthood. There they emerge as work addiction, rage, or as Happy Go Lucky Joe, who never takes anything seriously. Unfortunately beneath the masks we may carry feelings of not being worthy.

The masks, or protective selves, become a new means of connection with others. When we've been hurt, we tend to protect ourselves by making any similar future connections through our masks. Tracy put it well: "My dad messed around with me sexually when I was a child. I carry this extra thirty pounds to protect myself from getting hurt by him or any other man today. If a man wants to connect with me now, he needs to do so through the protective shield that I literally wear on my body." Tracy's friend, Bill, also carried an extra thirty pounds and for the same reason.

As you can see, the young child does whatever he or she can to stay connected and to avoid the pain of disconnection or abandonment. Yet in the course of normal development all of us at one time or another have felt disconnected, which does not in and of itself lead to problems in life. The goal is to maximize the moments of connection and to minimize the moments of disconnection. If there are babies around, watch the pain in their bodies as they're forced to disconnect with, say, their mothers before they're ready to do so. Ideally babies disconnect when they choose to do so out of their own needs and not out of their mothers' needs.

This works for us as adults too. Carolyn put this well: "In an ideal world it works best for me to be able to choose when, where, and how to connect with those I'm close to. This obviously gets compromised given that you, as my partner or friend, have needs and desires of your own." Nevertheless when you yearn for, need, or want connection, a sense of disconnection can feel devastating.

You might want to watch your own dance with connection and disconnection with the people around you.

- When and how and with whom do you choose to connect?
- How does it feel inside when you do connect?
- How does your body feel?
- What's going through your mind?
- Does connecting always feel good?

Although connection—whether negative or positive—is a goal of a child, and an adult goal as well, connections don't always feel good. Let's take little Susie Q. She's three months old, feeling needy, and wants to be held and fed. At the moment she's reveling in the safety and security of nursing from mom's breast—warmth and comfort inside and out—but suddenly something toxic starts coming from mom. Mom has become preoccupied with something else; she no longer wants to nurse. She wants the baby to hurry up and finish. She doesn't even have to say anything or take her breast away. Susie picks up the negative energy in the connection: "Mommy doesn't want me." From the bottom of her baby booties it feels like the bite of a black widow spider—a shattering abandonment. What was but a moment ago a warm and positive connection has turned into a negative and, to the baby, a devastating experience. Connection, though sought, is not always good.

Take another baby, Scotty. He wants to stop nursing, but his mother forces him to keep going. He feels engulfed and taken over by her. How about the young child who tries desperately to get daddy's attention, only to have dad say something caustic to her when he does come close? Or take the five-year-old who can't wait until daddy gets home. She jumps up on his lap for him to hold her—to connect physically—only to have him pay absolutely no attention to her as he spaces out watching the evening news on TV. Then there's the seven-year-old whose favorite uncle comes to visit only to molest her. Is this a connection? Yes, you bet. But is it a healthy one? Obviously not. Positive connections and self-chosen disconnections enhance self-development, and they make you feel better about yourself as well. However, negative connections, half or missed connections, and disconnections imposed by another, may wound you.

Who Am I?

The second job that a child has in growing up is to answer the question Who am I? This quest for a sense of self takes a lifetime. It begins the day you're born as you interact with significant others in your world, and it ends the day you die. People from mostly nurturing families seem to emerge from childhood with a more solid, integrated, and empowered self. The dominant child part is curious and happy. Those from more troubled families tend to be catapulted into adulthood with a more fragmented, compartmentalized, and dismembered sense of self. The dominant child part of them is buried, victimlike, and often frightened.

Children are like little scientists. They go around collecting data. "Am I pretty? Am I not? Am I smart? Am I not? Am I a nice person? Am I not?" When these children are consistently validated for who they are, they take on that particular characteristic as part of their self. And over time, with consistent validation inside and outside the home, these children develop a solid sense of self and begin to know who they are and who they are not. They feel more and more secure in themselves. Layer after layer they develop a solid, integrated, unified sense of self.

At home Paige was told she was inconsiderate. Her caretakers implied that she was a bad girl. They inconsistently reinforced her behaviors and they did a lot of name-calling. Yet Paige consistently got Excellents in citizenship in school. Under circumstances like these it was hard for her to know whether she was "nice" or not. As Paige began to grow up, she learned that who she is varied, based upon circumstances outside of her control. She found herself becoming more and more dependent on other people's moods and upon what they said about her. She looked outside herself to tell her who she was rather than within her self.

If this happens to a person across several characteristics, then she or he will develop a chameleonlike self that changes with the environment. Layer after layer there will form a less-than-solid sense of self.

By contrast Wendy was consistently reinforced both at home and school for her "nice" behaviors. When she got in trouble, her parents and her teachers simply reprimanded or punished her for her behavior. They did not tell her or even imply that she was a bad girl. Over time she developed a solid sense of who she was. She found that it was important to rely less and less on what others said about who she was and more and more upon who she knew she was inside. Layer after layer she developed a more solid, integrated, and empowered sense of self.

Each of us is like a little bit of every person with whom we've had a significant relationship since we were infants. We're like our caretakers—like our mothers, our fathers, our stepparents, our brothers, our sisters. And we're like our special teachers, our partners, our lovers, and our friends. We take a piece of everyone, and these pieces become what psychoanalysts call *introjects* and what cognitive psychologists call *schemata*. We take these significant people with us in the form of little selves within our large overall sense of self. We build our own internal "nesting toy." Thus, in a sense, all of these people form a part of our self.

Have you ever wondered why you are "driven" at work just like dad? Have you felt lost and all alone in a crowd, not a part of the activities, just like you felt when you were growing up in your large family? Have you ever felt isolated and alone the way you did as an only child in a world full of adults? Did you marry a second alcoholic when you swore that you'd never again marry someone just like your first husband? Do you find yourself laughing like your father, or having the same facial expressions as your mother? Have you ever found yourself standing with your hands on your hips just like the uncle you didn't like? Have you ever found yourself screaming at your children when you vowed you'd never, ever do what mom did to you? Do you hear yourself analyzing things the way your brother does?

We're all very much like those who influenced us—both the good and the bad. This seems to be true even though many of us work very hard to be different from our caretakers, different from our moms and from our dads. Sometimes it seems that the harder we work at being different from them, the more like them we become. The messages we heard during our growing-up years have become the messages we give ourselves today as grown-ups, whatever being grown up means. The voices that were once external to us as children become internalized as adults.

As we leave home physically as well as emotionally, we may very well take with us many parts of our parents. It's as though we take our parents' puzzles with us. Those of us from more nurturing families tend to take the good and leave the rest behind. On the other hand those of us from more troubled families oftentimes take the negative pieces with us and leave the positive behind.

Many who did not have their needs met as children find themselves feeling needy and empty as adults. Those who come from families where the distinctions between "what's mine" and "what's yours" were not clearly delineated may take on other people's issues. For example, they may take one parent's guilt and shame and/or the other's anger and fear into adulthood. Or they may take their parents' disordered sense of sexuality. In other words children may take their parents' "baggage" with them. What was once outside, in your external family, now lives within you as your internal family.

Let's look specifically at how you have internalized your external family in the following exercise:

WHO AM I?

To Begin
Take out a piece of paper and fold it into eight sections.

Me
1. In the first section quickly write down as many words as you can think of that describe you. Some of these words may be things that you do or ways you are. Fold up the paper and put it aside for a while.

MOTHER
2. Later in the day, or even the next day, take out this piece of paper and in the second section describe your mother or motherlike caretaker. Some of these words may be things that she does/did or ways that she is/was. Fold up the paper and put it aside for a while.

FATHER
3. Later in the day or the next day take out the piece of paper and in the third section, without looking at the other two, describe your father or fatherlike caretaker. Some of these words may be things that he does/did or ways that he is/was. Again fold up the paper and once again put it aside for a while.

IDEAL MOTHER/FATHER
4. And again, after a period of time, take out your paper. Without looking describe in another section how you wished your mother had been, that is, describe your fantasy or idealized mother. Then do the same for your male caretaker or father figure.

SIGNIFICANT OTHERS
5. Once again, after a period of time, take out your paper. In some of the remaining sections identify siblings and/or significant others (e.g., teachers, grandparents) in your life. Repeat this exercise for each of your other siblings, teachers/mentors, and/or significant others. Should you have the need for more sections, use the back of your paper; save one section for the instructions that follow next.

ME AS OTHERS SEE ME
6. Finally, take out the piece of paper and in the last section, without looking at the others, describe yourself as others see you. Some of these words may be things that others would say that you do, and some may be ways that others believe that you are.

SIMILARITIES AND DIFFERENCES
7. Now open up the paper and look at the similarities and differences between the sections. Place a star next to the sim-

ilarities, and underline the differences. You may be both like your mother and unlike her, like your father and unlike him, like your siblings or significant others and/or unlike them. What are the similarities and differences between your fantasy mom and dad and the real ones? Are there some similarities and some differences between how you see yourself and how others see you?

The ways that we're similar to the people from our past shows us very graphically how much like a quilt we are today. The threads were all spun and woven together as we interacted with all of these significant others. It's exciting to look at these threads and to discover where they come from.

However, some people have reacted very negatively to this exercise. Jenny exclaimed, "I don't want any of my father's parts!" Some find it hard to admit that they are at all like mom or dad. But just remember, we're not saying that you take on *all* the parts of your external family. We're simply trying to help you identify the parts you did internalize. None of us is either one of our parents in total. But we are a representation of many parts of them and others in our lives with whom we've interacted over the years. Interestingly enough, what counts in terms of our own sense of self is how we perceive our parents as well as how we interpret that perception. Our self becomes a series of three-dimensional images that represent all of the significant relationships in our lives.

Resistance to this exercise may be particularly strong if you were raised in a more traumatic type of family. We simply ask that at this point you try the exercise, and if you need to, you can box off in some way the parts of, say, mom or dad that you're sure you're not like in any way, shape, or form. That's okay for now. There's no right or wrong way to do this exercise, but we do ask that you at least try to do some of it.

At the same time this is a great exercise for being able to see others in their humanness—even when we don't want to. We can see their strengths and weaknesses, their masks and vulnerabilities. We also get to see why we have some of the internal struggles we have. This is not a time to be critical. Rather it's a time to develop a little empathy toward yourself and the generations that preceded you. Things that were done to you that caused you pain were most likely created by your parents in an attempt to protect themselves. They may never have healed from their own woundedness, and what they did to you may have been the result of that.

It's also true that it was their responsibility to heal themselves and not to pass their pain on to you. You did not deserve to be wounded. But now, perhaps unlike your parents, you have the opportunity to heal your wounds. That's what this book is about—healing yourself and taking responsibility for your life today. We were all raised in one kind of external family or another. That family has indeed affected who we are today. In spite of the fact that we may have moved miles away when we left home, we've taken our families with us.

Now let's take a look in the mirror to see how you'd describe yourself today. Take out a piece of paper and do the following exercise with us:

A LOOK IN THE MIRROR—I

WHAT TO DO
1. Quickly write down as many words as you can think of that describe yourself. Some of these words may be things you do or ways you are.
2. Now set this paper aside for one week. Then, without looking at what was written previously, repeat the exercise.
3. Set it aside for one more week. Then finally, for a third time and without looking, repeat this same exercise.

QUESTIONS TO ASK
- Are the lists the same from one week to the next?
- If someone were to challenge you about one of these characteristics, would you stick to your guns?
- Are you pretty sure of yourself in many areas? Do you know not only who you are but also who you are not?
- Are your lists full of mainly positive words or negative words?

You may find that you describe yourself very differently in different circumstances. It's almost as if you were a willow tree bending with every shift of the wind. You may find that you have described yourself more positively than negatively or more negatively than positively. No matter what's on your paper, though, and no matter how it feels, it is all a description of who you are — the beauty and the beast of it all.

FACTORS THAT CREATE MISSING PIECES

Many things along the developmental spiral affect you today. Wounds in your self continue to crop up as you try to stay connected. These are the missing pieces in our puzzles, and we've all got some; it's a normal part of the process. No one is raised in a perfect environment, no matter how many self-help books one's parents have read.

Everyone's sense of self has some holes in it. The question becomes how many, where they are, and how profound are the injuries. We have narrowed down the factors that produce these missing pieces to five:

- Society and culture
- Power
- Gender
- Trauma
- Age and stage of development

Let's look at these pieces one at a time and see how they affect self-development.

Society and Culture[4]

As you have seen, your family and the context you were raised in affect the development of your self. In the larger environment societal and cultural values also affect self-development. Those who are raised in non-Western cultures, such as Japanese children, develop a different sense of who they are compared with persons from Western cultures. Their self is more communal than autonomous and independent. Children in such cultures are stroked for being part of a team or a cog in a big wheel. Those in the West who are raised in predominantly white Protestant families are validated for being able to manage all by themselves. Because of the cultural diversity in this country it is not possible to generalize and say that all Americans have a self with an autonomous and independent bent. Within this country there are cultures such as the Asian American or Native American that emphasize a communal self similar to the one Japanese children acquire. Thus when we speak of Western culture in this section, we are speaking of a dominant white Protestant culture.

Look at Japan from a geographical perspective for a moment. It's a small country, and the population is dense. There isn't much elbow room. To survive, people need to be able to work together. As a result almost everything revolves around a sense of community, from a child's earliest days in the family to the work setting in adulthood. Homogeneity is emphasized. The Japanese are praised for how much they blend in, not for how much they stand out above the crowd. Everything is "for the family," "for the company," and "for the country." Individual needs are often sacrificed for the good of the whole. It is as if for the Japanese child the answer to the question *Who am I?* is defined in terms of relationship to the whole.

Japanese children are frequently raised by mothers who have sacrificed their personal hopes for the sake of the family. And then in school, children learn from year one that their group, their community, is what counts. They begin every day with a school song and a school cheer—their sense of self comes from being part of such and such school. Later this carries over to the workplace as well. The workday begins with everyone as a group singing a company song and chanting a company cheer. They may even do group calisthenics. They believe that when the mind and body are in sync, the individual will work better as part of the overall whole. Japanese workers are not pushed to climb up the corporate ladder the way Americans are. Typical Japanese workers dig into their jobs for life. If they can be good at a particular job and that helps the company, then they feel fulfilled.

The self that people develop in Western culture tends to be grounded in being independent and autonomous. Watch a group of children from the dominant culture play for a while and listen to what we praise them for: "Oh, Johnny, you're such a big boy." "Come on, Stephanie, let's be a big girl now." They're reinforced for how grown-up they are, and in this culture that means being independent and autonomous. This sort of reinforcement continues on into adult life. When was the last time that you heard white Anglo-Saxons being praised for how needy they are, or for how well they were doing when they cried profusely at their father's funeral? "Oh, she's doing so well" means that she's not crying, that she's tough as nails and is independent and resourceful.

Families in the dominant culture in this country tend to judge how well young men and women are doing by the amount of separation and independence they have developed from their families. Independence, not relationship, is emphasized. Not until recently have researchers studying women's development begun to suggest that this model of separation-individuation might not work for everyone, that instead what we need to be looking at is how well young people are doing in their relationships with family members.

On the corporate level, too, independence and autonomy are reinforced in this country. President Clinton's economic package and the Republican "Contract for America" both emphasize a stimulus for small independent businesses. Independence and autonomy are the backbone of this country's economic structure.

Power

Those of us who have grown up in the West have been acculturated to believe that power lies outside of us but that it can be acquired and that we deserve to "have it all" right now. What we have, what we own, defines who we are, and this in turn affects our development of self. This is reflected on a popular southern California T-shirt that says "Those Who Die with the Most Toys Win." Many believe that those who have the biggest and the best—the most and best clothes, cars, houses, time-shares, stereos, televisions, VCRs, and computers—those who have it all and have it now have the most power.

Power is defined as the ability to have influence. When most of us think of power, we think of how we as individuals influence or control others outside ourselves. All in all it's not unusual for children to see adults as the ones with power. They learn that those bigger than they have power over them. Children experience difficulties in their lives when they fail to believe that they have power over their own lives. Unfortunately so many of us as children had few, if any, models of people who were truly in touch with their own internal power. Even more hurtful, many of us had models of people who used power over others in a hurtful way. "Oh, yeah," said Joan, "I know about power. My dad was all-powerful. What he said was never to be questioned. He was the family dictator. Next in line for the throne were my two older brothers. I learned that men have the power, so I learned early to align myself with men. I had few girlfriends; I mostly hung around men. I wanted to think like a man and be like a man. I wanted to be all-powerful!"

At forty-eight Susan reflects on her grandmother as a model of power:

> You know, my grandmother (I called her Nana) seemed to have a lot of power with her love. She loved me for who I was. In her presence I felt empowered. But she didn't seem to own her own power. She let my grandfather take her power from her. He used to beat her up. This hurt her a lot. I think she turned to alcohol to assuage her pain. I guess that she learned to believe that power was outside her. Her husband had the power, and then later her bottle of bourbon had power over her.
>
> I was confused by all of this, but essentially what I learned was that in my world men had power over women and that men took power away from women. I learned that power was outside of me and that the way you got rid of pain was to put something external to you inside you to ease the pain, something like alcohol.

Susan, like Nana, became an alcoholic. The difference is that Nana died from alcoholism, and Susan has over ten years of sobriety.

Children like Susan and Joan grow up with very little sense of internal power. Their role models are either predators or prey. Adults like Susan and Joan tend to blame others for their problems and for their lack of power. They are vulnerable to those with *power over* them. They feel alone and let others define who they are. Many people stay victims as they fail to claim their own *power within* and as they fail to join up with others like themselves to actively attempt to make changes in the society in which they live. Many of us lack role models for how to claim our own power; we are not encouraged to learn what in life we do and do not have power over, and equally what we do and do not have influence over.

When we are so vulnerable to those who had power over us, we often turn outside ourselves to look for strength. Tim, who grew up with a dogmatic, overbearing father, joined a religious group led by a charismatic minister, who essentially told every member of the congregation how to live from dusk till dawn. Tim became a member of this group for support, but the members of the group seemed to turn their power over to the leader. Once again the power was outside Tim—first with dad and now with the minister.

It's both healthy and important for children to begin to question their parents and others and to distinguish themselves as separate entities. Yet so often we see parents take it as a personal affront that their child prefers orange over blue, or that their child prefers the Orioles over the Braves, or that their child wants to stay home rather than go on a family outing.

Most of us over the past decades have been raised in a male-dominated or patriarchal society. Power has been closely tied to gender. We have learned that the real power in our society is with men, with those who have money, with those who are white, and with those who are part of the dominant social and economic class. For instance the mother who says or implies to her children, "Wait till Daddy gets home," is actually power-identified with men, not other women, and perceives power as being outside of herself rather than within her. In our society, whether or not they work outside the home, and regardless of what we might believe is fair, mothers still have most of the responsibilities in the home and in raising children. Yet fathers often retain the ultimate power over child discipline, major household decisions, important family decisions, and how the money is spent. Children who receive these messages learn that power is related to gender.

Although not all males and females manifest these patterns, it is true that we live in a predominantly patriarchal society. Whether they abuse power or not, men reap the benefits of the power that other men have, whereas women still have to work harder to be accepted.

Increasingly there are women and men who have made their way to the top by claiming their power from within, in a nondominant, nonpatriarchal manner. They have learned to live by more humanistic principles and have continued to respect the rights, choices, and dignity of others.

People like this live by a program of attraction, not promotion. They respect the uniqueness of those who are different than they are. They try to be nonjudgmental and tend to support personal freedom and choice for themselves as well as for others. They attempt to enhance power within themselves and others. They do not have the need to step on others on the way up the ladder. They sense that there is enough for all and that they don't need to take from others in order to get what they need for themselves. They live the way they believe and allow you to do the same, with the same dignity and respect. These are the people who are becoming our role models for learning how to tap into the power that we all have within ourselves. *Power* is not always a bad word.

Take a few moments to reflect on what power means in your life and who has that power.

POWERFUL PEOPLE

- Identity five powerful people in your life.
- List them by name and describe the ways in which they were powerful:

Name   Ways They Are Powerful

1. _____
2. _____
3. _____
4. _____
5. _____

- Was their power positive or negative?
- How has their power influenced you and your sense of who you are?

Both how others have used their power over us and how we use the power we have influences who we are.

Gender[5]

Males and females are both different and similar—different due to how they are raised, and similar inasmuch as both struggle with the same basic issues.

There are two schools of thought that support the notion of differences in male and female development.[6] The psychoanalytic school believes that the genders are innately different. It views a boy's major task in growing up as one of separating from the one who "feeds" him (mom), whereas a girl's primary task is to find a new way of relating to her mother (and subsequently to others). The sociocultural school of thought, on the other hand, believes that males and females are innately similar but that because of gender-role socialization they develop differently. In our culture boys are often reinforced to be tough, nonfeeling, independent, goal-oriented, rational problem solvers. And girls are generally taught to be soft, process-oriented, emotional, nurturing, and dependent.

However, studies on gender are showing that there are more differences *within* groups than there are *between* groups. For example, if you were to observe a group of women, you'd find that there is quite a range in their gender-based behaviors. The same would hold true for a group of men. Yet if you were to bring these same groups of men and women together, the differences that you would have noticed when the groups were separate would now be much less visible. Women as a whole tend to be much quieter and less individualistic in mixed groups than when they are in groups of other women. Because gender is such a strong influence, the main difference that will be noticed when all of these people are together is that some in the group are men and some in the group are women. That is to say, when men and women are together, we tend to minimize other differences and to put more of an emphasis on the one obvious difference—gender. In fact we tend to magnify that difference and anything that can be attributed to it.

Interestingly there is no one trait or characteristic peculiar to only one gender. Nevertheless, gender is such a strong cue that it plays a major role in how each of us defines who we are.

Despite the differences between men and women that we tend to overemphasize, it is also true that the pieces that make up our self-images are quite similar. Whether we are male or female, we all have the same fundamental core issue: We are all scared of abandonment and will do anything we can to avoid it. Our differences show themselves in the various protector selves we develop or construct to guard ourselves against abandonment.

When we asked groups of men what they do to protect themselves against abandonment, the most common responses were: don't get too close emotionally; don't become emotionally invested; dictate levels of intimacy; manipulate the person or the situation through money; and make sure that someone else is always available in the background.

When we asked groups of women what they do to protect against abandonment, the most common responses were: acquiesce (do what the other person wants); try to be perfect; be "nice"; and anticipate and attend to the other person's needs (often before he or she even knows there are any).

We are similar and different in other ways as well. We all have feelings, yet we tend to demonstrate them differently. Women tend toward tears while men tend toward anger.

Another example of our similarities is that we all seek validation. Whereas in our society men are praised for their work, people are more likely to give women strokes for their "good looks." Clearly many factors—gender being just one of them—influence self-development.

Trauma[7]

Sometimes, when there's too much stress in our lives, our system goes on overload. We can no longer take in what's happening as rapidly as it occurs. Sometimes there is too much emotional and/or physical overload for us to protect ourselves from it.

Traumas can occur at different ages and stages, have varying impacts, and differ in duration. The younger children are when trauma occurs, the less likely they are to recognize that they're not responsible for what just happened. Young children believe that the world revolves around them—the good and the bad of it. They tend to believe that they're responsible for everything from mom and dad's divorce to Santa's bringing them lots of presents if they were "good little girls and boys."

The more significant the person who hurt you is in your life, the more profound the pain. For example if the father who raised you called you stupid, the trauma is more likely to be deeper than if you were called a name by your stepfather, who didn't raise you. And of course the injury to self is more profound if your partner tells you that you're not sexy than it would be coming from somebody you don't even know. They both hurt, but one goes deeper than the other.

Wounds that are perpetrated upon the self from ongoing trauma seem to differ from those that happen in one acute episode. The more repeated and long lasting the trauma, the more a child learns chronic helplessness. Experiencing repeated physical abuse is more damaging than having to witness or experience it once. While it may be difficult to deal with the issues of loss that come with changing schools a couple of times as you are growing up, it's not nearly as severe as moving fourteen or eighteen times. Traumas for some children are acute and situational—say, a negative look from dad. This kind of trauma hurts and certainly affects self-development but in a different way than a trauma that is chronic in nature and occurs repeatedly over time.

In families that experience chronic trauma, children often internalize the belief that there is something inherently wrong with who they are. They may come to believe, *I am basically a bad seed. I'm unlovable.* Year after year they live with inconsistencies, unpredictability, chaos, and stress. They live with fear, chronic disappointments, and loneliness. The saddest aspect of all of this—whether the trauma is acute or chronic—is that childhood traumas occur at the time in their lives when they are developing their identities and their sense of self-worth. All traumas hurt. They just hurt differently.

Wounds affect the puzzle of Self in different ways, that is, each one of these wounds can cause different kinds of missing pieces. The key to the kind and nature of the missing pieces, or, to put it another way, the size and shape of the wound left by the trauma, seems to be how the person experienced the trauma. Childhood injuries can wound the self in many ways. Some traumas are like puncture wounds, piercing their way down to the core of self to the earliest developmental layers. Some wounds are like surface abrasions; others are like gashes, ripping across several layers.

Let's take the example of a thirty-five-year-old woman named Marla, who felt betrayed at work. A fellow employee did not back her up on something they'd mutually shared and agreed that they would each take to the boss. "I can't stand it!" Marla exclaimed. "Sandy let me down just like every other woman in my life, way back to my mother, who left me when I was only two." Marla's pain is the result of a puncture wound. The pain is piercing. In order to heal from the wound, she will need to travel back to her original betrayal by her mother.

Scott, age forty-nine, has recently gone through a divorce. His wife left him for another man, and his ego was deeply wounded. He hurt. He was angry. He felt betrayed. Yet these feelings did not tap into old, unresolved losses because his early home life had been quite stable. This wound was an abrasion. Scott's grief process is less complicated and will probably take less time to heal than Marla's.

Bill, age forty-two, a recovering alcoholic, was recently fired from his job for sexually harassing several of the women he supervised. He felt bad about this for several reasons. He was scared about how he was going to support his family with no job during a recession. In time he felt bad about the women he'd hurt. But he was also mad at the friend who'd told his boss how he treated his female supervisees. And then, on top of all of this, he recalled being sexually assaulted by the priest at church when he was a choirboy at age twelve. He began to wonder if any of this was related to the fact that he was on his fourth marriage, each having ended because of his infidelity. Bill's pain from all of the "yesterdays" felt as real as his pain from today. This traumatic situation ripped across several layers of Self— through wounds from age twelve to his twenties, thirties, and forties. His wound is like a deep gash.

What were the sources of pain in your life while you were growing up? Divorce? The death of someone close to you? Did you move? Were hurtful words said? Was there physical, sexual, or emotional abuse? Did you have to live with mental illness or with addiction? Was a sibling always treated better than you? What age were you at this time? Did you miss out on being a kid when you were young? Did the age and stage you were at, the person involved, and the acute or chronic nature of the trauma affect how you experienced the trauma? Were there any missing pieces because of the trauma(s)?

Age and Stage of Development

As we have seen, self-development is affected by many things— family, society, and the culture in which we are raised; the ways in which power was used in this context; our gender; our experiences; and the perceived traumas of our lives. All of these things have different effects upon people, depending upon their age and stage of development.

Do you remember Erik Erikson's stages of development, which we transposed from a linear to a spiral framework (see page 50)?

Let's look at how society, power, gender, and trauma affect these layers at different ages and stages of development and how they produce different kinds of missing pieces in our inner development.

Vigilant Child/Shamed Child/Wanderer Child

Children who are hurt when they are very young experience trauma in the first layer of development—the one that has to do with trust. They are liable to grow up with a part of themselves being quite vigilant, scared, afraid, and certainly not very trusting of others. Let's call them *vigilant children*.

Children who suffer a trauma of some sort in the second layer out from the core—the one having to do with autonomy versus shame—are liable to grow up with a part of self that hides behind doors and is ashamed. We will call them *shamed children.*

When children are hurt when they're three or four—in the initiative-versus-guilt stage—they're liable to have difficulties being consistent in what they do. They probably have difficulty following through. They may have a tough time both starting and finishing projects. We'll call them *wanderer children.*

Inferior Child/Ambivalent Person

If children are traumatized between five and twelve years of age—during the stage of industry versus inferiority—they are likely to have difficulty in relationships with friends and they may very well feel that they're not very good at doing things. We'll call them *inferior children,* since that's exactly what they're feeling a lot of the time.

If the injury to self occurs during adolescence—the stage of identity versus role confusion—the young people are liable to act like chameleons, trying to please everyone all the time. As a result they feel ambivalent about everyone and everything. We'll call them *ambivalent persons.*

Withdrawn Person/Bored Person/Despairing Person

If the injury occurs one more layer out, in early adulthood— during the time that the issues of intimacy versus isolation are so prevalent—these people may very well be isolated and withdrawn. We'll call them *withdrawn persons.*

If the injury comes about during the middle-age layer of self-development—the stage of generativity versus stagnation—people are liable to feel a profound sense of boredom and that something is missing in their lives. They feel stagnant as opposed to having some sense of purpose in life. We'll call them *bored persons.*

Finally, if the injury occurs later in life, when one is an elder— during the stage of integrity versus despair—the trauma will lead to feelings of despair and to asking, "Has this all been worth it?" We'll call them *despairing persons.*

Imagine all of these people in one room—the vigilant child, the shamed child, the wanderer child, the inferior child, the ambivalent person, the withdrawn one, the bored one, and the despairing one. What a sight for sore eyes! Most of us were not injured profoundly at each and every layer of development, although many people from troubled families were injured in one way or another at many of these levels.

Remember Marla, who is feeling betrayed at work? Her trauma was a puncture wound, going back to when she was two and feeling betrayed by her mother, who moved across the country leaving the children with her parents. This wound pierces the first level of development near the core of self—the layer of trust versus mistrust. It also touches into the level of shame as well as initiative versus guilt, where a wound leaves one without a sense of ability, purpose, and direction in life. A child hurt here may feel like a wanderer.

Or take Scott, with no known childhood wounds. His wife leaves him to be in another relationship. His wound is an abrasion. He's embarrassed and withdrawn, and isolates himself from his friends. Not only is his hurt different from Marla's, but so is his recovery. It's not that one trauma hurts more than another, it's just that they're different.

Real life hardly ever falls into neat little packages. If you were injured at an early stage in your development, you were quite probably set up for injuries in later stages of your life. It's not hard to understand how issues with trust might permeate many areas of your daily life. Having difficulties with trust would be like the bottom girders of a multistoried building being off center. Even if the structures are in place in the rest of the building, the building will still tilt to one side. Perhaps for someone else the girder in the middle floor of their development is out of place, leaving only the top couple of floors out of balance.

Just to make things a little more complex and certainly more complicated, imagine that the girders are out of place on several floors of development. How would you feel if this building were you?

Physical, Cognitive, and Emotional Development

There are three major areas of development that can be affected by all the variables we have just discussed: the physical, the cognitive, and the emotional. In profound cases of abuse a child's physical growth is impaired. A pediatrician can actually read the differences in a child's growth chart after the child has experienced a major trauma. Another noticeable developmental delay is in the arena of arrested cognitive development, for example children who see everything as all right or all wrong. Finally, emotionally impaired children may get stuck with the feelings of a two-year-old, for instance, they may have a great deal of difficulty delaying gratification and in holding back their impulses. The point is that when there is an injury to the self, it can affect people in any and/or all of these three areas of development.

When children develop normally, they first see things as all or nothing. Either Mommy is honest or not. Through a child's eyes there's no such thing as a justified stretching of the truth. If you say you're going to be home after they go to bed, then you need to be home then. A child will think you've lied to him, even if you leave because of an emergency (and even if you left him with a responsible adult). Or if you say that you'll pick the child up after school, then being late is just like not being there. The truth is the truth. Trust is trust. Leaving or being late is just that. There are no excuses. Things are or they aren't. There are no grays. In a child's eyes there is only black and white.

If children get injured emotionally when they're in the midst of this stage of concrete thinking, their thinking development may get stopped as well. They may find that they continually think the same way they did when they were children. They may be grown up in other areas of their life: They may look older, act older, and even think older at work. Yet sometimes in interpersonal relationships they may find themselves thinking in all-or-nothing terms.

Cindy found herself thinking and saying to Paul, "I can't trust you anymore," after he was late once. Vera said accusingly to her therapist, "You lied to me about me being special," after she saw her therapist give a child patient of his a hug as the child was leaving a session. From a child's perspective trust is an all-or-nothing phenomenon and so is lying, whereas through an adult's eyes there are clearly defined degrees of trust and of telling the truth. As both Cindy and Vera heal, they will find that they think in these all-or-nothing terms less and less.

Picture three people walking down the path of life next to each other. One is your physical development, the second your cognitive development, and the third your emotional development—each one is a part of you. A trauma crosses your path and stops one or more areas of your development dead in its tracks. Let's say it's your emotional development that gets wounded and drags behind the other two. This happened to William. When he was five, his sister was in the hospital dying of leukemia. This is an age when a child thinks that the world revolves around him, that all of the good that happens is because of him and that all of the bad that happens is also because of him. In his own little mind William thought that he caused his sister's illness. And because of this trauma his emotional and cognitive development was arrested at five. His physical development marched on, but his feelings and thinking processes dragged behind. And as the years rolled by, to the outside world William looked and acted like a grown man. Decades later when he went into therapy, his cognitive and emotional development played catch-up. Does this make you wonder if any of the three—body, mind, and heart—are dragging behind for you?

DIMENSIONS OF SELF

As you develop in relationship to others over the years, layer after layer of the puzzle of Self is put in place. How your puzzle develops will affect how you see, perceive, and experience the world today. What follows are seven possible ways in which you can look at your sense of self. You may find that you identify with several of these dimensions.[8]

1. Integrated or fragmented self
2. Internally or externally defined self
3. Consistent or inconsistent self
4. Sure or suggestible self
5. Vulnerable and real or protective self
6. Positive or negative self
7. Congruent or incongruent self

You might think about your own sense of self as we more fully describe these seven dimensions. Keep in mind that there is nothing absolute about these categories. People tend to fall along a continuum on each of these dimensions. Sense of self, like life, tends to be full of shades of gray, not just black and white.

Integrated or Fragmented Self

Those with a solid and integrated sense of self know who they are. They are essentially the same person today they were yesterday and will be tomorrow. There is a thread of consistency in how they behave, even in different situations—a sense of I-ness. They feel solid. They may be flexible and adaptable, but they have some strong bottom-line definitions of who they are and how they behave. They look inside themselves to define who they are.

Those with a less-than-solid or fragmented self have more pieces missing in their puzzle. Cynthia described this well when she was faced with having to make a big decision—whether or not she would take a job promotion on the other side of the country.

> I want the promotion, but it's so far away from home. It's a good opportunity, but I'm petrified. My boyfriend really doesn't want me to go. Half of my women friends cry the minute I begin to discuss it with them, and the other half say, "Go for it!" My mom clearly will miss me. My dad has no comment. I feel like it's a real adventure! At the same time I feel like rolling into a little ball and crying. I really don't have a clue about what I should do. It's like a tug-of-war outside me and inside me. I'm frozen in ambivalence. I don't know what to do, and it feels like I'll never, ever know.

This confusion is not an unusual response for anyone faced with a major decision. The person in this example is able to hear the feelings of all those around her and to see the positives and negatives about the move. The problem develops, however, when she becomes permanently frozen in ambivalence. It's normal to have difficulty weighing all of the factors involved in a big decision like this. But people with an integrated sense of self are eventually able to work with both the positives and the negatives in a way that enables them to come to some sort of decision.

When people have a fragmented self, they become stuck as they listen to their internal dialogue. The external stress seems to shatter any sense of internal strength. Such individuals have difficulty getting enough distance from their own process and literally find it impossible to make a choice. They become immobilized by indecision. Individuals with a solid and integrated sense of who they are have learned to look inside themselves for validation. People like this still appreciate others' approval, but they aren't dependent upon it for their very life.

Internally or Externally Defined Self

People who come from families where there is consistent and reliable reinforcement for who they are learn to do the same for themselves. Those who did not get consistent reinforcement continue to look outside themselves for approval. They may "keep coming back for more," hoping that they will find validation the next time they ask. This sort of person develops a sense of self that is externally defined and dependent upon others. He or she becomes what is popularly called *codependent*, that is, one who is defined by others, not by self.

Sue, who has an internally defined self, demonstrated this when she was out with her friends. She was loud, boisterous, and funny. She was having a good time. But then Sally, a friend of Sue's, was critical of Sue's behavior. Sue thought about what Sally had said and weighed the circumstances. She decided not to change her behavior. "I wasn't being intrusive or hurtful. In fact I believe my behavior is actually much more positive than negative. I still want to be sensitive to Sally and her feelings, but I'm okay with myself. I think Sally has a problem with 'kicking back and letting loose.' " When someone is internally defined, she is able to consider other people's feedback or criticism, but she doesn't automatically change her behavior. People like this trust themselves and act accordingly.

Consistent or Inconsistent Self

Adults who are consistent in their behavior probably come from families where the caretakers were also consistent and predictable. Such people can adapt if the circumstances call for it, but they tend to maintain a core way of being. They have a consistent sense of self.

On the other hand the people who come from families where inconsistency was the rule of the day may themselves not be very consistent as adults. When the caretakers in a family were inconsistently available, the children may very well act one way today but behave differently tomorrow. Their behavior is unpredictable. This comes from what we would call an inconsistent sense of self.

Mary found herself acting inconsistently and talking out of both sides of her mouth, fearful of committing herself to an opinion. "Did you hear what Dan Quayle said about *Murphy Brown?* Wasn't that absolutely atrocious?" she exclaimed to her friend Betty, who quickly agreed. But then at work Mary articulated the merit of Dan Quayle's 1992 election remarks. And later that week she had lunch with Betty again, this time telling her that she agreed totally with Mr. Quayle. Needless to say, Betty was confused as to what Mary believed. It seemed as if Mary's basic beliefs, in this case about politics, were in flux and that she had an inconsistent sense of self. The exercise entitled "A Look in the Mirror," which you did earlier in this chapter, can be a good way to get an idea of how consistent you are. How consistently did you define yourself over a period of three weeks? Are you the same person today that you were a few weeks ago? If so, you have a fairly consistent sense of self. If not, your self is more inconsistently defined.

Sure or Suggestible Self

People who are sure of themselves today, who are not overly malleable and suggestible, come from families where they were able to develop a solid sense of who they are, year after year, layer after layer.

Those who come from troubled families tend not to be very sure of themselves as adults and can be extremely suggestible. They will be whoever you want them to be. If you ask them what they want for lunch, they'll say, "I don't know. Whatever you want." And they don't just say this once; they always say it. They are like human chameleons, Zelig-like. Remember Zelig from the Woody Allen movie? He became who everyone around him wanted him to be. He was externally defined, looking to others to tell him who he was.

Eight-year-old Karen seemed to be having difficulty deciding whether she should have dinner at her mother's house or at her father's house. "I want to go to Dad's house. But then my sister, Tammy, wants to stay at Mom's. Maybe I'll just stay at Mom's. But what happens if Dad calls and he wants me to come over now? Then I'll probably go over there, but if Mom wants me, then I should stay here, don't you think?"

Tim has been dating Holly for six months and is comfortable in the relationship. His good friend has a cousin in town who wants to go out with Tim, and at first Tim declines. Then the friend begins to question Tim about how solid his relationship is: "It's only been six months. What makes you think Holly wouldn't go out with someone else? Besides, Holly doesn't have to know. You'll really like my cousin! Come on, Tim! You're not married to Holly." Tim, who is quickly influenced by his friend's opinions instead of looking at his behavior in relation to Holly, allows his insecurity to be tapped and dates his friend's cousin.

Vulnerable and Real or Protective Self

When children are given the appropriate focus and attention, they will develop a vulnerable self, one that allows people and experience in. Over time a healthy person will weave both vulnerabilities and strengths into a fine and rich tapestry. Those from more troubled families develop a protective self in order to defend against the pain of chronic loss—against the pain of not getting their needs met and of not getting emotionally filled.

Children from troubled families develop a hard exterior shell. The shell serves two functions. One is to defend against the internal wounding—the fear, shame, guilt, and pain. Secondly the shell offers them a way of connecting with other people when being real is not acceptable. For example, being honest with your mother about how frightened you are when she drinks may only get you a smack in the face. Developing an exterior attitude of being tough and not caring makes it easier to deal with your parent. Sometimes when the losses are chronic, the exterior shell or protective self develops more than the vulnerable self. The protective self seems to become inflated at the expense of the more approachable vulnerable self. How such people present their real selves to the world may very well be different from what they feel inside.

Joey, who is always good for a laugh, doesn't appear to take anything too seriously. He keeps people at a distance. His laughter allows him to be with people without taking risks. The laughter keeps others from seeing how afraid he is that they don't like him.

A person who's always laughing (protective self) may be hiding some pain inside (vulnerable self). The macho man (protective self) may be hiding a needy child within (vulnerable self). And the person with a stiff, plastic smile (protective self) may be frightened inside (vulnerable self).

Candy put her smile on when she was eight and never took it off again. She kept insisting she was just fine in spite of the fact that her father had just died. Then her son had a serious accident and was in a coma for twenty-four hours, and her husband left her after twelve years of marriage "I'm just fine. I'll be okay. I have myself and my kids," she kept telling herself and others. Not too much later she developed a malignant tumor. "I'm fine," she continues to say, as the tears run down her face. The outside protective self works hard to protect the inside vulnerable, core self. Many of us have invested so much energy in our masks that we don't have a sense of who we really are behind the protector's mask anymore.

The journey of finding the answer to the proverbial *Who am I?* question seems to be one that involves seeking the vulnerable core self, which is often buried underneath layers and layers of protective self. Some of us have more layers than others because we needed more protection than others. The protective parts of us were and are essential. When it wasn't safe to feel and to be real, our masks protected us from going crazy or from dying at a time when we might not have made it without them. Today, although we do need protection from time to time, our protective selves can often be laid to rest. They've worked hard, but we no longer need them quite so much. Today it may be safer to feel and to let the vulnerable parts of our self out.

We all have a vulnerable self deep at the core of our being. And most of us have a protective self to some degree—the self we put out to the world. As we grow and get to know who we really are in the fullest, it becomes safe to experience the vulnerable self more and more.

Candy's protective self makes her look as though she has it all together, but her vulnerable self, which is scared, lonely, and in great pain, is hidden beneath that mask of smiles she wears to protect herself. Most of us have created a false exterior that we use in at least some instances.

What does your mask look like? How do you present yourself to the world?

Positive or Negative Self

Some of us feel good about ourselves. We call that high self-esteem. Some of us look inside and see varying shades of darkness. We feel negative about ourselves. We call this low self-esteem. How we feel about ourselves is certainly related to who we are, but it's not exactly the same as our sense of self. Those of us from more nurturing families, in which we received positive reinforcement, tend to develop a mostly positive sense of self and have high self-esteem. Those of us who were raised in an atmosphere of criticism and negativity tend to develop a negative sense of self and have low self-esteem.

Our self is the container that represents who we are. As you know, it is formed layer by layer, year by year. How solid that container remains depends on the consistency of the validation we get along the way. Self-esteem is what lies within that container. It can be more positive or more negative depending upon whether the person received more attention for positive or negative behaviors.

How positive or how negative we feel about who we are depends upon which of our characteristics received the most validation. Those who were consistently validated for positive things will grow up to have a positive and solid sense of self. They will have high self-esteem. Those who were consistently validated for negative aspects of self will probably grow up to have a negative sense of self—solid, yet negative. They will have low self-esteem.

At thirty-one, Teresa says, "It's just as well I haven't gotten married. I'd probably have had kids. Most of my friends do. I was really never very suited for a long-term relationship. I'm short-tempered and basically very selfish, so I'd never make a good mother. My two sisters are much better mothers and wives than I could ever be." As Teresa talks, it hurts to listen to her futility, her acceptance of being a difficult person, and her inability to believe she can be lovable and have more choices in life. She has a negative sense of self and low self-esteem.

Congruent or Incongruent Self

When what you do, what you say, what you think, and what you feel do not match, you develop what we call an incongruent or fragmented voice. This is a result of incongruence between your thoughts, feelings, and behaviors. Your outside doesn't match what's going on inside you. The outer layer of the Self puzzle—the protective self—is defending against the hurt, pain, and vulnerabilities of the inner layers of the puzzle. The vulnerable self has been so buried and defended against that nothing is in sync and this is when you feel askew and off center. The person presented to the world is not who you really are inside.

Celeste is a motivational speaker who speaks with conviction, compassion, and great energy. Yet she returns home with great doubt about how she is received despite standing ovations. She wonders to herself, *I know if they find out who I really am, they'll know I'm an impostor, that I'm not good enough, that I don't have anything of importance to say. They'll give me a standing room full of boos and jeers. It's just a matter of time.* The persona that Celeste projects in her behavior is inconsistent with her own self-talk and feelings. Her thoughts, feelings, and behavior do not match. She is incongruent.

• • •

Take the opportunity to assess yourself within the different dimensions we have explored. Fill in this Sense-of-Self Scorecard:

SENSE-OF-SELF SCORECARD

Place an X where you perceive *yourself* to be on the continuum of each of the seven dimensions:

Integrated	———————	Fragmented
Internally defined	———————	Externally defined
Consistent	———————	Inconsistent
Sure	———————	Suggestible
Vulnerable	———————	Protective
Positive	———————	Negative
Congruent	———————	Incongruent

Now do the same thing for *Mom* and then for *Dad* (primary caretakers). Place an X where you perceive your *mother/female caretaker* to be on the continuum of each of these seven dimensions:

Integrated	———————	Fragmented
Internally defined	———————	Externally defined
Consistent	———————	Inconsistent
Sure	———————	Suggestible
Vulnerable	———————	Protective
Positive	———————	Negative
Congruent	———————	Incongruent

Place an X where you perceive your *father/male caretaker* to be on the continuum of each of these seven dimensions:

Integrated	———————	Fragmented
Internally defined	———————	Externally defined
Consistent	———————	Inconsistent
Sure	———————	Suggestible
Vulnerable	———————	Protective
Positive	———————	Negative
Congruent	———————	Incongruent

You can also do this exercise for your sibling(s) and/or other significant others.

What did you discover about yourself and about your caretakers and/or significant others? Where are their similarities? Where are their differences? Don't be critical of yourself. There are reasons for your being where you are. This scorecard may very well change as you work on the exercises in this book. You may want to come back to it.

Even if your sense of self is somewhat fragmented, externally defined, inconsistent, suggestible, protective, and/or negative, and even if you speak with what we call a fragmented voice—meaning that your insides do not match your outsides—there is definitely hope for you. In order to straighten out this fragmented voice, you may choose to look deeper into the layers of self to discover more about yourself. That's what the rest of this book is about.

HOW MISSING PIECES AFFECT YOU TODAY

We hope that you see by now how your self mirrors the family and the environment you came from. If you come from a more nurturing family, it's highly probable that you've developed a solid, internally defined, consistent, sure, true, positive sense of who you are, and that you are congruent. As an adult you may tend to feel internally fulfilled and may do well in both solitude and relationships. On the other hand if your family was troubled, whether they were too lax and/or chaotic or too rigid, and if your needs were mostly not met at each age and stage along the way, you have probably developed a self that mirrors this family. Oftentimes such a person's adult relationships tend to be chaotic as well. Many from such backgrounds feel scattered and stressed out. When alone they feel an internal, never-ending emptiness.

Children who come to believe there's something wrong with them will later see the world through shame-colored lenses as adults. Five-year-old Tammy, who blames herself for her parents' divorce, may very well grow up taking the blame for everything that goes on in her adult life as well.

Ned comes from a family where everything looked picture-perfect on the outside yet was chaotic and stressful behind closed doors. As an adult he often looks as though he has it together. Yet behind his own closed doors in adult intimate relationships, he is often lost.

Sharon, the supermom, who was raised in a troubled family, today heads a family of eight, is married to a politician, and runs many volunteer organizations. And yet she easily moves into acting like a needy three-year-old in her marriage when she's scared and hurt. She has trouble accessing the parts of herself that could negotiate on her own behalf to get her needs met.

It doesn't matter how old we are, or how many years we've put between ourselves and our past, or how many miles away we move from our family, we still take with us the messages we grew up with. As Bill said, "I don't need my dad to live with me. I still hear his words fourteen hundred miles away. Every time I run into difficulty at work, I hear how stupid I am. I hear how I'm never going to amount to anything. I feel like I'm twelve years old all over again, and then I do make stupid mistakes." These messages have become part of a belief system—beliefs that have never been questioned or challenged. Our experiences of yesterday are the lenses through which we see and experience the world today.

Perhaps an exercise will bring this closer to home for you. You might simply want to read the exercise and then go back and do the things it asks you to do. Or you might want to record the exercise into a tape recorder and then play the tape back while you're in a relaxed state.

LENS EXERCISE

GETTING READY

1. For just a moment relax. Let all your troubles and worries go. Don't worry—they'll still be there when you return.

2. Put your attention on your breathing. Follow your breath in and out, in and out.

3. Listen to your heartbeat over and over and over again. You might even choose to close your eyes and feel a warm energy, like warm, soothing water, begin to trickle throughout your whole body, from the top of your head to the soles of your feet, slowly washing away your worries and troubles. Washing them all away. Watching the worries go. Letting go, one breath and one worry at a time.

GOING BACK IN TIME

1. Now picture a photo album of your life. You might even choose to put actual pictures of yourself at different ages and stages in front of you.

2. Begin by reviewing your life as an adult, going back in time, through the album, one page at a time.

3. Review your life page by page until one picture appears that best represents your childhood, a picture that most encapsulates your experience. This picture may be time collapsed across the span of your life. It may be a picture of something that actually happened, or it could even be a picture that only represents what it felt like for you in your family.

4. Be with that picture, just that one picture. Open all your senses to that experience.

5. Let that picture come to life by turning it into a video.

BEING WITH IT AND COMING BACK

1. What do you see? Who is there? Who is not there? What is being said? What is not being said? What do you smell? Taste? Touch? What is this really like for you?

2. Be with this experience for a few moments.

3. Now, in your own time, bring back into this room what you choose to remember.

4. Slowly, one breath at a time, turn the pages of your album back to this time. Come back into the here and now.

Take a few moments to write down your experience or to tell a friend about it. Doing this makes it real. How has this experience from your past influenced how you see and experience the world today?

Jerry's picture was of when he was fourteen with his mother, father, and sister downstairs on the couch watching TV together. He's upstairs in his room reading a book. He quietly remarked, "That's my whole life. I have always been separate from, never a part of. Reading was my escape then and still is today. I have never felt comfortable with people. My mom and dad never talked, and when they did, they never had anything nice to say to each other. I never even knew my sister because she was always glued to my mother!"

Joan saw herself in a picture at age eight, sitting on a porch surrounded by boxes and luggage on moving day, looking very sad. She said that this picture was her life in a nutshell. "My father couldn't keep a job, so we moved a lot. I lived in six different cities prior to graduating from high school. Then I married a military man, and we moved from base to base every three years for the next twenty years. Today I still keep a suitcase packed, ready to go. This image is so clear. It's as if yesterday were today."

How does your snapshot picture influence how you see and perceive the world today?

In case you skipped over this exercise or others in these first two chapters, you might consider going back now and actually doing the exercises. Remember that healing and growth come through experience. These exercises and others in this book are meant to give you such experiences. But if you simply read what's here without going through the process yourself, then you'll miss out on some of the healing and growth that are possible. It takes work to change lifetime patterns, and doing these exercises is part of that work. Remember, there's no right or wrong way to do the exercises, just as there are no right or wrong answers. There are simply *your* answers. And they're not to be judged by anyone else, not even by you or your inner Critic. It's okay if you draw blanks on some of the exercises. You can come back to those later if you choose.

Part I of *The Missing Piece* has been designed to help you raise your level of awareness about the context in which you were raised—your family, your society, and your culture. Because all of these influences have affected who you are today, it's important that you develop a real sense of them from more than just an intellectual level before you move on. We're not simply healing our perceptions here, we're healing our emotions and our bodies as well. In fact where we most deeply feel the loss of the missing pieces in our self is in our body and emotions, our heart and soul.

The next stage of our journey along the Spiral Path is to begin to look at who we are today, in the here and now. Now that we've gathered our tools for the journey and know how the pieces of our Self puzzle end up missing, we're going to to take a deeper look into Pandora's box than we did in chapter 1. We're going to look directly into the mirror of the Self.

PART TWO

JOURNEY
TO THE
DEPTHS
OF SELF

CHAPTER 3

Naming the Pieces

So you ask yourself, *Who am I? Who am I really? Do I wear a mask? And if so, what's beneath this mask that protects me? What are my vulnerabilities?* In this chapter we are going to give you the opportunity to begin that process of recognizing the many parts that ultimately create the whole of you.

We recognize that looking inside oneself is like opening up Pandora's box. What so many of us fail to remember is that beneath all of the demons, troubles, and chaos in that box lies hope—the opportunity to get to travel down the path of self-knowledge. It takes time and patience. While you are on this journey, you will name, get to know, and embrace all the aspects of self, and as a result you will form a more integrated and unified sense of self.

We have seen that those who come from more nurturing families tend to develop a solid and integrated sense of self. There seems to be both an internal and an external consistency in their lives. What they say, how they feel, and what they do tends to be consistent more of the time. They speak with an *empowered-self* voice.

However, those who come from more troubled families, where there is inconsistency and stress, tend to develop a sense of self that is less integrated, less stable, and less cohesive. Oftentimes the self that they present to the world is different from the real self that is buried deep inside. They may have a chameleon self that changes with the wind. They may wear a protective mask that hides their real or vulnerable self from the world. It's as though they've glued down the pieces of the puzzle called Self, but some of the pieces have been glued in the wrong places. The result is that what they do, what they say, and how they feel do not match. This is what we are calling speaking with a *fragmented-self* voice.

In order to heal this fragmented self, it is sometimes helpful to look at what lies behind the mask. This involves taking the puzzle apart and naming and getting to know the pieces one by one. Then, after we've relearned what we need to know about who we are, we put the puzzle back together.

While we're looking at each piece of the puzzle, we'll speak with the *fragmented-self* voice. This allows us to put all of the pieces on the table and look at each one of them with a high-powered magnifying glass. During this process we will become acutely aware that each one of us has many selves within us.

TAKING IT APART SO THAT YOU CAN PUT IT BACK TOGETHER

Science has taught us the value of both the process of analysis and the process of synthesis. When we analyze and break down the substance called water into its parts, we have the individual components of hydrogen and oxygen. These elements each have unique properties and functions of their own, yet when we integrate them, they become a third, unique substance—water—that we can't live without. Your sense of self is similar. It is a unique entity in and of itself, and yet each of the parts that make up the whole of you is also unique when considered on its own.

If the pieces of your self were put into the wrong places as you grew up, you may now need to go back and take the pieces apart one by one and examine them to see if there are any missing or misplaced pieces. Then you'll be able to reclaim them one piece at a time until the whole puzzle called Self is in place—the right place, the place that allows you to speak your Truth. When this kind of synthesis or integration happens, what you think, what you feel, and what you say all match.

This part of the journey is about naming all of the aspects of this puzzle. In the process of looking at your parts, you will not break apart. We will help you look at each part in relationship to the whole. When you're done, we promise that you'll be able to remember how to place the puzzle pieces back together. You won't lose the "whole" during the process. You will become more, not less whole.

MULTIPLICITY[1]

It's important to note that at this stage of the game, when we talk about parts of self, we mean just that—parts or aspects of one whole self called you. We're most definitely not talking about multiple personalities here.

We believe that all of us have numerous aspects of self that form an entire internal family of selves. For some of us that internal family is whole and integrated. But for most of us the integration process was not totally completed as we grew up. We've ended up, to one degree or another, with what psychologists call an *ego-state disorder*.[2]

For others—a very, very small number—the trauma in childhood was so profound and the abuse so pervasive and so chronic that they developed totally separate personalities and became true Multiple Personalities. In response to overwhelming stress the psyche sometimes resorts to the miraculous and lifesaving coping strategy of dissociating and ultimately forming separate personalities that operate as independent persons within one body. In Dissociative Identity Disorder, or D.I.D.[3] (formerly called Multiple Personality Disorder, or M.P.D.), the psyche develops a ravine between the individual personalities so that they don't even know one another. Whenever an individual personality takes over, the person may very well experience a lapse of time. The person can't account for the lost time, because he or she has no idea that another personality has been out at that time. The true Dissociative Identity Disorder has little, if any, control over when a particular personality comes out.

Most of us are *not* D.I.D.'s. Dissociation and multiplicity do, though, occur along a continuum. The more stress, chaos, and trauma there was during your childhood, the less cohesive and integrated the parts of self within you are likely to be.

In people with an integrated sense of self, their many parts work together in a cooperative whole. People with an ego-state disorder also have many parts of self. But they do not lose large chunks of time, nor do they have a total lack of awareness of other parts. They simply have many parts that do not work together in a well-integrated fashion. Most of us have these numerous parts, over which we have varying degrees of control.

To understand someone with Dissociative Identity Disorder, imagine a band made up of musicians who only play when they feel like it.[4] There's no sense of a harmonious piece of music being created by the group as a whole. It's as though each player were in a soundproof booth, and no one can hear anyone else. Each instrument plays its own well-developed song when it feels like it, or when something in the environment triggers it. The conductor is just there taking up space — she or he has no power. And the many beats go on.

On the other hand those of us who speak with a fragmented-*I* voice play in a different sort of band, most often unruly, with a more or less weak conductor. But while in the first band, members each play their own song, this band at least plays the same song. It's just that the musicians play different parts of the same song. Sometimes the piccolo will play out of turn or the bass drums will get all excited and go off passionately playing solo. All of the instruments hear one another, but the sounds may be discordant and out of sync.

In *The Missing Piece* we're working toward creating an orchestra with someone as wonderful and talented as the late Leonard Bernstein or Jo Ann Falletta or Seiji Ozawa conducting, in which there are many different instruments playing their own unique and awe-inspiring music but all blending together into a rapturous symphonic form. This is what it's like to speak with an empowered-*I* voice.

Most of us fall somewhere along the continuum between integration and D.I.D. or M.P.D., the ultimate in fragmentation. Most of us have several parts of self that are integrated into our whole to one degree or another. And most of us are fragmented to some degree.

We are not promoting, nor could we possibly create a true Multiple Personality or Dissociative Identity Disorder in the work that we are asking you to do. The coping pattern that makes one a "multiple" is generally thought to begin before the age of five, when the psyche is naturally prone to dissociating in response to exceptional trauma. All we're asking you to do is to look at the parts of yourself for the purpose of better integration. We are promoting a process through which you will get to know yourself better and through which you'll come to feel more integrated.

Nearly a century ago Sigmund Freud noted that creativity is regression in service of the ego. The process of naming and getting to know the individual parts for the sake of future integration is similar. We are inviting you to analyze parts of yourself in service of the ego so that you can better re-member the parts into a more solid, integrated, and congruent whole. We are inviting you to analyze your many parts of self for the sake of later synthesizing self. We are inviting you into a creative process, one that enables you consciously to get to know all of you.

STEPPING STONES: NAMING THE PARTS

The first part of this expedition into self is about identification. It involves *naming all of the parts of you.*

Look in the mirror. Whom do you see? Someone who is special and unique? Do you like what you see? How do you respond to the external you? There's an internal you, too. You know the saying "Beauty is only skin deep." What you find when you look inside, into your internal mirror, will be unique and special. No one else in the entire universe will find the same thing. You are you, and no one else is exactly like you. No one else's parts of self will be the exact replica of yours.

This diversity is important. This is why it can be so painful to take on someone else's definition of you. When you become solely who someone else wants you to be, when your pleaser part is on overdrive, you are said to be codependent. This principle applies both to your external characteristics and behaviors as well as to your internal parts of self. Remember this: Don't let anyone else name the parts of you for you—not even the authors of this book. This is your puzzle, not someone else's. This is your sense of self, not someone else's.

To help you clearly to delineate the parts of yourself, we're going to take you through an eleven-step process called "Stepping Stones." They are eleven steps to get to know yourself better and better. This is a circular process. You can visualize it as a series of stepping stones around the edge of a circular pond. Since the pond has no beginning and no end, the steps do not need to be taken in any particular order. You can step on 2 before 10 or on 4 before 3 if you choose. These steps are simply ways for you to look at the many answers to the question *Who Am I?*

STEPPING STONES
  1. An External-Family Look
  2. A Chronological Look

3. A Traits Look
4. A "What Do I Do?" Look
5. A "What Hooks Me?" Look
6. A Common-Parts Look
7. A Physical and Mental Look
8. A Male/Female Look
9. An Expanded Look
10. An Imaginary Look
11. The Center of You

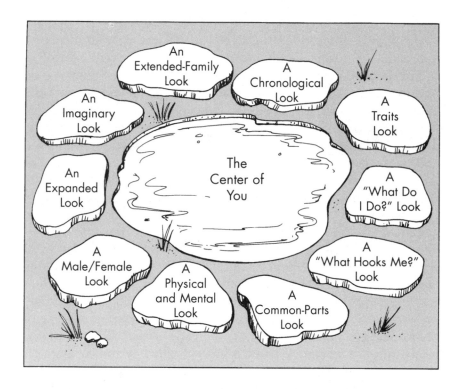

We have found that it works best to do all of these exercises, but in any order you choose. If you decide to skip a step, we would like to encourage you to go back later and do the exercise associated with that step. Each step will present you with an opportunity to look at yourself from a different angle.

It's as if you were looking at a rare gem, turning it around in your hand and letting the light shine through each different facet. As you hold this gem, the light will shine through in a different way, depending upon how you are handling it. Each stepping stone exercise is another turn of the gem. You will find that as you step along the path, you will get to know yourself better and better. When you've completed the journey, you'll be able to look at yourself in the mirror in the center of the pond and clearly name all the parts of your internal family of selves.

You may find that this part of the journey is like a smorgasbord. We encourage you to sample from each step. Some things will taste good; others won't. Some things will fit, others won't. Pick what feels right and leave the rest behind.

We suggest that you read each exercise first and then try it on your own before you read the examples we offer. This way you can use the stories to help you flesh out your own writing. It may be very helpful to write these exercises down in a journal and to date when you did each exercise. This journal is yours, for your eyes and for your eyes only to see. Remember that the goal in the end is to reach the final look in the mirror when you name *You*.

Stepping Stone 1: An External-Family Look

One of the most profound ways that we define who we are is through the holograms of the significant others in our lives that we've taken inside us. These people have all become part of us. They are major contributors to our sense of who we are.

There are two different ways that we would like you to look at how your external family has influenced your internal family. First of all, go back to the "Who Am I?" exercise in chapter 2 (pages 57–59). In this exercise you listed characteristics of yourself, your caretakers (your mother, your father, or whoever cared for you), yourself as others see you, and significant others. If you did not do the exercise before, then please do it before you begin the "Stepping Stones."

After you have done this exercise, you might find it helpful to glance at the list of descriptors in Appendix 1. Are there any new words on that list that you would like to add? Be careful not to take on any of these terms that do not truly describe you. Remember Woody Allen's Zelig? He probably would have taken on the whole list. We don't want you to become Zelig-like. Something shy of taking on the whole list will do nicely. What follows is an example of how Judith responded to the "Who Am I?" exercise.

Self	Mother	Father	Self as Others See Me	Nana (grand-mother)	Mrs. Smith (my second grade teacher)
spontaneous	judgmental	intelligent	powerful	spunky	smart
intuitive	caring	persistent	self-assured	playful	witty
spiritual	critical	intrusive	assertive	sad	loving
creative	lonely	funny	nurturing	serious	believable
sensual	active	passive	intelligent	hurting	determined
sensitive	uptight	distrusting	creative	cuddly	beautiful
nurturing	dramatic	aloof	sensitive	loving	
intelligent	martyr	patriarchal	patient	caring/	
scared	dependable	dishonest	energetic	nurturing	
insecure	strong	sad	angry		
lonely	scared	judgmental	aloof		
strong	fragile	scared	persistent		
honest	childish	destructive	hard worker		
open	distrusting	abusive	caring		
willing	aloof	rigid	dependable		
hard on self	intrusive	angry	macho		
driven	insecure	strong	strong		
compulsive	sensitive		driven		
			dominant		

The second way to look specifically at how your external family has made you who you are today is by looking at the masks that you and others wear. Let's look not only at the self you present to the world but also at the vulnerable self you may keep hidden and protected.

INNERS AND OUTERS

1. Taking one person at a time, step into your caretakers' (mother's/father's/significant other's) shoes for just a moment. What do you imagine is really going on for this person deep down inside? Beneath the mask what is she or he really feeling? What are some of the characteristics of this person's real or true self?

2. Now draw two concentric circles. Put the characteristics that your caretaker/mother/father/significant other shows to the world in the outside circle. Then put the ones this person hides behind the mask in the inside circle. The ones in the inside circle are the protected, real, or vulnerable selves. The ones in the outside circle are the masks, defended, false, or protective selves.

3. Do the same exercise for your father or mother or additional significant others, whomever you chose. Put the vulnerable or real self in the inside circle and the protective or false self in the outside circle.

Judith's "Inner and Outer" portrait looked like this:

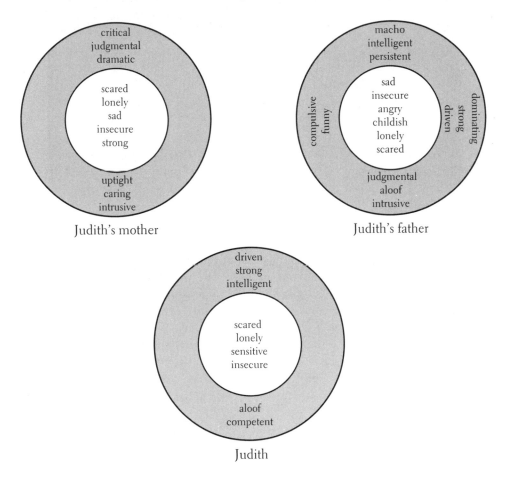

Judith's mother

Judith's father

Judith

Continue with the inners and outers of any other significant people you charted in the "Who Am I?" exercise. Now it's your turn. Let's look at the masks that you present to the world today. Again draw two concentric circles and list the characteristics you present to the outside world in the outer circle. Then show how you're really feeling in the inside circle. Even a quick look shows us how we have internalized those who have been important in our lives. Judith's circles show that in her inner circle she is scared, lonely, sensitive, and insecure, like her mom. But to the outer world Judith looks driven, strong, intelligent, and aloof, like her dad.

How do you present yourself to others? How do others see you? Are all of your masks simply ways that you protect yourself from being hurt, or are some of them a real part of you? Are you as tough as nails on the outside and just like a marshmallow on the inside? Or are you really strong on the inside while you present a weak and needy face to the world? Or are you both weak and strong, sometimes weak on the inside and strong on the outside and sometimes strong on the inside and weak on the outside? Your masks are an important part of you. They are you. We all need our masks to survive.

Take a moment to reflect back in time. What masks or protective selves did you develop around the ages of three, six, nine, twelve, fifteen, eighteen? What are the circumstances under which you wear these masks today? When do your "inners" and "outers" match? When do they not match? What causes you to speak with the fragmented voice?

It's important that you become aware of your masks, what they look like, what they do, how you can access them when you need to, and how you can set them aside when you no longer need the protection. Sometimes we forget to take our masks off, and then we wonder why we can't get close to our partner or friend. Other times we may need to own that the mask is really a part of us.

For example Judith discovered that what she thought was her mask, the appearance of strength, competency, and intelligence, was in fact a part of who she was. She was in fact strong, competent, and intelligent. It was not simply a mask employed for the purpose of survival but a real part of her sense of self as well. Your mask is very much a part of you. It is you. The goal is for each of us to be able to recognize our masks and to take ownership of them rather than them owning us.

Stepping Stone 2: A Chronological Look

Another way of looking at who you are is to do it in a linear or chronological fashion, that is, to move along a time continuum like the one Erik Erikson developed (see page 48). Each of us have several parts of our self that fit into a linear, chronological framework. These may very well be a little-child and an older-child part, a younger and an older teenage part, a young-adult part, a middle-aged adult part, a mature-adult part, an elder part, and a wise part. Here is an exercise that will help you define your self along a developmental continuum. You may choose to tape record this exercise and then to play it back to yourself.

A LOOK OVER TIME

1. Get quiet and comfortable. Follow your breath in and out, in and out. Note any tension that you may be carrying with you from your everyday world and release it. When you're ready, picture a scrapbook of pictures of your life from when you were born to now. Choose a safe place to begin and start turning those pages, one at a time, back through time until you reach a point where you're a small and very young child.

2. Be that **little child**. Step into your child self's shoes. What are you feeling? What are you doing? How would you describe yourself? Just be with your little child self for a time.

3. When you are ready, turn the pages in your scrapbook forward a little to when you are an **older child**. Be that older child. Step into those shoes. What are you feeling? What are you doing? How would you describe yourself? When you are ready, be with this older child self for a time.

4. When you are ready, turn the pages of time forward to when you were a **young teenager**, say junior high school or so. Step into the shoes you wore when you were between twelve and fifteen. What are you feeling? What are you doing? How would you describe yourself? You might even want to use some of the adjectives on the checklist on "Stepping Stone 1" to help you describe yourself at this age. Be your teenage self for just a few moments.

5. When you are ready, turn the pages of time forward to when you were an **older teenager**, high school or after. Step into the shoes that you wore when you were between sixteen and twenty-one. What are you feeling? What are you doing? How would you describe yourself? You might even want to use some of the adjectives on the checklist on "Stepping Stone 1" to help you describe yourself at this age. Be that teenager for just a few moments.

6. And once again, when you are ready, turn the pages of

the scrapbook forward to when you're a **young adult**, say age twenty-one to thirty-five. If you are not yet this age, imagine what you'll be like at this age. Step into those shoes. What are you doing? What are you feeling? How would you describe yourself? You might even want to use some of the adjectives on the checklist on "Stepping Stone 1" to help you describe yourself at this age. Be with your young-adult self.

7. When you are ready, turn the pages forward to you as a **middle-aged adult**, even if you're not yet that age. Step into those shoes when you were, are, or will be age thirty-six to fifty-five. What are you doing? What are you feeling? Describe yourself as a middle-aged adult. You might even want to use some of the adjectives on the checklist on "Stepping Stone 1" to help you describe yourself at this age. Be with this adult self for just a moment.

8. When you choose, turn the pages forward to you as a **mature adult**, even if you're not yet that age. Step into those shoes. What are you doing? What are you feeling? Describe yourself as a mature adult, age fifty-five to sixty-nine. You might even want to use some of the adjectives on the checklist on "Stepping Stone 1" to help you describe yourself at this age. Be with this grown-up self for just a moment.

9. When you choose, turn the pages forward to you as an **elder**, even if you're not yet that age. Step into the shoes you'll wear at age seventy or more. What are you doing? What are you feeling? Describe yourself as an elder. You might even want to use some of the adjectives on the checklist on "Stepping Stone 1" to help you describe yourself at this age. Be with your elder self for just a moment.

10. When you're ready, turn the pages forward to you as a **wise person**, even if you don't feel you've worn these shoes. The wise person can be any age. How old or how young are you? How does it feel to step into these shoes? What are you doing? What are you feeling? Describe yourself. And once again, you might even want to use some of the adjectives on the checklist on "Stepping Stone 1" to help you describe your wise self. Be with this self, knowing you can step into these shoes again any time you choose.

11. Gently, taking your time to collect your selves, return to the here and now. Below, write down descriptions of the nine selves you've just looked at. Put a picture of these nine

you's on the page as well. If you can't find a real picture of you at any given age, or if you haven't been that age yet, try to find pictures of others in magazines who look the way you envision yourself being at that age.

young-child self	older-child self	younger-teenager self	older-teenager self	young-adult self	middle-aged adult self	mature-adult self	elder-adult self	wise self—any age
0–5	5–11	12–15	16–20	21–35	36–55	56–70	70+	any age

What did you learn about yourself as you took a chronological look at who you are? You may find that this way of looking at the parts of your internal family of selves works well for you. This is simply one of ten stepping stones that will help you take a clear look in the mirror at your internal family of selves.

This is what Jannie did with this look at her self across time:

My young-child self is age three. She is playful, fun-loving, free-spirited, funny, spontaneous, cute, happy, sensitive, inquisitive—and also a little scared, lonely, and angry.

My older-child self is ten and awkward and sad.

My younger-teenager self, age thirteen, is free-spirited, funny, impulsive, sensitive, try-it-all, rebellious, angry, and lonely.

My older-teenager self, age nineteen, is sullen, philosophical, independent, and pensive.

My young-adult self is twenty-eight years of age, and she is independent, compulsive, dependable, judgmental, energetic, driven, and an explorer.

My middle-aged adult self, age forty-two, is dependent, angry, impulsive, sad, scared, self-abusive, sensitive, insecure, caring, intelligent, athletic, and depressed.

My mature-adult self is sensitive, secure, warm, and nurturing.

My elder-adult self is playful and free-spirited, though sometimes she moves slowly to conserve energy.

My wise-woman self is ageless and spiritual. She is opinionated, nurturing, caring, inquisitive, patient, peaceful, and serene.

Jannie found that there were positive and negative ways that she described herself at each age and that the descriptions reflected things that had gone on in her life at different ages and stages of her development. She reported to us, "The wise-woman part of me has been there since I was a child."

Stepping Stone 3: A Traits Look[5]

Traits or characteristics are ways of describing ourselves. Sometimes they reflect things that we do. Sometimes they describe ways that we approach things. Sometimes these traits are indicative of how we see and perceive the world. Looking at traits is another way to look at self. Cognitive psychologists have associated different personality styles with ways of thinking and perceiving the world. They have noted that each personality style or pattern of protective selves has a set of traits associated with it. It's possible that we have collected these traits from all the various personality styles within us. Some are more dominant than others. In fact we may get locked so deeply into one set of traits that we can't see or perceive the world in any other way—we overidentify with our primary selves.

One way for you to look at these traits would be to do the following exercise:

TRAITS

1. For just a moment let down your defenses. Ask the parts of you that protect you the most from hurt, pain, and vulnerability if it's okay for them to step aside for just a moment. Listen to your body and settle into being as honest with yourself as is humanly possible.

2. Check off where along the continuum you see yourself with each of these traits most of the time:

rigid _____ spontaneous
dependent _____ self-sufficient
passive-aggressive _____ assertive
mistrusting _____ trusting
self-centered _____ sharing
withdrawn _____ emotionally intimate
avoidant/inhibited _____ gregarious
controlled _____ expressive

3. Now that you have delineated which traits tend to describe you, please give each trait a rating from 1 to 10, with 1 meaning "I have this trait some of the time, but not much," to 10 being "I have this trait virtually all of the time." Put the appropriate number in parentheses at the end of each trait. This rating tells you how often you see yourself engaging in each particular trait. You can also rate each trait on each side of the scale. For example let's say on the "avoidant/inhibited _____ gregarious" dimension you sense that you are avoidant/inhibited in very few situations. You give it a "1." However, you see yourself as gregarious about half the time, so you give it a "5."

4. Then, if you find it helpful, in the same parentheses after each line in your traits list, note those situations in which you most commonly experience each trait. For example, if you've scored yourself a "5" for being gregarious, next to the number 5 also list the situations in which you are gregarious—"at parties, with friends, with my children," and so on. If you've given yourself a "1" next, at "avoidant/inhibited," you might also add "at work but only when my boss is hovering over me and I'm scared."

As we look at Bob's example below, it's clear that for the most part he feels good about himself today. Most of his traits are positive, and those that are less positive may very well be dependent on the situations he finds himself in. Notice that Bob gives himself a "5" at "gregarious," and a "2" at "avoidant/inhibited." He sees himself as "10" at "self-sufficient," and "0" at "dependent." The traits we see ourselves exhibiting most of the time form part of our overall personality. They are considered to be *states*. When a trait is more rare, it is seen as *situational*.

BOB'S EXAMPLE

(3, at work when scared)	rigid _____×_____ spontaneous	(3, with my partner)
(0, not at all)	dependent _____×_____ self-sufficient	(10, all the time)
(1, at work a little re: my boss)	passive-aggressive _____×_____ assertive	(8, almost all the time)
(4, at work, usually cautious)	mistrusting _____×_____ trusting	(5, friends, family)
(3, at work some)	self-centered _____×_____ sharing	(7, friends, family)
(2, at work a little)	withdrawn ____×____ emotionally intimate	(5, friends, family)

| (2, at work a little) | avoidant/inhibited___×___gregarious | (5, friends, family, parties) |
| (2, at work a little) | controlled___×___expressive | (9, most every place) |

Remember that Bob's sketch of himself is simply a snapshot at this particular time of his life—age forty-five. Your picture will probably have different parts and different scores than Bob's.

As you do these exercises, keep in mind that labels are simply convenient words that we choose to use at times to help us communicate our ideas and thoughts. However, labeling can also be used in a judgmental way to back people into corners. Labels can imply that things are all one way or another, that everything is absolute. When you label someone, you may be distancing yourself from that person. We're not using labels in this negative, limiting way. These labels are simply meant to serve as shorthand for some ideas and behaviors we're trying to describe. We don't believe that a person needs to become the label. If you, like Bob, tend to be assertive, and self-sufficient, this does not mean that you *are* those words. After all, at a given time and under given circumstances you may very well be the opposite of those words. You are not the label. You are not one single self. Perhaps in certain circumstances you can also be withdrawn and avoidant. That doesn't mean that you are those labels either. In other words just because you act in an avoidant and withdrawn way at times, it doesn't mean you are necessarily "Avoidant" and "Withdrawn," in capital letters.

Stepping Stone 4: A What Do I Do? Look

Many of us define who we are by what we do. Think for a moment about how you introduce yourself in social situations. If we were to ask you who you are, what's the first thing you'd tell us? Are you a partner; a father, mother, daughter, son; a grandfather or grandmother; an artist; a nurse; a teacher; a lawyer; an employee? This exercise is one more stepping-stone in this journey to look at the self.

WHAT DO I DO?

1. Follow yourself around for the next few days noticing what it is you do. Notice the different roles you take on, and the many hats you wear. List these roles on a piece of paper.

2. What adjectives describe each role for you?

3. Now imagine yourself surrounded by all of your roles. Can you see them all? That's the you that you present to the world.

4. Imagine for a moment that each of these roles is being eliminated. You're no longer what you do. All the hats you wear have been set aside. Who are you now?

Mary Anne discovered that she wears many hats, sometimes all at once. Here is her writing on this exercise:

> I do lots of things. I wear many hats, sometimes too many. I'm a partner, a mother, a teacher, a chauffeur for my kids, a house-cleaner, a gardener, and a friend. And being a partner means doing things all the time—picking things up after my partner, and doing the wash and the dishes and cooking and the like. Being a mother is all of that and more. It means being responsible for my kids' every move.
>
> When I wear my teacher hat, I'm in charge of a hundred students—the lectures, their grades, and all of their questions. As the family chauffeur I put five hundred miles a week on our van running everybody and anybody anywhere and everywhere. I'm the family maid too. Somehow I've gotten myself in charge of delegating all of the household jobs. And then there's our garden; well, it's all mine to keep up too. My partner likes to read and watch TV a lot. I also do the books for my partner's business. That's a bunch of busywork. And sometimes when all of the work is done, I get to relax with my friends. They're not much work, but everything else is.

Like Mary Anne we tend to act out roles as we define or see them. Mary Anne sees most of her roles as a burden. Is it any wonder that this thirty-seven-year-old woman is tired sometimes!? The real eye-opener for Mary Anne in this exercise was when she discovered that if she set aside all of these hats, there wasn't much left. She, like so many of us, had come to be her roles. When she imagined setting the roles aside, she felt empty, lonely, and sad inside. How about you? Who are you if you aren't doing something?

Stepping Stone 5: A "What Hooks Me?" Look

We all run into people who really bug us, who get under our skin, who we never ever in our worst nightmares would want to be like. Nancy said facetiously, "I gathered all of the men who really drove me nuts into one room. I ran a lottery, and I married the one that won." Jim said, "The kind of person who bothers me the most is someone who's a sloth and a wimp. I can't stand someone who just sits around and 'veges out.'" Emily, another Missing Piece group member, said that "people who are passive-aggressive get under my skin," and Sandy said, "I can't stand people who are pushy and aggressive." The list goes on. Everyone has someone or something that gets to them at some point in time.

WHAT HOOKS ME?

Follow yourself around for a few days. Who bothers you a lot? What movie stars or TV personalities can't you stand? What is it about one of your relatives, your partner, your friends, or even your children that you can't stand?

Write all of this down, because this is the kind of material you're liable to forget very quickly.

Nevertheless, much as we don't want to believe it, very often—as Larry so wisely said—"What bothers me most about you is something that I can't own about myself. Something that I so far haven't been able to embrace in myself. Something I haven't been able to learn to use productively for myself. When there's a part of you I can't stand, it simply may be that I'm jealous that you have that part and I don't."

Billy brought up the example of the band. "Maybe I don't have all the instruments in my band that you do in yours. Maybe I want what you have. Or maybe I have the instrument, but to make my music sound even better, I need to learn to play some new notes—notes that you know how to play and I don't. Maybe if I just learn a few new notes or even if I simply rearrange the music, the piece will be just as exquisite as yours. So if I own in me the parts that bug me in you, then I'll be exquisite too!"

Teri had it all figured out—intellectually at least:

If I can't stand it when you're really messy around the office, then there's probably a disowned part of me that's pretty messy too. It must mean that I haven't learned to use my less structured part of self to let go of the need for total tidiness around me at all times. It means I'm rigidly neat at the expense of spontaneity. If I can't stand it when you are late, then there's probably a part of me that keeps people waiting too. Or perhaps that there's a part that hasn't learned to let go of time in service of process. If I can't stand it when someone uses dominant, hierarchical power over me, then there's probably a part of me that uses that same kind of power over others at times.

We all seem to defend ourselves heavily against some characteristics we find in others, and try as we may, we still end up being like those we defend against to one degree or another. Disowned parts pop out when we haven't learned to use them and when we fail to value their energy. This would be like a piccolo in the band that has been ignored and has been locked in the band-room closet. Much to everyone's surprise this forgotten piccolo periodically runs onto center stage and makes loud, ugly piccolo squawks, just to "assert" itself. "I AM, even though you say that I'm not," it seems to be declaring. Needless to say, it helps to be aware of all of the parts of self, even the disowned ones like the hidden piccolo.

Stepping Stone 6: A Common-Parts Look[6]

We've found that there are some common parts that most of us have in our internal family of selves. These parts are known by many names. Here's an exercise that will help you recognize some of these common parts:

COMMON PARTS

Check off on the following list any parts that may be inside of you:

____ the Nurturer	____ the Protector	____ the Judge/Critic
____ the Cautious One	____ the Responsible One	____ the Patient One
		____ the Sensual One
____ the Spiritual One	____ the Wise One	____ the Playful One
____ the Mimic Self	____ the Rebel	____ the Creative One

_____ the Innocent
Child

_____ the Impulsive
One

_____ the Emotionally
Hungry One

_____ the Sad One

_____ the Athlete

_____ the Obedient
One

_____ the Humble One

_____ the Victim/the
Oppressed One

_____ the Frightened
One

_____ the People
Pleaser

_____ the Comic

_____ the Physically
Sick One

_____ the Patriarch/the
Oppressor

_____ the Angry One

_____ the Pusher

_____ the Scholar

_____ the Suffocated/
Smothered One

Now check off any of these parts that you think describe your mother, father, brother, sister, partner, friend, teacher, and so on.

What follows are Bill's answers to this exercise. He has bravely marked off even the ones that he's not so proud of. Bill saw himself as "Protector of the world. And I have a big Critic in there too. I've been a Victim a lot in my life, but I can also be an aggressive Oppressor as well. It amazes me, but as much as I consider myself a feminist, there's a patriarch inside me as well. Sometimes the Impulsive part of me comes out, and for sure the Rebel is rampant when I'm mad. My internal family is rounded out by a Playful Child part, as well as a Frightened One."

Bill described his mother as having a very Nurturing part, a Patient One, along with a strong Judge and inner Critic. He described his father as having a Patriarch, an Angry part, and an Athlete. He perceptively noted, "I think he's got a Frightened One hidden inside there as well." Interestingly enough, Bill describes his life partner as having exactly the same parts as his mother. His tennis partner, Jack, has an Athlete, a Judge, and a Sensual part. He sees his secretary as mostly a People Pleaser.

What are your common parts of self? Are there some that you are proud of as well as some that you don't want anyone to see? Look around you. What parts do you seek out in others? Why not make this into a game that you quietly play during this next week?

Stepping Stone 7: A Physical and Mental Look

Another way we define who we are is by our looks. "I am tall. I am short. I am thin. I am fat. I have big shoulders. My legs are long and lean. My hair is too curly. My nose is too big. She has quite a figure. He needs to work out. She looks the same today as she did twenty years ago—how does she do it? The tan makes him look wonderful. I'm a leg man myself. Watch how she walks. I love her eyes. I love his mouth. His jaw is so tight. She dresses like a guy. He looks like a swimmer. His pants are too tight. Her hair is to die for. He has some weight to lose. Look at those lines under his eyes. Have you ever seen hands like those? She looks great. He looks wonderful." And the list goes on.

Whether it's fair or not, we all judge each other and ourselves by physical appearance, and thus our sense of self is at least in part defined by our physical being. Many of us have an unrealistic view of what we should look like, and some of us even have an unrealistic view of what we do look like. Our society promotes such views.

Sometimes the physical self is part of the protective self. Sometimes it's part of a mask. Andy, who is twenty pounds overweight, carries his weight to protect him from being hurt. Sara, a college beauty queen, found "that people only see my beauty—they never listen to me. What I say is always discounted." Martin, a short man, defines who he is in part by what he looks like: "I always have to speak up so much and I have to be so aggressive. It's as though people expect me to be like Napoleon."

How do you see yourself as a physical being? A young college student who is proud of her near six feet in height told us with a smile, "I'm vertically advantaged." List as many words as you can to describe yourself from a physical perspective. Has that view changed over the years? Whom do you look like? Whom would you like to look like? Look in the mirror. What do you really see? That's a part of your sense of self—your physical self.

Do you consider yourself to be smart or not so smart, quick or not so quick? Intelligence is another way that we look at and define who we are. Some of us are smart and yet we doubt our intelligence. Some of us flaunt our intelligence and some of us hide it. Our society reinforces our having some intelligence but not too much. People are said to be "slow" if their intelligence is below normal (e.g. Forrest Gump), and "weird" if their intelligence is way above average (we call them eggheads). How do you judge yourself by your intelligence? What kind of impact does this have on who you are? Is your level of intelligence part of your protective self, or is it a part of the vulnerable you? Is it an important or major part of who you are, or is it simply a minor part? What weight does it carry in your sense of self?

Samantha told us, "I'm just average—fast on some things and not so fast on others. My intelligence is no big deal to me. Other things are more important." On the other hand Tom, a medical doctor, candidly told us, "I'd just die if my brain power left me. My dad has Alzheimer's disease, and the idea of my ever losing my mental faculties like that is overwhelming to me. I am my mind, and my mind is me."

Stepping Stone 8: A Male/Female Look

In our society we tend to be influenced by how those around us define what it's like to be female and what it's like to be male. Whether we believe that women and men are different or similar because of genetic wiring, or hormones, and/or because of the effect of the society in which they're raised, the sense of self is in one way or another most definitely affected by the notion of gender.

Whether or not it's logical or rational or even scientifically based, most of us tend to associate some traits with men and some traits with women. We tend to forget that men and women have more similarities than differences. We tend to forget that we all have one basic core issue—abandonment—and that much of our lives is spent dancing around (or sometimes even acknowledging) this fear. With this in mind, here are two exercises that will help you get in touch with what being male or female means to you:

MALE/FEMALE

1. Being a girl in my family meant:

_____.

2. Being a boy in my family meant:

_____.

3. Being *female* means to me:

_____.

4. Being *male* means to me:

_____.

5. If I were a woman, I would:

_____.

Or, if I were a man, I would:

_____.

6. Describe the person (someone who embodies all the traits that you value) you would most like to be like:

_____.

Barbara, thirty-eight, answered these gender questions as follows:

BARBARA'S EXAMPLE

1. *Being a girl in my family meant* being second best, being quiet, being helpless, waiting passively to have things done for you even if you knew that you could do it yourself.
2. *Being a boy in my family meant* getting hit. It meant being tough, being irresponsible, getting to play a lot.
3. *Being female means* life is tough, being victimized, and not trusting men.
4. *Being male means* being domineering, angry, ineffectual, adventurous, and having lots of excitement.
5. *If I were a man I would* have most of the power and make most of the money.

It's easy to see Barbara living a life where she does not value her relationships with women as much as she does those with men. While men are not to be trusted, at least they represent fun and excitement and power. Life does not have to remain caught within this frame. By attending to her healing process, Barbara may be able to tap into healthier beliefs and come to realize she has more positive options.

We agree with Carol Tavris in her landmark book, *The Mismeasure of Woman*, in which she states that women in our society have been measured against the standard of men and as a result have been seen as less than men. However, Tavris warns that the solution is not the opposite of that—to begin measuring men by the standard of women. Rather it seems more appropriate to look at each individual's unique characteristics. Measuring one by the standard of the other simply creates divisiveness.[7]

There's nothing in our genetic wiring that says that only women are the nurturing gender or that only men are superior at analytical thinking. Reliable research does not show anything in the human brain that makes a woman more passive and a man more aggressive. Women can be aggressive and analytical, and men can be passive and nurturing. These traits are no more feminine than they are masculine and no more masculine than they are feminine. It is certainly true that there are biological differences between the genders, but the bulk of the differences seem to be those that have been promoted by the culture, society, and context in which we live.

As Tavris suggested, the solution may be to look at each person as an individual, whether he or she is male or female. Research on "healthy" adults shows that we tend to define health by a combination of traits. Being emotionally healthy means having traits that have been traditionally associated with being female as well as those associated with being male. Consider for a moment how you look at yourself as a woman or as a man. Are there traits from both genders that you would like to (and perhaps already do) have? Barbara's answer to question number 6 reflects this:

> 6. *The person I would most like to be like* is soft, open, and receptive. She can let go. She is warm and tender. She listens well. She is serene. She is spiritual. She is very self-caring. She is creative, adventuresome, and playful. She feels her feelings deeply. She uses her anger constructively, not destructively. Power exudes from her cells, and her power is attracting. She is strong. She is direct. She gets a lot done. She is determined. She is honest. She knows how to say no. She is forever growing. She is comfortable in her body. She knows how to let things be and to let go.

The second exercise is a guided imagery. You might want to tape-record this so that that you can play it back for yourself.

BEING A MAN/BEING A WOMAN: GUIDED IMAGERY

1. Close your eyes for just a moment. Visualize yourself in a quiet, restful place where you can begin to look deep inside. A place where you can begin to rehear the messages that you got from your mother and from your father about being male and about being female.
2. Focus on your breath. Follow it in and out, in and out. Listen to those messages about being man, about being woman. Listen to those messages, one at a time, for some time.
3. Now become aware of your body as you listen to those

messages. Become aware of your breath, of your heart, of your head, of your legs, of your arms, of your hands, of your feet.

4. For just a moment listen to the messages that you got about being a woman, about being feminine. Are there some messages from Mom, and some from Dad? Where in your body do you store these messages? Where in your being do you feel you've kept these messages all of these years?

5. And the messages about being masculine, about being male? What are those messages—those from Dad, and those from Mom? Where in your body are you storing those messages? How does your body feel when you hear those messages?

6. When you are ready, come back into this room, and this time write about what you experienced just now.

Here's how Beth responded to this exercise:

The messages from my mother about being a woman are about being a victim, about being somewhat powerless. She taught me that women need to work hard because they can't trust men. "Don't trust men!" That's my mother's main message about being male. *These messages are stored* in my gut and they are visceral. *The messages from Dad about being female are* about women being "less than" and that I need to keep trying harder and harder. *Those messages are stored* in my feet, and these messages ground me in who I am. *The messages from Dad about being male are* that I need to do things, lots of things. I need to achieve to be worth anything, I need to work before I can play. And when I play, I'm to play hard. *Those messages are stored* in my shoulders, in my back, and in my neck—all of which are hurting as I write this. It feels like both my mom and my dad are all over my back as I listen to these messages.

Clearly Beth is going to struggle with feeling empowered as a woman. For her, strength was only supported through driven performance. Outside of performance there were no more positive attributes. Beth, like so many of us, is restricted by her narrow definitions of male and female. She sees being feminine as being passive, quiet, demure, helpless, gentle, warm, tender, nurturing, needy, serene, emotional, irrational, and process-oriented. She sees being masculine as being strong, assertive, domineering, determined, driven, outspoken, rational, logical, and goal-oriented.

Beth found that her body gave her clues about the messages she experienced and when. Her shoulders, back, and neck hurt when she considered whether the feeling might be a clue that she was operating under her dad's messages about being driven.

The messages that any and all of us have received about being male and being female profoundly affect our sense of who we are. Some of the reasons we feel the way we do are because of the stereotypical messages about gender that we have taken into our sense of self—parts that we're just beginning to take a look at here.

Stepping Stone 9: An Expanded Look

A number of other variables—such as ethnicity, social status, class, religion, education, sexual orientation, and physical ability— are also important parts of our definition of who we are. Much of what we see and read is geared toward individuals who are white, middle class, Protestant, heterosexual, college educated, and physically able. This is often regarded as the dominant culture because these are the people most likely to control economic resources and to wield power over others in our society. These are the predominant images that we see on TV, in magazines, and in the news. We tend to forget that not everyone fits into this mold. We forget that those who do not are often disenfranchised and left to feel that they are outsiders. This is a painful experience.

Stop and think for a moment. In addition to how you defined your sense of self before, how else might you see yourself? How do you identify yourself in terms of race, social status, class, education, religion, sexual orientation, and physical ability? Are you African American, Asian American, Native American, Hispanic, or Caucasian? Are you rich or are you poor? Do any of these things make you feel better or less than others? What do you have in common with others in your group, and what differences do you see between yourself and others? How strong a role do these issues play in how you define yourself and how you view others?

Have you been taught to feel ashamed of some particular aspect of your identity? Do you measure yourself by the standards of white, middle-class Anglo-Saxon America? Is that a standard that even fits you? Are you a part of, or different from, that? If you graduated from college, do you consider others who didn't have that opportunity to be less than you on some level? Or just because you had a rich uncle, are you better than others? Is your Jewish heritage accepted among your peers? Do your friends really understand what it's like to be a lesbian?

Those of us from the nondominant culture go through the process of forming an identity in many of the same ways as those from the dominant culture. However, we may not place the same importance on exactly the same parts of that identity. A large part of our identity may be as a member of a group and as a part of a particular community. If the group we belong to is an "out" group, we tend to emphasize group membership more in terms of how we define who we are. Group membership may become a major part of our identity, in many instances, a part of our battalion of protective parts of self. It's even possible that this whole notion of a missing piece in our sense of self is experienced differently depending on membership in one of these groups and whether or not the group that we belong to is an "in" group or an "out" group. For example if you are gay or lesbian, it's highly probable that your membership in that particular group is a large part of how you define yourself, whereas if you're a man with brown hair, you probably don't consider your membership in the group of men with brown hair to be a major part of your identity.

A person's identity is determined by more than just a simple interaction between "How I see myself," "How others see me," and "How I see myself in relation to others." The development of this identity is embedded in a context, and group membership is a key variable in that context. In other words we all belong to various groups, but some are more relevant to how we define ourselves than others.

For example, being Asian American in a predominantly white society may make one's racial self more salient on a daily basis than it would be for Caucasians. By contrast, if you are heterosexual and you mainly associate with other heterosexuals, your membership in that group is not likely to be as salient in your definition of who you are as it would be for a gay male. Take a young woman on full scholarship at an expensive liberal arts school. In that setting, class will be a more meaningful part of her self than it would be for her wealthy counterpart in the same school. Or take a physically challenged person—he's much more likely to define who he is by his physical self than someone who is not physically challenged.

Thus, if you are not part of the dominant culture, you have a duality to sort through as you define who you are. In such situations these more salient factors become a filter through which you view all aspects of life. You might even find that this dimension of who you are influences other ways you define self. For example you might find that there are female and male stereotypes in your culture that affect your identity differently than they do people from the dominant culture. The values that you place on individuality, autonomy, community, and family may also vary from the norm. The importance of religious or spiritual practices in your life may differ from that of the mainstream. The value of education may vary from culture to culture. All of this affects who you are in different ways.

It's likely that these issues influence us in ways we may not always be aware of. We want you to consider the impact of the issues of ethnicity, social status, class, culture, education, religion, sexual orientation, and physical ability in the following exercise. Respond to the sentence parts that are relevant to you. (The questions are repeated at least once in order to force you to take an even deeper look.)

GROUP MEMBERSHIP

1. I am _____.
(name your ethnic group: African American, Middle Eastern, Asian American, Hispanic, Native American, etc.)

2. Being _____ means _____ to me.
(name your ethnic group: African American, Middle Eastern, Asian American, Hispanic, Native American, etc.)

3. Being _____ means _____ to me.
(name your ethnic group: African American, Middle Eastern, Asian American, Hispanic, Native American, etc.)

4. Being a light-skinned or darker-skinned (circle one) _____ means _____.
(name your ethnic group)

5. Being a light-skinned or darker skinned (circle one) _____ means _____.
(name your ethnic group)

6. Being part of the _____ culture means _____ to me.
(e.g., Irish, Italian, Jewish, Polish, Lebanese, Chinese, etc.)

7. Being part of the _____ culture means _____ to me.
(e.g., Irish, Italian, Jewish, Polish, Lebanese, Chinese, etc.)

8. Having a(n) _____ education means _____ to me.
(e.g., eighth-grade, high-school, college, graduate-school)

9. Having a(n) _____ education means _____ to me.
(e.g., eighth-grade, high-school, college, graduate-school)

10. Being part of the _____ religion means _____ to me.

11. Being part of the _____ religion means _____ to me.

12. Being part of the _____ class means _____ to me.
(social class)

13. Being part of the _____ class means _____ to me.
(social class)

14. Being lesbian or gay or bisexual or heterosexual (circle one) means _____ to me.

15. Being lesbian or gay or bisexual or heterosexual (circle one) means _____ to me.

16. Being differently abled means _____ to me.
(hearing impaired, blind, chronic illness, etc.)

17. Being differently abled means _____ to me.
(hearing impaired, blind, chronic illness, etc.)

EXAMPLES

1–3. Being Hispanic means having strong family values to me.

4–5. Being a dark-skinned African American means not being accepted by the kids at school when I was growing up.

6–7. Being part of the Italian culture means being very affectionate.

8–9. Having "only" a high-school education means that I have disappointed my parents and that I'll never be enough.

10–11. Being Buddhist means having deep spiritual ties to my family and community, but it also means feeling left out of the dominant culture.

12–13. Being part of the working class means I know what it's like to work hard and that I'm a great example of the Protestant work ethic in America.

14–15. Being bisexual means not fitting in anywhere.

16–17. Having cerebral palsy means people often stay away from me.

Whether you are Caucasian, poor, and a high-school dropout, or an African-American doctor, your race, social status, class, education, religion, sexual orientation, and physical ability influence your experiences, both internally and in the world at large.

Stepping Stone 10: An Imaginary Look

Sit comfortably in a safe place and get really quiet. We want you to enter an inner space where you can be in touch with the intuitive side of yourself. We want you to use your imagination. We want you to tap into some creative energy. We all have that kind of energy, whether it comes out when you cook dinner, when you garden, when you solve a problem at work, or when you write a poem.

Children have great imaginations and they tend to be very connected to animals—through their family pets or through books and pictures. We would like you to use your imagination just like a child would. Imagine for a moment that you are an animal, any animal. What animal would you be? Picture yourself being that animal. What would you do if you were that animal? What animal would you never want to be? Picture yourself being that animal for just a moment. And what would you do if you were that animal?

Shelly said she'd be a cat because cats get held and loved. They are stroked. She wouldn't be a dog because they get put outside; they get kicked; and they're given away (or at least they were in Shelly's family). Shelly wept as she became aware that she, like the dog described above, was the one kicked, put outside, and given away.

Alec said he'd never want to be a parrot. Then Alec realized that he was the one in the family who told family secrets and felt like he was kept in a cage because of it. Today he'd like to be an eagle soaring everywhere high above the world. He said it offered him a way of seeing everyone and everything.

Sometimes when you come up with the animal you'd least like to be, it helps you get in touch with disowned parts of yourself. Robert, a Missing Piece group member, said,

> I'd hate to be a snake. Snakes are ugly. They slither in and out of places and surprise their victims. If I were a snake, I'd probably slither and sneak into places where I didn't belong. I'd scare people. I'd hurt people. I'd make people my victims. I can't stand people who put their noses in other people's business, and I can't stand people who are nosy and get into my

business all the time. I can't stand people who are dishonest. It used to really bother me when my brother would do that.

My mother would always slither into my room and go through my drawers when I was little. I'd see her do the same in Dad's workroom. I couldn't stand her when she'd do that. It really bugs me when someone gets into my things without asking, and when they're sneaking around and are dishonest.

Robert learned a lot about himself from doing this exercise. He's spent a lot of energy in his adult life in trying not to be snakelike. Others have perceived him as being aloof and standoffish because he didn't ask questions and didn't seem curious or interested. He thought he was being nonintrusive and nonsnakelike. Yet he found himself snooping through his lover's wallet and drawers when in the passion of the moment he just couldn't stand the distance he'd created between himself and others another minute. Sometimes he'd show up unannounced or arrive early as if to catch his partner doing something he wouldn't like. Thus, much to his dismay, Robert found that he could be snakelike too.

For some people the power in this exercise lies in discovering what they would like to be. This is the ideal self. For others the power of this simple exercise is in realizing what they don't want to be. This is the bad or negative self. Let's take one more step in order to resolve the tension between ideal self and negative self. If you couldn't be the animal you most want to be, and you didn't have to be the animal that you never, ever wanted to be, what animal would you be?

Sam would like to have been a lion, "so I could be king of the jungle," and he never, ever wanted to be an ant, "because they get stepped on." He said that if he couldn't be a lion and if he couldn't be an ant, he'd choose to be a giraffe in order to "keep an eye on everything."

Our ideal self, our negative or bad self, and the reality-based resolution self are all part of who we are. Sam, for example, has a part of him that is very powerful and aggressive, like the lion. And he has a part that is a victim, like the ant. But he also has a part that can see everything, like the giraffe.

So what animal would you like to be like and not like? If you couldn't be either of them, what animal would you be? Are these animals all parts of you?

Stepping Stone 11: The Center of You

In the center of the pond that the previous ten stepping stones have gone around is the core or "I" of you. This new stepping stone is the whole of you. It pulls all of you together like the hub of a wheel. The core "I" allows you to get out of a part and to not get stuck in it. It is the sum of all of the parts of you. It has within it a little bit of each of the other parts of you. It is the "me" that allows you to just be you. It is powerful and empowering. Power emanates from the "I," and consequently from you when you're in it. The "I" is the essence of you. Here is an exercise that will help you see the "I" of you when you look in the mirror:[8]

THE "I" OF YOU

- Look deep down inside you to your very core. What do you see?
- What do you sense?
- Is there an image or symbol that comes up for you that represents the whole of you? Something that pulls together all the parts of you?
- Picture that image. Let it work through you. Let the image "do you."

One of our Missing Piece group members said "The 'I' of me is my heart. When I put my hand over my quietly beating heart about an inch from my chest, I can feel everything inside of me come together. I feel whole." Another group member also had a heart image, but hers was when she was running. As she moved, she felt her heart beat. It had energy and power. She could feel the essence of herself. "It's like I become whole when I feel my heart beating fast like this. I am strong and powerful, and all of the parts of me are pulled together when I feel this racing heart." Another group member's image of his core was "a ray of light that runs through me from my feet to the tip of my head. When I picture this and feel it deep inside of me, I actually feel together and whole."

Cindy said that the image of her core was like the picture on the cover of the video *A River Runs Through It*. "It runs through me, pulling me all together like the peaceful, calm river that runs through life. I, too, feel whole when I sense this river running through me. I can sense the parts of me, but they are all just little offshoots from the main river that runs through the essence of me."

Dave said that the image that pulls him together is of the flowers in his garden—"all the tulips around the pond. They're so vibrant and full of energy, and when I envision them, I feel whole." Samantha said that her image was the music from Beethoven's Fifth Symphony: "I can feel myself come together when I feel that music play throughout the all of me, one part at a time. This music is at the core of me."

Sonya's image was that of a triangle that she placed over her heart as she talked. "When I feel this, all of the parts of me come together in the center. I am one and I feel powerful." Cathy pictured the globe as viewed from the moon by the Apollo Seven crew as her core. Patrick said his image was his girlfriend's hair blowing freely in the wind as she was running across a meadow near their home. "When I picture this, I feel the freeness of spirit in the center of me as well."

Clarissa said her core image was that of the bones that make up her skeleton. "When I get in touch with my bones, particularly as my bones touch the ground, I feel the center of me. Every part of me becomes a part of the core of me."

Before you move on to do any more internal-family work, it's important that you at least have a working image of your core so that when a part of you begins to take over, you can center yourself and return to the core of you. We do not want you to collapse into any one part. Such a collapse will hinder, not help, your healing. When you feel as though a part of you is totally taking over, you will want to step back into this position of "I"-ness so you can become all of the parts of you, not just one. You might need to practice getting in touch with your "I" so you'll be able to access your core self when you most need it.

A LOOK IN THE MIRROR:
A YOU-AND-ONLY-YOU LOOK AT SELF

There truly is only one you in this world. You are unique. There is no Self puzzle in this whole universe that is the same as yours. This look in the mirror is one that you need to do by yourself. This look comes from the depths of your own creative processes. It pulls together everything you've learned about your self as you journeyed across the Stepping Stones.

A LOOK IN THE MIRROR—II

1. Take out your journal—the one in which you put your answers to the Stepping Stone exercises.

2. Spread out your responses to the eleven Stepping Stone exercises from this chapter in front of you. Place your image of the core of you from "Stepping Stone 11" in the center. Take time to reflect upon the work that you've already done. Carefully look over all of the exercises. What strikes you as common threads that run throughout all of the characteristics that you have listed in these stepping stones? Which characteristics have some energy for you? Which ones stand out? Take a look in the mirror. What do you see?

There is no precise, systematic way of finding your most common characteristics. It works better just to surround yourself with as many characteristics from your stepping stones as you can, to look at them, and then to go inside and listen to your intuition. Ask yourself, "What are the five to ten best words that describe 'just me'?" This process works best when you've done all of the footwork in the stepping stones. Now it's time to look into your internal mirror.

3. Combine the words that you've used to describe you into groups that have some common characteristics. These are your traits.

4. Now combine the traits into parts of you until you have about five to ten different parts or aspects of you.

5. Can you hear any of those inner parts of you speaking up? Can you begin to picture them? Do these parts look like someone you know, or like a movie or TV or cartoon figure, or even like an animal?

6. Can you give these parts nicknames? It's okay to call them Critic or Nurturer or Protector or Crybaby. We encourage you not to forget the parts of you that you aren't proud of, the ones that you'd like to forget.

7. List the parts of you, or draw a diagram or picture of those parts on a piece of paper and date it. This should be fun—

make it into a game. The goal is to come up with about five to ten or so parts of self. Each part may have several characteristics within it. Each part may be a conglomeration of traits that seem to fit under the same heading.

8. Either make a list of the parts of you that you have just come up with or put them all inside a large circle that's the size of your paper. Remember to place the "I" of you at the top of the list or in the center. You might even want to do both. Here's a place for you to do this:

MY SENSE OF SELF PUZZLE

• Here's a list of the parts of me: _____

_____

_____

_____

• Here's what they look like in the following puzzle. Put the ones that are the closest to the core of you—that is, the "I" of you—close to the I on the page. You might even want to box off parts of you that you don't like or that you can barely accept, if at all.

• Do this inventory of parts of self each day by asking yourself, *What parts of me were out today? How big are they and how close to the core of me are they today?* Draw a picture of the puzzle of you each day. This should take only a few minutes.

Andrea recently came up with the following answers to these questions:

> I saw a lot in my stepping stones. When I let my imagination go wild, I realized that there were a lot of different voices that I could hear inside my head. There are many different messages that I can hear. I could see all these different aspects of me as if they were sitting around a round table. There are lots of women figures. This is really different from when I first did this exercise ten years ago. Then there were lots of male figures in my internal family around this same round table. I thought that

was weird, because I'm a woman. But I was very masculine back then. At that time I was a woman straight out of a patriarchal mold. Today what I see is very different. Today the people around the table look familiar. They seem to have developed faces and personalities of sorts over time.

After months of working with my parts, here's what I came up with as names for them: Psyche, Heardt, M. Power, She, Spirit, Soul-be, Lonestar, Whole, Vic, Bull Witch, Andie, When, Obie, Humbe and Earth.

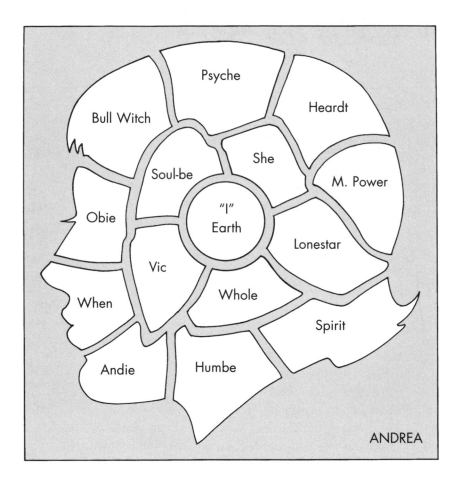

The "I" of me is the earth. Psyche, nicknamed after a Greek goddess, is my sensitive, sensual, creative part. Heardt is nicknamed after one who listened to and heard my hurt and pain.

While Andrea is in the process of developing her own nurturing part, Heardt has became the part of Andrea that takes care of self and that takes care of others.

> M. Power is a play on words for that part of me that truly feels empowered and powerful. It shows itself by being assertive, competent, confident, and secure. She is my part that just lets things be, the part that is accepting. This part is nicknamed after a therapist of mine who helped me learn just to let things be, not to always stir things up, and to make time to stop and smell the flowers.
>
> Spirit is the wise woman within me—a grounded, balanced, serene, peaceful, spiritual part of me. Soul-be is my part that is very much in touch with not just my body but with my essence and my soul.
>
> Lonestar embodies many of the characteristics of my father—his determination, perseverance, willpower, obsessiveness, compulsiveness, and strength as well as his loneliness. This part helps protect me from hurt and pain. This part helps me stand up for myself.
>
> Whole is the name I call the empty hole inside me that I step into when I am depressed and insatiably needy.
>
> Vic is my victim part. This is when I feel so burdened and helpless that I can't find any choices. This is also where my anger is.

Right next door to Vic is Bull Witch, for the bully and witch/crabby part of Andrea, the part that can be overbearing and dominant. This is the oppressive, patriarchal part of this forty-five-year-old woman.

A child part of Andrea is Andie, a nickname her younger sister called her when she was a child. Andie is about two years old, the age she was when her sister was born. Andie is sad, emotionally hungry, needy, and depressed at times. There is also an adolescent part of Andrea—When, the nickname she was called during the sixties when she was a teenager. This part is hyper, rebellious, and superindependent.

Andrea has an observer part of self. She calls that part Obie for the wise Obiewan Kenobi, from the movie *Star Wars*. Last and certainly not least is Humbe, the humble part of Andrea. This part reminds her that she puts her pants on the same way as the person next to her. Humbe is the part that helps her keep her feet firmly planted on the ground.

Susan found four parts of self when she did this exercise. Her "I" symbol was a heart. Susan named her parts with adjectives. The names (and the ages they represented) reminded her of clear parts of her personality. She named one part of her Baby Susie. She was seven years old, and she provided Susan with an awareness of her vulnerabilities. "It was Baby Susie who reminded me last week, that 'I am tired and I need to get some rest.'" This part got Susan's attention when she needed to rest.

Sassy Susan's (age thirteen) role is to tell the truth and to take care of self (and not others). This is a strong protective part of Susan. It was also where she felt a lot of her strength.

"The Nurse Sue (age twenty-two) part of me is there to make sure that people like me, so I listen to all of their problems." This is

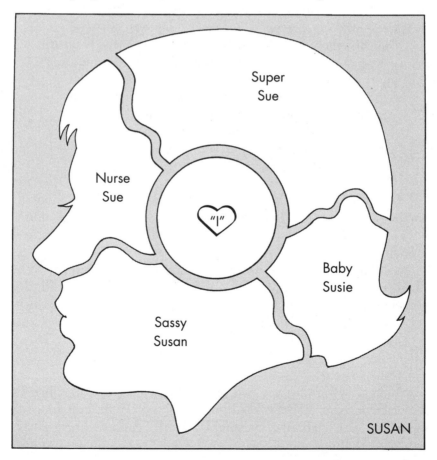

Susan's projected identity—how the world sees her. This is where she finds herself being liked by people. This part is very reinforcing, so you can imagine that Susan wouldn't want to give up this part very readily.

"Super Sue (age thirty-five) is my responsible self, my organized self, my controlling self. It's my protector, too, in that it assures that I will take care of what I need."

Andrew identified ten parts of self. He named them after animals. His "I" was a lion. One part that was very much a people pleaser he called Golden Retriever. Another part that was a real pusher he named Bull Dog. Another part that just liked to cuddle with his partner he called Kitty. A part that seemed to copy and

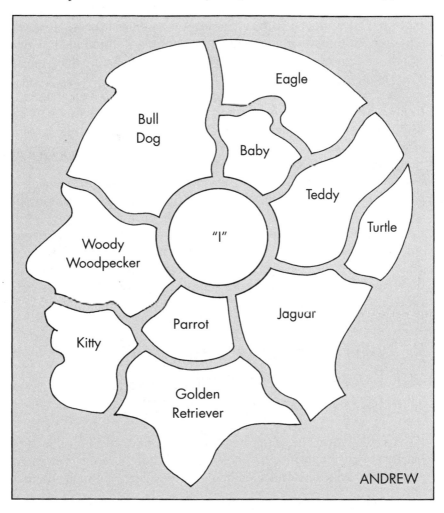

mimic everybody he called Parrot. A part of himself that was very defended and didn't let anyone in unless they were very safe he called Turtle.

A part of Andrew that watches over all of the rest of the parts of him he named Eagle. A little child part he called Baby, which was the name of his puppy when he was a little boy. The picky part he called Woody Woodpecker. The nurturing part became Teddy after his cocker spaniel that licked the tears off his face when he was going through a divorce. The tough, macho part of Andrew he named Jaguar.

Andrea identified fifteen parts of self, Susan identified four parts, and Andrew, ten. All of these are okay. There are no right or wrong ways to do this. There are no magic numbers. You may have five parts, ten parts, fifteen parts, or more. Any number is okay. However, you do need to have enough parts to give you a well-rounded picture of self, and enough parts to work with, but not so many that you get overwhelmed. Remember the "I" at the core.

You can add and/or delete parts as you work on yourself and get to know yourself better. No matter what, though, name the parts before going on. Write them in your journal and then set them aside while you read and do the exercises in the next few chapters of this book.

You won't forget these names, especially if you begin to check in with all of the parts of you once a day or so. Quickly inventory the parts each day by drawing them in a puzzle form or by simply listing them. A week or two from now you might check to see if the names still fit, if you have forgotten any parts of you, or if you want to change any of the ones that you've named. Other than keeping this daily inventory, you don't need to do anything with these parts right now. Just let the parts of self "work you" for a while.

SO WHAT HAPPENS IF SOME OF THE PARTS OF ME LOOK MORE LIKE THE BEAST THAN LIKE BEAUTY?

It's possible that many of the parts of you may very well appear to be negative, that they will seem more "beast" than "beauty." For example, if you had a very critical father, you may very well have internalized a critical part. If people always told you that you were not enough, you may very well have a part that constantly reminds you that you're not enough. If you were abandoned as a child, there may be a part that abandons others and even abandons you at times.

If you had a parent who didn't listen to you very well, who may have watched TV or hidden behind the newspaper while you tried to talk to her or him, or who did twenty other things while "listening" to you, then you may have a part that has difficulty being present while someone is talking to you.

If a caretaker of yours was lazy, you, too, may have a lazy part. If your mother or father was negative for whatever reason, you may very well have a part of you that is negative (no matter how hard you have tried not to be like that parent). To make matters worse, if you had a caretaker who hit you, you may have an oppressor and/or violent part inside of you.

If you are a victim—if you were verbally, emotionally, physically, or sexually abused—you may have both a victim and an oppressor part inside you. You may very well be capable of doing unto others what was done to you. This "beast" part may be there no matter how hard you've tried or how often you've sworn on a stack of Bibles that "It'll never happen to me," or "I'll never do what was done to me."

These beastlike parts may be very difficult to own at this time. That's okay. Remember your strengths. You're not all bad, you're not all beast. And you're not all good, you're not all beauty. You are human. And that means that you are not perfect. You may have some flaws. For now all we're simply asking you to do is to list the parts of you, whether you like them or not and whether you accept that they are a part of you or not. In fact it's okay to box the parts of you that you're having a hard time owning off into a corner for a while.

For a moment go back to the image of the band from earlier in this chapter. Sometimes there are instruments in the band that are not tuned properly or that are played poorly, and when this happens, the entire piece of music is thrown off. Your parts are like this. The part of you that you don't like is but a poorly tuned instrument, or perhaps one that plays too loudly. Now is not the time to fix that, or even to look into it. Now is simply the time to name the instruments, the tuned ones and the out-of-tune ones. We'll play the piece later.

The key concept in doing this work is: *Just because you acknowledge a part of you doesn't mean that you have to become that part. Just because you have a part inside of you doesn't mean that you have to act out that part.* If you have a violent part inside of you, you do not need to be violent. If you have an oppressor within, you neither need to step on nor abuse others.

In fact it seems that when you simply acknowledge that part (and maybe later when you get to know that part better in chapter 7), you develop more choice in your life about whether or not to act out that part. Acknowledging your potential for violence instead of denying it seems to reduce the need to act it out. After all, if someone were to attack you, you might need to be able to call on that violent part.

Schindler in *Schindler's List*[9] defined power as "when you can kill someone and you don't." You may need that powerful part of you if you need to take immediate control of a situation in a disaster. Acknowledging the power that you have over others may very well allow you to choose to act in a nonoppressive manner.

All of the parts of you have a part to play in the overall picture of you—even the ones you don't like at first glance. As you work with all of your parts, you'll find that your deficits have assets and that your assets have a flip side as well. And just like in the award-winning Disney movie *Beauty and the Beast*, sometimes you may find beauty in the beast.

Another important thing happens when you acknowledge (and later get to know) a negative part of you that you've denied over the years: A lot of energy is freed up inside of you. This is most obvious with addictions. Take the alcoholic who struggles and struggles and uses lots and lots of energy in order to control his drinking. But once he surrenders and owns that he is an alcoholic, and chooses on a daily basis not to drink, he finds that he has more energy to do other things in his life. Or take the woman who has worked her entire life not to be negative like her mother. When she owns that there's a negative part of her, she, too, has more energy and more choice about whether and when to let that part out of the closet.

Sometimes the positive parts are the hidden parts. This is especially true for people who feel bad about themselves or who have low self-esteem. Some people believe that they're rotten to the core and that consequently they have mostly negative and very few positive parts. If this is you, we urge you to search deeper. Trust us, there are more positive parts waiting for you to discover, even if you can't own them yet. Try to suspend your disbelief for just a little while. You might want to write down some positive parts of you on your list of parts. Remember that you can box off those parts (even if they are positive) if it's too uncomfortable to accept them for now. In fact you can box off any parts you choose.

If you're still struggling with naming parts of self, that's okay too. We simply ask that you try to be open to the process. It may be uncomfortable; we understand. Just name what you can. Date the piece of paper and set it aside. Keep reading and don't stop here. This is not the place to stop the process. Naming and acknowledging parts of self, which is what you've been doing, is only part of the process of finding the missing parts of you. It's not the whole thing. Actually, because this part of the process may feel fragmenting, that's all the more reason not to stop here. The goal of this process of finding the Missing Piece is integration, not disintegration, so keep your commitment to yourself.

You may find that the parts of you that you've named in this chapter and listed and/or drawn in your journal may change over time. Because of this we'd like you to check in with yourself once a day for a minute or two just to see if any of your parts have changed. In essence we're asking you to do a mini-inventory each day. Ask yourself with your list or drawing of parts of self in front of you, *Which parts of me were "out" today? Which parts spoke up and which parts were silent? And which parts could I use tomorrow?*

If you find that a part of you shows up on any given day, and if you find that the part is not on your list and it stays consistently over a period of time, add it to your list. If, on the other hand, you find that parts of you on the list never actually show up in your daily life even when you're watching for them, then you might want to remove them from your list. Add parts and subtract parts as you check inside each day. Revise your list so that it matches the insides and outsides of your Pandora's box. This is key to the whole process—looking inside, not outside. The answers are within you, not outside you. Begin or end each day with a brief look inside as you read on in this book.

Remember that the you inside of you is special and unique. It is different from that of any other person. Each and every one of us has our own puzzle. It's not your parents' puzzle. It's not your partner's puzzle. It's not your friend's puzzle. It's not even your therapist's puzzle. Each of us creates our own rainbow, our own prism, our own tapestry, and our own Self puzzle.

As you've discovered in this chapter, you're not just a single self. Each of us is made up of many parts. Our chance to put the puzzle together only comes after we've first recognized and named those pieces. You have just done this. Yet without first having looked at the roots of who we are, it will be difficult to put your puzzle together.

In chapter 4 you'll take a look at where you came from, the context in which you were raised, your family of origin, your neighborhood, your social class, and your culture, all of which form your external family. The parts of self you've just identified often mirror these relationships and influences. And because of this they continue to orchestrate your responses to the events and circumstances in your life today. But once you understand how the process works, you can begin to be the conductor of your own orchestra.

CHAPTER 4

Your Family Portrait

Our past is a part of who we are; it is not everything. We must ultimately attend to the unresolved parts of our past to be able to be present in the here and now. In this chapter we're going to help you begin to find answers to the question What's missing for me? Paradoxically the first step toward freeing yourself from the yesterdays that tug at your being is to look at those yesterdays, to take a picture of them, to create a family portrait.

In our culture it's been popular to blame others for our personal unhappiness. However, as you begin to take a look at how we internalize beliefs about who we are from our growing-up years, our intent is *not* to have you indulge in finger pointing but rather to help you let go of unresolved issues from your past. Today we need to take responsibility for our own lives and what we do with them. The purpose of exploring past history is to develop an understanding of our familial and cultural influences. To deny such influences would be to emotionally cut off a significant part of who we are. It would be to dismiss how we develop various parts of our self.

When we continue to disown our experiences, we betray ourselves. We're being dishonest with ourselves. Not allowing yourself to think and remember feelings associated with the past keeps you from becoming acquainted with all of your selves. When you deny the past, you become emotionally disconnected from self, and that directly interferes with your ability to become your own best friend and to be intimate with others.

We recognize that many readers have done as much reflection

about their growing-up years as they care to. We hope, though, that you will use this chapter as a review, as a way to straighten out any leftover hooks from your childhood and to heal that which has not as of yet been healed. If you find yourself resistant to this part of the process, feel free to skip this chapter and go on to chapter 5. If you feel too much pain or fear as you travel down this path, stop for a while. Pick up your "tool bag" from chapter 1. Use the tools to help you walk through reflections on your past. Remember, the past is only worth looking at in the context of who you are today, to get to know all your parts of self today.

MISSING PIECES LINKED TO THE PAST

As we travel down the path and you get to know your selves better, we will offer you many exercises. We would like you to do them all, even if that just means taking a taste of each. Pick what works for you and let the rest go.

Stop for a moment and think about your family. Think about where you grew up and how you grew up. You may want to tape-record this message and play it back for yourself later.

AT FIRST GLANCE

1. Find a comfortable place to sit and relax. Loosen your clothes and breathe deeply. Close your eyes and let your mind and memory travel back in time.

2. For a moment reflect back on your childhood. Picture your father. What's he doing? What's he saying? What's he wearing? How's he standing?

3. Picture your mother. What's she doing? What's she saying? What's she wearing? How's she standing?

4. Do the same with your sister(s) and brother(s) and any significant others in your life—grandparents, aunts, and uncles—whoever was most important to you.

5. Can you imagine them all in the same room? Who's talking to whom? Who's speaking the loudest? Who's withdrawn? Who's in charge? Who has the most power? What are they all saying?

6. What's the atmosphere like in the room—energizing, playful, tense?

7. Keep these pictures in mind as you think about whether as an adult you ever hear yourself saying, "I don't need my father to be critical of me, I rag on myself worse than he ever did." Do you hear yourself saying the exact same words to your child that your mother once said to you when you were a child?

8. Be with that childhood image. Listen to your inner thoughts and feelings. What are you thinking? How do you feel? Do you feel sad? Happy? Full? Empty?

9. Then, once again, step into the shoes you wear today. Have you taken yesterday with you?

The family you grew up in now lives inside of you. Without even realizing it, you took them into yourself as you were growing up.

We all started off in some sort of family. Perhaps yours was the typical American family with 2.3 kids, a mom, and a dad. Perhaps you were raised by your older sister or your grandparents. Perhaps you haven't seen your father for twenty years. Perhaps your mother became both mom and dad to you.

These are all *families*, and they have all had a tremendous impact on who we are today. Our family doesn't actually have to control who we are today, but it has left its imprint on us. When we come to understand this imprint, we get a better understanding of who we are. Ironically the family that once was our "problem" may now hold the key to our "solution."

Leaving an Imprint

For a few moments let your imagination run wild. Picture yourself on a beach at sunrise. It's foggy, and each wave of fog rolls along the beach like a billowing cloud. A foghorn sounds in the distance. It's low tide and the sand is still wet. You're the very first person to walk on this virgin beach. The sand is velvety smooth. The whole beach as far as you can see looks like a blank slate waiting for someone to create her or his mark on it.

You do just that. You walk, one step at a time, one footprint at a time, down the beach. This is your time, your moment, your life. Each of these footprints belongs to you, yet no two are the same. Each imprint you make on this virgin beach is different from the one before it. Each one creates a unique story, a special picture in the sand.

The scene changes. It's 9:49 A.M. A mother has just given birth to a child. The beautiful little girl child is placed gently on her mother's belly. The parents marvel in wonderment. What a miracle! A sense of awe fills the room. Will this precious little infant become the first woman to be president of the United States? Will she be an artist? An engineer? A rabbi? Is the world at her command? Is she a blank slate?

Is the virgin beach a blank slate? Is the newborn baby? This is a question that psychologists have asked for decades: Is a child a tabula rasa, a blank slate, or is a child's life predestined by the circumstances of its birth? There's no easy answer to this nature-versus-nurture question. It appears that both are true: We are prewired for potential, and we are also heavily imprinted by the context in which we are raised. Our mothers, our fathers, our aunts, uncles, and grandparents, as well as our friends, teachers, and lovers, literally make an impression on who we are. It's as if we make a hologram of our interactions with each of these significant people and carry them around inside of us. These people, and our experiences of them, become part of who we are. Relationships leave imprints on our soul.

FAMILY IN FLUX

The notion of the family itself has changed over the past few centuries. Families developed as cooperative units of human survival. People grouped together first to hunt and gather and then to grow and harvest farm crops and for purposes of defense. They came together to raise children, who in turn would continue the family line and the work of the group.

Interestingly, of all the species of creatures on earth, human offspring stay in the family context the longest. Children actually have to stay for about two to four years for physical survival. But they remain with their parents to learn the puzzling and seemingly contradictory system of rules that will help them cope with the complex human world in which we all live. We hold on to our offspring so that we can teach them how to survive physically, emotionally, and spiritually. Some of us transfer these rules to our children more effectively than others. Researchers have found that the dolphins, another highly developed and intelligent species of mammal, don't need to stay in their families to learn the rules of survival yet they choose to do so. It's intriguing to wonder how our family constellations differ from dolphin families given that we have to stay in the family unit, whereas dolphins choose to stay.

A family in an agrarian society is different from a family in an urban environment. The agrarian family consists not only of the nuclear family of mother, father, and children but also the extended family of grandparents, aunts, uncles, and cousins. It's not unusual for everyone within the family to live under the same roof or nearby. However, in an industrialized environment, the role of the family changes. Large families are no longer needed to provide all of the food, shelter, education, and labor. In many parts of the United States decades ago we shifted from an agrarian to an industrial society. At that time children began to work outside the home in factories. At work and in school they were taught by people other than their parents. Family members began to look outside the family for things that used to be provided by the family. The development of the railroad, the car, and air travel, as well as the telegraph and the telephone, made it easier for family members to separate. In other parts of the United States the agrarian family remains in place, confused as the world around them so drastically changes.

So today we find that the very definition of *family* is in flux. The question of the hour—in this time of divorce and single-parent households—is What is a family? The role of mother has changed, as has the role of father. To help sort out this confusion, the field of family therapy has emerged. And with it have come health professionals and agencies that offer services to meet the need of sustaining family unity and cohesion. It's no wonder that "family values" became a major political issue in the 1992 presidential campaign. People are confused about what it means to be a family. Are Murphy Brown and her baby a family? Does "family" mean simply mom, dad, and kid(s)? Or does it include the generation before us and the one that follows us? Is "family" the *family of chance*, which we were born into, or is it the *family of choice*, the friends we have made for ourselves today?[1] Is family only those who show up for Hanukkah or Christmas?

When we speak of "family" in this book, we mean the *context* in which we were raised. In addition to being influenced by immediate and extended family, the society and culture we grow up in influences who we are as well. You, the white Christian city boy, are different from your white Christian friend who grew up on a farm, and you're both different from the African American who grew up across the street from you, and different also from your Italian friend whom you sit next to at school, and from the guy in your Cub Scout den who grew up with maids and chauffeurs.

Our internal worlds are a representation of all that we've experienced in our lives—a tapestry of threads woven together from the day we were born until the day we die that create the pattern and fabric of our lives.

Few of us grow up all alone on a desert island, but even there the environment would affect us. Some imprints are positive and some are not. Some imprints wound us. For example what happens if you were never treated as special as a young child? What happens if someone criticized your every move? What happens if you were pushed to play football by your father when you really wanted to paint portraits or write stories? Imprints like these hurt. You may wonder, *How do I undo the imprints that hurt? Do I have to remain a victim of my past?*

We wish the answers to these questions were as easy as "Read this book." It's a start, though. For many who have traveled a path of healing before, this book may be a homecoming. *The Missing Piece* is about walking away from being a victim of your past. It's about walking away from being a victim of those harmful imprints. This chapter in particular is about looking at those imprints, working through them and moving on.

YOUR EXTERNAL FAMILY

Who we are is strongly influenced by the family and context in which we were raised. We are calling that your external family. We all have an external and internal family. The external family includes those people, places, and things who have made an imprint on who you are today. In contrast your internal family is all the parts of you within you. Let's zoom in again for another look at your external family. Who's there? What do they look like? Who's standing next to whom? What are the expressions on their faces? What do you see in their eyes? How does this picture make you feel?

We're going to take you through a journey of self-reflection that will help you to view how those with whom you grew up form a part of who you are today. It will give you an opportunity not just to understand yourself better but to actually see that you have choices about what you want to keep in terms of family influences and what you would like to change. This process will help you identify the strengths and weaknesses of your family, as well as your own personal strengths and vulnerabilities. This is not a process of blame. It's not even a process of asking others to be accountable for how they've influenced you. It's a process of identifying and developing an appreciation for the textures and complexities of your life. It is an empowering process.

In answering the following questions you are no longer looking at a one-dimensional picture. You are adding depth, intensity, and color to your family portrait.

External-Family Questions[2]

Please note that when we say *mother* or *father*, we mean the people who were your male or female caretakers when you were a child, whoever they may have been. If you like, you can fill in the answers on the External-Family Scorecard in the Appendix.

YOUR BEGINNINGS

- What is your name? Who named you? What do you like to be called? Were you named after anyone in particular?
- Do you carry a legacy in your name?
- Do you or did you have a nickname (and at what ages)? What does it mean or stand for?

Some of us were named after specific people. Who those people were and how our parents felt about them is very significant. To be named after a loving family member often instills pride, but as Leigh said, "When I found out that I was named after my father's girlfriend, it immediately made me feel that I was the source of my parents' anger." She said her father never once in his life referred to her by her given name. He created his own nickname for her—Babe—a nickname that was his attempt to save his daughter from being trapped in the middle of his marital conflict.

Steven's name left him with much better feelings about himself. He'd been named after his mother's brother, his uncle Steven Rey, who'd died shortly before Steven's birth. This uncle was remembered most fondly, described as fun to be with, bright, and caring. Steven never met this uncle, but he became the model Steven aspired to be like.

• What do you know about the circumstances in your family and the world surrounding your conception? And what do you know about the circumstances and the world around your birth (before, during, and after)?

As you learn about the circumstances of your birth, you'll begin to understand how and why you came to play the role you did in your family. Kate was the second child in her family, and she was a much-wanted child. Yet the pregnancy was difficult due to her mother's previous medical problems. Kate's mom was bedridden the last four months of her pregnancy. However, at Kate's birth, which went very easily, there was much celebration; all were involved. Kate's father witnessed the birth. Her sister was at the hospital with a nurturing grandparent, and gifts abounded for both Kate and her sister. It is not surprising that this was a family that would continue to enjoy rituals, celebrations, and a sense of family community, with Kate often the center of attention.

Marcia was also a very much desired child, like Kate. But Marcia would be the first and last child for her parents—after three previous miscarriages. Marcia's birth had much anxiety around it. Her father was very tense and emotionally unavailable to his wife, who was petrified. Marcia was surrounded with many gifts, but most were gifts that had been offered at the times of the previous miscarriages. By the time Marcia was born, it was clear she was seen as the salvation to her parents' marriage. The parents never did adequately grieve the loss of the three unborn children, and consequently they were unrealistic in their expectations for Marcia, who had to represent all four children. Today, at age thirty-seven, Marcia is still trying to be everything to her parents—the glue that binds her parents in a marriage that lost most of its life over four decades ago.

Tom said his father was too busy to get to the hospital when he was born—he was out drinking with the guys. Tom's father would be out drinking for most of the other significant events in Tom's life. Tom not only had an absent father, he had a very angry and bitter mother. He didn't feel wanted by either parent. Unfortunately that would become the theme of Tom's life. He, too, would become an absent father, off drinking, married to a woman who, like his mother, had become very angry and bitter.

YOUR CARETAKERS

Who are the members of your family?
In one sentence describe your father.

- What was your father's most common advice to you?
- What is the best thing your father ever said to you? What did you feel?
- When, or in what kind of situation, did you feel closest to your father?
- What is the worst thing your father ever said to you? What did you feel?
- What was it that your father, way down deep, really did *not* want you to do?

In one sentence describe your mother.

- What was your mother's most common advice to you?
- What is the best thing your mother ever said to you? What did you feel?
- When, or in what kind of situation, did you feel closest to her?
- What is the worst thing your mother ever said to you? What did you feel?
- What was it that your mother, way down deep, really did *not* want you to do?

Draw a family tree or genogram. If you have never drawn one, you may find it helpful to see page 384 in the Appendix for an example.

Joe remembered that his father's most common advice was "to treat others as you want to be treated." He laughingly commented that there were times growing up that he hadn't wanted to hear that, particularly when he became angry at one of his sisters. But to this day he says that this advice has served him well in life, and it's a major message he has instilled in his three children.

Paul says his father was not a verbal man. He was quiet and not very emotional. However, when Paul was sixteen, and his twelve-year-old dog died, it was his father who left work early so that he could be the one to pick Paul up at school and tell him about Sarge. Together they buried the dog. Paul said, "In my dad's quiet way, the truth was he felt my pain, and I always knew that. I counted on it, and I trusted it."

Susan said the most frequent advice she heard, the best thing her mother said, and the times she felt the closest to her mother, were all around the theme of getting an education. "My mom never had much time for us kids. She was a single mom, and I felt she liked being at work more than she did being with us. She was pretty distant, and very critical of me. Yet she pushed me toward a college degree, for which I am most grateful, because most of the girls I grew up with hardly finished high school. The closest time we spent together—the memory that still warms me up—was when I was real little and she would read to me at night."

Lynn's message of advice she most remembers came through teasing, "Sometimes my mother got impatient with me because I have always been slow and methodical. She called me poky, but I knew she was teasing me and it didn't hurt me. My dad would tell me to hurry up. I am still slow and poky, and they still tease me. In my family we didn't do things to hurt each other. Tease, yes—hurt, no."

But there are also people who grew up in more traumatic families. "My dad didn't notice me until I was about fifteen and old enough in his eyes to go drinking with him. We were drinking buddies. We got along great until I got sober, and now we have no way to relate again."

When people are raised in abusive or addictive families, they often hear shaming messages and can easily identify the worst things they heard:

"I wish I never had you!"
"You are so stupid! Can't you do anything right?"
"I don't have time for your questions!"
"Why can't you be more like (somebody other than who you are)?"

"You're just like (someone they intensely dislike and perceive to be bad)!"

"You'll probably leave your children just like your dad left you."

FAMILY MESSAGES

- What were the messages that you heard and that may still reverberate in your mind today?
- Have you internalized a belief from "the worst thing" that was said?
- Are you able to appreciate and savor the "best thing" or the "close moments"?
- What did you do about the thing your parents didn't want you to do?
- Did you do it to spite them?
- Did you value their input?
- What does that tell you about how you listen to others today?

It's in answering these questions, and in ascertaining whether or not you're still hanging on to those that were so hurtful, that your healing will begin to occur. We can learn a lot about ourselves when we think about those things our parents told us, either verbally or nonverbally (but we felt in our hearts), that they really didn't want us to do. These kinds of messages tell us whether or not we needed to please them, whether we were intimidated by them, or whether in our anger we would rebel against them. Our reactions also give us clues to who we are today.

Sometimes the thing a parent never wanted us to do was to tell the truth, or to show certain kinds of feelings. Cindy said,

> I knew my mother never wanted me to show anger. She told me good girls always keep a smile on their face, so they never disagree. She told me that if I found the right man, he would take care of me and that I should never have any reason to question him. If I was upset about something, I was to ask myself what it was that I needed to do differently. Well, I have smiled through two of my husband's extramarital affairs (that I

know about). I smiled each time we moved because he said the next job would be better. I said nothing other than, "Dad really does know best," when all of this caused my children great pain.

Others of us may have had a parent who didn't want us to go to college, didn't want us to move to a particular place, marry a particular person, or choose a particular career. Jim said,

> My dad didn't want me to pursue my artistic interests. He wanted me to have a business degree. I can still hear him screaming at me: 'You will never make a living! There is no money to be made there! You'll never support yourself!' So I gave in and didn't do what I wanted. I have never enjoyed my work. I have a partner who is self-supporting and I don't feel the need to support her, but I feel guilty when I take time for my art because the message is still that I am not being productive.

Only now, at the age of forty-six, is Jim beginning to look at how significant this influence has been in his life. His dad would be proud of his business accomplishments, but Jim is not happy at all.

Anita's response was to rebel against her parents and to do exactly what they most feared.

> My parents didn't want me to marry Terry when I was sixteen, but I was bound and determined, and I did. They told me that if I would at least wait five years before I had children, that would help. So I had my first child before I turned eighteen, and had two more children by the time I was twenty-two. Needless to say I was not a mature teenager, and life has been very difficult. I still have difficulty believing that what anyone else says is important. I follow my feelings of the moment! I am a recovering alcoholic now and learning that self-will runs riot. I'm learning the hard way!

SIBLINGS

- Describe your brother(s) and/or sister(s).
- Answer the questions listed under the Mom and Dad section with each of your siblings.
- How did/do your mother and father feel about you compared with your brother(s) and sister(s)?

Jan said that because she was the only girl in the family, she was the "prized child." Both parents prized her, and each of her three brothers felt she was "special." It simply fueled her self-esteem. While Jan felt prized, she also felt she had to be and do for her parents what they had not been able to do for themselves. Being the oldest, more was expected from her. As a result she could never fully live up to their expectations and always felt she was a disappointment to them.

LOOK-ALIKES

- Who looked like whom in the family?
- Who acted like whom?
- Was it positive or negative to look like or not to look like this person?

Sally said that she was the one who looked more like her mother than any of her sisters. She wondered if that was why she was the one singled out for her dad's physically abusive behavior and not the others. Phil looked exactly like his dad, who divorced his mother to marry another woman. His mother's response to her own intense guilt and extreme anger over her failed marriage was to give Phil great latitude in his behavior when in fact he needed more limit setting. In therapy Phil's mother realized that she could easily see her ex-husband in her son. She tried to offset this by going to the other extreme. Whenever she was angry with her son, she became excessively tolerant of his behavior, whatever it was. She was fearful of setting limits because she didn't want him to leave her and go live with her ex-husband. She didn't trust that she could separate out her anger at her son from that at her ex-husband, and she was fearful of overreacting.

Jan said that in her family she was just like her mother, and her sister was just like her father.

My dad did what he wanted without considering anybody else. He was selfish, and that didn't bother him.
He actually seemed happy and probably was because
his needs were met. Well, my sister has always been
like him. She always did what she wanted. She would
never do anything around the house to help. She never
did what she was asked. I was always busy doing my
part and her part, just like Mom was busy doing her
part and Dad's. Mom financially supported the family. Dad played. I took care of the house, and my sister
played. Today I am a major support of my family, and
my sister is still happily playing and has someone to
support her.

SIGNIFICANT OTHERS

• Describe additional significant others—grandparents, relatives, friends, teachers—who have affected your life by doing
the things listed in the questions under Mom and Dad.

Parents aren't the only ones who have an influence on
children. Others often play significant roles. Grandparents
are often key figures in a child's life. This was certainly true
for Bob. "I always felt I was loved by both of my grandparents
when I wasn't so sure about anyone else. When I went to
their house, I slept well and felt safe. They were patient with
me and made me feel that I could accomplish whatever I set
my mind to. They would get me involved in projects around
the store and not just leave me, but would work with me for
hours. They paid attention to me."
June reflected,

My parents had these friends who were our unoffi-
cial godparents. They made holidays very special. My
parents didn't have much money, so although we
got presents, they were always practical. Well, these
godparents made holidays fun. At Christmas they
would take us out into the woods to get a tree, and
we would sing our way into the mountains! At Easter
they would bring baskets that were so pretty. It seems
that in our family, at home, life was very serious. Our
godparents would hide the baskets, and we would have

to find them. They would make a game out of things. They were fun and made me feel liked. I don't think they ever said anything special, but they made me feel something warm and good that I didn't always feel otherwise.

"In high school, life was pretty tough," said Joan.

I didn't talk about home, but I guess the people in town knew things weren't very good—with my dad not being home much and my mom always working. There were so many of us kids. There were these three different teachers over the course of high school. In their own way they paid attention to me and gave me confidence. One was a teacher who gave me extra assignments that he didn't give others and told me that he thought I was more capable than others. He challenged me, and I met the challenge.

Another teacher would actually ask me questions to see if I was being offered any direction regarding school plans after high-school graduation. He made sure that I knew what the next steps were. A third teacher was a lot like the first. He kept giving me unusual challenges. When I was elected band president, he sat me down and told me I didn't have to do all of the work. He literally taught me about delegating. Then, without asking, he offered me a second instrument. I played the clarinet. But one day he walked up and handed me a set of drumsticks for the timpani. He said he needed me to learn how to play because we needed someone to represent us on these drums at a county event. He expected me to perform. I was petrified, but I felt honored. I met the challenge with pride.

When kids are not given the amount and the appropriate type of attention that they need at home, significant others become primary in their lives. There are very few of us who can look back and not find someone who said something or did something that offered us just what we needed at the time—confidence, direction, or support.

TROUBLE AT HOME

- Were you the target of physical or sexual abuse?
- Were you a child of an alcoholic parent? A schizophrenic? A manic depressive? Or someone who was depressed?
- How has that influenced you, both negatively and positively?

The loss, the denial, and the shame that are part of an addictive or abusive family, or part of a family that has been affected by mental illness, has a major impact on who we are. When an individual denies and is unwilling to own these more extreme family influences and consequences, the result is a distorted picture of self.

We encourage you to face the pain if your family was one of those more extreme types and to get support in doing so. Your willingness to identify addictions, illnesses, and sources of dysfunction in your family will ultimately allow you to heal from them. If you have not begun to address these issues and you need help, please see page 386 of the Appendix for referrals.

Family Rules and Roles

What were the rules in your family? They may not necessarily have been verbal ones. Nonverbal, unspoken, but implied rules can hurt as much, if not more, than verbal ones. For some people their family's messages were stronger than rules. For them the rules had become family law.

Here are some rules that lead to a more positive and mostly nurturing family environment:

- Ask for what you want.
- It's not okay to hit.
- Listen when others talk.
- Treat others the way you want to be treated.
- Ask, don't take.

More hurtful rules include the following:

- Children are to be seen and not heard.
- Family business is strictly family business and does not belong outside these doors.
- If you want something, take it.
- You can't trust other people.
- Don't show your feelings.

Often, without consciously realizing it, we still operate by the rules of our early years. What are the rules you operate by today? Are they helpful or hurtful? Would you like to change any of them? As a child what roles did you play in your family?

Another way of asking this is: Looking back now, what was your primary job? Susie found she played a variety of roles. "When I was young, I got to be the baby in the family because I was the youngest child and everyone wanted to take care of me. But when I was twelve, my parents divorced and the whole family split up. Suddenly I became the family housekeeper. With the divorce my two brothers went with my dad, and my sister and I stayed with Mom. I became the housekeeper and my sister became the cook. And both of us became parents to Mom. She fell apart, and it was really scary, but we did a pretty good job taking care of her."

Some typical roles in families include: a child who becomes the family clown, bringing humor into the family; a family hero; and an overly responsible child. In addition there may be a family social worker, who takes care of everybody's emotional needs; and the family communicator, who does the talking for everyone else. Finally, there may be a family scapegoat, who is the one everybody blames things on; and an angry child, who looks as if he or she is the problem in the family, deflecting the focus away from others.

We all play roles in our families—some of us play more than one. These roles only become problematic when the children and their roles are what maintain family stability, thus keeping the roles rigidly assigned. When we live in an insecure environment, we take on roles out of fear in order to feel safer. Years later many of us discover that these rigid roles have become our only source of identity, leaving us with an inner emptiness.

POWER, SURVIVAL, AND SAFETY

- Who had power in your family?
- How was power wielded in your family?

These questions are often useful in helping us understand how we relate to our own sense of power and the power of others. Knowing who had power in what situations and whether or not it was used in a positive manner may help us identify hurtful or healthy situations today. It can also help us reflect on how we use power ourselves. Do we mimic those we were raised with, and is that something we desire? Do we "pound" people down in the same way that we were verbally, or perhaps physically, "pounded" down when we were children?

- How did you survive some of the hurt and pain in your family—no matter what kind, or how little or how much you were wounded?
- Where did you go to feel safe? To whom did you go to feel safe?

How we dealt with pain or hurt as a child often reflects the way we still respond to it as an adult. It's not until we know how we responded yesterday that we can respond differently today. Often one of the ways we deal with pain is to attempt to deny or minimize it: "Oh, it wasn't that bad. Mom didn't mean to say that." "It didn't really hurt."

Sometimes we convert one feeling into another, for example cracking jokes when we get scared. When we're sad, we may become angry to cover it up. Some of us use sarcasm to cover over fear or hurt. Many of us isolate ourselves when we're in pain. We may withdraw into our books or into an absorbing hobby. We often seek out places that feel good, or we seek out certain people who either make us feel good or offer us opportunities for escape.

When children are hurt, they sometimes go to a certain part of the house—their bedroom, a closet. Lee went to his sailboat, and Tim went to the schoolgrounds and played on the swings. Bob went to his room and got his trains out. Sara played with her dog. Sally went to her grandparents'. Sam went to a rock out in the woods near the family farm. As teenagers, many people go to their boyfriend's or girlfriend's house. For many children extracurricular school and church activities create places of safety.

It's wonderful when we find positive outlets for our pain. But if we only use them to cover up our feelings, we'll soon find that we're left with unresolved pain. It helps to know what we used as children to survive hurt, and whom we chose to bring us a sense of safety. This can give us cues about ways we can deal with our pain today. It's likely that Lee still sails and that Tim has found another outdoor activity. Bob probably has hobbies to distract him. Sara still spends a lot more time with animals than she does with people. Sally has good friends. Sam seeks nature, while others may seek relationships to lessen the pain and to feel safe.

For many children, such as Sara, their family pets were a source of major comfort. Our pets would listen to us and always agree, and sometimes they would lick the tears right off our faces. They would come when called. Their love was so unconditional, they were great friends. In a few cases they may have literally been our escape: "I would get on my horse and ride for hours." "Cuddling my cat made me feel warm when life was cold." "My dog was my best friend! We would even bicycle and run together." It can be very comforting and healing to talk about the animals in your life. Your animal may very well have been the "safe person" in your life.

HAPPY MEMORIES

• What are your fondest memories of growing up?

For many people this is a fun question. "Oh, my favorite memories are about going to the mountains when we were kids. Several families would go together with sleds and toboggans, and hot chocolate and chili—we'd go for the day." "Oh, it was when I would go to work with Dad or Mom. It was fun to watch them and see all the people come into the store. I can remember my dad being so helpful and Mom laughing with the customers." "The holidays I loved." "We had great family vacations."

Some people can relate to many fond memories. But others can do this exercise quickly because they remember so few good family times. "I remember the one time my mom came to my school open house and was sober. It was great. I was so proud of her." Some of us seem to have to search. And yet in spite of how traumatic one's growing-up years may have been, nearly everyone has some fond memories.

If there is resistance to this question, you need to ask yourself if you need to hang on to your anger or to a totally negative image. We aren't saying you shouldn't hold that image, but if you are, it's helpful to know the purpose it serves.

Deborah was really angry with her family. She hadn't talked to either parent or sibling in four years. She had disowned them. She certainly didn't want to think about the possibility of having any fond memories. Yet in her group therapy fond memories came up for discussion. Finally, after much physical tension and hostile glaring, she broke down in tears: "If I find any good, it will just prove they could have been loving when they weren't. If I find any good feelings, it will take away my anger, which I know is justified. If I find any good, it may mean I really do need them."

Those were very loaded statements for Deborah. She was right—if she got in touch with any fond memories, it would tap into the fact that she has needs. The truth is these needs may never be met. But if she never acknowledges them, she cannot grieve for what was lost. And without the grieving she can't free herself up for more positive and healing energy. We don't think this part of everyone's journey will be as difficult as Deborah's was for her, but we know that when there has been trauma in a family, this question can be even more potent than the others.

THE MAGIC WAND

- If you had a magic wand, what would you keep and what would you change about the family in which you grew up?

"I would keep everything and change nothing." That is the response we hear from people who most often were taught to be grateful for what they had, and that they don't have needs, that their needs are not important, or who believe that to say that everything wasn't perfect is an act of disloyalty. Some take a philosophical view, that we wouldn't be who we are if things hadn't been the way they were in our lives.

As you respond to this question, know that you aren't changing anything about the past by waving a magic wand. The past stays intact. You aren't ungrateful or ungracious by having your own needs, or by wishing that parts of life could have been different. Chances are your parents wished they could have done it differently too! You're not being disloyal to their love. Let the magic wand take a sweep and see what little or big things you would change. Don't think about outcomes, just allow yourself this moment of fantasy.

Sandy waved her magic wand and brought happiness to her family. "I saw a smile on everyone's faces. My dad came home every night rather than staying out drinking. My mom tucked us into bed instead of isolating herself in her own room with a bout of depression. We all ate dinner together and thoroughly laughed and enjoyed one another."

For some individuals such as Sandy the magic-wand exercise opens up an awareness of losses, which can then put us in touch with our unresolved pain. This was also true for Dale. When he waved his wand, he brought back his brother, who had died at the age of twelve. This was a memory Dale had tried to escape. He never talked about his brother's accident and subsequent death. Yet that was the first thought that came to his mind when he was asked this question.

After you've answered these questions, step back for a few moments and look at what you have said. There may very well be some valuable information here for you.

STORIES
Childhood Stories

Stories, both real and imaginary, also help us get a picture of our external family. One way of exploring this is to identify your favorite story as a child, one that pulls you back into your childhood. It could have been a fairy tale, or a television show, a cartoon, a movie, or a comic book. The stories you remember best are typically the ones where you identify with the characters, where you wanted what happened in the story to happen to you, or where you valued something it said. Think back when you were a child. What story were you drawn to?

For some women the story was about Cinderella, the one who was always waiting to be saved. For others, it was a television show such as *Father Knows Best, Ozzie and Harriet, The Brady Bunch,* or *The Bill Cosby Show,* which were all about the "perfect" American family. These may have been the families you wished you'd had. Did you want to be like them? Did you feel bad when your family wasn't able to live up to that standard?

The story Andrew remembered the most was "Hansel and Gretel." He and his sister had quite a sibling rivalry. Sonny remembered "The Ugly Duckling." He'd always felt left out, just like the duckling that looked different from all the other ducks.

Amy's favorite story was *The Little Engine That Could.*[3] The little engine kept trying harder and harder to make it up to the top of the hill with its load of toys for all the little girls and boys, and along the way it kept saying, "I think I can. I think I can. I think I can." Amy said that because of this book she knew her whole life that she could escape the pessimism of her family, as well as the pessimism of her community that told her that she wouldn't amount to "a hill of beans." She did this by telling herself every day, "I think I can. I think I can. I think I can," as she tried to offset the pessimism. And just like the little engine, Amy made it to the top of the hill. Her spirit of optimism won out over the pervasive family spirit of pessimism. Amy is, though, "driven" like the *Little Engine That Could.*

What's your favorite childhood story? How old were you when you read it? Be that age for just a moment if you can. Get little. How does the story go? What's the most important part of it for you?

Family Stories

Over the generations families also create their own stories. These family stories tell us who we are, where we came from, and the context in which we were raised. Typically these stories will have a theme. It helps to know what you've been told, what you've been able to surmise in letters or pictures, and what themes appear to repeat themselves from one generation to another, from your grandparents, to your mother, to your father and now to you and your siblings. How do they play themselves out? Karen's family story, which was spun around a strong work ethic, spoke of hard work leading to success. She heard how her grandparents came from the eastern part of Canada to the Pacific Northwest in the late 1800s. They sold goods in a small retail store. Her father went to work at the age of nine in the store, as did his two sisters. Today she and her brother are owners of a major retail clothing chain.

Randy's family story was about individual travel. He came from a small family—there had only been one or two children in each family for three generations back. It seemed that each person was given permission to travel as far as he or she wished and didn't need to report back in. While there was little sense of family connection, this attitude encouraged a strong sense of adventure and independence. Today Randy is a photographer for magazines such as *National Geographic* that take him around the world. He thinks fondly of his parents and brother, seeing them a few times a year, often in an exotic area of the world, since they all enjoy travel.

What is your family story? See if you can identify a theme. Tom was bewildered with this exercise, insisting that he could not find themes. To him family members were very disengaged from each other and they didn't even try to maintain connections. He could ascertain very little history. He wondered how to get a theme out of the pool of nothingness. Finally out of frustration he said that if there was any theme, it was of everybody being disconnected. "We're always disconnected, and that's still the story today."

Take a few moments to reflect and then to write your family story. How does the story go? Does it change over time? Can you begin to imagine your family portrait turning into a family video and the snapshots turning into a moving picture? Slowly run the movie forward and then slowly rewind it and watch it in reverse. How does this make you feel? Where are you in this story? From your perspective what's the most important part of your family story?

YOUR FAMILY IN TECHNICOLOR[4]

Reflect back on what you wrote on your Family Scoreboard. Which questions offered you memories that felt good? Which memories were painful? Now look back at the picture that came to mind when you first began this chapter. You've probably found that your family portrait changed over the years, right?

Take a few moments before we bring this chapter to a close and once again picture the family you grew up with. Picture your family at various stages of your life. What does that picture look like when you were very young? Before you went to school? When you were in grade school? When you were a preteen? And as a teenager? Now in your twenties? thirties? forties? fifties? sixties? seventies? eighties? nineties? and so on. How do you look and feel in each of these pictures? How do you see yourself looking older?

In the space provided below, if you can, put a family picture from each of those periods in your life.

Baby Family Portrait	Pre-School Family Portrait	Grade School Family Portrait
Title_____	Title_____	Title_____
Preteen Family Portrait	Teenager Family Portrait	Young-Adult Family Portrait
Title_____	Title_____	Title_____

Mature Adult Family Portrait	Elder Family Portrait
Title_____	Title_____

Now make this a game—try putting a title under each picture. What would you call each one, and what would you title the whole set? Was your external family one that offered you most of what you needed to become whole, or was it one in which a great deal was missing?

Does your perspective change over the years, or do things look the same today as they did when you were a young child? Close your eyes and imagine this series of pictures turning into a three-dimensional portrait—a family video, one that shows the world through your eyes and fully explains what it was like to be you in your family. Watch that video in your own mind's eye. How is it arranged? Is it linear or does it go by themes and cross back and forth over time? Hold these images with all of their depth and motion in your mind's eye. These are a representation of the imprint that your family has had on you.

The vehicle that takes you through childhood and adolescence and brings you into adulthood is your sense of self. This sense of self is the answer to the question Who am I? It is the core part of you that has been created over the years as you have taken inside you the experiences of growing up. What was once outside you in your external family is now inside you in what we call your internal family. Before we continue to look at the internal family—parts of self—it can be helpful to have a picture of the road ahead of you. The formation of self is a spirallike, circular process and so is the healing process; we refer to it as the Spiral Path.

CHAPTER 5

The Spiral Path

Your sense of self forms in a spiraling process, layer by layer from the inside out, year after year. Each time you face a new situation in your life, your self attempts to take in the new information and to incorporate it. This ongoing dynamic process makes you a product of your experiences. It begins the day you're born and lasts until the day you die. The Self is forever changing and growing.

A solid core develops if there are a minimal number of crises in your life and if you are consistently reinforced and supported for who you are. Sometimes, though, growth is less smooth for some people than for others. One of the layers of self may get injured or even infected. In such cases new layers form that temporarily cover over the old wound. In other cases, if the spiraling process of forming a self is truncated by acute or chronic crises or traumas, then the layers fail to form smoothly. These chinks are like missing pieces in a puzzle.

Chinks in your sense of self can affect how you experience the world in the here and now. The more wounded you are, the narrower your life's path becomes. As this happens, you may find yourself caught in a spiral where you experience less and less joy, see fewer options, and experience greater fears.

Eleanor, age fifty-two, an accountant and a married mother of two, found that she had become sadder and sadder over the years. By the time she no longer had to struggle on a daily basis with the task of raising children, and with more time on her hands, she became increasingly more anxious and depressed. The joy that she had looked forward to after the kids "left the nest" was not there. The wounds from her childhood that she had so carefully evaded had caught up with her. As year after year passed, Eleanor felt like her life was leaving her behind. She became more and more frightened and isolated. One day it became clear that something needed to change in her life, that the wounds to her sense of self had become too painful to bear any longer, that her masks could no longer keep out the pain.

Janis Joplin[1] once sang, "Freedom's just another word for nothing left to lose." And it's when Eleanor felt she had nothing left to lose that she "hit bottom" and surrendered. Too many years of feeling that life was passing her by, of becoming increasingly frightened of the world and more isolated, had caught up with her. Eleanor knew she had to find a way out of her ever-widening hole. She confided her feelings to a friend, who introduced her to a personal-growth process that ultimately led her to a deep healing.

With surrender the journey of growth and recovery from the woundedness begins.[2]

This whole process—both the formation and the healing of self—seems to be circular, not linear, in nature. When we heal a wound from yesterday, we spiral round and round, weaving from the surface back to the core of the wound until it is healed. Here is a picture of how we see this process: As we search for the missing pieces of self, we travel around the spiral again and again at deeper and deeper levels. Each time around, the steps and stages of healing look strikingly similar, even though the issues may be different.

The wound from being abandoned by your mother or father as a child does not have to be dealt with all at once. Chances are that a wound like this spirals through a number of layers of self-development. It will take several turns around the spiral to reach the inner layers of self where we will find our missing pieces.

The stages that we are about to describe can be clearly delineated when looked at in isolation, though in the real world these steps can be taken out of order and sometimes it may even feel as though you're on more than one step at a time. You may move in and out of steps. Your growth requires you to spend some time on each step, but the exact order and the pace is different for each of us. Sometimes you may move along the path at a rapid pace. Sometimes the healing process may proceed at a snail's pace. And sometimes you may experience flashes of insight and sudden change. Looking for your missing pieces will become part of your daily life, a process that begins the second you look in the mirror, throw your hands up, and yell, "My life just isn't working for me this way." This is when you take that first step on the Spiral Path,[3] the journey where you rediscover your real self, your authentic self. This journey is about becoming real, the journey so aptly described in the children's book *The Velveteen Rabbit*:[4]

> "What's it like to be real?" asked the Velveteen Rabbit. "Does it happen all at once, like being wound up, or bit by bit?" "It doesn't happen all at once. You become. It takes a long time. That's why it doesn't happen to people who break easily, or who have sharp edges, or who have to be carefully kept. Generally, by the time you are Real, most of your hair has been loved off, and your eyes drop out and you get loose in the joints and very shabby. But these things don't matter at all, because once you are Real you can't be ugly, except to people who don't understand." ... "I suppose you are Real?" And then he wished he had not said it, for he thought the Skin Horse might be sensitive. But the Skin Horse only smiled, "The Boy's Uncle made me Real. That was a great many years ago; but once you are Real you can't become unreal again. It lasts for always." The Rabbit sighed. He thought it would be a long time before this magic called Real happened to him. He longed to become Real, to know what it felt like; and yet the idea of growing shabby and losing his eyes and whiskers was rather sad. He wished that he could become it without these uncomfortable things happening to him.

The healing process is also very much like the one experienced by the Little Prince in the Saint-Exupéry book. The Prince goes from planet to planet looking for the answer to his questions. He discovers that the answers had always been at home and that he finds them when he speaks his truth. Like the Prince, we often travel around looking for answers outside ourselves, only to discover that they're right here, close to home. They emerge readily when we're able to identify, speak, and be congruent with our own truth, when we stay true to our nature, when we are real.

Dorothy in *The Wizard of Oz* also found this to be true. In the end all she had to do to get back to Kansas was to click the heels of her ruby slippers and say, "There's no place like home"—such a simple solution after such a long journey. But the truth of the matter is that Dorothy probably wasn't ready to hear the simple solution about how to get home until she traveled along her path of self-discovery.

Johnny, a young boy in an Alice Walker story titled "Finding the Green Stone," has a similar journey. He loses his magical glowing green stone due to his own mean-spirited behavior. He, his family, and his entire community go around in search of this green stone. He finds that the key to finding the stone actually lies within him, deep within his heart. The love that glows bright in his heart helps turn an ordinary stone into his special green one. With the support of his community Johnny sets out to find the green stone.

> He was puzzled that everyone in his community wanted to help him do something he could only do himself, and in his puzzlement, he began to feel as if a giant bee were buzzing in his chest. It felt exactly as if all the warmth inside himself was trying to rush out to people around him.
>
> He noticed that as soon as the warmth that was inside him touched them, they began to shine . . . and when Johnny followed Katie's gaze and looked down at his hand, what did he see? Not the dull and lifeless rock that he'd thought he was holding, but his very own bright green stone!

In these stories the characters first look for answers outside themselves but in the end discover that the answers are within them. They find the answers at home and the key in each story was about getting real. Eventually, after they have journeyed, the Velveteen Rabbit, the Little Prince, Dorothy, and Johnny find their missing pieces inside themselves.

The specific nature of the growth process is unique for every one of us. The walk on the Spiral Path of Healing is, in and of itself, not always smooth. It can be a struggle. Sometimes you may take two steps forward and two steps back. Sometimes you may even trip and fall. There are, however, signposts along the way.

SIGNPOSTS ON THE SPIRAL PATH

What follows is a picture of the Spiral Path with eight signposts delineated. This is the path that you will travel around as you search for your missing pieces of self. We are numbering the signposts for the sake of clarity. However, we ask you to remember that sometimes you will take these steps out of order and that you may pass by them many times as you go up the spiral path of your inner growth.

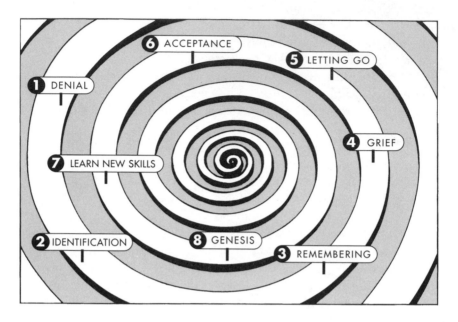

We will first briefly describe the eight signposts, and then we'll discuss them more fully.

You meet the first signpost when you set out on your journey. It is (1) **denial**. This leads you to signpost (2) **identification**. For many, saying "This is what's not working in my life" shows that you're willing to take a long, hard look at what it means to be a workaholic, or a controller, or a peace maker, or a perfectionist. It means that you're now willing to identify and own the difficulties you may have faced when you were growing up. It means that you're willing to own that these experiences are all part of who you are, part of your sense of self.

Sometimes the road gets rough. You may encounter snags in signpost (3) **remembering**. It may be painful remembering what was and what wasn't in your life, remembering where you may have lost some of the pieces of your Self puzzle, and remembering what got you to where you are today. And yet, in order to find the "missing piece," these memories must be reexperienced, worked through— and released.

As you do this work, you'll pass by the (4) **grief** signpost. This marks your spiraling passage through anger and rage, blame, sadness, and despair, as well as guilt and shame. Grief is about loss. All of us experience loss in our lives. Loss itself does not cause missing pieces in the puzzle. However, when we fail to grieve, when we drag the past with us like an albatross around our necks, we end up with old pain continuing to weigh us down today. This is how we end up with missing pieces.

But remember, the reward for working through the grief is a release from pain—this is when "the good" comes. It's then that you begin the process of (5) **letting go** and begin to move on in your life. It's at this point in the process that you come to some level of (6) **acceptance**.

Now, as your life starts to change, you begin to (7) **learn new skills**. You begin to alter old life patterns. You begin to have more choices in your life. And it's in this virgin territory that you discover (8) **genesis**—a new beginning. It's here that you complete one of the many spiraling rounds on your journey to find the pieces of your missing self. It's here that you experience rebirth, that you experience wholeness.

We will now describe each one of the stages in detail with examples from the process of healing your relationships with both your external and your internal family. Later we offer examples of how this process works. Remember that your external family is made up of both your birth family and the environment from which you came, and that your internal family is the parts of you that have been formed over the years in interactions with significant others in your life.

Signpost 1: Denial

Denial is the state we're in before we actually begin to circle the growth spiral. Denial is the defense that we fall back on when we fear loss, when we sense that what we're going through is too much, and when everything is overwhelming. Indeed denial can protect you, but it can also fog your vision. Denial can skew your perceptions.

Denial is not all bad, though. Without it, in the midst of trauma you would become overwhelmed. You would fragment. You might fall apart. Denial protects you. Denial can be both your friend and your foe.

When there is a trauma in our lives, we naturally go into shock at first. After the shock wears off, we may experience a flood of emotions and thoughts. And when that gets to be too much, the pendulum swings to the other side, and we go into denial about the real events occurring in our lives. As one works through the grief process, it is normal for the pendulum to swing back and forth between flooding and denial. Grief only becomes complicated when the pendulum ceases to move, when you get stuck in the flood of feelings or when you get stuck in denial.

When we constantly use denial, it becomes ingrained. This is when denial becomes like cataracts instead of disposable contact lenses. When denial takes over, our ability to make choices is limited and our life path narrows. Whit was in denial about his father's diagnosis of having Alzheimer's disease. He expected his father to understand and follow through with his instructions, getting agitated when he would not. He didn't provide for caregivers and spent hours in fear as his father repeatedly became lost. Whit would lament, "My father is too young to be senile, he is only sixty-nine! He is just being stubborn!"

At fifty Martha's primary identity has been as a wife and mother, but then she discovers that Jack, her husband of twenty-five years, is having an affair. It's too much for her to accept that. She can't believe it. She's so dependent on him. What can she do? She denies that the affair is even going on. She becomes more and more dependent on Jack. Her self-esteem plummets to a lifetime low. Like Whit she begins to walk down a narrow life path with blinders on, which makes it less and less probable that she will be able to survive financially, let alone emotionally, out there in the big bad world without Jack.

Whereas denial is a defense that is used by the healthiest of us in situations that occur in the normal course of living, denial can also be used in more problematic and troubling situations. The most profound example of how denial is used is when someone who has been abused denies that the abuse ever even occurred. Suzanne has been married thirty-three years to a prominent dentist who has beaten her, both physically and emotionally, on a daily basis since the day they got home from their honeymoon. Her childhood was uneventful. "This [the battering] doesn't happen to women like me," she said to reassure herself. She found out the hard way that it can happen to you. She denied the black eyes, the sore ribs, and even the cutting caustic comments that bludgeoned her self-esteem.

Over the years of abuse she came to believe that "he says he'll kill me if I leave. I believe him. I know that I'll die if I leave."

The denial was broken, though, the day Suzanne's husband threw an iron at her. In the flash of a moment when the iron was flying across the room, Suzanne stopped and thought, *Oh, my God, I'm going to die if I stay.* The iron kept flying, and Suzanne ducked. Within twenty-four hours she was in an attorney's office, and a week later in our office. The denial that had allowed her to stay in the marriage had just been broken. Within one week of the iron incident she had moved into a battered-women's shelter.

The denial that we speak of is part of the abuse cycle that Lenore Walker,[5] the nationally known psychologist who has authored pioneer work on the dynamics associated with battered women, has so clearly delineated.

While everything appears to be going smoothly behind closed doors, the tension begins to rise. There is the act of abuse—whether it's a husband striking his wife, a parent physically or verbally hitting a child, or a few sarcastic and cutting yet subtle words said by a wife to her husband. Abuse is followed by chaos and confusion. Everyone may go their own separate ways. This is followed by an "I'm sorry" moment and promises of "It'll never happen again." The two make up. Lovemaking for the adult partners may be "the best ever."

Children who have been hit by mommy are now showered with presents by her. Nothing is talked about. Everything is swept under the carpet. The abuse is denied and all is forgiven. In due time tension rises, tempers flare, and the pattern repeats itself again: Abuse occurs; the abuse is denied; it is followed by chaos; forgiveness follows; tension increases; and the abuse follows over and over again.

If the abuse cycle is to be stopped the denial must be broken. The greatest probability that the cycle will be stopped is if someone intervenes during the time of crisis. In Chinese the character for the word *crisis* means "an opportunity for change." It is often the only time that there's an opportunity to break this cycle, to end the denial, and to change the pattern. This is true for any kind of growth process. For the process of change to begin, denial first needs to be broken. The crisis needs to be seized as an opportunity for change. On the other side of the denial step lies the beginning of healing—the process of traveling on the Spiral Path.

Signpost 2: Identification

As you leave denial, you will come to a signpost called identification. It's during this stage of the growth process that you begin to develop a core member of your internal family of selves. You recognize yourself as a person who wants to change and you see what specific pattern you want to change. This is where Suzanne says, "I am a battered wife," or Whit comes to terms with his father never again being who he once was. Martha finally owns that her marriage is in trouble and, in fact, there are things she doesn't understand about the marriage.

It's at this signpost of the spiral that you will begin to identify your individual core issues of difficulties with trust, control, and/or dependency; your sensitivity to abandonment, rejection, and loss; and any problems with intimacy you may have. This naming of the problem may sound simplistic: "I need to look at ways to be less judgmental of others and less critical of myself." But it can also be complex and painful for some as they own being an abuse victim, a gambler, a perfectionist, a placater, a critic, an alcoholic, and so on.

No matter how difficult it is to get past this signpost, it is a crucial one. Naming and labeling the problem is basic to any change process. By calling an issue what it is, it's harder to deny it. When Carol wrote and said out loud, "I am a shopaholic," she was in a better position to look at the effect her compulsive shopping had on her life.

Take Pat for example, an adult child of an alcoholic, who has for a lifetime taken a vow of silence about what went on in his family. When he begins to talk openly about his father's drinking, he is quickly confronted with a sense of being disloyal. "It's one thing if I say something about my father to myself, and it's another thing if I say something to you about him, let alone to a group of people. It's a totally different story if *you* say something about him. He's my dad, and even though I'm bugged at him, he's mine, not yours, to rag on. If I've got a problem with him, it's mine, not yours, to name."

You will experience this stage of the Spiral Path every day. For example, identification occurs when a widow is having struggles with accepting her husband's death. Or it is when you realize that bankruptcy is inevitable and is ultimately going to be the answer that you choose.

A word of advice: Many people remain in the identification stage and consequently become stuck in their process of healing. When they name the problem, they experience a major rush of relief, not realizing that there's much more to the process and even greater benefits in continuing the journey. It is thus easy for many people to stay with the problem and not move into the solution. Remember on your journey around the Spiral Path that the identification signpost is just that—a signpost. Identification in and of itself is not the whole journey; it's just part of it.

Signpost 3: Remembering

The next signpost is remembering. It's about remembering what was and what wasn't, about putting back together the various "members" of your past. All of us have memories of life experiences, of when things in our life worked for us as well as of times when some things were not working. The exceptional times—both the good and the bad—stand out in our minds. Sometimes, though, we forget the extremely bad times, especially those that involve trauma. Experiences in the here and now can rekindle these buried memories. Sometimes something you hear on the radio, read in a book, hear in a group, or see in a movie can trigger a memory of a specific event from your past. Memories can be cognitive, that is, your *head* remembers. Other times you may have feeling flashbacks, when your *heart* remembers. Sometimes the memories are somatic ones, when your *body* remembers.

Steven, a young business executive whose wife has just left him for another man, remembered more than the good and bad about his marriage. The trauma of his wife's affair also triggered concrete memories of other losses. In the midst of his grief in the here and now, Steven began to remember how betrayed he felt when his mother left him alone with his baby brother at age five while she went out drinking with her lover. The losses of today triggered a flood of memories from yesterday. His head, so to speak, remembered.

Anne was visiting with her ex-sister-in-law, whom she had not seen in years. As they were sitting around talking, for no apparent reason Anne suddenly felt inadequate, just like she felt in her family as a child—never good enough. This visit from a family member had triggered off old feeling memories—memories that had been stored in her heart for all these years. It was an emotional memory, an emotional flashback.

Memories are also stored deep down in your being, in your body. Often these memories are of things that physically happened to you.

Sometimes these are memories of things that happened to you before you had words to name them. Memories like this tend to surface when there is a similar event in the here and now that triggers off the old buried memories. Cathy, who was sexually abused as a child, had her first memory of the abuse as a thirty-six-year-old adult when she experienced numb hands. Her hands made her remember—and feel—exactly how she felt at age five when her teenage brother made her masturbate him.

Remembering buried experiences is a step in your journey around the spiral, but memory alone isn't enough. One must not only remember, one must feel the feelings once again connected with those memories. Armed with the tools and support of today, you can walk back into the pain of yesterday. This time you don't need to walk back with the vulnerabilities of a child. You can walk back with the strengths of an adult. While it's important to feel the feelings, remember you do this with your adult resources.

Childhood events are often forgotten when there are multiple traumas for the child to deal with. When Cathy was five, her younger brother was in the hospital dying of a brain tumor at the same time that she'd been left at home with the older brother who molested her. What she remembered at first was her baby brother dying, and how she'd been left by her parents, who quite naturally were at the hospital with him. What she'd forgotten was the molestation. But this traumatic abuse memory had been stored in her body. And finally, thirty-three years later, she was able to remember the second trauma. When there has been trauma but it's not yet safe to respond to that trauma, we often bury the feelings of loss and the memory itself. Multiple traumas quite often result in multiple buried losses. Many of these losses may very well be buried in the body.

Recently a major controversy has arisen in psychology—the recovered memory debate. Can adults recall previously forgotten memories (of childhood sexual abuse), or are such memories false and the result of suggestions made by therapists? An American Psychological Association Working Group[6] recently issued a report concluding that both occur. Some people forget and some therapists suggest. Further research is called for to determine the mechanisms within the human brain that allow one to remember some things and not others.

This may leave you wondering about your memories: Are they real or imagined; did they actually happen? Good question. There is not a simple answer. If your intent in exploring your memories is to recall each detail and construct one hundred percent of the facts, you may very well have a rough road ahead of you. The only sure-fire way to know if an old memory is totally accurate is to find independent corroborative evidence that supports your perception. If, on the other hand, your intent is to put the pieces of the puzzle of your life together, to make sense of your life story, to understand why you are who you are today, then your task, though difficult, is not impossible.

We do have one very strong piece of advice for you that emerges from this repressed memory debate. Your answers are inside you. Don't let anyone (your friend, your partner, your lover, your therapist, or your doctor) tell you about a memory and what it means.

Resist anyone who tries to tell you that "Oh, this memory sounds like such and such." We repeat: Your memories are yours and no one else's.

Be open to whatever comes up for you. Remember what you can. Your memories will help you grieve and to eventually let go and move on in your life.

Loss from trauma can manifest itself in various forms. Many repress the pain, which can in turn manifest in obsessive thoughts or compulsive behaviors, which can over time turn into full-fledged addictions. The results are predictable. People who have many unresolved losses seem to have multiple difficulties in interpersonal relationships. In order to move on to the next step in their growth process, they must first connect the head memory with the feeling memory, and with the physical memory as well. This allows them to be present for the grief work that follows.

Signpost 4: Grief

On the next part of the spiral you may experience a flood of feelings—many of which are associated with grief—grief for what was, grief for what wasn't; grief for the errors of omission and grief for the errors of commission. This signpost is a major one. Loss is a part of daily living and it can be the result of a crisis. All of us grieve whenever we experience a loss in our lives. This could be the small loss of saying good-bye to your partner each morning as you leave for work, or of breaking a favorite cup. It could be a large loss, such as the end of a twenty-five-year marriage, or a partner's being diagnosed with cancer, or the loss of a job. It could be the loss of letting go of children as they leave home, or of an elderly parent dying. It could be the losses associated with addiction.

The grief process is similar for all kinds of losses, no matter how big or how small. The only way to resolve grief is by walking through it, not around it. You will find that you need to pass by each of these feeling states in the grief process, though not necessarily in this order:

- The sadness and the despair
- The anger, the rage, and the blaming—of self and of others
- The guilt and the shame

Please make sure that you have close at hand your knapsack of "tools for the journey" that you picked up in chapter 1. It is true that the way to heal old wounds is to walk back through the pain and to feel the anger that it wasn't safe enough to feel at the time you were originally wounded, but the idea is to walk back through those feelings in today's safety, and with today's support. You won't be able to accomplish a thing and you'll only hurt yourself further if you walk back through the pain without your tools and your safe support person(s). Traumatizing yourself all over again is not the goal. Healing is the goal, and healing takes safety. Fast does not necessarily mean better.

The worst pain was yesterday. It already happened. You're not going to die from the pain today even though it might feel like it at times. If you get stuck, or if you get overwhelmed, you have a Plan for Getting Unstuck and you have an Overwhelm Plan (see pages 30 and 31). Remember your healthy defenses. They're yours to call upon as you need them. Remember your boundaries. Your new ones can be firm, but not rigid. Remember how to be present, how to get grounded, and how to stay in balance. That's especially important.

Remember your commitment and keep walking even when the going gets rough. And whatever you do, don't forget your strengths. They got you where you are today. You're a survivor, and as you travel the Spiral Path, you learn more and more about how to live beyond survival. Keep your tool bag on hand, and travel on.

Sadness and Despair

All of us feel sad when we lose something. If we feel the sadness and let go of it, we can move on to other steps in the grief process. Problems develop, though, when we avoid the sadness step. Sadness buried over time becomes despair, the kind of pain that takes your breath away. The sadness that many adults from troubled families have to walk through is profound. It comes from the core. The pain is incomprehensible at times and it often feels as though it will never end.

Grief, though, is like waves that break up on the beach. Waves come and go, one wave at a time, in and out. Sometimes these waves feel like tidal waves. That's when we need support to ride out the next one and the next one. But what we know about despair is that if it is really and truly felt, or, to put it differently, if you walk through it and not around it, in time it will end. As you travel along the spiral, you will come to see that eventually you, too, will be able to let go of the grief and move on. In time the waves will roll out.

Anger and Rage

Another step that many people trip over is anger. Buried anger in time becomes rage. Most of us only know about destructive releases for anger. But anger can be a very constructive energy. It's the backbone of healing. There are many ways we deal with anger—or avoid dealing with it. Few of them are healthy. Some people learn to deal with anger by repressing it. Some ignore it. Some people, when they are angry, withdraw. Some deal with anger by intellectualizing it, by working harder in school, and by being the extra-responsible one at home. Some deal with anger by holding it inside and having it seep out by being sarcastic and hypercritical of others, that is, by being passive-aggressive.

Some turn their anger on themselves. They become self-destructive. They overdrink. They overeat. They overwork. Some are hypercritical of themselves. They constantly blame themselves for everything that goes on around them. Suicide is the ultimate anger turned upon self. Others rage outwardly. They yell and scream at their children and/or their partners. They may even hit them. They hurt others in ways that they, too, were hurt as children.

For anger to become a constructive energy, it needs to be worked through and released. When anger is blocked within, so is the pathway around the spiral.

The goal is ultimately to let go, not to collect anger. The first step in letting go of anger is to own it. When anger is collected over time it grows and weighs you down. When left unresolved anger can overcome and bury you. One of the ways we have found helpful is to look at feelings as if they are cards. When you look at anger in this way, it becomes like a game and becomes easier to deal with.

Sue, who is a single mother, had no difficulty addressing her an-

ANGER UNO GAME

Date/ Time	Describe the incident that caused you to get angry, frustrated, or irritated.	Describe the root of your anger.	Rate the intensity of your anger. More cards = more intense anger.	Describe how you are going to release your anger constructively.	What number of cards did you release?

Daily Total of Cards Collected   _____

Daily Total of Cards Released   _____

Total Cards Held on to at End of Day   _____

ger when she felt she had recourse and was confident about what to do—as seen in her two situations in the morning. But her anger with her son in the afternoon was strongly fueled by her helplessness and fears, and the greater seriousness of the situation.

Use the blank chart on page 172 to ascertain how you respond to anger. What did you learn about yourself? Try to develop strategies so that you don't keep holding on to your anger.

Here are some constructive **ways to release anger**:

- Tell the person who is the source of the feeling.
- Find a different way of looking at the situation and then reframe it.
- Exercise, for example, running, walking, working out, swimming.
- Pound a pillow with your fists.
- Hit a pillow with an old tennis racket.
- Scream in a solitary place.
- Shred paper and put it in a basket as you do it.
- Lie on your back and do scissor kicks with your legs.
- Throw back your shoulders and arms as you say, "Get off my back!"

Here's a sample Anger Uno Game that Sue filled out for a day:

SUE'S ANGER UNO GAME

Date/ Time	Describe the incident that caused you to get angry, frustrated, or irritated.	Describe the root of your anger.	Rate the intensity of your anger. More cards = more intense anger.	Describe how you are going to release your anger constructively.	What number of cards did you release?
Monday 8:30 A.M.	Angry with oldest son for oversleeping, missing school bus. I had to take him to school.	His not taking responsibility for self—a repeated pattern.	4	Tell him I'm angry, and set stronger consequences, I won't drive him to school next time.	4
Monday 10:30 A.M.	Work meeting was canceled.	I had worked hard to prepare. Was anxious and wanted meeting over with so that I could stop being anxious.	4	Took a 10-minute outdoor break/walk when meeting was to have occurred. Sought out rescheduled time.	4
Monday 3:00 P.M.	Call came from school—oldest son absent all afternoon.	Angry. Son's problems interfering with my work. Angry with son. Angry with self for feeling helpless.	9	Don't know. Go look for him.	2

Daily Total of Cards Collected   17

Daily Total of Cards Released   10

Total Cards Held on to at End of Day   7

While anger is a natural emotion that we all experience, some people have experienced greater childhood trauma than others. This can lead to the potential for more intense anger and possibly rage. To feel protected and safe in expressing your anger, it's important to allow yourself the opportunity to work with a helping professional skilled in facilitating the safe expression of anger and/or rage. We suggest this most strongly for anybody who has a history of physical and/or sexual abuse.

Some people have repressed anger, and for them the release of those repressed feelings is the goal. On the other hand, some people spew out their anger in destructive ways, and the goal for them is to release it constructively instead. The constructive release of anger allows you to progress through your grief work and to continue on the Spiral Path. The point that is true for both groups is this: Violent expression of anger is destructive, nonproductive and essentially ineffective. Violence hurts, not heals.

Anger is energy—the energy that can and will fuel your healing when it is released constructively. When energy is blocked, so is your recovery. For many people anger is released when they change how they think about the thing that they were angry about.

Sandy's partner abruptly left their relationship of seven years. Sandy woke up one morning to find a note saying he had not been happy for a long time, was sorry, but he had to leave.

> I was so angry. I was enraged. I couldn't believe, first of all, that he'd leave—but to leave with a good-bye note! Then I found out he already had another love relationship! It felt like a poison inside me. I couldn't think straight for months. In my mind I ran through all the things I wanted to do to him. My imagination went wild. I never knew I could be that enraged. My images were vivid! And I knew I needed to talk. I talked to everyone—those who would listen and even those who wouldn't. One day I said to a stranger that I met while waiting at a crosswalk, "Do you know what happened to me?" Before he could get away, I told him my story. I think he thought I was nuts, but I didn't care.
>
> Some friends got tired of hearing my anger. Some friends withdrew. Some friends worked hard to take my anger away. While I believe my fantasizing and need to talk were vital to my getting through the pain, I began to realize that I needed more help. My anger was all-consuming. I finally sought a therapist who for seven weeks walked me through a process where I walked and stomped my feet. I got lots of exercise! I ripped newspapers. I yelled and screamed. Sounds crazy maybe. It was highly structured. We began at a certain time. I followed her directions. We ended at a certain time. It was a physically safe purge of the anger and rage I felt within. I hurt no one and the hurt inside me stopped too. I turned something that was eating me up into something that fueled my healing.

Sandy's example serves as a model, even for those who have comparatively small pieces of anger that we have held inside. The goal of anger work is to identify it, to work through it, and to actively release it in a nonviolent manner.

Blame

Destructive anger can come out as blame—the blaming of self and the blaming of others. Whether that blame is directed inward or outward, it needs to be reframed as an issue of responsibility. Blaming ourselves is different from taking responsibility. True self-blame is a finger-pointing process that is shaming; the message is *I am responsible and therefore I'm bad*. Recognizing when we are responsible for certain behaviors is a wonderful strength that allows us to be accountable. We can then change our behavior and apologize if appropriate. We're in a position to take action. Yet for many people the blaming of self is hurtful. So often the process simply stops with the finger pointing or with a person's taking blame when it isn't theirs. The solution is not to take responsibility for the behaviors and actions of others, nor is it incessantly to blame others. The solution is to learn healthy boundaries: (a) to take responsibility for your part and your part only; (b) to learn what you have control over (yourself); and (c) to let go of blaming or controlling that which you truly don't have control over (others).

For example, Cathy, the thirty-six-year-old incest survivor, has suffered from chronic depression her entire life. She has blamed herself for anything and everything that has gone wrong. In order for her to be able to move beyond a spiral of self-defeating self-blame, her healing begins by holding her perpetrators responsible for their part of her pain. That doesn't mean that she can force them to own their part, but she needs to recognize that she wasn't responsible for what happened to her as a child. In this situation the perpetrators were Cathy's parents, and their part is theirs, whether they chose to pick it up or not. Her recovery lies in recognizing that truth. Once she does that, it will be more possible for her to begin to recognize where she is responsible and where she is not responsible in other areas of her life. When she lets go of the shackles of blame, she is taking a big step toward freedom from her past.

In contrast to Cathy, many people seldom take responsibility for their own behavior and have the tendency more chronically to blame others for their trials and tribulations. John, age twenty-seven, began his journey around the spiral totally blaming others for everything that ever happened to him in his life. As he heals, he'll need to see his own part in problematic situations in the present. He'll need to see clearly what he was responsible for as a six-year-old little boy and what he did not have responsibility for at such a young age. Even if he did talk back to his father, this behavior did not deserve the constant barrage of critical and judgmental messages that his father laid on him. Six-year-olds talk back. They're asserting their individuality and need to learn the right way to do that. Nothing justifies any kind of covert or overt abuse by a parent—whether that be physical, sexual, or emotional. John was not responsible for his father's yelling nor his father's unreasonable expectations of him. John's responsibility as an adult is to learn not to yell obscenities at his boss, the way his father did at him, when he's angry. His father was responsible for his behavior when John was six. But as an adult today John is responsible for the verbal abuse he dumps on others. Finger pointing—at others or at self—is not the solution. Learning from your past mistakes and from the mistakes of others is.

Mother Blame

Nowadays parents and most specifically mothers tend to be the recipients of the greatest amount of blame for their children's problems well into adulthood. How many times have you heard or even said, "It's Mom's fault that I'm the way I am." So often we blame the person who was there, the one who was around, and in our culture that person most often is good ol' mom.

If this is you, you might begin to ask the question, "Where was Dad all this time?" Whereas most of us developed the core part of who we are in relationship to our mothers, who most likely were our primary caretakers when we were young, not all of the missing pieces in our puzzle of Self are the fault of the mothering that we received.

Some of our missing pieces are the result of the context in which we were raised, and that context may very well include more than a mother who didn't do a good enough job. That context may very well include a physically or emotionally absent father and/or a culture that promotes dominant or patriarchal power. When we are simply into "mother blaming," or for that matter into "family blaming," we're not seeing the whole picture, and we tend to get stuck. It's important to keep in mind that you not only came from your external family, but that your caretakers came from their own external families as well. All of you are products of your social context—of the culture, society, religion, and community you were raised in. Simply put, your caretakers were the product of their environment—one that itself may have been nonnurturing and perhaps even abusive. You will know that you are ready to pass by the blame signpost on the Spiral Path when you are able to assign appropriate responsibility, not blame, for whatever you are grieving about.

Male-Female Differences

Grief work tends to be different for men than it is for women. Although this isn't always the case, men tend to express themselves through anger, while women use tears. The differences are not genetic. These differences are created and enhanced by Western culture. Males are reinforced to overemphasize anger. Females, on the other hand, are reinforced to avoid anger and thus get stuck in the sadness. It's much more socially acceptable in our society for men to show their anger outwardly. Little boys are taught that it's okay to fight, but little girls are criticized for fighting: "Oh, honey, that's not ladylike." Little boys are called crybabies if they cry. Few little boys ever see their daddy cry. Little girls, though, tend to be comforted when they cry. They watch mommy cry and think, "Gee, she gets attention when she cries and so will I."

Those little boys and little girls grow up to be adult men and women who have feelings both of anger and of sadness. Men tend to emphasize the anger and bury the sadness, and women tend to emphasize the sadness and bury the anger. Whether we are women or men, we need to work through both the anger and the sadness at the grief signpost.

Guilt

Oftentimes in the healing process what follows the anger is guilt. Sometimes guilt is just the flip side of anger. Guilt is a feeling of regret about something you did or did not do. There is *real guilt* that you feel when you act in a way that is not in sync with who you are, that is out of line with your values. And there is also the *false guilt* that you feel for others' actions, that is, when you feel guilt for your mother's abuse, for your father's drinking, for your sister's bad mood, or when your partner is rude to a friend of yours.

In our culture women tend to accept responsibility for much more than they have power over. The result is profound self-blame and excessive guilt. Excessive guilt hinders, not helps, the growth process. Excessive guilt keeps one stuck as a victim. The guilt step is a steep one for many of us, but especially for those of us who are females.

Shame

Guilt is what you feel when you make a mistake. Shame is what you feel when you *are* the mistake. Shame is the painful feeling that comes with the belief that there's something inherently wrong with who you are. It is the painful feeling that comes with the belief that you are bad, inadequate, or defective. Shame is what Mandy felt after she lost her job: *I'm not worth anything. I'm no good to anyone.* She couldn't differentiate the feedback she was given about her performance from how she felt about herself. A blanket of shame had overcome her ability to reason. Shame is the belief in your unworthiness that hits at the core of your being—a belief that seems to hold even though others may continually tell you that you're just fine as you are.

Many troubled families are shame based. The parents in these families make shaming statements, such as "Emily, you are just a worthless pile of _____ [expletive deleted]." Or "Bill, I can't rely on you for anything." Or "Marie, listen to me. This is your mother speaking. You should know better than to let your sixteen-year-old daughter go out that much! If you'd kept her home, restricted her activities like you know you should have, she wouldn't have gotten sick." Or "John, you'll never find a job if you sit around on your rear end like your dad did." Or "Amanda, you should know that girls can't do that kind of thing. You'll never get into medical school. Don't even waste your time applying."

Adults who are raised in families that give messages like this quite often take the family shame with them. The shame that once bound the family may now bind the person. You can imagine that Emily might say to herself when she's trying to get a job done at work, *Oh, I can't do this. I'm not up to it.* Or Bill will tell himself, *I don't need to follow through on that. I'm not very reliable anyhow.*

Marie found herself really depressed after the phone call from her mother about her sixteen-year-old daughter, but she didn't know why. John, who has been unemployed for the past fifteen months, has come to believe that he really is just like his dad. He looks in the mirror and reminds himself of that every morning when he shaves. Amanda, who was class valedictorian, now works as a receptionist for a local insurance company. It would be one thing if she enjoyed the job, but it's a whole different thing since she not only hates what she does but who she is. Shameful messages planted in the depths of self grow in a cancerous and insidious manner until they take over our whole lives.

Healing from shame involves breaking the silence. Shame withers on the vine when it is exposed. The healing begins as you talk with people you trust about the things about which you feel shame. Ultimately you'll need to identify the shaming messages that you heard and events that you experienced in order to separate your real self from them. When something hurtful has been internalized, you need to be able to say, *But that's not about me. It's not about my worth or my identity. Yes, it hurt. Yes, it felt horrible. Yes, it caused me problems in my life, but it's not about me. I'm not my shame. I am me.* As you put into words how bad you feel, ultimately owning the sadness, hurt, fear, anger, guilt, and shame, your woundedness will heal and you'll be able to let go and move on.

Developing Support

Do you remember in chapter 1, "Tools for the Journey," when we had you create a safe place and find safe persons to be around you while you do your growth work? It is on this part of the Spiral Path that you will need this particular tool the most. If you have not already done so, this is the time to create that safe place and to call on the people that you consider to be safe. It will actually help your process if you surround yourself with safety. It does not help to go back and retraumatize yourself. You surely did not feel safe when you were originally wounded. But it's crucial that you feel safe now as you heal these wounds. Here are some suggestions that a safe person might make to help you work through the anger and rage, sadness and despair, guilt and shame:

A SAFE PERSON MIGHT TELL YOU TO . . .
- Crawl into bed with the covers over your head, hold yourself tight, and just rock yourself to sleep.
- Take a walk.
- Take a wonderful bubble bath.
- Slowly drink warm tea through a straw.
- Stand up and from the depths of your soul scream into a pillow how angry you are about what you missed out on as a child.
- Pound pillows.
- Lie down on your bed on your back and in a scissorslike man-

ner kick your legs up and down, screaming over and over again, "NO, NO, NO, NO. GET AWAY. NO, NO, NO, NO."
· Write and write and write until you have nothing else to say about how unfair it all was.

What is your safe person asking you to do right now as you move through the grief step on the Spiral Path?

Signpost 5: Letting Go

The next signpost along the Spiral Path is about letting go. This is when you're no longer willing to let the past dictate how you live your life today. Letting go involves a willingness to let go of resentments and judgments. Letting go is not forgetting. Letting go is not condoning. You never have to condone someone's hurtful behavior. But when you truly let go, it means that you're no longer trying to get a statement of guilt, an apology, respect, love, understanding, and/or financial compensation for your wounds. When you let go, you accept that the debt that they owe you will never be paid and that the score will never be even. You're no longer invested in changing the other person or hoping that he or she will change. When you let go, you take the capital letter out of *He/She*. *He/She* becomes *he/she*. And for you *i* becomes *I*.

Forgiveness can be a part of letting go. It is *not*, however, a mandatory part of your healing. Forgiveness is a gift that comes as you move along the Spiral Path. You don't need to forgive someone who hurt you in order to let go and move on. In fact the only forgiveness necessary is forgiving yourself. In order to move on, to let go of your past, you do need to forgive yourself. Remember that when you were wounded, you were only a four-foot-two-inch eight-year-old child, not a five-foot-eleven-inch adult. You weren't responsible for the other person's behavior then and you aren't now.

Linda, age twenty-seven, let go of her father when she finally realized through all of her being that the only kind of relationship she could ever have with him as an adult was one that was distant and at best oblique. She let go when she finally lowered her expectations and quit wanting something from him that he was not able to give. And when she let go, she realized that she had freed up lots of energy to use in the here and now in other areas of her life.

It appears that letting go leads to an acceptance of what has occurred. It involves accepting that nothing we do to punish others will heal us. There also comes a time when trying to get something from someone who doesn't have it to give keeps you stuck in your growth process. There comes a time when moving on is more important than dealing with those in the past who hurt you. There comes a time when letting go of the past and taking care of yourself today is more important.

Letting go is an internal process. It occurs within. It results in a feeling of freedom. Letting go is empowering. Letting go results in an inner peace—perhaps, the missing peace that you have been looking for.

Signpost 6: Acceptance

While you have not erased your history, by the time you have reached this step, you have certainly acknowledged and examined it. By now most of the time you will find that your feelings, your thoughts, and your behaviors are usually in sync. Not only can you talk the talk, you can also walk the walk. Acceptance seems to be the next signpost to pass on your journey. The Serenity Prayer is the embodiment of acceptance.

God grant me the serenity to accept the things I cannot change,
The courage to change the things I can,
And the wisdom to know the difference.[7]

This prayer teaches us to accept the fact that "I cannot change" you no matter how hard I try. The painful reality is that I have no control over people, places, and things. "The things that I can" change are things about *me*. According to this prayer, I pray for the wisdom to know the difference between *you* and *me*.

This signpost involves both an acceptance of others and an acceptance of oneself. Acceptance of others involves the willingness to let go of other people and their faults, to be willing to allow others to be who they are, even if we don't like their actions. While we might accept them for who they are, we still have some choices whether or not and how we interact with them. Acceptance is not synonymous with passivity. Acceptance is an active process.

Acceptance of self includes the acceptance of oneself as human. This kind of acceptance involves really believing that you cannot be perfect, that you do make mistakes, but that you try to learn from them. It means that we have come to accept the limits of our power. When one feels acceptance, one feels a certain level of serenity as well.

Acceptance involves humility. A friend, Michelle, said it well: "When I'm at the signpost of acceptance, I humbly accept that no matter how many signposts I have passed on the Spiral Path, I know I still have more to learn about myself. When I'm in 'acceptance,' I embody a spirit of humility. And that humility leaves me with a 'beginner's mind.' "

Everyone is your teacher—both women and men; both those who are victims and those who are empowered; both those who are more wounded and those who are less so; both those who are rich and those who are poor; both those who are younger and those who are older; both those who are smarter than you and those who are not; both those who are differently abled and those who are not; both those who are people of color and those who are not.

Acceptance involves being willing to move on from your woundedness, not hang on to it and thus no longer give it power over you. You empower yourself with acceptance. Those who get stuck on their journey on the Spiral Path, especially those who get stuck in the grief process, give their power away to others. It's when you reach acceptance that you take your power back.

Signpost 7: Learning New Skills

It's at this point on the journey that changes begin to occur in your life. You begin to notice changes in your thinking, in your feelings, and in your behaviors. There are changes in how you see and experience the world. These changes are often small at first. You might not even notice them until later. In fact others may notice that you have changed before you do.

This part of the process is like putting on a new pair of glasses.[8] You may notice new perspectives shifting your point of view:

- From believing that you can fix your family, or from believing that you can make them into the parents you need, to accepting that what you see is what you get
- From all-or-nothing either-or thinking to inclusive thinking; recognizing a "middle ground"
- From idealistic to realistic and respectful expectations

These changes involve a willingness to look for the pockets of health in your family's behavior—an acknowledgment of the good as well as the bad. When you learn new skills, you can take your father's stubbornness that has angered you for years and look at it from a different perspective. You can see that the positive side of stubbornness is the ability to persevere that you, too, have picked up, and you can see how it has served you well. It means acknowledging the times your mother was there for you, not just the times she was not.

The change that occurs for you at this signpost on the Spiral Path allows you to accept a more complex, broader, more integrated parental portrait, one that includes shades of gray as well as colors. These changes involve taking responsibility for what you have been given to do and letting go of the rest.

Changes this profound and this deep don't happen overnight. Our patterns of behavior are deeply rooted, and they take a great deal of time and effort to break. You may well feel awkward as you try out new patterns. So, if you're on your first circuit around the Spiral Path, just be patient and accepting of where you are now. Don't expect to taste the fruit of these changes until you have passed by this signpost several times. These are our long-term goals. Reaching them can be a lengthy and enduring process.

Robert has just begun his work on his external family. He did notice that he felt some relief after doing the exercises in the chapter on the family portrait. He saw that it was actually helpful to see where the family negativity came from. He reported, "Some things did change for me. I'm trying to do affirmation statements every day. And I'm just beginning to see the glass as half full, not as half empty. I'm working on it. Maybe if I keep trying, things will change. What do you think?"

What we think is that on subsequent rounds past this part of the Spiral Path, as Robert goes deeper and deeper into the depths of his self, he will find it easier and easier to see the bright side of things. He may someday even forget that the glass was ever half empty.

As the rules for living change in your life, you will need to find mentors who will work with you and be models for what it's like to be a powerful woman; or how to be a nurturing parent; or a warm, sensitive man; or a powerful yet humble business person. The mentors will teach you new living skills. They will provide examples of how to be, but they cannot define your standards. Your standards are yours for you and you alone to define. Your mentor will help by giving you guidance and support and by letting you know how to live life in a more empowered way.

Sara's mentor was Ethel, a woman she knew at work. This was someone she looked up to. At first Sara did everything like Ethel. Sara was the student and Ethel the teacher. But then, over time, Sara picked what fit of Ethel's ways and left the rest behind. Reciprocity developed in the relationship, and one could even see where Sara had become the teacher and Ethel the student. Ethel, who began as a mentor, later became a peer, an equal, and a lifetime friend of Sara's.

As you begin to use the skills your mentors have taught you, and as you teach others, the seeds of integration will begin to take root and sprout.

Signpost 8: Genesis

As you reach what may appear to be the end of your journey, you will experience a new beginning, a genesis. This is when there is a rebirth of self, when the adult woman, for example, feels as though she's giving birth to herself. Genesis is a rest stop, a time of integration, a time to just let things be, a time to stop to smell the flowers. This is when you are able to say, "Hi, my name is Marie. I am grateful for who I am, and who I am is a sum total of where I have come from." Genesis, as the term implies, is not the end but a new beginning. The beginning of walking around the spiral at deeper and deeper levels, the beginning of healing more and more of self, the beginning of getting to know yourself. The beginning of finding more and more missing pieces.

There may be some sense of fear and some sadness as you reach this signpost. There may be a new kind of grieving. This is because this is where you give up your identity as a victim. It's at this point that you begin to take responsibility for your own life, that you learn to respond, instead of react, to situations. The question arises, If I am no longer a victim, then who am I? Who is the real me beneath the mask?

If you were without models of what it means to be a responsible adult, this step in the journey is understandably tinged with mixed feelings. It may actually feel safer to blame others for what they didn't do rather than to take responsibility today for what you need to do for yourself. When you are in genesis, you will have compassion and understanding not only for others who have wronged you but for yourself as well. You will feel a deep appreciation for all that you've walked through to get to this point on the Spiral Path.

Genesis is also tinged with feelings of bliss. Genesis is when one begins to feel whole, not full of holes. Genesis is when one feels connected with self and with others. Genesis is when the selves become one. Genesis can be exhilarating. Genesis is a time of celebration. Genesis is about widening your range of choice in life. Genesis is about living in freedom.

Once you tap into what is real and genuine within you, it will be with you forever. Sometimes the realness feels exhilarating, and sometimes it hurts. Genesis is the step that helps you find the meaning in your suffering. Genesis is the signpost at which life turns from being a burden to being a challenge.

ROADBLOCKS ALONG THE SPIRAL PATH

People get stuck along the way to genesis. They run into two main roadblocks: *fear* and *resistance*.

The way past those roadblocks is through the process of *surrender*.

Fear

Change—what the whole journey on the Spiral Path is about—is scary. For example Sally laments, "I've needed my perfectionism. It's given me positive attention, even awards and accolades. It's given others a picture of me as strong even when the real me is weak. Yet I need to let go of my perfectionism, because it creates rigidity. It fuels my fear because I never feel good enough. It's killing me."

What lies ahead is unknown. It is a path with uncharted waters. Some turn around and run when they face the fear, which can be present each step of the way. The fear can be either general or specific. It can be experienced as lack of sleep or the inability to concentrate. It can manifest in being scared of a specific person, place, or thing. It can even show up when we promise ourselves that we're going to work on the exercises in this book but then find jillions of excuses not to do it.

When fear is concentrated, we begin to resist the change process and to find reasons to stop walking the Spiral Path. When we run into the roadblock called fear, we need to own it and see it for what it is—a cue, a signal. Fear is a feeling attempting to tell us something. It's telling us that we need more—more support, more information, and a safer environment. Look at your expectations; be realistic. Beef up your support system. Take your time. One step at a time you can walk through your fear.

Resistance

Resistance is a nebulous wall. We may resist moving on in our growth process for a variety of reasons. We resist because of our fear and because we don't feel safe. We resist because we don't have the information about how to move on. Resistance is there for a reason, and our task is to find out the reason, to make it safe enough, and to move on.

Trust your inner guide, your inner wisdom. Deep down inside you know what's best for you. You may be resistant to moving on because you need to slow down. Many people try to recover from their problems too fast. For example they try to do a "fast food" version of recovery from alcoholism in thirty days; from sexual abuse in two months; from divorce after a twenty-year marriage in a year. They find excuses for not doing the exercises in this book. They tell themselves, *Oh, those are for people who really need help.* They "forget" to deal with something important. They say that trying something for their growth process that a friend recommended is silly, so they don't even try.

The great wall of resistance becomes a signal to slow down; to smell the flowers along the way; to walk through, not around, the grief; and to fully integrate the changes that are occurring in your life. Be patient. It may take time to work through resistance. Remember that there's no right way or wrong way to do this work. There's simply your way. And that way is perfectly okay.

It takes energy to hit a wall, to get up again, and to finally move around it. It helps sometimes to hear how others have walked through their fear and resistance. This is where being in a support group is valuable. You hear others' stories and realize you're not alone. Sometimes time itself helps. Time allows you to get a different perspective on the problem, to see it more clearly, to be able to respond instead of react.

Sometimes doing role-playing helps. A man who is petrified to go into a group meeting at work, for example, may be able to get through his resistance by role-playing his walking into a simulated group with a friend, sponsor, or therapist. It's in the midst of the role-play that he may make it through his resistance and be able to let go of old defenses that have become roadblocks.

Sometimes creating metaphors helps one walk through resistance. The adult woman who realizes that her whole life has been like her favorite childhood story, *The Little Engine That Could*, may now be able to see how she has other choices about how to run her life. She may realize that there are other ways to get back on track, more supportive ways than to keep chugging up the hill all alone in a driven manner.

Sometimes the resistance forms itself in your body as a physical symptom, perhaps as a knot in your stomach. It may be helpful in working through this resistance to imagine how a knot might move or unravel if it were to get untied. Joe realized that to untie a knot, he needed to look at the knot carefully in order to identify the problem. Then he needed to get help untying the knot from an expert. Sometimes it takes a long time to untie knots. And it certainly takes patience. But as Joe spoke about this knot, he told us that the feeling in his stomach dissipated. He was already beginning to work through his resistance. He was finding a new way of dealing with the physical symptom. He was getting at the fear by breaking it down into small steps, one part of the knot at a time. He was working through his resistance by utilizing other support and resources—both external and internal.

Resistance is a normal part of any change process. It's normal for any system to put on the brakes once a change has occurred. Look at what happens to you when you lose weight. Your body naturally resists the change and seeks to return to its previous set point.

Change is powerfully resisted in the larger context of our society. For example look at what happened in the women's struggle for rights in the mid-nineteenth century: The initial momentum was followed by resistance to the changes later in that same century. Then look at the upsurge in the women's movement in the early twentieth century. Then in the 1940s, in the 1970s, and again in the mid-1990s each spurt of growth has been followed by societal resistance—a backlash.[9] Today women's concerns have become key issues in political campaigns. Nineteen ninety-two was called "the year of the woman," yet by the 1994 midterm elections with the conservative backlash, women's issues have once again taken a back seat. The women's vote in 1992 was the swing vote in many state and local elections. Any way you look at it, resistance is just part of the process, whether we are talking about your resistance in walking the Spiral Path or the resistance that precedes each step of the process.

It's not until we've created a safe enough environment that our wall of resistance comes down. When we've created a supportive group of friends and when we've created a place and a time in our lives to look for missing pieces, the wall will crumble away. Resistance may in fact be a friend, not a foe. Resistance may be your signal. Embrace it. Trust yourself. Trust the process. Trust that you will work through this roadblock when it's safe enough.

Surrender

The way to walk through your fears and that great wall of resistance is by surrendering. This ability develops as you really "get it," down to your core, that your old way of running the show is no longer working. With surrender there comes a willingness—a willingness to change, to do it another way. This frees you up to have the courage to do what you need to do. There seems to be a different sort of surrender needed at each signpost along the way. And this surrender leaves you ready and able to take the next step.

To many of us who have been raised in Western culture surrender means waving the white flag. It's equivalent to losing. However, we'd like to suggest that surrender during the process of change represents internal strength, not weakness. You can only surrender to change when you become willing to give up your *false self*—when you're willing to set the masks aside, when you're willing to reveal your vulnerable *real self*. Surrender tells us we're in touch with our own internal vulnerability and power. It's a measure of strength, the beginning of winning, not losing, of changing old patterns, of creating a new way of life.

Can you think of a time when surrendering was a measure of strength for you, a time when surrendering was a win, not a loss? Felicia experienced surrender as a measure of strength at forty-nine, when she let go of her grief about her ex-husband. "For a long time I ranted and raved about how unfair it was that he left me for her. I cried for what seemed like forever. My friends said that it was all for the best, but I didn't believe them. Life didn't feel better. Out of my fear I tried to control him. I tried to control everything. It didn't work. I still felt bad. I felt horrible. I was miserable. Then one day something inside me changed. I just let go. I had decided that life was too short to live in this misery." Felicia had surrendered.

Another example of surrender as a measure of strength is presented in the movie *The Prince of Tides*. It's not until Tom has the courage to remember and reexperience the traumatic events of his childhood that he is able to surrender. It is his surrender to the pain, to the rage, and to the healing process itself that eventually leads him to freedom—the freedom that one has when one can choose to return home. He metaphorically returns home to find himself and he literally returns home to be with his family in South Carolina.

One of the unique gifts of the Twelve Step programs is that they offer the participants a way of living that embraces the process of surrender. For decades Al-Anon has worked with family members who have done everything imaginable to fight, control, and insist that their alcoholic family member stop drinking. Al-Anon teaches that in the act of surrendering one moves from being a victim to a position of strength, assertiveness, and empowerment.

Surrender is an active, not a passive, process. Surrender is not about rolling over and letting others walk all over you. Surrender involves owning the power that you have and letting go of whatever it is that you don't have influence over. People, particularly women in our society, are taught to surrender. But what is often meant by that is giving in and giving up—lying down and becoming a doormat. This is not what we mean by surrender. The kind of surrender that we're advocating is part of the growth process; it involves activism and reciprocity.

Phyllis said, "If I stop trying to control how you treat me and I switch the focus to actively taking care of me, then I free up energy I can use in other areas of my life." This kind of surrender is empowering. It does not involve further victimization. Surrendering takes courage. It takes strength to continue doing it. But it makes you feel stronger in the long run. The self gets stronger and more empowering with each surrender.

GETTING STUCK AND UNSTUCK ALONG THE SPIRAL PATH

Not everyone makes it to genesis, the final signpost. Some run into fear and resistance that they're not able to work through. They find that they don't feel safe enough, or supported enough yet, to surrender. Sometimes travelers stay on one step for a long, long time. They plateau.

Three distinct stuck points, or roadblocks, stand out as common ones that travelers may come up against along the Spiral Path:

- Labeling their problems
- Confusion about loyalty
- Taking too many shortcuts from identification to letting go or acceptance

Labeling

People get stuck labeling their problems over and over again. Jill put it well: "Oh, I have control issues. That's why I did that." Jim said, "I have trust issues with women. That's why I can't be close to you." Robin said, "I'm an alcoholic. That's why I act this way." Labeling something as a problem is only a small part of the process. Hiding behind that label as a defense is not the solution. The label in and of itself is not the answer.

Loyalty

Many people get stuck as they walk along the spiral because of their confusion around loyalty. When they begin to own their own sadness, fear, and anger regarding family members, they feel as if they're being disloyal. They believe that they're saying they no longer love that person. It's important to understand that we often have our most intense feelings about those we've loved the most. To talk about one feeling does not take away from, erase, or negate another feeling. You can feel anger and love for the same person. By not being able to speak your truth, you are betraying yourself.

Shortcuts

Another way that people get stuck on the Spiral Path is when they take a shortcut between identification and letting go or acceptance. They try to skip the steps and signposts in between. What happens, though, is that people who take this route miss the crucial part of the journey—the walk through the feeling steps and into and through the grief process. They do only the intellectual part of the work and try to skip the emotional work. They may understand in their heads what has happened, but they bury their fear, their sadness, and their anger in their body.

People tend to look hardened when they take this shortcut and skip the grief work. Their false self becomes rigidified, like a protective shell. They use their energy to control others in order to fend off their own feelings of rage and utter despair. Those who skip this part of the climb sound flat and feelingless. This is because when you shut down one feeling, you shut them all down. What they say, how they feel, and how they act do not match. They speak with that fragmented voice. They may have healed their heads, but they have not healed their hearts, and they probably haven't healed their bodies either.

All of us seem to get stuck somewhere along the way. It's simply part of the process. In fact sometimes it's a very helpful part of the process, because what may look like being stuck may in fact be a time of integration or even a time to buttress up our support system.

Remember that healing is a process. Your map for this process of the Spiral Path is on page 162. It will help you find your way as you walk through these steps. Remember also that if you need support, ask a friend, your support group, your sponsor, or your therapist. Their support and perspective are invaluable. And, most important, remember to have faith and to trust in yourself and the process.

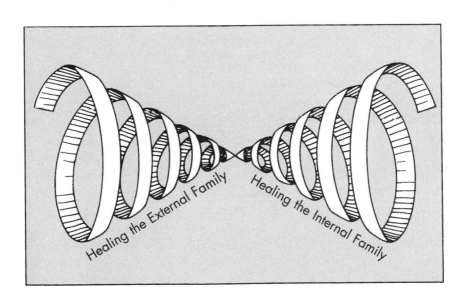

THE SPIRAL PATH FOR HEALING THE INTERNAL FAMILY

As you walk around this spiral, you are actually going deeper into self to heal yourself and to heal your experiences with your "external family." Then you will walk around a similar spiral as you get to know all the parts of your "internal family of selves." This is necessary because what was once outside you in your experiences with and interactions between you and significant others in your life is now inside you. It has become your own internal family. The process of healing your internal family of selves is similar to the one you took to heal your external family.

You might, for example, be in denial about the nurturing part of you if you came from a family where nurturance was not valued or encouraged. When you first identify this nurturing part that takes care of you, you've moved into this part of the healing process. You will then begin to remember the people who have and have not nurtured you in your life. This may bring you into some grief. Perhaps you feel some sadness and anger about the ways in which your mother and father may have not been very nurturing at times. It's also possible that you'll feel guilty for not having spoken up about your needs sooner. There may even be shame if you feel there was/is something inherently flawed within you that attracts nonnurturing people into your life. However, as the grief is worked through, you're likely to let go, learn new skills, and come to a point of acceptance about this nurturing part of you. Next comes genesis, or a new beginning, in which the nurturing part of you is integrated into who you are on a daily basis.

Andrea went through these steps when she was forty-five and discovered her inner child. She'd denied that she had "one of those inside me" until she began to do the exercises on the inner child in the next chapter. At that point she began to picture and then to name that part of her—"Andie." Slowly she began to remember more and more about Andie's experiences as a child—fond memories as well as painful ones. Grief followed, but not before some fear emerged: "This is too scary to remember. I'll be too needy if I step into Andie's shoes." And some resistance as well: "Oh, this inner-child stuff is silly. I have a business to run. I can't afford to be needy."

Then, when the grief hit, Andrea experienced waves of sadness for what it was like to be a little girl who rarely had a daddy around. She got angry. She experienced some guilt and even some shame before getting to the place of letting go and moving on to accept Andie as part of her. And then, after passing the genesis signpost, she repeated the whole process for another part of self.

In the next chapter you will get to know not just your inner child but the many different members of your internal family of selves. You'll meet your nurturer, your protector, your critic, and the victim. Together, you and your internal family of selves will traverse the Spiral Path journey just described.

As you journey, you'll come to the warning sign that says, Please Keep Going. It's okay to take a time-out, but it's not in your best interests simply to label these parts of self and just leave them at that. That would be too fragmenting. This is not the place to stop. Naming the parts and understanding the spiral-like nature of the journey is important, but it's not the whole process. It's just part of it. Your goal is to take your puzzle apart, to get to know the parts, and then to put them back in place, to get them all to work together, and to move on to a place of empowerment in your life.

If you stop at the fragmentation phase of the process, you could conceivably feel more scattered than you did when you began. After all, if you stop there, the pieces of your puzzle—and you—are all over the floor. So the bottom line is that if you get stuck, overwhelmed, or even bored, go back to your plans, your "tools for the journey" from chapter 1. Once again, a temporary time-out is no problem and may very well be healthy, but a permanent detour from the Spiral Path is not advisable.

Remember that people move through their own unique Spiral Paths at different paces and that your path may be somewhat different from that of others. The pace at which you traverse your path usually has to do with the complexity of your family background and the depth of your woundedness. Make a commitment to keep on going until you get a sample of the joy, ecstasy, and fulfillment you're liable to feel when you reach the step that allows you to speak with an integrated and empowered "I" voice—the voice that represents the whole of you. You can do it. We have faith in you and your inner strength.

Walking around the spiral is a journey. If the end seems to be getting farther and farther away, then you might want to remember that the true goal is the journey itself.

I said to my soul, be still, and wait without hope
For hope would be hope for the wrong thing, wait without love
For love would be love of the wrong thing; there is yet faith
But the faith and love and the hope are all in the waiting.
Wait without thought for you are not ready for thought.
So the darkness shall be the light, and the stillness the dancing.
—from "East Coker" by T.S. Eliot[10]

PART THREE

KNOCK,
KNOCK.
WHO'S THERE?

CHAPTER 6

The First Look Inside

Before you examine the specific parts of self that you named in chapter 3, we would like to have you take a look at a few of the more common parts:

- The Lost Child (the wounded one and the innocent one)
- The Nurturer
- The Protector
- The Critic
- The Victim

Most of us have a lost child. And many of us have a nurturing part of self as well as a part that protects us from getting hurt. And, like it or not, most of us have an inner critic that keeps us doing our best. Some of us who were wounded as children, or even as adults, have a victim part of ourselves as well.

Many readers, particularly those who identify as being adult children or codependent, have already begun the process of going inward to meet their lost child. If this is true for you, you may have a head start on exploring your many different parts of self, but if you only look at your lost child, you'll get stuck and miss a lot of other important pieces. If you indulge one part of self, you may ignore and abandon other parts of your internal family of selves. You may be denying your strengths.

Although we believe that the lost child may be the portal to your soul, you must recognize and ultimately embrace all parts of self, not just one inner child. Without the adult parts, the lost child feels lost, unprotected, neglected, and abandoned. You need all of you in order to heal and become whole.

We hope that you'll be able to take the information you find in this chapter and blend it into what you've already learned about your internal world. One's inner child, nurturer, protector, critic, and victim parts do indeed have common threads, but we would be remiss if we led you to believe, even for a moment, that everyone has identical inner parts of self. While both of us, Claudia and Leslie, have inner critics, protectors, and so on, our inner parts are different because our life experiences have been different.

If you come from a troubled family and/or if you intuitively know that you have a very wounded part, please proceed to the section in this chapter on the nurturer and protector parts of self (pages 200 and 225 respectively), and work with these parts first. Your wounded parts will heal more quickly as you develop the protective and nurturing parts.

Therefore we urge you to read what follows in this chapter with your own parts of self in mind. We hope to spark your interest and to help you get to know your parts even better than you already do. Remember, you, not we, are the expert on your internal world. We are simply your guides. If, for example, we say something about your nurturer or protector that doesn't strike home with you, then simply set what we have said aside. Filter what we say through your own internal experience, through your internal family, and through your own sense of self.

THE LOST CHILD

Many of us do not want to look at our lost child. Some of us don't even have a clue about what we mean by the term. Some of us are curious, whereas others may not care to know. Here are some reasons many of us don't look inside at our lost child:

- We're scared of our feelings.
- We don't want to be childish like our parent(s).
- *Child* means being vulnerable, and *vulnerable* means being hurt.
- Being a child means having no choice, no power, and no control.

- Being a child means being a victim.
- We don't know who or what the lost child is.
- We don't know how to find our lost child.
- We don't have the tools for this work.
- Our very survival has depended on our ability to cover up our vulnerabilities.
- We have painful memories of being a child.

Do any of these strike a chord for you? These are the elements of resistance. Respect and honor your resistance as you look at your lost child. Try, if you can, to hang in here with us while we ask you to stretch a little bit more.

FREE TO BE

Sit quietly in a safe place. Take out a piece of paper and some crayons or marking pens. Relax for a few moments. Take a few deep breaths in and out. Can you begin to picture a little child? Do you see him or her? Write the word CHILD in the center of your paper. Now write down every word you can think of that is associated with this word. You may write the words anyplace—all over the page if you like. It's even okay if it looks messy. Write more and more words that remind you of the word *child*. Write right side up, upside down, and sideways. Write in circles, write in lists, or in any way you choose. Keep writing until no more words come to mind and then write some more and more . . . and more . . . and even more.

What do you see? What do you think? What colors did you use? What did you learn about yourself in doing this exercise? You might want to make this real by sharing it with a friend.

Do you see the child within as all negative, as a victim who has no choice, a powerless being with no control, one who is in a lot of pain—the wounded one? Or do you see the child in all of her wonderment and glory—the innocent one? Just accept where you are today with this snapshot picture. Let it be what it is. It's okay if the word *child* brings negative associations to mind, and it's okay if it brings positive ones. What you just learned may help you understand your readiness and/or your resistance to moving on.

In peeking into your child self, be open to realizing there's more than one way to view the inner child. The child within has distinct aspects. We hold not one child but possibly many. It's the innocent child (sometimes called the natural child) that people hear the most about and want to access. Yet it's the wounded child (the abandoned child, vulnerable child, etc.) that we are the quickest to access. In getting to know your parts of self we'll help you delineate these two particular child parts. There may be other ones that you'll want to look at later.

When people resist looking inside the self, it's often because the wounded lost child makes you want to hide from yourself. This child is the one who makes you resist doing this work, resist looking within. For this child it seems just plain foolish to look at things that are going to hurt. The wounded child is scared and will drag her or his feet.

There is, though, another child part inside you that you may find a little easier to connect with. This child is not hurt or wounded. This child is innocent, playful, and incredibly wise. Although she's not wounded, she holds the key to healing your woundedness. Looking at this child will ultimately allow you to recognize your own needs better. And with the help of a nurturing and protective part of you, you'll be able to take better and better care of yourself. The innocent child will make you laugh, and when you're in pain, laughing helps. It's as if the innocent child takes the wounded child's hand and helps her or him keep walking down the Spiral Path. These two—the wounded and the innocent child—become buddies, and together they will make you feel better. As you connect with your innocent child, you will experience more spontaneity, and you'll have more fun. Whereas the wounded child may weigh you down, the innocent child lightens you up.

How Does the Child Within Get Lost?

The Innocent One

Many of us have difficulty getting in touch with this lost child. It's as if we never knew this child, never experienced her or his energy. Children raised in troubled families quickly learn that it's not safe just to "be." It's not safe to be themselves. They learn early on to protect themselves from the pain of rejection. Many of them learn that the only way to stay connected with mom or dad is to please them, and if that means burying the innocent/playful child, then that's a sacrifice that they're willing to make. They build a false, protective shell, one that shields them from further rejection, disappointment, and despair. The child within, who embodies the real self, becomes a prisoner, walled in by a protective, yet false self.

As these children grow up, they have difficulty getting in touch with the fun-loving part of them. Some feel as though they were never children. They had to grow up too fast. They never learned to play. They just learned to be ultraresponsible. They lost their childhood, and in fact became *prisoners of childhood.* If this is you, it may be very difficult to open yourself up to that little girl or that little boy because your survival has been dependent on covering up your vulnerability. Even acknowledging the fact that you were a child can be very threatening. It means remembering a time when you didn't have the power to protect yourself. It means remembering and reexperiencing your vulnerability, your shame, and your pain. If this is your story, it's no wonder that you hid your innocent inner child behind a protective shield so that you wouldn't get wounded anymore. That was good judgment.

The Wounded One

When we look at the lost child from a wider perspective, it seems as if children can be wounded whether they are given too little or too much. Many children are wounded by not getting enough love and attention. Others seem to be given too much, showered, for example, with toys instead of love. They're smothered in overindulgence. On the surface it looks as if such children are given enough, but they aren't. They're missing the love and attention they're starving for. All the toys in the world cannot replace a child's needs for a safe, nurturing, emotional connection with a caretaker.

Some children are overly sheltered. They're not given the opportunity to try their own wings. It's almost as if their wings are clipped. The souls of children like this aren't allowed to flourish. They're every bit as wounded as the child who doesn't get enough.

Sometimes the wounding results in too much hurt and pain. The child learns that "when I'm being real, being me, I get rejected. I can't be me and be accepted." Children learn that the only way that they can stay connected is to give up being real. Wisely they put up a wall of protection. They develop a false self, one that pleases the parents and allows them to stay connected—a self that denies loss and therefore denies life. At the time, though, from the child's perspective, the sacrifice of this real self seems like a small one.

However, in his or her attempt to defend against wounds to the sense of self, the child raised in a troubled family comes to identify more and more with the false self. The real self becomes buried under more and more layers of protective shell. The child within is lost and buried deep inside.

If you come from a troubled family and you ignore your wounded child, you're ignoring your pain and missing out on any chance of wholeness. Your lost child may be hurt; she or he may feel weak, scared, frightened, self-centered, neglected, and needy. It's going to be okay. Your child can be healed and needs to be healed in order for you to become whole. Even if you come from a less troubled background, ignoring your inner child may very well perpetuate a joyless way of being.

Remember, children take time and energy to raise. They take resources. It's important for you to have some choice here. Ask yourself very seriously if you truly have the time and energy to have a child right now? Just because your lost child says, "Now," it doesn't mean that now is best for you. If you do have the time, resources, and energy, proceed. If not, consider when would be a good time. Make yourself a deal about when you'll get back to healing your lost child. Both of you deserve it.

Meeting the Innocent and Wounded Children

The Innocent Child

It's the innocent child part of you who can be very playful, spontaneous, and a joy to be with. It is the innocent child part of you who leads you to your sense of true inner wisdom and knowingness. Let's meet this innocent inner child. Sometimes the innocent and playful inner child peeks out from behind the curtains when you don't even know she's there. Just the other day as we began to write this chapter, we sat down to play a game of jacks. Remember jacks? It had been a long time for both of us, but somehow we remembered. Claudia grew up in a small town in the Pacific Northwest, and Leslie in a southern California coastal community. We had two very different homes, two very different childhoods, two very different experiences, yet we both were kids, and many kids like us played jacks. We fumbled as we tried to regain the concentration that we once had. The rings on our fingers got in the way. They had to come off. Sometimes when it was our turn, we didn't even manage to pick up one jack. We were so awkward, we weren't even sure we could really call this playing jacks. But, oh, did we laugh a lot! We laughed so hard that there were tears in our eyes. We laughed so hard that the game itself really didn't matter anymore.

There were other times like this for us too. We rode the merry-go-round round and round and round at Disneyland. We played Charades until the wee hours of the morning. We had a slumber party and told ghost stories until we shivered ourselves to sleep. What we were doing didn't matter. What did count was that we felt connected and we felt close to each other.

You might be asking yourself as you read this, were we two adults playing, or were we two children playing? Could we have been two adults playing in a childlike way, or were we two lost children playing? You pick. To us it really doesn't matter. It was just fun, and that was all that counted!

Some years ago Cynthia, who is a prominent attorney, found herself befuddled. She began to collect stuffed animals and plastic cartoon characters. She began to spend a little time each day sorting through and playing with these animals, but she didn't know why. She had no logical explanation for her own behavior. Was Cynthia's innocent, playful child peeking out from behind her mask of competence?

When he turned fifty, William began to collect miniature trains. All he knew was that he enjoyed it. It was fun. He had no words for how he felt. Maybe his innocent child had surfaced and was speaking through the trains.

The innocent inner child of yours that may have been locked away for years—especially if you had to grow up very fast—may be the best friend you've ever had. This friend could very well be buried deep inside you—just like she was for Claudia, Leslie, Cynthia, and William. Find your innocent child. She or he holds the key to your happiness.

The work we do on our lost child offers great benefits to our adult selves. The child within, especially the innocent child, helps us know what we want, what we feel, and what we need. As we come to listen to and value our own inner innocent children, they will come forth bearing gifts. They'll provide us access to trust, wonder, playfulness, imagination, creativity, spontaneity, and bliss. They help us access our own "jack playing" energy. The innocent child has been and always will be there—inside us, as a part of us. It's our job to get to know her or him a little bit at a time.

The Wounded Child

Often we do unto ourselves that which was done unto us. If we were abandoned as a child, we may abandon the child within ourselves. If we were ignored, we may ignore our lost child. If our mother did ten things while she was listening to us, without some recovery we may tend to do the same to our lost child. If we were once shamed as a child, we may be ashamed of ourselves today. If our caretakers did not take care of us, we probably didn't learn to take care of ourselves. It's the wounded child part of you, on the other hand, who gets addicted: "I want it—whether it be alcohol, drugs, clothes, sex, food—and I want it now!!" It's the wounded child who thinks nothing is ever good enough. It's the wounded child who gets jealous. It's the wounded child part of you who sees things as all or nothing: "If you really loved me, you'd be home on time every night." These are all good reasons to look at our inner self and to learn to do for ourselves that which was not done for us.

Nothing bad has to happen to you as you work with your wounded inner child today. You may feel vulnerable. It may hurt to remember, but nobody is actually going to hurt you. No one is going to take advantage of you. As you work with your wounded child, you're not giving up control. You're not going to be victimized.

Sometimes we begin the journey of looking inside ourselves when there's a "crease" in our lives. This could happen when a lover leaves, when someone gets sick or dies, when we move, when a child leaves home, when we have lost a job, with the discovery that one of our children is in trouble with drugs or alcohol, or even when we see ourselves acting as our parents once did. We were dancing along when we stumbled and fell. We realized that something wasn't right. How we'd been running the show wasn't working any longer. We "hit bottom."

So often we don't see our wounded child until something in our adult life strikes a childhood chord. Then, and only then, do we look at ourselves in the mirror. What we find is a cloud of hurt that is raining pain. This is when we find that scared wounded child—that very vulnerable young part of us that we buried years and years ago, a part that's crying out for help from our grown up parts of self. A scream bellows out from deep inside us: "I need you. Help me. I'm down here. I need you."

Sometimes the wounded child surfaces when we least expect it. We may be in the middle of a business meeting, or giving a lecture, or talking to a friend, and we feel that we are three years old in a thirty-five-year-old body, or ten in a fifty-year-old body—vulnerable, little, small, and not the age that we truly are. Sometimes we may just ache. We may be hurting so much that we can't stand it and yet we don't know why. The key question to ask yourself at such times is, *How old do I feel right now?* The answer may lead you to some part of your being that arose around the time when you were wounded.

The lost child within who emerges is often wounded and power-less, unable to take care of herself, in need of nurturing, in need of quality time, in need of connection, and in need of parenting—*good enough*, nurturing parenting. This child is often shy, and sometimes cries. This child may not be able to talk. Your wounded child may not trust even you, although you are this little person. She or he may have no feelings, or all the feelings in the world. This child is needy and cries, "I want my mommy to take care of me. I want my daddy to protect me. Does anyone hear me? Is anyone home?" This cry for help from the wounded child is a cry for you—all the parts of you—to help her. Don't reject or abandon her as happened before. Listen to her. Hear her. Hold her. Make it safe for her.

Tim, who was very angry and who was experiencing problems with intimacy, discovered his wounded inner child in a therapy ses-sion. He was talking about how his father was "never there for me" as he showed his therapist childhood pictures. The therapist com-mented on how happy and carefree he looked when he was two and how proud he looked as a five-year-old. Then she asked him to look at himself at age nine. What he saw was a very, very angry, depressed, and forlorn little boy. The therapist asked, "What happened between the innocence of two and the despair of nine? What does that little boy need?"

The thirty-year-old man began to cry. Years of silent tears poured forth. Tim cried and wept and rocked himself. He seemed to rock back and forth forever. It had become safe enough for his wounded child to begin to speak: "I want my daddy. Please don't leave, Daddy. What is this work that you go to when I wake up and don't get back from until after I go to sleep? Don't you care? Daddy, I need you to play with me. I need you to hold me. I need you to listen to me. I need you to show me what it's like to be a guy. So far I don't like what I see."

Everyone thinks Allison "has it all together." Then she started pushing her friends away. She remembers feeling out of sync, more and more crabby, and sadder and sadder, but she didn't know why.

And then one day, when a friend left town on vacation, Allison burst into tears. It didn't seem logical. It didn't make sense. It was as if the "leaving" had tapped into a well of tears. She suddenly discovered a deep pocket of neediness, feelings that she had buried behind a mask of competence.

Her needy wounded child had been abandoned to some degree by her friend, who went on vacation, but mostly by Allison herself. It seemed that the more time Allison spent in her adult competent parts, the more she neglected and in fact abandoned her own wounded child, who by this point had become quite needy. She, too, cried out, "I need you to be there for me. Where are you, Allison? I need you."

Our wounded children need us. They need to be able to trust us. They need our consistency over time. They need to learn to trust that we will not leave them, that we will love them just for who they are. They need to trust that we will allow them to just be and that we won't neglect or abuse them in any way, even though other adults may have done so. Unfortunately—and fortunately—we cannot heal our wounded child overnight. Unfortunately because we'd all like the pain to be over immediately, and fortunately because often it's through this wounded child's pain that we learn so much about ourselves. True healing takes a while. Fast healing often doesn't "take." It's just a Band-Aid.

RECOGNIZING YOUR LOST CHILD

You might want to tape-record this exercise and play it back to yourself.

As you prepare yourself to do the following exercise, find a safe, quiet place to relax and get comfortable. Gently close your eyes and surround yourself with a soft, protective light. Gently breathe in and out.

Listen to your breath—deep and slow. Imagine yourself on a walk in a beautiful setting of your choice. Feel the sense of peace and safety. Let an internal protective light guide you. As you view the horizon, notice that it is familiar. See the home that you once lived in growing up.

Know you are safe—in a protective light. From this safe place ask yourself the following questions: *What does this home look like? Who lives there? What do they look like?*

*Where are you in this home? How old are you? What words
best characterize how life is for you in this home?*

Now approach the home. Outside of the house under a
large tree you sit with the younger you. What would this self
say? Be with this younger you—listen. Listen more and
more. And now, knowing that you have more time ahead of
you with your lost child, begin to come back into yourself.
You're not saying good-bye: you've only begun this rich new
relationship. As a gift to your younger self, before you begin
your journey back down the path, share your protective light.
Feel it surround you both with safety. And when you are
ready, slowly open your eyes.

How was this experience for you? Did you sense the light? How
old was your lost child? You may have found that when you picture
a little boy or a little girl, you see this little child as all good or all
bad. If you see him or her as all good, that's probably the ideal child
that you are in touch with, whereas if you pictured this child as all
bad, then that is probably a wounded or lost child. There are a host
of adjectives you may attach to your lost child and to the experience—*awkward, stupid, okay.* You may see the child as cute, small,
scared, angry, curious. You may be very touched by this child. It's all
okay. There's no right or wrong way to do this. Just be open to the
experience, whatever it might be.

Sometimes the child who emerges is the fun-loving, innocent
one that peeked through for Claudia and Leslie as they played jacks.
But the part of the lost child that first emerges may also be the
wounded child—one who wants others to fix her—a child who
needs to be taken care of, who demands to be the center of your universe, who needs your undivided attention, who is jealous, who
needs to be understood, who needs your unconditional love, who
needs you now, right now. Try not to judge what comes up for you.
Be gentle with yourself. Can you tell the difference between the innocent, fun-loving inner child and the wounded one? Have you
been able to get in touch with both?

Finding Your Lost Children

Sometimes the innocent and the wounded children come out on their own and sometimes they refuse to come out. Sometimes one hides behind the other. As we delve into our self, it's the wounded child we're most likely to encounter first, and the innocent child we ultimately want to embrace. When they hide, you need to invite them out. You need to make it safe enough for them to surface. We have found numerous techniques helpful in working with these lost children. But before we share them with you, there are certain principles that seem even more important than the techniques themselves. So we offer you a set of guidelines for working with your lost children—both the innocent one and the wounded one:

GUIDELINES FOR GETTING IN TOUCH WITH YOUR LOST CHILDREN

- Listen not only to what they say but to what they don't say.
- Listen to how they say what they say.
- Listen carefully. They may speak softly.
- Understand them.
- Be patient with them.
- Respect their need for boundaries.
- Make them feel safe.
- Be consistent with them.
- Make only promises that you can keep.
- Talk to them in their own language.
- Be simple, specific, and concrete.
- Treat them with the respect and dignity that you would a peer.
- Talk with them, not at them.
- Validate their feelings and perceptions.
- Put yourself in their shoes.
- Play with them.
- Believe that they know what's best.
- Trust them.
- Let them guide you.
- Be with them.
- Allow them to be all of who they are.

You will notice, no matter what exercise you pick, that the goal is for you to experience your inner child in all of her or his woundedness or innocence. It's not enough just to think about or simply to talk about your lost child. You cannot talk your way into her or his innocence or wisdom. Experience is the way in. Experience alone is what will heal the wounded inner child. It was experience—often troubling or traumatic experiences—that wounded the child. And it is experience, in a safe, healing environment, that will heal the inner child.

Techniques for Working with Your Inner Children

We're now going to look at several techniques for getting in touch with both your inner children—the innocent one and, most especially, the wounded one. The techniques are aimed at helping you identify and make peace with your wounded child. Until you do that, your perceptions will be distorted and you will lack the freedom to move on in life. It is in the healing of the wounded child that the innocent child is free to emerge. Try these techniques and use those that work best for you.

Childhood Pictures

As you first begin to work with your lost child, you may find it helpful to locate a childhood picture of yourself. This will help your inner child become real to you. Remember, in chapter 4 of this book, when we had you find some childhood pictures of yourself with your family? Now we want you to find some pictures of just you. Maybe you'll find some where there's a sparkle in your eyes. Maybe there are pictures of you at an age when you look very innocent. What do you see when you look into the eyes of the child in these pictures?

Put these pictures somewhere that you can frequently pass. As you walk by the picture, pause and say, "Hi." Do it today and do it tomorrow. Say "Hi" for many days in a row. After you've done that for a while, pause to listen. Let your child speak back. What is she or he saying? It's okay if you feel silly. Just continue with the dialogue—talking out loud is fine. Your internal self needs to be heard, and if you haven't found it out already, it can be fun.

Who is it you hear and see—the wounded child or the innocent child?

LETTER WRITING

If you get tired of talking, you can try writing a letter to your child. Find a safe place where you feel secure, comfortable, warm, and nurtured, a place where you won't be interrupted. Sit down with paper and pencil. And in very simple language begin to write a letter to the child you've come to picture within you—the one you see when you close your eyes.

Speak simply. Be direct. Be specific. Tell your inner child all the things you wished had been said to you when you were that age. What messages do you want your lost child to hear? What words of wisdom do you have for this child? Take the time you need just to be with these inner children, whether they're wounded or innocent.

Put a picture of your lost child in a place where you can see it easily. Be open. Read your letter out loud. Allow the child within you to hear what you have to say. You might even invite her or him to write you back. Which one is willing to come—the wounded or the innocent child?

Opposite-Hand Writing

If your lost child is willing, sit down for a few more minutes, and with your nondominant hand let your child write to you. You'll have to keep time for your child because she or he probably doesn't know how yet. How about ten minutes to begin with?

Take out some paper, maybe even paper that is superwide-ruled, like you had when you were first learning to write. Take out some crayons, or even a wide dark-leaded pencil. Do you have a kitchen timer or a stopwatch, something that'll let you know when ten minutes are up?

Sit in a comfortable place. Do you remember how you used to sit when you were a kid?

When you're ready, pick up the crayons or the big pencil with your nondominant hand and begin to write whatever comes to your mind. Keep the pencil or the crayon on the paper. Don't take it off the paper the entire time.

Even when you don't know what to say, keep writing, even if you say, "I don't know what to say . . . this is dumb. I don't know what to say." Let your mind wander. Let the pictures flow.

There's only one rule, and you're already doing that. You are keeping the pencil/crayon on the paper each moment, one moment at a time. You're writing whatever comes to mind. Say it without judgment. Say it all.

When your time is up, put your pencil or crayon down and look at what your inner child wrote. Take a moment to read what was written to you, and let this lost child know that she or he has been heard. Or if your child self wants a response, say when you're going to get back to her or him. It is very important to keep your promises so that your child will learn to trust you. We've found over the years that in working with inner children, consistency and predictability are crucial.

What is your wounded child saying, or not saying, to you now?

What is your innocent child saying, or not saying, to you now?

Here's an example of something that Howard's wounded child wrote to him:

> Hi! Where have you been? It got scary. Yeah. I got scared. I know you did all you could. But I just hid. That's all for now!

Howard's adult side responded by writing with his dominant hand:

> Hi. Yes, it's been a long time. I'm sorry, but I got scared too. I didn't know what to do. So I just pretended that I didn't care. I got angry and tough and forgot so that no one would notice how lonely and scared we were. I bet we have a lot we'd like to say to each other. I'd like to talk some more. Mostly I'd like to listen to you. I'll be back to talk to you again tomorrow morning, okay?

If you haven't already done so, try this exercise and the journaling afterward. Remember, there isn't any perfect way to do this. This isn't about right or wrong. It's just about allowing yourself to be who you are.

Active Imagination and Voice Dialogue[1]

There are many other ways to experience the healing of your wounded child and innocent child. You can simply talk to these inner children through *active imagination* or *voice dialogue*, which are very similar to the letter writing. We'll work with this technique more extensively in chapter 8, but we offer you a brief example below in which the inner child talks to the adult self:

INNER INNOCENT CHILD: Hi! I want to play with you today. Can we blow bubbles all over the place?

ADULT SELF: SURE. THAT WOULD BE FUN. CAN YOU SHOW ME HOW? IT'S BEEN A LONG TIME SINCE I BLEW BUBBLES. I'M A LITTLE SCARED.

INNER INNOCENT CHILD: Okay. I know how. I'll show you. It'll be fun!

ADULT: HERE ARE THE BUBBLES. LET'S GO.

Games to Play, Things to Do

You can also make things for your wounded and innocent inner children or have them make things for you. How would you like to do finger painting, sculpt with Play-Doh, make buildings or forts, or play with Legos, or Lincoln Logs, or trucks? You can be with both your innocent and your wounded inner children by playing with Hula Hoops, trains, or stuffed animals. Your playful child may like to watch TV shows—such as *Sesame Street, The Electric Company, Mister Rogers' Neighborhood, The Simpsons, Mr. Ed,* or *The Mickey Mouse Club.* When two people play, it is often their inner child parts that are playing with each other, games such as Charades, Monopoly, Checkers, Candyland, Waldo, Mr. Potato Head, jacks, hopscotch, Tic-Tac-Toe, or card games such as War or Go Fish. Some kids like to play with dolls or puppets. Some like to play in the sand. It's even fun to make a collage with your children, to paint or draw with them, or to read comic books with them.

Bedtime Stories, Movies, Videos, and Songs

Some lost children like to have bedtime stories read to them, books such as *Good Night Moon* or *Where the Sidewalk Ends.* What was your favorite childhood story? Do you remember that from chapter 4? Sometimes it's fun to take your child to the movies or to rent videos. Disney movies are always a good standby. Our favorites lately are *Aladdin, Beauty and the Beast,* and *The Lion King.* Children like singing songs—ones that repeat themselves over and over again such as "Row, Row, Row Your Boat" or "I Love You a Bushel and a Peck." Our favorite song today to sing to both wounded and innocent children is a song by Libby Roderick called "How Could Anyone Ever Tell You"[2]:

How could anyone ever tell you you were anything less than beautiful
How could anyone ever tell you you were less than whole
How could anyone fail to notice that your loving is a miracle
How deeply you're connected to my soul.

What songs do you like to sing to your innocent and wounded inner children? Try one today. It's okay if you can't sing. Neither can we. Your inner child won't judge you. It's okay if you can't think of a song. You can use one of ours. It's the experience that counts. Remember? You can't think your way through this.

Old Newspapers

Sylvia discovered more about how she felt as a child when she took a field trip to the library. She looked at the microfilm of newspapers during the period of time between when she was about three and seven. She wanted to see if she could begin to recall things by immersing herself in the times. She wanted to see if she could begin to remember what happened between the joy in her three-year-old eyes and the pain and silent rage that were evident in her seven-year-old eyes. She read the headlines. She looked at the ads. She laughed at the comics. And as she did so, she began to remember how frightened and lonely she felt as her parents were separating and when they ultimately divorced.

Oldies but Goodies

Sara went back and listened to her favorite albums from the era that she grew up in. The music took her back to what was going on in her life when she was ten—to the era of oldies but goodies. Elvis and the Beatles were her way back to buried feelings.

Bruce rented a video on world events during the 1960s, the period when he was in elementary school. The video took him "back home" too. He began to remember how he felt way back then in the "olden days." He remembered what he was doing. "It was strange. It felt for a few minutes like I was actually back on Elm Street and everything was the same as it had been then. I was playing basketball with my two best friends. We were joking about the girls we couldn't stand, complaining about our parents and teacher. I could hear the radio playing the Beatles' 'I Wanna Be Your Man.' "

Special Time

What's important here is to "just be" with your child. The game, the book, the newspaper, the music, or the movie are simply means to an end. They're all ways for you to establish a relationship with your lost children. The goal here is for you to spend *special time* on a regular basis with your lost child—time that your child can count on. "Special time" is a means through which you can establish a unique and special relationship with your inner children.

How about you and your inner children picking several of these projects? Action and experience are the keys. Simply reading about your lost child will not work; playing with your lost child will. Hoping against hope that the inner child will heal will not work; taking action to heal him or her will work. The proper healing combination includes the proper balance of action and just being. Take it slowly. Allow time for your child selves to heal. Try not to overwhelm them. Do things with them, but also allow them to just be. When and if you want to, try sharing your experiences with a friend. That will make it more real.

Healing Rituals

What often works best is to establish a ritual in which you make time and space in each day—the same time and place—to connect with your wounded and innocent children. Healing rituals are important in the creation of a safe enough environment for the wounded child to emerge and be healed. Safety is also important to the innocent child so that she or he can play or tap into inner wisdom. It's hard to do that when you're in crisis.

We want you to know that we understand that even with the best of intentions and efforts, sometimes it's just not safe enough for your inner children to surface. It's your job to create that safety, and a healing ritual is one way to establish it. All it takes is five minutes out of your busy schedule each day to light a candle and to write in your journal. Your inner children will emerge when they're ready.

The healing of any woundedness begins when you establish an intimate relationship with the children within you, and that means hearing, sensing, and living the depth of their pain. It means facing their terror and comforting them in the middle of the night. It means holding them with your arms and with your words. It means cherishing them for just who they are. It means recognizing, accepting, and embracing them. And it may mean saying no to them. Setting limits and boundaries is a part of being a nurturing and protective parent. Healing means doing this over and over again, not just once but many times, one day at a time for the rest of your life.

As you may already know, work on the wounded child may hurt. The pain from yesterday may have been buried deep in your being, and digging it up again is anything but fun. You may experience hours of tears and despair alternating with anger and rage. This is all part of the process. If the feelings were avoided back then, probably because it wasn't safe enough for you to feel them, then they need to be felt now in order for you to heal. The most important thing for you to do while you are dealing with your wounded children is to "be there" for them. They may need to be nudged, but don't push them. They need attention, but don't smother them. It was bad enough being abandoned as a child, but if you end up getting abandoned again and this time by yourself, it's even worse. We believe that the worst abandonment of all is the abandonment of self, and if you abandon your inner children, you are abandoning yourself.

Child Spirit

Are you willing to walk slowly down a path with us, one step at a time? We'd like to help you get in touch with the innocent spirit of the child, the spirit that you were before you were ever hurt, the spirit that you were before there were any missing pieces in your puzzle of Self, the spirit and essence that makes you you. For just a moment hold our hands—with one of us on one side of you and the other on the other side—Leslie to your left and Claudia to your right. Once again, you may want to tape-record this exercise and to play it back to yourself.

ONE STEP AT A TIME

In a safe space, gently close your eyes and observe each breath as it moves in and out of your body. In and out, in and out. As you read on, let yourself and your breath be one. Imagine yourself walking down a path—a path that may be surrounded by trees and birds and mountains that seem to reach to the sky. Or you may find yourself on a path that winds along the shore of the sea, with the wind blowing in your face and the waves spraying you as you walk. Or you may find yourself in the midst of your favorite meadow, sur-rounded by tall grass and wildflowers in all the colors of the rainbow. Whatever path you choose is the right one. Your path is yours. We will walk on either side of you on whatever path you choose.

As you feel the earth below your feet, you will notice that in the distance there is a small child playing freely, and happily.

And as you get closer, imagine for a moment, just a mo-ment, that this child may be you—the way you used to be. Free to be whoever you wanted to be. Notice the sparkle in your eyes. Hear your giggle. It's so contagious. Feel your own vibrant energy.

Allow yourself to be with this inner child for a moment in your day. This child is your teacher. This child has mes-sages for you. Listen quietly. Be with your child self. Hear and remember the messages. Now, slowly, gently, bring these messages back with you into this room, into this space in the here and now.

As we tap into this kind of childlike energy, life is indeed "for fun and for free." Life is just a delight. When we're in the energy of the innocent child, there is a sense of wonderment. There's a magic to living, and we seem to exist in a state of awe. The playful and in-nocent child holds the key to your creativity. S/he is the essence of your vulnerability, the part of you that helps you connect with others in emotionally intimate relationships. If you haven't integrated the innocent child, connections with others can be skewed.

When this innocent child is firmly grounded and implanted within you, you'll be able to work more effectively with the wounded child. If you come from a troubled family, your innocent child holds the key to your freedom from the bondage of your past. Can you begin to picture your innocent child helping out your wounded child, holding her or his hand as they walk along the Spiral Path together?

Let's practice going back and forth into this childlike, innocent, playful energy a few times. Release any here-and-now problems that you have. Ask the wounded child to step aside for a while. You might even bring a curtain down around yourself to separate yourself from these problems. Allow yourself the space and the time to let go. Let go of whether or not you've done the work you brought home from the office, whether or not your laundry is done, whether the living room needs to be picked up, whether or not you ran those last-minute errands. You might want to read through this whole exercise first. When you know what to do, close your eyes and begin to do the exercise. You might even want to record this exercise into a tape recorder and play it back to yourself later. There is something magical that happens when you hear yourself speaking with your own inner child:

THE CHILD COMES FORTH

REMEMBERING

Remember how you felt when you first found the innocent child just playing freely? Remember how the child looked? How the child was dressed? Do you remember the smells in the air? The colors that surrounded you? Was the air that you breathed warm or cold?

WATCHING

Watch your breath right now. Watch it go in and out, in and out. Notice the warmth of your breath as you breathe in and out over and over again. Feel how that warm feeling is beginning to flow throughout your whole body, starting at the top of your head and moving down with each breath. Feel that warm feeling flowing down into your neck and into your shoulders. Each breath out washes away all the tension in your body. Note how your mind is becoming more and more relaxed as you breathe in and out, releasing the troubles and stresses of your everyday life as you breathe. Feel that warm feeling flowing down, down, down into your chest.

Now focus your attention on your heartbeat, one beat after another. Allow the warm, cleansing feeling to enter all of the cells of your being. Feel it flowing into your abdomen. One breath at a time that warm feeling goes down into and through your legs. Releasing and washing out all of the tension in your legs. Flowing down into your toes. Filling each and every toe with a warm, cleansing, tingly sensation. Feel the energy move back up your spine and across your shoulders. Feel the warm feeling unknot the tension in your shoulder joints and flow down your arms and into your fingers, washing all of the tension in your being out through your fingers. And through your toes.

Now that you're totally relaxed and you're releasing any remaining tension, one breath at a time, you may choose to begin to remember a time when your child was close at hand.

RECONNECTING WITH YOUR INNOCENT CHILD

Can you hear her talking to you? What does she have to say? Remember the messages that your innocent child had for you, that you once heard her say to you? If you don't already have your eyes closed, do so now, if you feel safe. Can you remember, can you sense again, the feeling that's in the air when you two are close? Can you feel that right now? Feel it with all of your being. Feel that feeling with all of your soul. Feel the presence of the child in your heart and then ever so slowly, with each breath in and out, watch the child's energy seep into every cell of your body. Feel it enter your heart, your head, your neck, and down into your arms and to the tips of your fingers. Can you feel them tingle?

Now watch your little child enter your chest, your abdomen, your legs, and down into your toes. Now run her energy up through the earth beneath your toes into your legs, abdomen, chest, shoulders, neck, arms, head, and out the top of your head and back down again with each breath into your neck, your shoulders, arms, chest, abdomen, legs, and out your toes.

Run your inner child's energy up and down and through every cell in your being until you know it as well as you do your own ... up and down ... down and up ... again and again and again, over and over again continuing to notice her/his presence with each breath in and out, out and in. . . . Your innocent child is you, and you are your child self.

A SPECIAL TOUCH

When this feeling has filled your being, your whole being, every little part of your being, begin by touching your little finger on your nondominant hand to your thumb on that same hand and continue to feel that feeling. If you are right-handed, touch your little finger on your left hand to the thumb on that hand, and if you are left-handed, touch the little finger on your right hand to your thumb on the same hand.

Keep those fingers lightly touching each other until we tell you to take them apart. Feel those fingers—and continue to feel your child's presence in all of your being from the tip of your head to the depth of your heart to the tips of your toes. . . .

Continue to feel that feeling flow through your whole body up and down with each breath in and out. Let that feeling flow as you hold those two fingers together. Ground yourself in that feeling, the feeling of the innocent child within, who is in you with each breath in and out. Be with that feeling just a little bit longer, in and out, in and out. With each breath feel your inner child's presence in every cell of your being.

CONNECTING AND DISCONNECTING

Now slowly pull those fingers apart, and as you do so, see how this wonderful childlike energy leaves your body. Notice as you pull those fingers apart that your own natural energy returns to your being from head to toe. Continue to breathe in and out, in and out.

Now observe your own energy. Breathing in and out, notice how and where you feel different. . . . In and out, one breath at a time. Slowly watch those two fingers—your little finger and thumb—come closer and closer together until once again they touch. As they do, feel the essence of that child energy take over once again. As those two fingers touch, notice your energy begin to flow again from the top of your head, through your heart, and down to the tips of your toes. Watch it flow from the tips of your toes to the top of your head and back down again. Stay with that energy for just a few more moments. . . .

And then practice one more time pulling those two fingers apart. Then put them back together and pull them apart—each time noting the change in your energy. Let it be. Let it flow. You may very well find yourself many, many times per day practicing putting those fingers together and feeling that child energy in every cell of your being.

You may find yourself choosing to practice this exercise

when you first awake in the morning and before you fall asleep at night . . . and many times during the day. Watch those fingers come together and feel the energy over and over again.

COMING HOME

Breathing in and out, in and out, together and apart, until you're ready to come back into this room, in this time and place. One breath at a time . . . come back into this time and this place, counting to ten. By ten you will be fully awake, remembering what you choose to remember.

This exercise simply helps you make real what may seem unreal to you. Children need things to be real, and if the child within is not yet real to you, this exercise and others in this chapter are designed to make that happen.

Sean used this exercise in a business meeting in which he found himself getting very anxious. "I simply touched my two fingers to each other, and it was like magic. I felt my innocent child with all of his wisdom. He gave me awesome advice. The business deal went our way!"

Laurie accessed her innocent inner child right before an exam. "I didn't exactly want a child part of me showing up to take the test, but having her wisdom there helped answer most of the questions. It made me feel more confident and secure. I did great. No problem."

Another Missing Piece group member, Ann, showed up one night with only her child parts present. She expected us to help her stop her pain. She expected us to set all the limits and boundaries. We didn't, couldn't, and wouldn't. We were able to comfort her and guide her, but we were never able to take all of her pain from her. That can only be done by oneself for one's self over time. It truly does "take a long time to grow young."[3]

THE NURTURING PARTS OF SELF

Children need nurturing parents, who offer them support and validation for simply being, who applaud and celebrate them as children. It's not what you do that's so important, but that you're there for them. This is what children value. Obviously children do things that parents may not approve of, and this most certainly requires a response in which they appropriately express their disapproval. The teaching process works best if the child's essence is not devalued. Mostly nurturing parents offer support to children as they take risks and try new behaviors. They're supportive of children's feelings as they experience pain and joy.

In your external family who was your nurturing parent? Remember that these may not be your biological parents; they may have been your grandparents, stepparents, extended-family members, friends, or friends' parents. Who was "there" for you? Who helped you grow up to be who you are today? Did you have a model for a mostly nurturing parent? Did that model look anything like this?

IN A MOSTLY NURTURING FAMILY ...
- People feel free to talk about inner feelings.
- All feelings including joy and sadness, anger and guilt, are okay.
- People's opinions are respected.
- All family members are treated with dignity.
- The person is more important than the performance.
- All subjects are open to discussion.
- Individual differences are accepted.
- Each person is responsible for his or her own actions.
- Respectful criticism is offered along with appropriate consequences for actions.
- There aren't any "shoulds."
- There are clear, flexible rules.
- The atmosphere is relaxed.
- There is joy and laughter.
- Family members face up to and work through stress.
- People have energy.
- People feel loving.
- Growth is celebrated.
- People have high self-worth.
- If there is more than one parent, there is a strong parental coalition.
- Family members can let go and let things be.
- Family members have fun both together and separately.
- Family members can be trusted.
- Family members walk what they talk.
- Family members are consistent and predictable.

- People are treated with respect.
- Parents are loving and caring but not indulgent.

Does this sound too good to be true? The answer is probably yes. Remember, though, this is just a model and something to strive toward. The goal is progress, not perfection.

Over the past decade in Adult Child of Alcoholic meetings and in the many offshoots from those meetings, people have been told that the "solution" to their troubled childhood was to become their own parent. This sounds wonderful on paper, but it's certainly more difficult to put into action, especially if you don't have the appropriate models to build upon. So we offer the foregoing list to serve as just such a model. The next question, though, is How do I activate those nurturing qualities within me? If I never experienced them— only read about them—how can I make them real? How can I make them come to life within me? Is there really a nurturing part of me?

The answer is yes, yes, and yes. Yes, even if you came from an abusive background, somewhere, perhaps hidden deep inside, there is a nurturing part of you. Most of us had someone take care of us, at least somewhat, and maybe not perfectly by any means.

What we want you to do is to try to pull up those people in your mind's eye. Picture them and what they did for you. In what little ways were they nurturing? We're going to have you build on that.

Jamie remembered her grandmother, Nana, who cuddled her:

> She loved me no matter what just for who I actually was, without my having to do anything. It didn't even matter to her that I brought all of those swimming trophies home. Oh, she was proud of me. But it was me she loved, not what I did. I could cry on her shoulders about anything and everything.
>
> She stood up for me with my mom and dad, sometimes even though they gave her a hard time about interfering. She seemed to have my interests in mind most of the time. But it wasn't like she just took care of others all the time. She took real good care of herself too. I didn't like it much then, but now I respect her for telling me no sometimes, because I think she had her own life and that she couldn't always be there for me. Mostly she loved me and made me feel lovable. I really trusted her a lot. She was my buddy and she took real good care of me—kind of like what I need to do for myself today, huh?

What was once outside was now inside.

At first John couldn't think of any models for nurturance in his family. But then when we nudged him a little bit, he dug even deeper. That's when he remembered a Boy Scout leader who had taken an interest in him. "Now that I look back on it, he cared for me. He would take extra time with me when he showed me how to do things. He would ask me how I was, and I felt he cared. It doesn't seem like a lot, but he was one of the few people in my life who showed even those little moments of caring. I'm grateful. I try to be like him with my son today."

Those external people that we turned to or turn to today are models for how each of us can protect and nurture our own selves better.

THE NURTURER

Who were the nurturing person(s) in your life? Who do you try to be like when you try to nurture a child, friend, or lover in your world today? Who was there for you as a child? Who is there for you in your external family today?

Picture those persons nurturing you. What are they doing? What are they saying?

Experience it down to your bones. How does it feel? What would you like them to do again? Stay with this experience for a few moments. Feel yourself being very nurtured—the most nurtured you've ever felt in your whole life.

Imagine that person nurturing you from the inside as well as from the outside.

Staying with the feeling of being supported, cared for, and valued, create a symbol that represents the part of you that is a self-nurturer. Open all of your senses to that symbol. What does it look like? Does it have a smell or a taste? What's it like to feel? Does it make any noise?

Examine your symbol of nurturance in the light as if it were a rare gem. It's yours, all yours. Created from, by, and for you. No one can take it from you. It's yours to keep.

Felicia's protective symbol was a lake. She said it was a calm, warm lake with white ducks on it. "The calmness of the lake is what

I feel when I think of those people who have been loving toward me. I also think I chose a lake because my aunt and uncle were very important to me as a child and were strong nurturers of me. They lived next to a lake, and we used to walk around it. Having white ducks on the lake comes from the feeling of being valued. I felt like the white ducks—valued and beautiful."

CONTACTING THE NURTURER

Go back into the imagery and re-create your symbol of the nurturer. Be with the feeling. Again, think of messages you received that have been supportive of you—messages that tell you how valuable you are. Now give thought to those people in your life whom you nurture. Who are they? How do you offer them nurturance and support? What do you say? Be with those thoughts for a few moments. Now imagine those things being said to you. Imagine those loving looks, words, or touches.

Take your feelings and thoughts about nurturance and let them take over your whole being. Feel it—being nurtured—in all in its glory! Sense being a nurturer and being nurtured!

Staying in those feelings, raise their volume a little bit higher. Then turn them up higher and higher. Get them to 100 percent. You are *all* nurturer. Be with that 100 percent feeling of nurturance.

Now, very slowly, move from 100 percent to 80 percent nurturer. Be with the 80 percent nurturance. . . . Now move back up to 100 percent. . . . and back down to 80 percent.

Try going down to 25 percent. . . . Be with that. . . . Now move back up to 40 percent. . . . and back down to 25 percent.

Now let's try a scant 5 percent feeling of nurturance. . . . Be with that feeling a moment. And now move the volume back to 25 percent. . . . And again back to 5 percent.[4]

What does this feel like for you? Where is your own personal comfort zone? How much nurturance is enough for you? Where would you like to spend more time? Can you imagine different times in your daily life that you might find it helpful to utilize the nurturer to a greater or lesser degree than at others? Are there certain people you may spend time with where you feel you need to call on your nurturer more? Are there some people with whom you need your nurturer around less?

What's important in this process is to know that you can call upon the nurturer whenever it is helpful and to whatever degree you may need.

Dick decided that he felt silly talking about a nurturing person in his life. After all, he was a jock, an ex-USC football player. He didn't need to be taken care of, or so he thought. Still, Dick kept running into problems in relationships with women, who told him they were leaving because he was "too needy." Dick said, "I don't know what they're talking about."

And he really didn't—he wasn't in touch with any of his neediness. Because of this, Dick expected the women in his life to pamper him, to be there at his beck and call, and to care for him in ways that his mother and father hadn't years ago. This was because he wasn't in touch with either his "needy child" part or with the part of him that could actually nurture and care for his own inner child. He expected others—in this case women—to do it for him. "Why not?" he asked. "It feels like I've got to get it from someplace. Isn't that what women are for?" It's no wonder so many women left him!

After much work in therapy Dick began to discover his own internal world. He found both a needy child within as well as a nurturer—the embodiment of all of the women who had nurtured him over the years. With some help Dick began to turn to himself as well as to friends for nurturance. "This is a small miracle," he exclaimed. "There's no way that I ever thought of myself as nurturing. But now I feel more in control, and women seem to be sticking around longer in my life. I guess I must not be as draining and demanding as I used to be."

THE PROTECTIVE PARTS OF SELF

Children need nurturance, and they also need parents to protect them. When we were children, we needed our parents to protect us physically from being hurt and abused, and to protect us psychologically as well. We needed them to protect us from having to handle too much too fast. We needed them to protect us from growing up too fast, to challenge us to be the most we could be. We needed parents who prepared us from day one both to be in relationships with others and to be able to be alone.

Inner children need parents too—parents who are there for them, who protect them from having to handle too much too fast, from growing up too fast. Parents who challenge them to be the most they can be, and who prepare them from day one both to be in relationships with others and to be able to be alone.

In your external family who were your protectors? Was it both your parents or one more than the other? Was it a sibling? Was it a neighbor, or someone from church? Who in your childhood offered you some sort of physical or psychological protection when you needed it?

Sonny's older sister was like a mom to him. "Sandy protected me a lot from my stepfather. She stood up for me with my mom, too, when Mom would rag on me for not doing my chores. She made me do them still, but she tried to shield me from Mom's constant criticism. Today I try to be like Sandy with my daughter. I try to be understanding and to stand up for her when she needs me."

Karen remembers her neighbors being her protectors:

> When I'd get lonely, or scared, or so angry I couldn't stand being in my house, I would go to the neighbors'. My parents were drunk a lot and fought just as much. Well, I had these two neighbors, and I could go to their houses at any time of the day or night. They didn't question me. They were my nurturers, but they were clearly my protectors too. They let me sleep there so that I would be rested and able to go to school the next day. Sometimes they made sure I had money for lunch. They talked to me about what to do in certain situations when my parents would try to argue with me or call me really hurtful names.

THE PROTECTOR

Take a moment to listen to your inner self very carefully. Write down your answers to the following questions:

Who were the protective person(s) in your life?

1. _____
2. _____
3. _____

Whom do you try to be like when you offer protection to a child, friend, or lover in your world today?

1. _____
2. _____
3. _____

Who was there for you as a child, and who is there for you in your external family today?

1. _____
2. _____
3. _____

Picture those protective persons. What are they doing? What are they saying?

Experience it down to your bones. How does it feel? What would you wish them to do again? Be with this experience for a few moments.

Staying with the feeling of being valued and protected, create a symbol that represents the part of you that is a self-protector. Open all of your senses to that symbol. What does it look like? Does it have a smell or a taste? What does it feel like? Does it make any noise? Examine your symbol of protection in the light as if it were a rare gem. It's yours, all yours. Created from, by, and for you. No one can take it from you. It's yours to keep.

Ken's image of self-protection was a shield: "I could see this shield; it was as if the people who protected me held a shield up that said No! It is a bright, shiny shield with a big blue and red eagle on it with its wings spread. I think the bird is me, flying with a wonderful freedom. I think that when I felt protected, I also felt free to be me."

CONTACTING THE PROTECTOR

Go back into the imagery and re-create your symbol of the protector. Be with the feeling. Again, think of messages you received that have been protective of you—messages that tell you how valuable you are. Now give thought to those people in your life whom you protect. Who are they? How do you offer them protection? What do you say? Imagine those things being said to you—the messages, the looks, the behaviors.

Take your feelings and thoughts about protection and let them take over your whole being. Feel the sense of being protective and being protected!

Staying in those feelings, raise their volume a little bit higher. Then turn them up higher and higher. Get them to 100 percent. You are *all* protector. Be with that 100 percent feeling of protection.

Now, very slowly, move from 100 percent to 80 percent protector. Be with the 80 percent feeling of protection. . . . Now move back up to 100 percent. . . . and back down to 80 percent.

Try going down to 25 percent. . . . Be with that. . . . Now move back up to 40 percent. . . . and back down to 25 percent.

Now let's try a scant 5 percent feeling of protection. Be with that feeling a moment. . . . And now move the volume back to 25 percent. . . . And again back to 5 percent.

What does this feel like for you? Where is your own personal comfort zone? How much protection is enough for you? Where would you like to spend more time? Can you imagine different times in your daily life that you might find it helpful to utilize your protector self to a greater or lesser degree? Are there certain people you may spend time with where you feel you need to call on your protector more? Are there some people with whom you need your protector less?

Again, what is important in this process is to know that you can call upon the protector self whenever it is helpful and to whatever degree you may need. Many times your protective self wears a variety of masks, and these protective selves can have different names—such as the pusher, who pushes you to get more done; and the judge, who judges others so that you can make yourself feel better. Some have the perfectionist, who strives to be perfect to help you prove that you're a worthy person.

These are examples of ways you learned to protect yourself from having to feel the pain of what's happening in your life at any given time. Take a moment to see if there are some readily identifiable parts of yourself that, looking back, you can see were developed to offer you some protection when you weren't being adequately protected by others.

Whatever you call your protector self, it has a rather obvious role in your life—to protect you. It protects you from others and from your own vulnerabilities. The protector may come on strong at times. It may put up an impregnable steel wall, or the shield may be semipermeable. It helps you maintain boundaries between what is yours and what is someone else's. The protector helps you say no and mean no. It keeps some things in and keeps some things out, and helps you maintain your sense of integrity.

When the protector is out in full force, you'll find that it's difficult for you to connect with others. This probably works out just fine. When there's danger lurking, you probably don't want to connect. Sometimes, though, the protector takes on a life of its own and forgets to step aside to allow you to experience and to show some of your vulnerabilities. Its job is to protect you from being overwhelmed, from too much vulnerability. Thus when you feel safe both externally and internally, the protector may want to take a rest. It helps when the protector is strong and flexible as opposed to rigid and brittle.

The nurturer is there to care for you in ways that you may not have been nurtured as a youngster. The protector is there in a similar manner, to protect you in a way that you weren't before. We firmly believe that you have these parts inside you. They may be buried. They may need to be enhanced. But they are there.

The protective part is there to defend you from hurt and pain in your life and to shield your vulnerabilities. The nurturing part is there to care for you. Are you there for your nurturer and protector? Can you get in touch with them? Relationships work best when there's reciprocity. You need to be there for each other, and your part is to pay attention to them.

THE CRITIC

Many of you have said, "I'm my own worst critic." Most of us at least seem to have some part of ourselves that judges us—sometimes harshly. Take the woman who is on diet number 4,679, who looks terrific but who's ragging on herself because she just had a delicious chocolate chip cookie that her boyfriend made for her. Or take the salesperson who has just put in a successful sixty-hour week. But he loses his last sale before he leaves the office for the weekend, and he's ferociously hard on himself all the way home: *You fool. If you were any good at all, you would have closed that deal. What an idiot. You should have known better.*

The primary job of the critic part of each of us is to protect us. Ideally it offers us constructive criticism before someone else does it for us. That sounds like a good idea, right? Noble, right? Well, while the critic may have honorable intentions, and originally may have had your best interests at heart, something often goes wrong along the way. The critic takes on a life and identity of its own. The critic becomes a big part of you. It dominates the picture, and when it does, it feels like it *is* you at times.

Who was your original critic? Who tried to protect you by pushing you to be the best when you were a kid? Whose motto was "If you can't do it right, don't do it at all"? Who kept on your case all the time? Was it Dad? Was it Mom? Was it a sibling or a teacher? And who has taken on that role in your life today?

THE CRITIC IN YOU

Take a moment to listen to your inner self very carefully. Write down your answers to the following questions: Who was critical of you?

1. _____
2. _____
3. _____

What were the messages you heard?

1. _____
2. _____
3. _____

Do you remember hearing the following statements? If so, fill in the blanks.

The trouble with you is _____.
The trouble with you is _____.
If only you had _____.
If only you had _____.

You should have (have not) _____.
You should have (have not) _____.

Now picture those person(s) talking to you. Can you hear them? What do their voices sound like? Exaggerate their voices, and play them over and over again in your mind like a broken record.

How is that for you? What do you feel like? Do you feel anything in your body, or do you go numb? How do you handle criticism? Is it all bad?

Does anyone today sound like this old critic to you? (It may not be someone else—it could be you yourself.)

Do you listen to him or her? Hear that person say whatever he or she says to you over and over again. How is this for you? Now what do you feel like? How does it feel in your body as you hear this current person in your life tear you apart today?

It's important that you do the best you can at coming up with the critical messages you've heard over and over again in your life. Odds are that you give yourself the same messages today that someone else gave you back then. You may very well have become your own worst critic. Once again, what was once outside you has come to be inside you. The external critic of yesterday has become the inner critic of today.

Ultimately we can only let go of the hurtful critic as we come to recognize its voice.

CONTACTING THE CRITIC

As you have with the nurturer and the protector, create a symbol for your critic, for example a gigantic finger aimed at yourself. Again think of messages you received that have been critical of you that you have internalized. What are the words, the body stance, or the face of that critic?

Take those feelings and critical thoughts and feel them all. Go back to the feelings and raise their volume, higher and higher . . . a little bit higher. Get them to 100 percent. You are *all* critic. Be with that 100 percent.

Now slowly move from 100 percent to 80 percent critic.

Be with the 80 percent critic. . . . Now move up to 100 percent . . . and back down to 80 percent.

Try going down to 25 percent. . . . Be with that. . . . Now move back up to 40 percent . . . and back down to 25 percent.

Now let's try a scant 5 percent feeling of criticism. . . . Be with that feeling a moment. Move the volume back to 25 percent . . . and back down again to 5 percent.

What does this feel like for you? Where is your own personal comfort zone? How much criticism is enough for you? Can you imagine different times in your daily life where you might find it helpful to utilize the inner critic to a greater or lesser degree than others?

Again, what is important in this process is for you to know that you can call on your critic whenever it is helpful and at whatever level is comfortable. The critic is a source of discernment. The critic can help you pick things that are important out of a mass of trivia. The critic can help you choose what to do when there are too many choices. We all need the positive side of the critic.

Sometimes it seems as if the inner critic has to work overtime. Ruth complained, "My critic never thinks I'm enough. She runs my life. She's been doing this since I was two. I think that she needs a break, but she's too scared to let go. She thinks that if she isn't there bugging me, I'll fail at whatever I'm doing." Critics need a time-out just as we need a time-out from work periodically. We call that a weekend, or a vacation. Does your critic ever sleep, rest, or go on vacation? In one of our Missing Piece groups the participants came up with a list of ways to give their critic a rest:

- Do something nice for yourself.
- Listen to what the critic has to say, thank it for sharing, and take what it says with a grain of salt. Still, it may have something useful to say.
- Do something that you know you're good at.
- Tell someone else about what the critic says to you.
- Try to find something funny in what the critic has to say.
- Offset the critic's negative statements with positive self statements.

- Set a time limit on how long in any given situation you will be willing to listen to the critic.

Your critic has several first cousins who were first designed as masks to protect you. They are the perfectionist, Mr. and Ms. Right, the driver or pusher, and the judge. All of these parts may very well have caused you pain at one time or another. As you think about the messages of the inner critic, listen to what the cousins may be saying as well. The perfectionist seeks nothing less than absolute perfection, 100 percent in whatever you do. Mr. and Ms. Right insist that they're always right and that you're never wrong. The driver or the pusher pushes and pushes and drives you until you get something done. And the judge often criticizes and judges others with the same ferocity that the critic judges self.

Sometimes the critic simply doesn't know how to take a break. It needs a helper, someone to hold its hand and set limits. The critic can, as we're sure you know, be quite harsh. An out-of-control critic can cut you up and spit you out in one easy move. This is where we suggest you bring in some other parts of you to help out. Perhaps the nurturer could help, along with whatever you call your protector. They may very well need to step in and protect you from the harsh critic. Those of us with brutal inner critics may need a lot of members onboard to help tackle the critic when it gets out of control.

Judy's nurturing part reminded her on a daily basis of all of the things she was doing right. This at least partially offset the critic's list of the things she did wrong. We all need to hear that we're doing a good job. In fact we usually need to hear it a lot, because odds are we've told ourselves plenty of times all the things we could have done better or that we did wrong. When the critic is in high form, it can devastate you. It can leave you feeling that you never do anything right, that you're incompetent at work, as a partner, as a mother, and as a friend. This is precisely why the critic needs to be offset by other parts. The critic assumes you're responsible for everything. While this may serve you well at times, it may well be overkill at other times. No one is responsible for everything—not even your inner critic.

Have you ever considered giving your critic a break? You could have some other part on call. That's what Vicki did.

I sent my critic to a WordPerfect convention in Hawaii. I thought she needed to have something to critique, so I figured better them than me. I was hoping that she might get a little sun, have a few Mai Tais, and relax a little in spite of herself while she was there. I reminded her before she left that she had taught me very well to be as perfect as possible and that it was time for her student, me, to show off. She liked that, insisting that I give her a full report when she got back. I told her "no problem" and assured her she'd still have a job when she returned—there'd always be things to criticize me about. She left, and I relaxed.

The critic may seem bad, but it does have a useful job to do and that is to protect you, to make you the best you can be, to push and motivate you, to make you do things, to help you be discerning, and to keep you in line. Without your critic you might not be who you are today. Respect your critic, but don't let it take over. It's been on your side for a long time. You may simply need to hire on a few assistants or send it off for a vacation soon. After that your critic may be able to stick to its primary, and certainly positive, job of discernment.

The Victim

Most of us have at one point or another in our lives been a victim of something. You know that you're a victim when you find yourself saying, "It's not fair! What happened to me is just not fair! Why me? Why me?" Or you know that you are or have been a victim when you feel burdened rather than challenged by something.

You are the victim of something when something outside of you has hurt you, and when you feel like you have very little, if any, control over it. In the course of daily living this happens to us all. You can't live without having been the victim of something. Maybe it was the IRS or that highway patrol officer who picked you out of a whole line of cars going 75 miles per hour on the freeway, and you were the only one who got a ticket. Not fair, right?

Some people seem to be victims all the time. In their own eyes it seems as though a pattern that started in childhood is still perpetuating itself today. Once a victim, always a victim, or so it seems. Jean was ignored a lot when she was a child. No one paid any attention to her. Her older brother, Bill, was the one who got all of the attention, in her perception. "I then ended up with a husband who always worked and never paid attention to me either. My kids don't even pay any attention to me. The list goes on. There's this guy at work who got the job I wanted. I was passed over. Figures, huh? How come it's only the men who get everything in this world? I can't stand it. It's not fair. It's my turn to have someone acknowledge me!"

Sometimes people get stuck in the rut of blaming others for everything, feeling that their entire life is outside their control. They can't seem to make their way through the muck to find another way to live. Victims such as Jean may have found their inner child, but that child is wounded, and she will stay wounded because a victim part of her has taken over. It's as though the entire self has been swallowed up by the victim in cases like this. Jean was most certainly a victim of unfair and uneven treatment as a child. And it's true that in the here and now she's being treated unfairly by her husband, and even by her boss. Jean clearly has many feelings about all of this—a lot of anger, and maybe rage, and certainly some sadness and despair. But if Jean doesn't work through and let go of these feelings, she will remain a victim. Only this time she will be a victim of herself, of her own feelings.

Jean's difficulty is that she has felt the anger and the sadness, but only in her head. She has hung on to her feelings. She has not released them in a constructive way. In fact when she has released her anger, she's done it in a destructive manner. Last night she said some really cruel things to her husband in a fit of rage—things that had certainly caused Jim, her husband, a great deal of pain and shame. And she had set herself up as a victim one more time because, as one might expect, Jim's friends aligned themselves with Jim, immediately heckling her. Jean was once again left standing there all by herself, devastated, and feeling like a victim.

Okay, let's bring this victim information home now. Here are a few questions that might help:

THE VICTIM IN YOU

Is there a victim part of you that keeps getting in situations where someone hurts you? Where it feels as though someone has done it to you one more time?

How do you feel when you're in that spot? What do you think before, during, and after the victim part of you has been out? How big a part of you is the victim part? When was the first time you remember being a victim? How has being a victim served you?

The last question is the tough one. Most of us who have been the victim of something in our lives, or who feel like victims all of the time, won't like this question because it sounds like we are getting blamed for yet one more thing. It feels like one more burden. Yet by answering this question, it will be possible to see the part you contribute to being victimized.

We all usually hang on to patterns and behavior when it does us some good, even though that may be hard to see. Can you stretch, and maybe for just a split second begin to imagine how the victim part of you has helped you out in your life? Sabrina said that her victim part "helps me avoid growing up." "After all," Walt said, "the victim is my out. He gets me attention. People always feel sorry for the underdog. I get lots of sympathy that way." And Mandy revealed in group that "I'd be lost without my victim. Who would I be without her? She's been around for a long time!" Sheila said that "I'd have to quit therapy, and I like the attention I get there. If I wasn't a victim anymore, there'd be nothing else left for me to work on." It seems as if the victim can indeed serve you as well as hurt you.

CONTACTING THE VICTIM

As you have with the nurturer, the protector, and the critic, create a symbol of your inner victim. What are the words you hear when your victim is speaking? What is the body stance? How does the victim feel?

We realize that when the victim part of us is tapped, it's not as if we have a lot of control. Most of us feel as if we have suddenly become all-consumed. But try this out anyway: Go back to the feelings and the internal messages and raise their volume, higher and higher . . . a little bit higher. Get them to 100 percent. You are *all* victim. Be with that 100 percent feeling of being a victim.

Now we are going to ask you to touch the dimmer switch

and slowly move from 100 percent to 80 percent victim. Be with the 80 percent victim. . . . Now move up to 100 percent . . . and back down to 80 percent.

Let's go back down to 25 percent. . . . Be with that. . . . Now up to 40 percent . . . back down to 25 percent.

Now let's try a scant 5 percent feeling of victim. Be with that feeling for a moment. And now move the volume back to 25 percent . . . and again back down to 5 percent.

What does this feel like for you? Where is your personal comfort zone? How much victim is enough for you? Can you imagine different times in your daily life that you might find it helpful to utilize the inner victim to a greater or lesser degree?

Most people believe they would never want to be in a victim role. Yet many of us go there very quickly when we're frightened. A part of what we want you to see is that much of the time you have some level of choice about what you do when you're scared. You may feel the feelings of a victim, but may be able to choose action that doesn't allow you to remain in those feelings or to be further victimized by others.

Susan said her symbol for being a victim was a bowl of Jell-O.

When I become scared, I feel I have no substance. That I've nothing to say that anyone would want to or be able to hear. I can't find a voice. I can't stand strong—I melt. I hear myself saying, "Don't hurt me. I can't get up. I have nothing to contribute." What might ultimately be of value is transforming my Victim symbol—I saw it while I was doing the Victim exercise. I visualized my Jell-O turning into pudding, which to me had more substance and strength. Then I was able to change my Victim image from Jell-O to pudding, and ultimately to a cake. It is as if I'm a cake that rises, takes shape, and has many different parts to it.

Much of this book is devoted to figuring out directly or indirectly how to get out of being the victim. When you stay stuck in the inner child, you're a victim of your past. When you forget the nurturer or the protector, you're a victim. And even when you ignore your inner critic, you are a victim of yourself because, as we have seen, an ignored inner critic is like a crazy person gone wild. Any way you look at it, you're your own victim if you don't look at, get to know, and become aware of all of the parts of you in your vast inner family.

The motto of the recovering victim is "What, if anything, do I have any control over?" And this motto may very well be the key to the next door that we need to go through on our Spiral Path.

The next few chapters are about getting to know all of the parts of you that you've named so far. Naming, as you have seen, is helpful, but the real healing, and the real finding of your missing pieces, comes when you get to know all of you from the inside out. You've started that process in this chapter as you have gotten to know your innocent child, wounded child, nurturer, protector, critic, and victim, if you have one.

Making peace with your wounded child is one of the goals of this work, and you are going to need all of you to be able to do that. Without healing your wounded child you'll continue to be weighed down by her or him. You'll feel burdened. You may very well feel like a prisoner within your own self—a prisoner of your own inner child. The answers, including the ones that will allow you to make peace with your woundedness, are all within you. Your task is to access and utilize them.

CHAPTER 7

Getting to Know You

Not only do you need to name the pieces of your puzzle, as you have just done in the previous chapters, you also need to get to know those pieces. Some of the parts of the puzzle may seem like good pieces, while some seem like bad ones. Some are beautiful, and others beastly. Beastly is not necessarily bad. Beast parts are simply disowned energies. They're like a little kid who's been locked in a closet a long time, and who's naturally gotten pretty loud and mad: not a "bad" kid, simply one who now needs to be heard. If you treat him lovingly and include him in your family, he'll behave. If you don't, he may act like a small wounded animal, who bites out of fear. This is what a disowned part is like. It needs the light to shine on it— slowly and gently.

With the help of the "observer self" you can begin to get to know not only the positive and the negative parts, but the owned and disowned parts. You don't need to *become* the Beast part of you to get to know it. You simply need to understand it and know that it exists. Some parts are like people who are not listened to, who are not understood. They tend to act out. It is through the process of naming, listening to, understanding, and embracing *all* of the parts of you that you feel whole.

Remember that the goal of the process of finding the missing piece is integration, but to do this, we must first name the parts as we did in chapter 3. Then we need to get to know them, as we're about to do now. Do you remember the steps on the Spiral Path that involved getting to know your feelings—your anger, your sadness, your guilt, your shame? Getting to know the parts of your internal family of selves[1] is the internal equivalent of that part of the walk around the Spiral Path.

Before you move on in this process, you might want to get out the work you did in chapter 3, especially "Stepping Stone 10", in which you named all of the parts of you. Look at the diagram of your internal family. It may have been hours, days, or even months since you named those parts of self. Are there any new updates or changes in your internal family? If so, add them now. Take a look at the overall list. Do the five to ten parts of self you've listed and/or drawn represent a true picture of all of you? If so, great. You're ready to move on. Remember that you don't need to have done this step perfectly. You should, though, at least have some pretty solidly identified or the work on getting to know parts of self won't make sense.

In this chapter we're going to give you guidelines that will help you to know each part of your internal family. This process is about making these parts of you real. Do you remember the story of *The Velveteen Rabbit*? The Skin Horse told the Rabbit that you become real when someone loves you so much that all the fur is rubbed off your nose. Your goal in this part of your growth process is to get to know each member of your internal family of selves so well that the fur is rubbed off each of their noses. By the end of this chapter, when you actually come up with an external concrete representation of these internal parts of you, you will know all the parts of your internal family of selves better than you ever have in your entire life. You will know yourself better than ever before.

A PHILOSOPHY FOR DOING INTERNAL-FAMILY WORK

Before we move on in getting to know all the parts of you, let's stop for a moment or two to reflect on a few prerequisites we feel are necessary for doing this kind of work on yourself.

1. A wellness approach works best in healing self. Each of us has the answers within.
2. There is an inherent value in and equality between all the parts of you. We have a great deal of respect for the integrity of, and diversity among, all the parts of you.

3. Ultimately we are all personally responsible for our own behavior.

4. As you integrate the parts of self, they do not die, they simply transform.

5. Everything is interconnected and interdependent.

6. Inner-family work is an active as well as a receptive process.

7. Once the change has begun, it's simply your job to allow the process to continue.

8. There will always be a pull back to the old ways of being.

9. We all naturally seek wholeness and balance—both in our internal life and in our external world.

10. Inner-family work is ultimately designed to help you put on a new pair of glasses, to help you widen your perspective, and to help you see things differently.

11. Inner-family work is about speaking your truth and daring to live it.

12. And, finally, this work is about you having choices in your life and feeling empowered.

Wellness Approach

A wellness approach works best when we're healing the self. Each of us has the answers within. Your job is to uncover and discover those answers. Sometimes we need others outside ourselves to support us in our journey to help us find the answers. We believe in the strength of the inner spirit of all. If you can get quiet, if you can listen, and if you can clear away enough of the problems, you will see the light. You will discover the solution to your problems within you. Rarely does that inner light get totally snuffed out, no matter how troubled our family may have been. It may be buried, but it still shines, if only just a little.

We believe that you can find your inner light. There is a healthy, nurturing spark in you. It is a positive, "can do" attitude that we are encouraging you to embrace as you approach the first step in healing your internal family of selves.

Value and Equality

There is an inherent value in and equality between all the parts of you. It's important to respect the integrity, dignity, and diversity of them all. Each part serves a purpose. Each part has a job. Each symptom has value. All of the parts of you serve the larger whole. It is with this kind of respect that we approach each piece of the puzzle, curious to discover its role in the larger picture.

Each part is important in its own unique way. You probably have some parts you've labeled good and some you've labeled not-so-good; some beauty, some beast. You may be loving and self-caring on the one hand, and crabby and irritable at other times. That loving part may contribute to the larger whole by helping you connect with others, while the crabby, irritable part may also serve to help you disconnect when things get to be too much. It may help you get distance when you need it. Both parts are important. Each piece contributes to the overall puzzle in its own unique way.

Personal Responsibility

Ultimately we are all personally responsible for our own behavior. It may indeed be true that the past can operate as an albatross around your neck. While you may have been victimized, it's ultimately up to you to see that you don't stay a victim. We can create change for ourselves. Having to take responsibility for yourself does not mean that you were necessarily at fault yesterday. It's your responsibility to do the best you can with the tools that you have at any given moment, to heal yourself, to establish new patterns, and to move on. You have responsibility to work through the pain of your past, to try to learn new skills, and to do the footwork at least in finding the missing pieces. Sometimes this means allowing yourself to be awkward while you change an old pattern and learn a new behavior. Your healing is up to you. But if you don't attempt it, there will be no healing. You need to take the first step.

Transformation of the Parts

Parts of you do not die, they simply transform. As you do inner-family work, you'll get to know all parts of you better—young parts and old parts, large parts and small parts, those you like and those you don't like. As you work with these parts in an attempt to get them to work together in the service of the larger whole called "I," you will find parts of you—and your attachment to certain ones and detachment from others—changing and transforming, but pieces of the puzzle never totally disappear or die off. The essence of them still remains, though they seem to change. For example, the part of you that may appear to be "selfish" and "self-centered" at first, may evolve into a very "loving and self-caring" part. The "controlling" part of you may transform into the "protective" part. And even the "rebelliously acting out" part of you may become a "high-energy, spontaneous, playful" part of you. Parts of you do not die; rather they grow and shift and develop.

Interconnection

Everything is interconnected and interdependent. What goes on inside you affects what goes on in your outer world, and what goes on outside you frequently mirrors what is going on inside you. All of the parts inside you are connected and interdependent in some way. Take Sal's situation, for example. Sal is having marital difficulties and at the same time he and his wife are having difficulty with their fourteen-year-old son, who is being disruptive at school and emotionally distant at home. At work Sal is having difficulty concentrating. He has stopped working out at the gym, which had been a routine for over two years. He feels alienated and disconnected from everyone and is avoiding spending time with friends. In moments of quiet he feels scared and empty. His internal and external worlds seem to mirror each other.

Another example of interconnectedness and interdependence on a larger scale can be found in nature. The study of ecology has shown us that all systems are connected. We earthlings have found out the hard way that destroying rain forests in South America affects the climate in North America and that a volcano erupting in the Philippines affects the weather in California. Just as things in our external worlds are interdependent and interconnected, things in our internal worlds are connected or interrelated as well.

Active and Receptive Process

Inner-family work is an active as well as a receptive process. It takes action to change. You need to do things differently in order to change patterns in your life. You also need to be open and willing to change and to be teachable, that is, to be receptive.

This active-receptive dimension is a thread that winds throughout most change processes. People in Twelve Step programs know how some of the steps (1, 2, 3, 4, 5, 8, 9, 10, and 12) are ones of action while others (6, 7, and 11) are steps that call for a more receptive mode. If you've ever watched a young child learn to walk, you can see that this process is both active and receptive. Little by little the child actively learns to roll over, then crawl, and then walk with help. And finally the child begins to teeter by itself one step at a time. Before you know it, the child is into everything. If you watch carefully, though, you will see that at each step of the way the child has to wait and be open to a new way of approaching things—that is, be in a receptive mode—until muscle abilities and coordination catch up.

The process of finding your missing piece is much like learning to walk. It is a process that moves one step at a time.

Being with the Process

It's your job to allow the process of change to continue. For people who grew up in turmoil, it's often difficult to simply be with the process of change. Most of us fight any type of change because we feel we need the assurance of knowing exactly what is going to happen, when, with whom, and where. Yet change is a constant in life. Change sometimes means not knowing the outcome. It means not being in control of others. When we're still operating from a basis of fear, we resist change. We fight it. We struggle. It's after we come to trust in ourselves, develop trusting friends, and create safe environments in our life that we can allow ourselves to be with change.

The Pull Back

You may feel a pull back to the old way of being—to being a victim of your past—if the new patterns that you have worked to change are not allowed to settle and firmly implant their roots. On the one hand you may no longer be a victim of your family, of a critical partner, or of a boring job. But on the other hand, you may feel pulled to the drama and excitement of an intense change process. You may feel compelled to stir things up. But if you've truly reached the acceptance stage, it may be better just to let things be for a while, that is, to allow some integration to occur before moving ahead. If you can do this, if you can allow things to settle, the pull back to being a victim will dissipate over time.

Seeking Wholeness

We all seek wholeness and balance—both in our internal life and in our external world. Balance is the goal of this inner-family work. Balance is the cure for what the Hopi Indians call *koyaanisqatsi*[2] (pronounced "coy-ah-ni-skat-see"), life out of balance. *Koyaanisqatsi* is a life gone crazy, a life in turmoil, disintegrating. *Koyaanisqatsi* is a state of being that cries out for another way of living. Inner-family work is a step in the process of finding that other way of living. It is a step toward living a life in balance in both one's external as well as one's internal world.

However, you don't have to get your life totally in balance before you do inner-family work. You don't need to be totally whole. You simply need to appreciate that this is the goal of the work. Wholeness and balance are goals, and seeking them is an ongoing process that takes a lifetime.

A New Pair of Glasses

Inner-family work is ultimately designed to help you put on a new pair of glasses, to help you widen your perspective, to help you see things differently. Inner-family work is about maximizing choice in your life. How you define reality, that is, how you come to understand and see things, influences how you experience life. At first you may feel like a victim of whatever specific behavior or pattern of behaviors you're trying to change. But as you continue to work through the process, you'll begin to see things differently, as though you've put on a new pair of glasses.

Speaking Your Truth and Daring to Live It

One of the goals of inner-family work is speaking your truth and daring to live it.[3] The real truth about each of us lies within us, and living that truth involves both identifying and experiencing what is going on. We're said to be living a lie when we deny our internal experiences, when we deny our thoughts and feelings. The biggest challenge in life is to be true to ourselves. In order to do that, we need to find out who we really are. Learning this is what putting together the puzzle of Self is all about.

Speaking and living the truth may be the most courageous thing you will ever do. It's not until you dare to speak the truth—to others as well as to yourself—that change can occur. It's not until you own the problem that a solution can be forthcoming. Courage is about grace under pressure. Courage is the quality of mind or spirit that enables us to face difficulty and pain with firmness, integrity, and honesty. Inner-family work takes courage. It takes courage to be aware of and to speak the truth, and it takes great courage to live that truth.

It's when you've begun to speak your truth and to dare to live it that you can develop a whole and integrated sense of self. The main message in the Academy Award–winning film *Scent of a Woman* was about just this. The young boy maintained his integrity, with Al Pacino's support and encouragement. The challenge for you is to put your puzzle together, to find your missing piece, and to live your truth.

Having Choices

A goal of this work is for you to have choices in your life and to feel empowered—for you to be able to facilitate change within yourself. When you can do this, you stop being a victim of others—and of yourself. You are your own best therapist, and your therapist's best co-therapist. The answers are within you. You are truly your own best guide. Sometimes this wisdom part of you may be buried or temporarily missing in action. But we believe that it is still there no matter how hurt you may have been as a child. Your wise self may be but a flickering light. Sometimes you may need someone outside you—a friend, a mentor, a sponsor, or a therapist—to help you gently fan this flickering internal flame and to help you access your inner guide.

As you come to realize that you have the answers within you, that your solutions are hidden deep within, you will feel empowered. When you take your own power, you will have choice. You will be able to facilitate change within you—within your internal family of selves. True power lies as much in your ability to influence those within you as in your ability to influence others.

And now, with your tools for healing in a bag on your back, and with this philosophy for internal-family work close at hand, let's continue the journey along the Spiral Path of Healing by getting to know all the parts of you.

GETTING TO KNOW YOU, PART BY PART

To get you to know yourself better, we'd like you to look at each of your parts through several different lenses. We want you to ask yourself the age of each part of this internal family and the role of each part. Then we want you to think about the positives and negatives of each part. Next, putting on different lenses, you'll try to see the opposite of each part.

Then you will ask yourself if you own that part of you, or if you've buried it within you in the depths of your soul and never want to see it again? Can you come up with a symbol for each part of you—a person, a figure, an animal, a cartoon character, a movie star, or an object or image of some sort? And finally we'll look at the size of each part compared with the whole of you.

Using a wide-angled lens we'll help you become aware of the similarities and differences between the parts of your internal family—the parts that you both own and disown, and the relationship between them. The point of this work is not to fragment you. You are doing this work for the sake of integration and wholeness. We hope that you will come to know yourself even better than you know your external family. We want to help you bring some color and dimension to your internal-family portrait, just the way you did to your external-family portrait in chapter 4. We want to help you make your internal family come alive, to make what goes on inside you as real to you as what goes on outside you. We want the parts of self to walk right off the page.

Picture your internal family of selves. You might even want to pull out the picture of this that you did on pages 122–123 in chapter 3. Note that in the center of that picture you will find the core or "I" of you. You are the sum of your parts. We are now going to get to know these parts one at a time. It is important, though, for you to remember that you have a core. If you feel too fragmented during this process, go back to the core of you for grounding. Use the chart on the following page as a guide for pulling together information about each part of you.

With your picture of your internal family of selves (see pages 122–123) on the table in front of you, you can use the chart below as a guide for pulling together information about each part of you. This is just a sample. You may want to enlarge this chart if you can't fit all the information about your internal family on one page. As you

VITAL STATISTICS: PARTS OF SELF

Date: _____

Directions: Fill out the following sections of this chart for each part of you:

Name	(1) Role	(2) Age	(3) Pluses/ Minuses	(4) Opposite	(5) Favorites	(6) Owned/ Disowned	(7) Making It Real	(8) Size

do the exercises in the following sections, fill in your chart one column at at time. Take your time. If you run into difficulties, turn back to the "Stuck" and/or "Overwhelm" plans (pages 30 and 31) you developed as you gathered your tools in chapter 1. This is a long journey. It will take you a while. But you'll find it well worth your time, for in the end you will feel much more whole and complete.

Each part of your internal family is special and unique in its own way. There are many lenses through which you can begin to look at parts of yourself. These lenses are ways of looking inside—ways of looking at you from the inside out.

The Role Lens

Each part of you has a job or a role, so to speak, in the overall functioning of your internal family and ultimately in your overall functioning. After all, you are your parts. Each part of you is an important piece of the puzzle. To begin to decipher that puzzle, it's important at this junction in your journey for you to get to know the parts of you well enough to understand each of their roles. Here is an exercise that might help you do this:

ROLES

Picture one part of you at a time. Look that part straight in the eyes and ask it, *How do you serve me? What is your job, your role in making me who I am?* And now pick up a pen and complete the following sentence for each part of you. Each of the three repetitions goes deeper into that part. Don't leave any of your parts out.

Hi, my name is ——————————————.
My job is ——————————————.
My name is ——————————————,
    and I serve you by ——————————.
My name is ——————————————,
    and one of the things I do is ——————.

Repeat this process for each part of you.

Did you answer these questions for each part? If so, it's time to work on the column on roles in your chart. Mary began this process with the part of her she calls Cutie Pie.

> My name is Cutie Pie. My job is to make people like me.
> My name is Cutie Pie, and I serve you by being vulnerable.
> My name is Cutie Pie, and one of the things I do is ask for what we need.

Next she went on to the part called Toots.

> My name is Toots. My job is to meet the world.
> My name is Toots, and I serve you by being spontaneous.
> My name is Toots, and one of the things I do is look for the good.

As you answer these questions, don't let your critic get in the way. There are no right or wrong answers with this. Anything and everything goes. You don't need to do this perfectly. This is for your eyes and your eyes alone. You can answer the questions in whatever order seems right for you. The questions will give you a more complete picture of who you are.

Mary has now begun to question how she lives her life. She doesn't feel nearly as happy as she'd like. Others don't seem to be filling her up in ways she hoped they would. We're going to follow Mary through the next several exercises while she looks inside Pandora's box. Here's how Mary filled in the Roles chart for herself:

MARY'S VITAL STATISTICS (ROLES)

Name	Role
Cutie Pie	My job is to make people like me by charming them. I act cute. I get dressed up. I look vulnerable and needy, so I'm not a threat to anyone. I'm the part of Mary that asks for what we need. People hardly ever turn me down because of my sparkle.
Toots	I meet the world each day looking for the good. I'm full of joy and fun. I'm uninhibited and spontaneous. I like life. I'm full of innocence.
Serena	I intuitively know. I'm the wise, inner self. I'm her inner wisdom. I am truth. My job is to "be still" and just to let things be.

Name	Role
Not Fair!	My job is not to ask for anything so that I am not disappointed. I'm a victim. I remind Mary not to expect too much from people.
Red	My job is to be the protector. I'm full of anger. I set the boundaries.
Controller	My job is to make sure Mary is safe. I do that by putting up a shield around her feelings. I anticipate things ahead of time to make sure we get what we want. I tell others to do things so that they get done. Sometimes when Mary doesn't trust, I am here to provide some sense of predictability.
Nurturer	My job is to support Mary. I affirm her. I am her kindness, her humbleness. I am only now starting to be listened to. I am present all the time, but Mary pushes me aside when Controller and Cutie Pie are out.
Observer	My job is to observe. I'm a detached part that can see the overall picture. All parts can talk to and through me. I'm like a conduit through which the other parts operate.
Critic	My job is to be the faultfinder. I find her faults. I make her be the best at everything she does, so that others won't find fault with her. I'm also good at finding fault in others. In that way I protect her by helping her correct herself before she gets criticized by others and by helping her see other people's faults before they get too close and hurt her. I protect her from getting hurt.

As you can see, diversity is often the name of the game. Mary has nine rich parts that seem to run the gamut. Paradoxically Mary says that as she gets to know all of these parts of her, she no longer feels totally torn apart or fragmented. As she gains a fuller appreciation of her complexity, she feels more whole and more integrated. As she asks what role each serves, she's able to develop an empathy for aspects of herself that she has run from or denied her entire life. Now she recognizes that all along she's done what she thought was best to take care of herself. She's just beginning to see that all the parts have served her in one way or another in her life.

Mary's friend, Phyllis, found that she was totally overwhelmed at this point in her journey. Almost all of the parts of her were negative, not nearly as positive overall as Mary had found her parts to be. Our advice to Phyllis was to "hang in there for a little while." We hope you're listening if you, too, are feeling like Phyllis. Everyone has some positive parts, even those who have terribly low self-esteem. With some help and support most of us can find a positive side to what may seem a mostly negative trait. This is what the next few sections of this book are about, so try to keep on with the process if you can. This may be the way out of the doldrums, even though at first it may feel as though you're plowing into them even more deeply than before. Owning who you are is not always easy. We admire your courage in going on. If you feel good, keep going. Even if you don't feel good, keep moving through this. We promise you, there is light at the end of the tunnel.

The Age Lens

The next lens that we want you to try looking through has to do with age. Each part seems to be a certain age. They may be younger than you, or they may be older. We all have both young and old parts of ourselves when we're young children, and we still have young and old parts when we're older. Have you ever heard a little child speak with the wisdom of a sage? Or have you ever seen an adult act childlike? Parts of these people are speaking up—old parts and young parts.

In order to survive your childhood, did you have to grow up too fast? Did you become an adult child? If the adult part of you had to come forward a lot, the child part may not have gotten to play much. Here is a brief exercise to help you fill in the age column of your Vital Statistics chart:

AGES

Close your eyes for just a few moments.

Picture each of your parts, one at a time. See them all sitting together around a large table.

Go around the table and check out how old each part seems to be. Is he or she an elder, an infant, young adult, or a teenager? How old would you say each one is? Can you tell their ages by how they look, what they're wearing, what they're saying?

As you open your eyes fill out the age column on your chart.

Here's how Mary filled out her age chart:

MARY'S VITAL STATISTICS (AGES)

Name	Role	Age
Cutie Pie	To be liked	2 / child
Toots	To enjoy life	4 / child
Serena	To be intuitive	Ageless
Not Fair!	To get Mary taken care of	13 / teen
Red	To protect	16 / teen
Controller	To protect and to put things in order	22 / adult
Nurturer	To be loving and self-nurturing; to take care of Mary	34 / adult
Observer	To watch over things	48 / adult
Critic	To find fault	16 / teen

As she filled out the chart, Mary laughed when she realized that her different parts were in fact different ages. "Sometimes I truly feel as if I'm four years old; other times, I'm sixteen. And now I periodically feel the maturity of being thirty-four." Not only do our parts often have an approximate age associated with them, but each part tends to serve a particular purpose in our lives as well. Each part has an age and a role.

The Plus and Minus Lens

Another way to get to know all of the parts of you is to look at the positives and negatives of each part. We're sure that you find some parts of you more positive than others. Sometimes it's difficult to find a positive side of something that seems so very negative. It can be difficult to switch perspectives. We simply ask that you try putting on a different pair of glasses, ones with "plus" lenses if you are used to dark ones, and, believe it or not, we want you to put on "minus" lenses if you are used to light ones. Look carefully at each part of you—one part at a time. We urge you to look at all sides and aspects of yourself.

Do you spend an inordinate amount of energy fending off some of your negative traits? We believe that if you stop pushing them underground and own them instead, they'll have less influence on who you are and how you feel. Yes, we know that it's difficult and anything but fun to acknowledge that you can be judgmental like your father, or as demanding and critical as your mother. But if this is at all true, and you keep denying it, we've found that it's better to stop fighting it and to acknowledge it. Then you can use the energy you've spent defending against it somewhere else. Stay with this exercise, and if you need to, turn back to chapter 1 to review your strengths. The following questions may be helpful:

PLUSES AND MINUSES

What positives can you find within each negative part?

What is the negative side of each positive part of you?

If you are having a tough time with this even after you dig as deeply as you can, ask a friend for some help. When you are ready, write the answers on your chart.

When Mary stretched herself and looked through different lenses, here is what she saw:

MARY'S VITAL STATISTICS (PLUSES AND MINUSES)

Name	Role	Age	Pluses	Minuses
Cutie Pie	To be liked	Child	I get positive attention.	People don't take me seriously. I'm lonely a lot, and I feel needy.
Toots	To enjoy life	Child	I have a genuinely good time. I laugh when my spirit is tickled. I'm attractive to people.	I'm not serious about things. I'm not taken seriously. Sometimes I don't get things done when I should. I'm impulsive.

Name	Role	Age	Pluses	Minuses
Serena	To be intuitive	Ageless	I feel inner peace. I give meaning to life.	Sometimes I know things I wish I didn't know.
Not Fair!	To get Mary taken care of	Teen	Others take care of me.	I keep getting hurt. I feel powerless. I'm a victim. I can't do things for myself.
Red	To protect	Teen	I make sure people don't mess around with Mary.	I'm too rigid. I shut out people and opportunities. I push people away.
Controller	To protect and to put things in order	Adult	I make life more predictable. I get my needs met.	I can't relax. All of my energy is consumed with this job. I have a lot of fear and shame
Nurturer	To be loving and self-nurturing. I take care of Mary	Adult	I bring love to Mary. I'm a builder of her strengths. I can listen to all of her parts. I'm empathetic.	Sometimes others who want Mary to take care of them and not herself don't like me. Others accuse me of being self-centered. I speak from the heart.
Observer	To watch over things	Adult	I can see not only the forest but also the trees.	Sometimes the overview that I see isn't a pretty picture.

Name	Role	Age	Pluses	Minuses
Critic	To find fault, to be discerning	Teen	I'm honest with my criticism. I can identify where improvements are needed.	I can only see faults, not strengths or assets. I speak bluntly and judgmentally. I am not liked.

As you can see, Mary found that there can be a positive side to every negative and a negative side to every positive. In recognizing both aspects we come to honor ourselves rather than being critical and judgmental, which can only hurt our spirit. Your puzzle pieces are multidimensional and multifaceted. Are you beginning to see yourself from many angles and from many sides? Can you see that you are more than a diamond in the rough, that you are a unique gem, flaws and all?

The Opposite Lens

Now that you have looked at the pluses and minuses of your puzzle pieces, the next pair of lenses will be easy to use. We believe that you will get to know the parts of you even better as you discover the opposite side of each of these parts. People in our Missing Piece groups have found this section most helpful because in order to do this, you need to step out of a part and into its opposite. What better way to get a different perspective on yourself?

If you've found mostly positive parts of you in your internal family so far, you may very well experience some resistance in this exercise. On the other hand, if you've grown used to your parts being fairly negative, then naming opposite positive parts may also feel uncomfortable to you. Do you remember toward the end of the chapter in which you named your parts of self (page 122) when we suggested that if this was a problem for you, you simply box off those parts you found hard to accept? You may want to do this now with the opposite parts of you. If you can't accept the opposite of a part of you, at least write it down to briefly acknowledge it. It's even okay if you box it off for now.

We want you to respect your resistance to looking at these opposite puzzle pieces. It may be there for a reason. Your resistance may be there to help you slow down. It may be there to remind you that you need to get in touch again with the tools for your journey that you discovered in chapter 1 before you begin to peek at some of these intense and perhaps painful pieces of the puzzle.

We suggest that you ground yourself firmly in your strengths before you do this part of the Spiral Path. It's also helpful to have a strong support system—both internally and externally—before you attempt these steps. If it's too scary or too hard, stop, and regather your resources. When you're ready, when you feel safe enough, you can choose to continue your journey to find the missing pieces.

We ask you to consider that there may be some value in working with the so-called dark or shadow sides of self. As you see and own the opposites, your perspective on yourself will open up. After all, it seems to be in the darkness that we see the light. Look outside on any dark night. The stars that light up the night aren't visible in the daytime, yet they're still there. Think about it. Try it. Most of all try to be open and nonjudgmental about the parts that you find uncomfortable. It is in the darkness that we can so often see the light. Have you noticed how much better you can see the stars when you get away from the city lights? Here are a few questions that might help you look at yourself through these particular lenses:

OPPOSITES

> List each part of you on a piece of paper.
>
> For each of the parts of you complete the following sentences by free-associating:
>
> 1. When I think of _____, the first word that comes to my mind is _____.
> Another word that comes to me is _____.
> 2. When I think of the opposite of _____, the first word that comes to my mind is _____.
> And another opposite word that comes to mind is _____.
>
> Now choose from among your free associations the one word that best represents the opposite of each part and write it down on your Vital Statistics Chart.

Here are a few examples of how Mary began this process: "When I think of Red, the first word that comes to my mind is *rebellious*.

Another word that comes to mind is *angry*. When I think of the opposite of *rebellious* or *angry*, I think of being a victim, hurt, and helpless." Once again here is what Mary added to her chart:

MARY'S VITAL STATISTICS (OPPOSITES)

Name	Role	Age	Pluses	Minuses	Opposites
Cutie Pie	To be liked	Child	Gets attention	Lonely and feels needy	Ugly
Toots	To enjoy life	Child	Attracts	Impulsive	Controlling
Serena	To be intuitive	Ageless	Serenity	Sometimes truth hurts	In pain and full of anxiety
Not Fair!	To get taken care of	Teen	People do things for me	Repeatedly victimized	Aggressor
Red	To protect	Teen	Protects	Pushes people away	Victim
Controller	To create order	Adult	Assures that my needs are met	Fearful	Powerless
Nurturer	To love myself	Adult	Empathetic	Self-centered	Critic
Observer	To observe	Adult	Oversees	Sees too much	Tunnel vision
Critic	To find fault, to be discerning	Teen	Identifies problems	Only sees faults	Nonjudgmental, nondiscon-cerning

As you work with all of these parts of you, you will find that when you are stuck in one part, perhaps in the negative side of a part, the way back is to find its opposite. For example, if Mary finds she's being rather critical about something, she might choose a healthier perception by going through her nonjudgmental, nurturing part, which is the opposite of the critic. On the other hand, if Mary is stuck in her Cutie Pie stance, she might find her way out by seeking guidance through the wisdom part of Serena.

You've worked hard to get to this point. Take some time now to reflect on the many aspects of who you are. Begin to appreciate your own complexity. At this point you don't need to go do anything but allow yourself time for reflection. Give yourself a pat on the back for getting this far. Take a break. Your break may take anything from a few minutes to a few hours or even a few days.

TIME OUT

Okay, did you take a long enough break to be ready to travel deeper into the depths of self? Did you let things simply "be" long enough? Did you allow some integration to occur? Did you allow some of the puzzle pieces time to set in place? Has the glue dried yet?

The Favorite Lens

Each one of your parts of self probably has favorites of its own— favorite things to do, favorite colors, favorite songs, favorite foods, favorite clothes, and the like. Some parts may look like abstract pieces of artwork, others like animals, and some even like pieces of clothing.

As you talk about a part's favorite things, that part will become more and more real, so real that it is literally going to walk off this page. When you're ready, complete the following sentences for each part of you. If you can't think of something for a part, just leave it blank. Try coming back to it later. You do not need to fill out every sentence for each part. Just take the ones that fit and leave the rest behind.

FAVORITES

I am _____ _____ and
(name of part)

My favorite color is _____

My favorite song is _____

My favorite movie is _____

My favorite story is _____

My favorite toy is _____

My favorite food is _____

My favorite thing to do is _____

My favorite place to go is _____

My favorite friend is _____

MARY'S VITAL STATISTICS (FAVORITES)

Name	Role	Age	Pluses	Minuses	Opposites	Favorites
Cutie Pie	To be liked	Child	Gets attention	Lonely and feels needy	Ugly	Food: milk and chocolate chip cookies. I like to be held and rocked and cuddled. I like to be sung to. I like lullabies. Color: pink. I like it best when Mary pampers herself with bubble baths and lotion.
Toots	To enjoy life	Child	Attracts	Impulsive	Controlling	I like ice cream; to play dolls; to tickle and rough house; to play with friends and go to Disneyland. Color: green. I like songs— "Row, Row, Row Your Boat." I like it best when Mary just plays and plays forever and ever.
Serena	To be intuitive	Ageless	Serenity	Sometimes truth hurts	In pain and full of anxiety	I love to watch sunrises and sunsets; to walk barefoot at the beach; to dance and become one with the music. I like things to be very simple. I like soft music that is peaceful. My favorite color is white. I like to travel and to explore. I like it best when Mary is centered and allows "life to do her."
Not Fair!	To get taken care of	Teen	People do things for me	Repeatedly victimized	Aggressor	I like black. I like to be alone. Things bug me. I don't like anything. Nothing makes me happy. I like to mope around. I like funerals and horror shows. I like overcooked Brussels Sprouts. I like country-Western ballads.

Name	Role	Age	Pluses	Minuses	Opposites	Favorites
Red	To protect	Teen	Protects	Pushes people away	Victim	I like to mess around. I like to tell jokes. I'm funny. I like to go bungee jumping and motorcycle racing. I like red. Food: hamburgers, fries, and shakes. I like oldies-but-goodies music and rock and roll.
Controller	To create order	Adult	Assures that my needs are met	Fearful	Powerless	I like everything to be in its little box. I like things in place. I like the colors black and white. My favorite story is *The Little Engine That Could.* I like potato chips. I like the waltz.
Nurturer	To love myself	Adult	Empathetic	Self-centered	Critic	I like to cook. I like any and all foods. I like to read to others and to myself. I like to pamper myself. I like to sit by a warm fire all cuddled up. I like to garden. I love wildflowers. I love roses. I love warm springlike colors. I like soft classical music.
Observer	Observe	Adult	Oversees	Sees too much	Tunnel vision	My favorite song is "On A Clear Day." My favorite color is orange. I like to take long walks up to the tops of mountains where I can enjoy the majestic view.
Critic	To find fault, to be discerning	Teen	Identifies problems	Only sees faults	Nonjudgmental, nondiscerning	I like to be in charge. Nothing is perfect, so it's hard to say what I like. No food fits my criteria and no music is right. My favorite story is *A Christmas Carol.* I like Scrooge. Bah, humbug!

Some people find a combination of ways to create and demonstrate their parts of self. What seems important to keep in mind is that there are no right or wrong parts, and there's no right or wrong way to do this. It's in the process that you'll find what you're looking for. The fact that you're even looking and listening inside is the important thing. Beyond that, seeing and experiencing certainly seems to be a major part of the process of changing patterns. We want you to tap into some sort of creative energy. We all have it. It's just that sometimes it's buried and our critic won't let it out.

It doesn't really matter what your parts look like. What does matter is whether you try to find the answers inside because, no matter how you do it, this is the way you'll find your missing pieces. This is the way you'll begin to feel you know yourself better, the way you'll feel more and more whole.

The Owned-or-Disowned Lens

All of us have parts of ourselves that we like and parts of ourselves we'd just as soon never let out of the closet. But some parts of our puzzle we've never even acknowledged; they're what we call disowned pieces. If you have low self-esteem, you may not have owned the more positive parts. The good is buried beneath pieces of rubble. When we're not aware of a part of ourselves, it becomes disowned. The process of finding the missing piece involves owning our disowned pieces. It's a process in which we bring to full consciousness that which was once unconscious.

This is no simple task. And once again, we'd like to remind you to check over the tools for your journey in chapter 1, because discovering and owning disowned parts involves a trip into the depths of self. Respect any resistance you may have about looking at these disowned parts. It may be a signal that you have some more work to do with your tools first. You may feel as though it's just too much. Or it may not feel safe enough. Do you have a good support system? You may want your friends there in case you need them.

It's not easy to own a part of you that's critical or judgmental. It's not easy to own a patriarchal part if you present yourself to the world as a feminist. It's not easy to admit that you have a soft, vulnerable part if you're a prisoner on death row. Can you even begin to imagine that a Pro Life man who blocks the entrance to abortion clinics may very well have an abortionist part hidden inside himself? You can see where owning disowned material can be a political hot potato in the external world. It may be just as hot in your internal world as well.

Owning your disowned parts may be both the most difficult and the most rewarding part of your walk on the Spiral Path. Take it slowly, one step at a time. If you're ready to begin the footwork that eventually enables you to put on a new pair of lenses—to find a new way to look at yourself—then read on. But be gentle with yourself, and take your time. You may even need to take time out. If you do, please make a commitment to your inner self about when you are going to begin the process again.

If you're ready, please pull out your Vital Statistics Chart. Look at the descriptions of all the different parts of you. In particular look at the opposites of the pieces of your puzzle. Can you remember times that you have acted in ways that you'd just as soon forget? Can you remember when you acted just like someone that you despise? Who bothers you more than anyone? Whom do you find yourself pointing the finger at quite frequently? What is it about your partner/child/friend that bothers you more than anything else in this entire world? What one word would you use to describe your ex? What movie star, TV character, or political figure do you just hate? What is it that you're very judgmental about, that you swear you'll never, ever in your wildest dreams be like? These are clues to help you begin this journey to find your disowned parts. This is like a treasure hunt because beneath the rubble of disowned parts are the riches that will unlock new doors for you as you find them.

This is like Pandora's box. Remember all the wild things that came flying out when it was opened? Those may be like disowned parts of self, but don't forget what was at the bottom of Pandora's box—hope—and hope is what we're after: hope for wholeness, hope for finding the internal missing piece. Here is an exercise that might begin to help you to find your disowned selves and to be able to differentiate between the owned and the disowned parts:

OWNERSHIP

We're going to go together searching in the dark corners of the puzzle called Self to find any hidden, lost pieces. Some of them you'll like, and some you won't.

Begin by taking out your Vital Statistics Chart. Look at the column called "Opposite." Take the characteristics listed in that column and come up with one word or name that best describes those particular characteristics. Add those descriptive words/names to your list of parts.

Now go down the list and ask yourself the following questions about each part: What role does it play in your life? How old is it? What are its pluses (the advantages) to this role? What are its minuses (the disadvantages) to this role? What is the opposite part? What are this part's favorites?

Ask your self the following questions about ownership of this part: Do I have access to this part on a daily basis? (and if so, do I acknowledge the part?) Or do I disown this part?

You will find what Mary found out when she did this exercise on the next page.

Mary found lots of things in her treasure chest—some good and some bad; some like Beauty and some like the Beast; some that she owns and some that she doesn't. Cutie Pie, Toots, Responsi, Serena, Nurturer, Critic, and Observer are today parts of the puzzle that Mary claims she owns or that she is trying to own, whereas Troll, Wild, Not Fair!, Red, and Controller are parts that Mary says that she does not own yet. She seems to own some positive and some negative parts and to deny some other negative parts. It's our sense that as Mary names, gets to know, comes to understand, and owns even the negative aspects of self, she will feel better and have a more whole and integrated sense of herself.

It's not hard to understand how some people have disowned negative parts. For example the nicest man in the world may have disowned the rageful part of himself. On the other hand, how about the woman who has low self-esteem, who mostly owns negative parts, but who may very well have some positive characteristics within her that she simply doesn't own yet? The nicest man in the world will do better after owning his angry voice because he'll no longer need to spend so much energy fending off his underlying rage. If the woman with low self-esteem can let some of the good parts surface, she will most certainly feel better about herself. This part of your growth process is simply about trying to understand some things about you that have been misunderstood up to now and perhaps even been buried in the corners of self.

All too often in life we seem to destroy things we don't understand. But in many instances it is these disowned and misunderstood parts that hold the keys to unlocking the treasure chest of self that

MARY'S VITAL STATISTICS (OWNED OR DISOWNED)

Name	Role	Age	Pluses	Minuses	Opposite	Favorites	Owned/Disowned
Cutie Pie	To be liked	Child	Gets attention	Lonely and feels needy	Troll	To cuddle	Owned
Troll	To keep people away	Old	Keeps boundaries	Lonely and scared	Cutie Pie	Nothing	Disowned
Toots	To enjoy life	Child	Attracts	Impulsive	Responsi	To play	Owned
Responsi	To be responsible	Adult	Very responsible	Overdoes, burns out	Toots	To keep busy	Owned
Serena	To be intuitive	Ageless	Serenity	Sometimes truth hurts	Wild	To watch sunrises and sunsets	Owned
Wild[4]	To be out of control and free	Ageless	Fun to be with	Out of control	Serena and Controller	To dance wildly	Disowned
Not Fair!	To get taken care of	Teen	People do things for me	Repeatedly victimized	Red	Nothing	Disowned
Red	To protect	Teen	Protects	Pushes people away	Not Fair!	To mess around	Disowned
Controller	To create order	Adult	Assures that my needs get met	Fearful	Wild	To put everything into boxes	Disowned
Nurturer	To love myself	Adult	Empathethic	Self-centered	Critic	To cook	Owned
Observer	To observe	Adult	Oversees	Sees too much	Not Fair!	Walk to high place	Owned some
Critic	To find fault, to be discerning	Teen	Identifies problems	Only sees faults	Nondiscerning, Nurturer	Bah, humbug	Owned

contains our missing piece. Acknowledging all of these parts seems to be part of the process of claiming ownership over the puzzle. It looks as though we may already be well on the way to owning more and more parts of ourselves as we journey the Spiral Path.

As you acknowledge and own each part, you need to take lots of time to let it become a part of you. Respect your resistance. As you acknowledge and later own and embrace a new part of you, you may very well feel a pull back to the old way of being, to the old pattern. Remember that this whole process of finding your missing pieces takes hard work and that is sometimes painful. It certainly takes time—perhaps a lifetime—to integrate the parts into the whole of you. But keep in mind that it is often in the darkness that you will find the most light. And it is in the stillness that you will find the dancing. This is what finding the missing piece is all about—bringing light to the darkness. It's also about having options. The more you know about all of you, the more options you have to choose. Eventually you will be able to choose which part or parts you want out at which time.

The Making-It-Real Lens

Now comes the fun part. The best way we know of to help you get to know all these parts is to have you do something that makes each part concrete, makes it live. This is where the part walks off the page. This exercise brings color and depth to the pieces of you. Be gentle with yourself as you get to know these parts of you, for they may contain both joy and pain. Take your time. Time and patience will be your best friends in this part of your Spiral Path. Here are a few suggestions on how to do this step.

MAKING IT REAL

Close your eyes and, one by one, picture each part. As you keep each part in mind, ask yourself who or what it looks like.

Draw a picture of that part or find a picture in a magazine that reflects that part of your inner self.

Think of a real person you know who's like that part. Think of a cartoon or storybook character who looks or acts like that part.

Does this part of you appear in your imagination in black and white or does it have other colors?

Is the part like some object you've seen? Perhaps a trinket or treasure around your home.

When you're ready, fill in your Vital Statistics Chart for this section. This exercise is a key piece of your Self puzzle. It may seem silly or a waste of time to come up with a tangible and concrete representation of what a part of you looks and acts like. But it's an integral step on your path to wholeness.

When Mary did this exercise, she had a picture in her mind of what her different parts looked like. She then looked through magazines and cut out pictures that best represented those images. Some of the pictures she found were right on, and some were only close to what she was after. She knew she could always go back and find new pictures later on. While she didn't glue the actual pictures to her chart, she did fill it in with descriptor words. We'll leave it up to you to imagine these pictures.

Some of the pictures, such as a cartoon of the critic that Mary found, were a perfect replica of how she saw and experienced a part, whereas in other cases, such as with the wide-angled picture of the sky, the images were symbolic. The key was that she chose pictures that spoke to her.

In order to make the parts of you real, it helps to keep your eyes and your senses open to anything and everything around you. A wide variety of magazines, ranging from *People* and *Popular Mechanics* to *Working Mother, National Geographic,* and *Newsweek* or *Time* will offer different possibilities. You may find daily newspapers helpful too. Sometimes the pictures in there are very realistic.

The important thing is to listen to your internal world while you keep your senses open to your external world. What speaks to you? What catches your interest? James, who used cartoon characters to make his parts real, found himself doing that instinctively when he went to a toy store. He was Christmas shopping for one of his nephews, and found plastic toy replicas of all his parts, which he placed in an old cigar box that he'd treasured since childhood. He had five parts: His mischief self was portrayed by Donald Duck; his helpful side was represented by Pluto; his Adventurer was the Red Baron; and his observer was Tweety Pie.

MARY'S VITAL STATISTICS (MAKING IT REAL)

Name	Role	Age	Pluses	Minuses	Opposites	Favorites	Owned/Disowned	Making It Real
Cutie Pie	To be liked	Child	Gets attention	Lonely and feels needy	Troll	To cuddle	Owned	She looks like a cute, small, blonde doll that is smiling.
Troll	To keep people away	Old	Keeps boundaries	Lonely and scared	Cutie Pie	Nothing	Disowned	Like a Troll doll.
Toots	To enjoy life	Child	Attracting	Impulsive	(Responsi)	To play	Owned	She looks like another small doll. She's playful-looking, with dark brown hair.
Responsi	To be responsible	Adult	Very responsible	Overdoes, burns out	Toots	To keep busy	Owned	She's very businesslike and uptight.
Serena	To be intuitive	Ageless	Serenity	Sometimes truth hurts	In pain and full of anxiety (Wild and Crazy)	To watch sunrises and sunsets	Owned	She looks like a picture of Mary Magdalene.
Wild	To be out of control and free	Ageless	Fun to be with	Out of control	Serena and Controller	To dance	Disowned	She looks like Janis Joplin.
Not Fair!	To get taken care of	Teen	People do things for me	Repeatedly victimized	Red	Nothing	Disowned	She looks like a sad young teenage girl, with one arm reaching out for help and the other pushing help away.
Red	To protect	Teen	Protects	Pushes people away	Not Fair!	To mess around	Disowned	She looks like an angry teenage boy who at times is mad and sullen and at times rebellious.

Name	Role	Age	Pluses	Minuses	Opposites	Favorites	Owned/ Disowned	Making It Real
Controller	To create order	Adult	Assures that my needs get met	Fearful	Wild	To put everything into boxes	Disowned	She looks like an airport control tower at peak hour. She's frazzled and trying to get things under control.
Nurturer	To love myself	Adult	Empathetic	Self-centered	Critic	To cook	Owned	She looks like an older woman reading to young kids gathered near her feet—like my grandma.
Observer	To observe	Adult	Oversees	See it too much	Not Fair!	Walk to high place	Disowned	She looks like a wide-angled picture on a crystal-clear day in which one can see forever.
Critic	To find fault, to be discerning	Teen	Identifies problems	Only sees faults	Nondiscerning, Nurturer	Bah, humbug	Owned	Looks like an old male judge sitting up above everyone, shaming them with a finger pointing down at them. Looks like my father.

Linda Sue, another group member, found items in her house that spoke to her different parts. One was a toy stuffed leopard that reminded her of a phrase her husband uses a lot: "You can't change a leopard's spots." This leopard represented her hopeless part. She also found an empty picture album that had been sitting around for two years; it was symbolic of her procrastinator self. A kite she found hidden in her closet represented her playful child, the one that she seldom allowed out.

Another Missing Piece group member, a very talented young elementary school teacher named Cindy, drew her parts, cut them out of construction paper, laminated them, and glued them on to popsicle sticks. She then placed the sticks in the top of an egg carton so that they could all stand up and she could work with them like puppets. Another group member put all of her parts on a mobile. Another pasted his magazine pictures on posterboard.

One woman couldn't come up with faces for her parts, so she simply put their names on the back of doll-house-size director chairs around a table. Later on, as she got to know herself better, she was able to make little figures to put in the chairs. A man in the group made a puzzle out of fiberboard. Each part of him was a piece of the puzzle. In the end all of the pieces with their faces fit together and there were no missing pieces.

It helps to actually give not only color, shape, and form to your parts, but movement too. One man in the group tried being a "Part for a Day," kind of like "Queen for a Day." "It was amazing," he said, "how people responded to me differently dependent on which part was out." One person made a collage of his parts. Last fall one of our Missing Piece groups voted to make their parts come even more alive. On Halloween night they all came dressed as their favorite part. Another group came dressed as a disowned part. And finally one Missing Piece group member found a different piece of music to make each part of him come alive.

The Size Lens

Our final pair of lenses is designed to help you look at the size of each piece of the puzzle. On any given day some of the pieces of the puzzle may be larger, more in the foreground, than others.

SIZE

Take out your Vital Statistics Chart. Look at all of the work you've done.

On a large piece of paper draw a large circle. Place "I" in the center of the circle to represent the core of you.

Place the other parts of you from your Vital Statistics Chart on this page. Represent the relative size of each piece of your puzzle on this page as well as how close they each are to the "I" in the center of the page.

Some parts will be larger than others. Some will be closer to the core of you, whereas others will be farther away. Some will be owned and some will not. Some will have connections with other parts and some won't. What follows is a graphic representation of how Mary sees herself today.

Sometimes it's helpful to do this little picture once a day. It's a great way of taking a daily inventory, that is, of seeing which parts of you have dominated or been absent from your life today. After you draw this picture, take time to thank the parts who've been doing all the work. You might also want to ask the others if they have anything new to add. Jo found that this was an excellent way for her to get in touch with and to know the parts of herself each day. "Now," she says, "I wouldn't miss drawing that picture. It only takes a few moments. It's such a great way for me to check in with myself each day. It lets me see if I'm out of balance. It gives me a read about other parts of me that might need to be invited out the next day. It's just become part of my daily routine, like brushing my teeth."

Today Mary seems to be owning many of the pieces in her puzzle. She's in the early stages of her therapy process. She isn't yet feeling as self-confident as she'd like, but she's made great strides in speaking from some of her adult parts rather than her child parts.

In the picture on page 271, the pieces that are more influential are the larger pieces of the puzzle. It seems as if Nurturer, Toots, Responsi, Critic, and Controller are her more dominant parts, with Observer close behind. Cutie Pie still has more power than Red. Wild is pushed off into a corner of the page but it's still there, and Not Fair! is hidden over in the opposite corner hoping that someone will notice her. Serena is in the background today, but tomorrow is a new day.

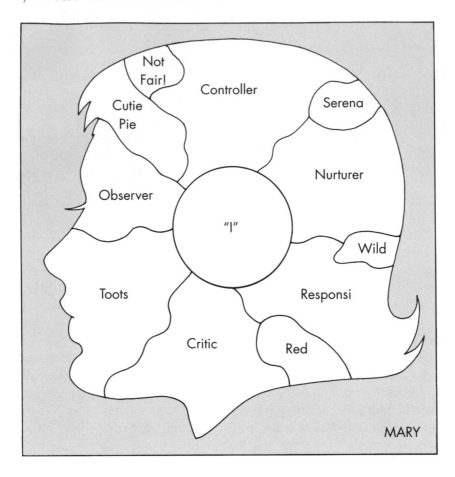

MARY

What does your puzzle look like? Have you drawn yours today? Each piece has a name and a job. That job may have changed since the part was originally conceived, but it still has a unique function in helping the overall you discover its wholeness. Mary, like you, has a very complex puzzle. She has pieces at all ages and stages of development. She even has two male parts—Red and the Critic. She's still searching for her missing piece. She readily admits, "I don't have it all together yet." A noticeable difference for her today is that she's no longer so critical of herself. She has hope. She doesn't feel as helpless and as much like a victim as she did when she began this whole process. Do you notice any difference in yourself?

A Closer Look

Now that you have all the parts of you down on a piece of paper and described to some degree, we're going to take a look at the similarities and differences between them all. The more common are the threads that you find between the parts of you, the more solid and integrated a sense of self you have. Those who come from more troubled families tend to have very few common threads. They may reach adulthood with a highly diversified family of selves, with each self sharing few features with other selves.

In the next part of your work you will paint a clear picture of the degree of diversity and/or unity in your internal family of selves. We encourage you to move on in the process—whether it's now or later. After all, naming the parts and getting to know them are only a few of the steps in the process of putting the pieces of the puzzle back together. Now we're about to turn a corner so that all of these parts of you can begin to work together. Integration is just around the corner. Keep on moving. You're getting there.

PART FOUR

PUTTING
ORDER
TO CHAOS

CHAPTER **8**

Coming Full Circle

Now that you've gotten to know all the parts of you one by one, it's time to open up the lines of communication between them and get them to work together in an integrated whole. You probably arrived at the doorstep of this book with a puzzle that had many pieces, some of which were owned, disowned, or unknown. We led you around the Spiral Path such that you journeyed into the depths of self and took the puzzle apart. You then held each piece up to the light and examined it as if it were a rare gem. You named each of the pieces and got to know them. By this point you've experienced much of the richness of each part of you.

Now it's time for you to experience yourself as a whole, multidimensional person. It's time to set the stage for integration, to put the pieces of the puzzle back together. We've come full circle on the Spiral Path.

There are three things we believe you can do to set the stage for this process of putting the puzzle back together:

- Create a safe internal and external environment
- Develop compassion for each and every part of you
- Establish empowering connections between parts of you, two by two and as a whole

CREATING A SAFE INTERNAL AND EXTERNAL ENVIRONMENT

In order to be free enough to experience your internal richness, you need to operate in a safe enough environment. In chapter 1 we talked about how to make a place where you can feel safe enough to grow. Traditionally we tend to look at this safe healing atmosphere as something we need to create in our external worlds. But to truly heal and become whole, we need to create a safe internal environment as well.

Are you able to speak up when you need to in your everyday world? Do all of the parts of you feel safe enough to voice their opinion? Do you treat others with respect and dignity? Do you treat all the parts with the same respect and dignity? Do you listen to everyone's opinion even though you may personally disagree? Do you listen to all the parts inside you—both the owned and disowned parts—even when you don't like a part of you?

The structure you create to provide external safety is the same one you need to offer your internal family of selves. In parenting yourself you need to

- Be supportive of yourself
- Minimize the chaos
- Develop consistency and predictability within your internal family
- Be flexible
- Respect each part
- Have ground rules that encourage the growth and well-being of each part, as well as of yourself as a whole
- Develop trust in each part of you so that you can talk and listen to it
- Identify your feelings and express them
- Find a safe place for speaking with your parts of self
- Develop rules that respect the privacy and dignity of each of your parts
- Develop clear boundaries and limits
- Create healing rituals for some of your parts

You can't even begin to find the missing pieces of your puzzle until you have created an environment that is at least somewhat safe both outside and inside. You need a safe enough place to find the pieces when they appear and to allow change to occur within you. As you set the stage for integration with safety, you will then be able to develop compassion.

DEVELOPING COMPASSION

Compassion is defined as "a feeling of deep sympathy and sorrow for another who is stricken by suffering or misfortune, accompanied by a strong desire to alleviate the pain or remove its cause."[1] Compassion thus involves both feeling and action. Part of the way we learn to work together is by being able to step into another person's shoes, by seeing things from another's perspective. This results in a feeling. Having empathy for others may sound easy on paper, but how well have you been able to do this in the partnerships in your life? Can you maintain this feeling with your life partner, with your friends, with your children, with your caretakers, with your employer, with your employees? Can you do it with the checker at the market, the teller at the bank, the examiner at the DMV, your friend who is HIV positive? Can you maintain compassion with a religious fanatic if you are an atheist, the ex-business partner who is suing you, your ex-wife of thirty years? Can you do it with a two-year-old who is having a tantrum?

It's not easy. You need to know what your own shoes are like first. You need to know what you are thinking, feeling, and doing before you can step into someone else's shoes. When you have a sense of boundaries, when you know where you begin and where the other ends, the process of developing compassion comes more readily. In order to be compassionate, you need to be able to keep one foot in your own shoes as you step into someone else's. You need to be able to get out of yourself while still maintaining your own inner connection. You need to be able to understand where the other is coming from and what the other's experience may be. Then, according to the definition of compassion, you need to be able to take some action.

Compassion—both the feeling and the action—produces a change in perspective. It is this broadening of perspective that lies at the root of any growth process. Compassion brings people together, whether they're in your external world or your internal world.

Amy and Randy developed greater compassion for each other

when they were working with a therapist who asked them each to role-play what the other one was thinking and feeling about a specific problem situation. Amy had an opportunity to take a job in a different state and wanted to go. Randy had one year left of graduate school, and while he could not see himself separated from Amy, he really could not see himself leaving his graduate program. They were very angry with each other, both seeing the other as selfish and unrealistic.

When the therapist asked Randy to put himself in Amy's shoes, he said, "Randy, please see this as a good opportunity for me. My boss believes in me and that feels good. Nobody has ever believed in me before. He is like the father I never had. I've never been very sure of myself, and this company makes me feel that I am capable. They push me, and I meet the challenge. I'm not sure they'll continue to support me if I don't go. I don't trust myself to go with another company because maybe I'm really not good at what I do."

When Randy was finished, Amy then put herself in his shoes and said, "I really do love you, Amy. But for the first time I'm really scared. We've always agreed on major issues before. If I don't go, my fear is that our relationship is over. Yet I've worked so hard, paying all of my own school fees and working while going to school. It's hard to be this close to someone and have it severely disrupted. Amy, I want you to be there for what's important to me. I've been alone so much of my life, and this tells me that I may be alone again unless I give up something else that's important to me too."

While Randy and Amy did not reach a conclusion about what they would do, they completed the session feeling much more connected to each other. They both felt much more understood, and they understood each other more. The process helped them identify the strengths of their relationship, and they were very hopeful that they'd be able to reach a satisfying decision. All of this was the result of being able to step compassionately into the other's shoes.[2]

Compassion is a wonderful feeling. When someone is compassionate with you and/or when you're able to be compassionate with someone, it brings joy into your life. You know that you matter and that someone cares. Most all of us strive for that kind of feeling in our external worlds. We believe this is the same feeling you might be looking for in your internal world.

In order to bring a sense of compassion to your internal parts, you need to do the same things in your internal world that we've just described can happen between you and others. What goes on in your internal world is simply a reflection of what happens in your external world. In the following exercise you'll experience stepping into the shoes of each of your parts. You'll also experience each of the parts of you step into the shoes of the other.

COMPASSION

With the help of your Vital Statistics Chart, complete the following sentences for each part of you:

_____, I, _____, value you
(part of self)   (your name)

for _____.
(characteristics)

When Sonya did this exercise with the different parts of herself, here is what she said:

Nurturer, I, Sonya, value you for your love of life and for being so soft, so gentle, and so caring of me and my physical being.

Protector, I, Sonya, value your ability to take care of us by protecting us.

Rocky, I, Sonya, value your ability to help us set boundaries and limits.

Bea, I, Sonya, value your ability to let go and to let things be.

Spirit, I, Sonya, value your calmness and serenity.

Doer, I, Sonya, value your determination and your ability to get things done.

Victim Sonya, I, Sonya, value your ability to get people to take care of us.

Will, I, Sonya, value your ability to get your way.

Sony, I, Sonya, value your ability to have fun.

Rebel, I, Sonya, value your bundles of energy.

Grit, I, Sonya, value your openness and integrity.

Observer, I, Sonya, value your objectivity.

You can take this exercise one step further, if you choose, by having each part of you fill out this sentence stem for every other part of you. For example, when Sonya did this from Nurturer's viewpoint, she had her say what she valued in Protector, Rocky, Bea, Spirit, Doer, Victim Sonya, Will, Sony, Rebel, Grit, and Observer.

In the first exercise you had the whole of you, the "I" of you, say what you valued about each part. In the next exercise, you are to have each part say to each other part what it values the most. In this exercise if you have three parts, for example, you will do this twenty-seven times. We know this sounds like a lot, but it's worth it. You're worth it. Just do a few sentences at a time.

Another way that people develop compassion for each other is to share their vulnerabilities when it feels safe enough. Here's an exercise to help the parts of you to do just that:

SOFT SPOTS

Once again take out your list of parts and their vital statistics. Complete the following sentences for each part of you:

I, _____, have the following vulnerabilities: _____, _____, _____, _____ and my fear is _____.

For example, Sonya did it this way for Rocky, the limit-setting and boundary part of her: "I, Rocky, have the following vulnerabilities: There is a part of me that doesn't trust, so I am too rigid and have a hard time being flexible. Then I get too needy and forget my strength. My fear is that I will keep seesawing like this and won't be able to hold on to my objectivity."

Will did this exercise, acknowledging his driver self, the part that pushes and pushes. "I, Driver, have the following vulnerabilities: I push so hard that Will sometimes gets sick. I push so hard that I'm blind to what's around me. I push so hard that I run over people. My fear is that if I loosen up, people will take advantage of me. They'll see that I'm not as smart and capable as I seem. If I slow down, there won't be anything there for me."

Sonya and Will developed many different perspectives as they stepped into the shoes of each of their parts. They were able to be more empathetic with themselves. They were able to hear their own vulnerability and at the same time be more honest and realistic with themselves. They even began to embrace some of the parts that had previously been disowned.

Now it's your turn. Actually do this exercise rather than simply reading it. It's the experience of compassion with each and every part of you that makes this worth the time and effort. We promise that if you do the exercise, it'll do you. It's simple but powerful. While the "Soft Spots" exercise is about developing compassion, it is also about opening up the lines of communication between parts.

Establishing Empowering Connections

It was in the family, community, and the social context in which we grew up that we were taught to communicate. How did your caretakers talk with you as a child? Did they talk at you, down to you, or with you? Most likely the way they communicated with you has become the way your adult parts talk with the child parts of you today. Were your opinions respected? This will govern whether or not you respect the opinions of the parts of you. Did you feel valued for what you said? Do you value what each of your parts say to you?

Did you learn to listen? Do you listen to all the parts of you today? Did people listen to you? This may very well determine whether or not you truly listen to each of the parts inside you today. Did you yourself learn to listen not only to what was said but to how it was said? And do you listen that way to all of what is said inside you today? For example do you allow the inner critic to drown out the other parts of you? Whatever you learned about communicating in your external family is probably what you play out today in your relationships with others as well as how the parts of your internal family communicate with you as a whole and with one another.

We have found that the following guidelines help improve communications with all the parts of you:

**GUIDELINES FOR BETTER
INTERNAL-FAMILY COMMUNICATION**
- Be open and receptive
- Be nonjudgmental
- Be nondefensive
- Be curious
- Be interested
- Take time to listen
- Understand the part's position
- Put yourself in the part's shoes

- Remember that all parts are equal
- Remember that all parts are to be treated with respect
- Be with the part without becoming it
- Mirror back to the part the content and feelings that you've heard

These guidelines may help you become a better listener and a better communicator in your relationships in your external world as well as in your internal family. These guidelines will help you be heard better. Being heard will make you feel valued and important, and isn't that what it's all about?

When it feels safe enough to be compassionate, another step toward getting your internal family together is to empower the connections between parts of self. This can be done by strengthening the connection between

- Any two parts
- Each of the members of your internal family as a whole through the use of internal-family meetings

Strengthening the Connection Between Parts of Self

When you grow up in a mostly nurturing family, you end up with your parts connected to one another. Each part is just that—an integral part of a larger whole. But when you grow up in a troubled family, some of the parts may be missing, and the ones that are there are definitely not very well connected.

Most likely you feel better when you're connected to the special safe people in your life. This applies in your internal world as well. Do you remember when we talked about how one of the main jobs in life for little children is to be connected? This is just as true for adults. And one of the best ways to be connected is through communication.

Can you remember a time when you felt connected to someone you cared about? Did you feel heard by him or her? Did it feel as though this person was able to step into your shoes and to see things from your perspective? Maybe this person didn't agree with you, but at least he or she seemed to understand where you were coming from. Most of us have problems with communication sometime in our lives. When we aren't able to say what we want to say or to hear what our friend or partner is trying to say, it doesn't feel as though they can step into our shoes, and we don't feel connected. This can happen internally as well.

This difficulty isn't irreversible, though. You can learn to communicate better both externally and internally. If the parts of you are not very communicative with you and with one another, you can facilitate that process by helping them listen to the other parts and by helping them talk to one another. Communication is the key. Difficulties in communication are the basic reason there are problems in relationships—whether they're friendships, intimate relationships, or ones between parent and child, employee and employer, Congress and the president, or nations. Difficulties with communication are also one of the primary divisive factors between you and the parts of you.

We've found two techniques helpful in facilitating communication within your internal family: the first is Voice Dialogue and the second is Active Imagination.

Voice Dialogue

Voice Dialogue is a process suggested by Hal Stone and Sidra Winkelman-Stone in which the parts can dialogue with a friend.[3] We are extending this concept to include dialoguing with the core or "I" part of you, and then to eventually have the parts of you talk to one another.

Do you remember the Tools for the Journey into the depths of Self that you put in your tool bag in chapter 1? You might choose to review them before moving on. We'd like to enhance and add a few new tools specific to doing internal-family work, and in particular to doing Voice Dialogue. Here are a few additional tools to check out before you journey on:

- Do you have access to your observer self?
- Do you know all of the parts of you, both the owned and the disowned?
- Do you have access to your core "I"?

You learned about the observer self in chapter 1. This is the part of you that can get distance from something; that can be with a part of you without melting into it or having to become it. In addition, you met the core or "I" of you in chapter 3.

Also before you move on, it will be helpful if you've come to know all your parts—both the owned and the disowned—so well that they've come alive for you (see chapter 7). In doing the dialogues you may very well find new parts, so it's useful to be well acquainted with the ones you've already gotten to know in the previous couple of chapters.

When you first begin to use this technique, it's helpful to have one of your parts dialogue with an external friend. It may feel strange at first, but it's worth it in the long run. Obviously you need to choose someone who understands and can support you in this process. As Steve said, "There was no way I was going to do this at first. But then on a bet I tried it. This was truly one of the most valuable techniques I've ever experienced. I feel one hundred percent better after doing this. I know it's going to take continuous work, but at least I made the leap and got past feeling awkward and, quite candidly, crazy. Now I use Voice Dialogue all the time."

Here are some guidelines and steps to help you try Voice Dialogue. We bet you'll be a fan of it after only a few tries.

GUIDELINES FOR VOICE DIALOGUE WITH A FRIEND

GETTING READY
• Choose a topic to dialogue about. Are there things in your life that you're having a hard time making a decision about? Are there any big deals going on that you could use another opinion on? Are there any places you feel stuck? What's happening in your life that you could use another perspective on?
• Choose a quiet time and a safe place to begin.
• Pick a safe friend to work with.

THE OBSERVER SEES IT ALL
• Step into the shoes of the observer self. Allow your perception to expand into a state of awareness where you can see all the members of your internal family of selves.
• Look at your list of parts of you. Can you picture them all?

CHOOSE ONE PART
• Which one part wants to talk with you today?
• From this state of awareness in the observer self's shoes, name that part. Picture that part. Allow that part to come into your mind.

• Where would that part of you be if it were in the room right now?

STEP INTO THE PART'S SHOES
• Prepare to move out of the place you're in. Prepare to leave your state of awareness and to go to sit where this particular part of you would be if it were in the room.
• Step into this place. This part may be behind you, next to you, in front of you, or even above you or on the floor below you. Now step into the shoes of the part of you.

BE WITH THE PART
• Feel the part's presence in your body. Just be with that part for a moment. Are you sitting differently? Do you feel tension anywhere? How do you feel as this part? How are you breathing?
• Feel and be with the part for a moment. You don't need to say anything. Just be with this part of you.

NOW IT'S TIME FOR YOUR FRIEND TO HELP
• Make contact with your external friend, who is here to help.
• Friend, ask whether the part wants to talk to you.
• If so, using the Communication Guidelines described on page 283, listen to the part's reply. If the part doesn't want to speak at first, be gentle. Be patient. The part will talk when it feels safe enough. It takes time and trust to build a relationship in which communication is open and direct.
• If the part is open to communicating, begin a dialogue. Listen. Make sure that you take some time, Friend, to step into the part's shoes. Try to understand the part's point of view. Mirror back as much as you can of what the part has been saying. Be as empathetic, understanding, and compassionate as you can. Friend, please try not to tell the part what to think, feel, or do.
• Allow the dialoguing to go on as long as either the part of you or your friend have something to say, and as long as you are still both up for listening.
• If your friend seems to collapse into one of the parts and can't seem to get out, ask him or her to step back into the observer's shoes or to step into the core "I."

SUM IT UP

• As the dialogue is ending, Friend, thank the part for its help. Then have the part step back so that the "I," the whole person, comes forward.

• Now, as your core "I," ask yourself, *What did I just hear? What did I learn about myself?* Say out loud what you learned. Say it so that you can remember it. Make conscious that which was once unconscious.

• Friend, now it's your turn to sum things up. Tell the "I" of your dialoguing partner what you heard the part say.

Voice Dialogue: Ron Talks to Sally

GETTING READY

Ron, a Missing Piece group member, decided to try Voice Dialogue. Here are the steps he went through and the dialogue itself. He chose to work with his friend Sally. Ron spoke from a part of him, his inner Critic whom he'd named Not. The situation that Ron concentrated on was a problem at work—he'd just received a negative evaluation from his supervisor. Here's how the dialogue went:

SALLY (external friend): Hi, Ron, how are you? Can I speak to the part of you that has an opinion about the evaluation Ron got today at work?

RON'S Critic, "Not": (*Ron checks inside himself with his Observer part, then picks the part that has an opinion about this evaluation.*) Sure, that's the inner Critic part of me named Not.

THE OBSERVER SEES IT ALL
CHOOSE ONE PART

SALLY: Hey, Ron, where would Not be in this room if he was here?

RON: He's back there looking over my shoulder. (*Ron points to a place right behind him.*)

Step into the Part's Shoes

SALLY: Ron, how about moving over there, so you can step into Not's shoes?

(Ron moves to where he indicated Not was standing.)

Be with the Part

SALLY: Hi, are you Not, Ron's critic part?

NOT: Yeah, so what's it to you?

SALLY: Well, I just wanted to talk to you, okay?

NOT: I don't know. Tell me what you want to know about first.

SALLY: Okay, I want to talk about Ron. You know him, right?

NOT: *(Nods his head yes.)* Oh, that's simple. He just needs to try harder. I told him all the things he needed to do better, but he just doesn't do them. The list is long, but at least I gave him the list.

Now It's Time for Your Friend to Help

SALLY: Wow, Not, it sounds like you have some very strong opinions about all of this. And it sounds like you've known Ron a long time.

NOT: Yeah, no kidding. I've been around since he was about two—that's when his sister was born. I tried to get him to be perfect because that was the only way his parents would give him any attention. You know, they really wanted a girl. Obviously he didn't fit that bill and competed for the attention his younger sister got.

SALLY: So, you've been really trying to protect Ron, then?

NOT: Of course. He deserves to be valued, and he deserves attention. He's good at what he does. I'm just afraid to tell him that in case he gives up and quits trying because he still hasn't gotten his parents' approval. As long as that is important to him, I am important to him.

SALLY: I don't know, Not. It sounds like you feel irreplaceable. It sounds as if your job is impossible.

NOT: Yes, it is an impossible job, but Ron hasn't figured that out yet. He doesn't listen to anyone but me. When he's scared, he comes to me first. I'm really tired. I've been at this for sixty-three years. But I'll be here as long as he comes to me. I really am here to be his friend.

SALLY: How about if we explore Ron's getting to know his other parts? I hear how valuable you have been to him. You have been a good friend and won't be discarded. But we'd like to get to know the other parts better too.

NOT: Well, you can't expect much from them.

SUM IT UP

Sally then asked Ron to step out of Not's critical shoes and back into his own. Then the two of them summarized what had just happened. Ron's main comment was,

> I've always felt the heaviness of the critic. But I never thought of him as a protector before. This makes it possible for me to be more forgiving of him, and obviously of myself. When I realized that I didn't have to totally let go of a part of me, it became easier to get to know the other parts. Now I'd like to hear from some other parts of me—the ones that aren't so hard on me. And I'm hoping some of the other parts can help me with this critical part, because when the critic takes over, I feel horrible. I feel I can't do anything right. My critic seems good at discernment, but he goes crazy at times.

The next level at which you might try this technique is between different parts of you. As strange as it may seem, you can actually have parts of you talk to other parts of you by moving back and forth from one part's space to another. The simplest combination and the one we want you to try next is to have the core "I" part and another part dialogue. Later, after you're more proficient at Voice Dialogue, you can have parts of you dialogue with other parts of you while the observer observes and you remain in touch with the "I" of you.

The guidelines for doing this type of Voice Dialogue are the same as you just learned for doing voice dialogue with a friend. In this case, however, instead of a friend asking questions of a part of you, your core "I" self will be asking the questions. The "I" part is nonjudgmental. It is extremely curious. It is open and interested. It can readily empathize with a particular part of you. The "I" seems to understand all of the parts. It can be with a part of you without becoming that part. It is the whole of you.

It may be awkward at first to move from chair to chair or even to speak through the parts of you as if they were puppets. Just give it a try. It's actually no less awkward than having a part of you talk to a friend, and it's equally successful and helpful.

GUIDELINES FOR VOICE DIALOGUE: PART TO WHOLE

GETTING READY
• Choose a topic for your internal dialogue. Are there any things in your life that you're having a hard time making a decision about? Are there troubles in one of your relationships? Are there any big deals going on that you could use another opinion on? What's happening that you could use another perspective on? You may very well find that talking into a tape recorder helps the process. That way you can replay what was said at a later time and perhaps get new insights you might have missed the first time.
• Choose a quiet time and a safe place to begin to dialogue between parts of you.
• Get your tape recorder out and ready to talk into.

THE OBSERVER SEES IT ALL
• Step into the shoes of the observer self. Allow your perception to expand into a state of awareness where you can see all the members of your internal family of selves.
• Look at your list of parts. Can you picture them all?

CHOOSE ONE PART
• Which one part wants to talk to the core "I" part of you today?
• From this state of awareness in the observer self's shoes, name that part. Picture that part. Allow that part to come into your mind.
• Where would that part of you be if it were in the room right this moment?

STEP INTO THE PART'S SHOES
• Prepare to move out of the place you're in. Prepare to leave your state of awareness and go sit in the place that this particular part of you would be if it were in the room.
• Step into this place. This part may be behind you, next to you, in front of you, or even above you or down on the floor below you. Step into the shoes of the part of you.

BE WITH THE PART
• Feel that part's presence in your body. Just be with that part for a moment. Are you sitting differently? Do you feel tension anywhere? How do you feel as this part? How are you breathing?
• Feel and be with that part for a moment. You don't need to say anything. Just be with this part of you.

BACK INTO THE OBSERVER SELF
• Now slowly pull yourself out of that particular part and come back to the place in the room where you can see all the parts of you and the core "I" of you.

BEING WITH THE "I" OF YOU
• Stand up and move to the place in the room where your core "I" is.
• Picture and sense the "I." Allow this core part of you to come into your consciousness.
• Now for another moment feel and be with the "I." Step into the "I's" shoes.
• Feel the "I's" presence in your body. Just be with the "I" for a moment.
• You don't have to do anything right now except to be with the "I." Keep breathing slowly and evenly.

THE "I" TALKS TO THE PART
• Allow the "I" to begin to talk to the part of you.
• Inquire whether that part wants to talk to you, the "I."
• If it is willing, listen using the Communication Guidelines described on page 283. If the part of you does not want to talk, be gentle. Be patient. The part will talk when it feels safe enough. It takes time and trust to build a relationship in which communication is open and direct.
• If the part of you is open, begin a dialogue between that part

and the "I." Allow the two of you to talk to and listen to each other.

• Move from one place in the room to another as you dialogue. When you speak as the "I," be where the "I" is in the room. Then move to where the part of you is when it is ready to speak. This may seem crazy, but try it—you'll like it. Once you get past any initial awkwardness, you'll find that this means of communication is an invaluable tool.

• If the part of you gets overwhelmed and seems to collapse, the "I" can either step in and take over or it can have you step into your image of wholeness—into the core integrative part of self.

The "I" and the Part Sum It Up

• As the dialogue is ending, have both the "I" and the other part of you sum up what they heard the other say.

• Then, when each has said what it has to say, when they've both listened to the other, step out of the shoes of the part and out of the shoes of the "I" and move back into your own shoes—the ones on your feet.

When Andie did this exercise, she found that she felt strange at first. "Hey, I feel like I'm Sybil with all of those sixteen personalities. Me talking to me, right? I can't do this. It feels too strange. It feels crazy." Then, with some encouragement from some friends in a Missing Piece group, Andie tried to talk to herself. "After all, I talk to myself all of the time anyhow. I just never did it so formally. Actually this structure helps a lot!"

Getting Ready, the Observer Sees All, Choose One Part

Andie wisely decided to try this in a place where no one could hear her talk to herself. She stepped into a state of awareness, the observer self, where she saw all six parts of her internal family: Katherine, the sensual part; Ann, the wounded child; the protector; the inner critic; Nana, the nurturing part; and the core "I." The topic that Andie decided to ask about was, "How do I deal with this situation where John [her partner] and I are disagreeing about how to choose a new couples therapist?" She decided to talk to "I," the core, and to Nana, the nurturer. Here is what was said as she spoke into her tape recorder:

Voice Dialogue: Andie Talks to Andie

STEP INTO THE PART'S SHOES

 ANDIE'S "I": *(Andie is sitting on the sofa.)* Hi, Nana. How are you today? *(Andie moves to the rocking chair across the room where her Nana part is sitting.)*

 NANA, THE NURTURER (A PART OF ANDIE): [This part is sitting in a rocking chair.] I'm good, "I." How are you? What brings you here today? *(Andie moves back to the sofa.)*

BE WITH THE PART, BACK INTO THE "I,"
THE "I" TALKS TO A PART

 "I": I just wanted to get to know you. Tell me a little about yourself. *(Goes to rocking chair.)*

 NANA: Well, I'm fifty-fiveish. I pride myself on how well I nurture others—and myself as well. I spend lots of time listening to others, that is, allowing others to be heard. But sometimes I need to be listened to too. *(Goes to sofa.)*

 "I": I can listen too.

 NANA: Good. I could use a little support today. There's this problem I have.

 "I": What's that, Nana?

 NANA: Well, when Andie was a little girl, she got hurt when she went over to her father's house to visit after her parents were divorced. He told her that he would always be there to take care of her and that she should trust him. But one night when she was real little, he left her all alone in his apartment while he went out with his girlfriend. Andie woke up and was terrified to find herself alone. Finally, when he got home and she cried, he told her to get in bed and not to be silly, that he'd been there. Andie made a clear decision that night not to trust anyone and not to accept help from anyone.

 "I": I can see that this was real tough on Andie. Did she learn to rely on you then, Nana?

 NANA: Well, not exactly. She was distant with me too. But after years and years of my just being here, she finally allowed me to take care of her. I had a little help from Andie's real grandmother. She really loved Andie a lot. She used to just rock Andie for hours. She'd read books to her and bake chocolate chip cookies with her. She just loved her no matter what. You see, I'm just like the real grandmother in Andie's life. I am like an "angel mother" to her.[4] Her name was Nana too.

"I": It sounds like you're really important to Andie, and that she trusts you a lot. How can you help Andie in the situation she's in with her husband—about choosing a couples therapist?

NANA: *(Rocking back and forth in her rocker.)* Well, I just need to listen to her fears about couples therapy. I need to hold her. I need to let her feel me being there for her. I need to hug her with my words. I need to reassure her. I need to reassure her that she's okay and that she's going to be okay.

"I": When people feel heard, they're less frightened. Let's talk about this more later. One last thing, how can Andie get in touch with you if she needs you during this stuff with her husband?

NANA: Good question. Maybe she can reach me each time she touches the blue sapphire ring I gave her—the one she wears on her right ring finger. I used to let her wear it when she was a little girl.

"I": Thanks, Nana. How about if we talk to each other tomorrow at the same time for a few minutes?

NANA: I'll be here!

"I": Wait, Andie wants to know the exact time. How about seven A.M., when she gets up?

(Nana nods yes.)

The "I" and the Part Sum It Up

When the dialogue was over, Andie summed it all up. She started to talk out loud to herself, and here is what "I" said:

> This felt weird, just like I thought it would. But I learned something too. I didn't know how Nana could help me with this stuff

with John. It just feels reassuring to me to know that she's there. I can actually feel her "warm fuzzies" as I talk right now. Maybe with her there I'll be able to feel less childlike when John and I are talking about which therapist to see. Before this I just felt so small when he disagreed with me about whom to see. Now maybe I can take care of me and rely less on him to do it all for me. I guess we'll see.

Then the part called Nana reviewed what she had learned: "I was sure glad to have Andie ask for my opinion on this issue. She has neglected me for years. I'd really like to be there for her. All she has to do is touch her ring."

Finally Andie stepped back into her own shoes to review what she'd heard: "I need to do this more. It really helps. It's totally amazing. When I touch the ring that my grandmother, Nana, gave me years ago, I can tap into this nurturing energy."

We've now demonstrated two of the three levels of Voice Dialogue. If you want, you can go one level deeper in doing Voice Dialogue. The first one you learned was when you have a friend talk to a part of you, like Sally did with Ron's critical part named Not. The second level is when you talk with a part of yourself, as Andie did when she had her core "I" talk with her nurturing part, named Nana.

There is a third level in which you have a part of you talk with another part of you. You can follow the Guidelines for Voice Dialogue: Part to Whole (page 291) that you just did when your core "I" dialogued with a part of you. On the third level you simply have two parts talk to each other, part to part. And once again you move to where each part is in the room when it's speaking.

For example, Andie might have Katherine, the sensual part of her, speak to her inner critic. The first time she did this, Andie discovered that the reason she felt so guilty after a sensual evening with her partner was because the critic had popped out to critique the entire evening from beginning to end. It had said things like "Well, the sex would be much better if you'd lose five pounds," or "Do you know how ridiculous you must have looked serving dinner in a negligee?"

From this Voice Dialogue Andie discovered what appeared to be an internal-family conflict between the sensual and the critical parts of her, a conflict that had made her miserable for years. Andie is currently working on a way to help the parts of herself resolve this conflict. Below is a portion of a dialogue between two parts as taped by Andie's recorder:

Voice Dialogue: Two Parts of Andie Talk

ANDIE'S INNER CRITIC: *(Looming over the foot of the bed.)* You're being very selfish these days.

ANDIE'S SENSUAL SELF—KATHERINE: *(Propped up on pillows on the bed.)* What are you talking about?

CRITIC: You're acting as if you're enjoying yourself. You take time with eating. I see you choosing clothes that give you a feeling of movement and softness. You're even using bubble bath a lot lately.

KATHERINE: But it feels good. I'm only treating myself with love.

CRITIC: That's not okay. There are others to think of.

KATHERINE: You sound like your cousin, the judge.

CRITIC: I'm not judging you. I'm frightened for you. If only you would spend more time working, and less on yourself. There isn't time to focus on yourself. There are things you have to take care of.

KATHERINE: Critic, that was a long time ago. You've been with me since I was a child. Mom and Dad didn't encourage me to take time for myself, or to appreciate touch, smells, or tastes. They had to have all of the attention. There was a lot for me to do taking care of them. There was no more time left for me.

CRITIC: But you've got to take care of others or else they'll hurt you.

KATHERINE: I know you're trying to protect me, but now so much of you is hurting me. You always rag on me and criticize everything I do. I'm going to turn down your volume.

Active Imagination

A second technique that helps your parts communicate with each other is called Active Imagination.[5] This is a process of dialoguing as well, but with this technique you do the dialoguing on paper. The rules are similar to the ones we just described for you for Voice Dialogue. You need to begin the process of Active Imagination in a safe, quiet place with a pencil and paper, your journal, or your computer or typewriter. Here are some guidelines that will help you with this process:

GUIDELINES FOR ACTIVE IMAGINATION

• Sit down in a quiet place. Relax. Place yourself in a receptive and open frame of mind.

• Begin to picture a great ocean, one that is as vast as your imagination will allow you to believe.

• Now picture a cork bobbing up and down in the ocean, up and down, up and down. This cork is your conscious mind. The vast ocean is your unconscious mind.

• Allow the cork to bob up and down as you go into the depths of your unconscious. Deep, deep within that vast ocean of you wait all the parts of you.

• See and sense all of these parts, one at a time. Be open to one or several of these parts as they come to the surface, one at a time. Be open to the one that begins to speak up. Be willing to listen.

• Allow the "I" of you to begin to open up lines of communication with this part that keeps bobbing up to the surface.

• Now pick up your pencil and place it on your paper, or place your fingers on the keyboard of your computer or typewriter. THE "I" OF YOU WRITES IN CAPITAL LETTERS, and the bobbing part of you writes in small letters. Speak Clearly. Listen carefully.

• Continue the dialogue until you both decide that you're done for today.

• Take a moment for each of you to summarize what you heard the other one say today. Let each other know when you'll speak with the other one again.

• Then slowly let the cork take over again as you bob back up to the surface and become more and more awake, more and more conscious of all the things going on in the world around you in the here and now.

· If you choose, read over what you and the part of you have just written to each other.

You might switch back and forth between Voice Dialogue and Active Imagination. You might even want to simply talk out loud into a tape recorder. When you start out with these techniques, it helps to do the dialoguing out loud, and perhaps to hold a part of you like a puppet in your hand and to speak through that part.

Samantha had made a collage for each of her parts and had pasted these on separate boards; she looked at the part's board as she stepped into that part's shoes. Cindy had put the part in a dollhouse-size director's chair and allowed it to talk to her. John looked at images of his parts as he spoke. Do whatever you need to do to be in a part's shoes as you speak.

When you first try Voice Dialogue or Active Imagination, remember to have the "I" or core of you talk with a part of you. As the parts of you become better established, you can have dialogues between the individual parts of you. Here's an example of Kim doing Active Imagination. Her "I" is talking with her shy self.

Active Imagination: Kim, Part I

KIM'S "I": HI, SHY. HOW ARE YOU TODAY? DO YOU WANT TO COME OUT AND PLAY? WE COULD TALK WHILE WE PLAY.

SHY: hi, observer. i don't know. i'm kind of shy and scared. who are you? can i trust you?

"I": I'M THE PART OF YOU THAT JUST LIKES TO LISTEN. I WON'T JUDGE YOU. I'M NOT CRITICAL. I JUST WANT TO GET TO KNOW YOU, TO LISTEN TO YOU. YOU CAN TRUST ME, BUT THAT WILL TAKE TIME. LET'S TAKE LITTLE BABY STEPS. WOULD YOU LIKE TO PLAY A GAME FIRST?

SHY: okay, how about pick-up sticks?

One day when Kim took a break from her work, she played a game of pick-up sticks with herself. Having done Active Imagination work, she creatively decided to let her shy part play too. They didn't speak much that first time. But as time went on, they slowly got to know each other better. Shy came to trust "I," who remained inquisitive and very curious to learn more about Kim. "I" began to deeply understand and to be able to put herself in this little one's shoes. The shy part of Kim—which is of course a part of Kim herself—felt heard, understood, validated, and cared for.

After Kim had done both Voice Dialogue and Active Imagination between her "I" core self and every one of her parts, she began to be willing to develop lines of communication between the individual parts. When you do this, have one part write in capital letters and another part write in small letters. What follows is a sample of Active Imagination between two parts of Kim: her rebel and her shy parts.

Active Imagination: Kim, Part II

REBEL: ARE YOU OPEN TO TALKING TO ME, SHY?

SHY: well, yes, sort of. you know i am not very good at talking. what do you want?

REBEL: WELL, HOW COME YOU'RE SO SHY? THAT'S NO FUN!

SHY: i'm afraid to talk to you. i'm afraid you'll laugh at me, then call me names. you scare me. you're always so tough. you always know what to say.

REBEL: WELL, WE HAVE TO TALK BECAUSE THEY TOLD US TO. I SAY TO HECK WITH THEM, BUT YOU KNOW I REALLY DO HAVE A SENSITIVE SIDE, AND SINCE YOU'RE LIKE MY LITTLE SISTER, I FEEL PROTECTIVE TOWARD YOU. THAT'S WHY I ACT TOUGH. I'M AFRAID FOR YOU. I DON'T SEE YOU TAKING CARE OF YOURSELF, SO I MAKE SURE NO ONE HURTS YOU BY INTIMIDATING THEM.

SHY: i really do admire you, and i like your strength.

REBEL: WELL, I LIKE YOUR SOFTNESS. YOU'RE ASTUTE. YOU CAN HEAR PEOPLE. ME, I JUST RUN THEM OVER.

SHY: but you know how to get things done. you make things happen.

REBEL: WELL, I COULD SHOW YOU HOW TO DO THAT IF YOU'D SHOW ME HOW TO BE SOFTER AND NOT SO LOUD. YOU COULD HELP ME LEARN TO LISTEN TO MYSELF BETTER, OKAY?

SHY: we could share things. i like that idea.

The conversation goes on with both parts as they try to be open, nonjudgmental, as they try to put themselves in each other's shoes. In this case these parts quickly recognized they were parts of a whole, and they saw themselves as internal siblings. They decided to like each other. They could see each other's strengths and they started to work together.

As these parts of Kim get to know each other, they may be able to talk about each other's vulnerabilities and fears. While they're most definitely off to a good start, it isn't always so easy. We suggest that you begin with parts that are more open to each other. We know that you'll have parts that are shyer than others, and some that are less trusting than others. A few of your parts may be so angry that they hold on to their rage at you with intense fervor. Other parts may be more withdrawn. It's okay. Just let them be. Be patient. This will take time, but it will work.

In doing your own Active Imagination it's sometimes best just to start writing—or talking if you're using a tape recorder. It may help to ask the part what he or she is afraid of. Sometimes it helps to let a part know that it's okay not to know, that it's okay to leave blank spaces in your writing when a part goes numb or silent. After all, most of us go numb or silent at times, right? Sometimes it may be best to let go and just go on to another part or come back to it another time. You have choices here.

If Voice Dialogue helps you connect parts with parts, then use it. If Active Imagination works better for you, then choose that. You might even choose a different technique depending on the situation. You're welcome to design your own way of getting parts to communicate with each other better.

Mary, who worked in a large medical center, had difficulty with Voice Dialogue and with Active Imagination, so she'd send faxes between her parts. "It was great. Everybody got to speak up that way. And I felt less silly doing that than I did talking to myself."

Andrew left voice-mail messages from one part of himself to another. Angela sent letters from one part to another. And Darnel used a tape recorder to record messages and send messages between parts. "It's actually kind of fun," she said. "You know I've never felt creative before, and this feels creative. I love it!"

Sandy drew pictures and sent them as messages from one part to another. "I love drawing. It was kind of like drawing bridges between the parts of me. It's amazing. I actually feel more whole now that I've done this. How can separating out the parts and giving them a voice make me feel more whole? It's kind of paradoxical! Who cares how come it works. It just works!"

It's our belief that you cannot become whole until you open up lines of communication between all the parts of you. It's when all the parts of you are working together as a whole that you'll find the strong and integrated sense of self you've been looking for.

Strengthening the Connection Between Members of Internal Families

The second of the two ways to establish empowering connections between parts is through the use of internal-family meetings.

We all had or have families of one sort or another. We're calling this actual family, the one you grew up in, your external family. The purpose of that family was for the nurturance and betterment of the children. Families are supposed to work together as a unit while they simultaneously support and promote the uniqueness and individuality of the members. Did your family operate as a whole? Did it promote and celebrate your uniqueness and individuality?

External-Family Values and Beliefs

Your external family taught you values both explicitly and implicitly. These values were in turn reflected in the way your family lived on a day-by-day basis. Unless you've stopped to think about it and worked very hard at changing it, you've already taken these family values and beliefs with you into your adult years.

Values are reinforced by beliefs and these in turn are supported by rules. All of this is learned through behavior. In troubled families the rules may be as basic as "Don't talk. Don't trust. Don't feel." In other families the list is more extensive. Ask yourself what were your family's rules—the ones that were spoken as well as the ones that were not spoken.

Wayne described the rules in his family: "My dad did all the talking. The children couldn't ask any questions. My mom had to placate. We all just showed up and shut up." Jim said that in his family he learned that "children are to be seen, not heard."

Because you are what your beliefs are, it is of utmost importance that you identify, look at, and challenge the beliefs that you inherited.

Behavior	Belief
Parents fight a lot. Mom ultimately acquiesces.	It won't do any good to stick up for what you believe in or want. Women always lose.
When children show anger, they are scolded and told to be grateful.	It's not okay to be angry. You're being ungrateful when you're showing anger.
When Dad and someone else disagree, Dad politely leaves and does what he wants.	You don't have to listen and consider others. You can do what you want.
Kids in our family are allowed to borrow items and are not expected to return them.	You can take what you want anytime.
My mom and dad always said no to everything. Sometimes I could convince them to make no into yes.	No may mean no or it may just be a challenge for me—a challenge to make no into yes.
When children cry, they are held and comforted.	It's okay to show my sadness. People will be there for me when I feel sad.
When mom is cooking dinner, her child interrupts her. Mom stops to listen.	When I am listened to I feel important and valued.

Beliefs are not genetic. They can be changed if you choose to do so. Here are a few beliefs that people we've worked with brought with them from their external families—beliefs which need to be challenged:

> You can't trust other people.
> No one is going to listen to what you're going to say.
> What you have to say has no value.
> Don't draw attention to yourself.
> There's no time to play.
> Don't ask questions.
> If you put yourself first, you're selfish.
> Never ask why.
> You've got to get things done first and then you can play and
>   have fun.

Boys don't cry.
Boys just want one thing.
Good girls don't get angry.
Children are to be seen and not heard.
When you're an adult woman, let the man in your life think that he's making all the decisions.
Girls go to college to get a Mrs. degree.
Men are rational and women are emotional, and never the twain shall meet.
Girls should do the dishes because men need to rest after a long day's work.
Girls are good at the arts, and guys are good at math and the sciences.
Women should never be believed "at that time of the month."
Children shouldn't speak up or disagree with you. That's being disrespectful.
Adults are always right.
Moms are responsible for everything in the house. Yet wait until Dad gets home to get advice and to make big decisions.

In spite of being raised in a troubled family, many of us still heard beliefs that we most likely will choose to maintain today, such as:

Treat others as you want to be treated.
Feelings are important.
Your needs are important.
We are all spiritual.
It's okay to take risks.
It's okay to make mistakes.
Cooperation is important.
Everything is interconnected.

Here is an exercise to help you identify, confront, and let go of the beliefs that may be hurtful to you today. It will also help you reaffirm or create beliefs you want to own today that are consistent with your true nature.

BELIEFS

Make a list of all your family's rules and beliefs. List the ones that were spoken out loud as well as the ones that were implied. Leave the list open-ended. There may be more as you begin remembering.

1. _____
2. _____
3. _____
4. _____
5. _____
6. _____

For each belief, ask yourself:

- Is this a belief that is helpful for me today? Does it allow me to live my life the way I choose to now?
- Is this a belief that is hurtful? To me? To others?
- Is this belief helping me stay aligned with my true self?

As you ascribe value to a belief, you're taking active ownership of it. As you do this, it becomes part of you. By challenging what you've been taught to believe, you'll become an owner, not a victim, of your beliefs.

- Reread our list of beliefs in chapter 7 (page 240). Which of our beliefs are yours as well? Add any new and different beliefs of your own.
- Affirm all of your beliefs through a ritual. Design the ritual to allow you to let go of the old hurtful beliefs and to reaffirm the ones that are helpful and that make you feel whole. Make the ritual something special that you will remember, something that allows you to let go, to heal, and to be all of who you are.

When Serena did this exercise, her ritual involved a fire at the beach. She wrote the rules and beliefs she wanted to release on individual pieces of paper and as she tossed each one into the fire, she spoke aloud a new belief that she wanted to have emerge out of the old, hurtful one. It was almost like the legendary flaming phoenix that rises out of its own ashes—a case where new is born from old. Serena's new list of beliefs did indeed emerge out of the old ones: "My feelings are important." "My perceptions are accurate." "I deserve to be listened to." "I deserve to be heard." "People can be trusted." Friends of hers joined in her celebration, one in which Serena was becoming the owner, not the victim, of her beliefs.

We hope that the beliefs you act out in your internal family and in your daily life will be in alignment with who and what you are. The more you look at your beliefs and the more you challenge and ultimately own them, the more likely you are to be in sync with your nature. We agree with Plato, who said that it is in our nature as humans to seek wholeness. Maybe it's also "in our nature" to seek, look for, and find the missing pieces of self.

Internal-Family Values and Beliefs

One of our beliefs is that everything is interconnected. Your external family is very connected with your internal family. Your family's values and rules become yours—not only in your external world as an adult but in your internal world as well.

It's time now to take a look at the customs and beliefs you choose to have for your internal family. You may want to use the same customs, values, and beliefs that you've chosen for your external family. You may want different ones. You might even want to do a poll of all of the parts of you by asking each of them what beliefs they would like to have that would help them maintain their own integrity. When Andrea did this, here is what she came up with:

ANDREA'S INTERNAL BELIEFS, PART BY PART

Psyche: All of us need to try to be open and receptive. We are all responsible for our own behavior. We all need to have choices. Our goal is wholeness.

Heardt: I'd like us all to try to listen intently to one another. We each need to take care of ourselves. We need to be self-nurturing.

M. Power: We should each have the right to say no and to have no accepted by others in our family.

She: I want us to take time out sometimes just to let things be. Whenever there's a pull back to an old way of being, just letting things be allows new patterns to root themselves deep in the soul.

Spirit: Let's all practice daily at letting things go. All of us are equals, and all of us are interconnected in some way.

Soul-be: It's important to us that we keep our feet on the ground one day at a time. It's just as important to keep listening to our mind, heart, body, and soul.

Lonestar: Work is important. Business is business. It needs to stay business.

Whole: Too much analysis can be bad for the soul. A little analysis can lead to understanding and, paradoxically, to synthesis, but too much can tear you apart.

Vic: I want everyone to be able to moan and groan and complain if they want to because sometimes life's just not fair.

Bull Witch: I want us each to be able to gripe and to be crabby if we choose.

Andie: Play is important. All my feelings are important too.

When: We can all mess around if we like—just for fun.

She: Trust the process. Letting things be, letting things flow naturally, is important. Sometimes we need to get out of our own way.

Humbe: I want us each to remember that our feet are made of clay.

Spirit: No matter how much pain there was yesterday, no matter what I feel today, and no matter how much anxiety I have about tomorrow, there is within each of us, if we choose to embrace it, hope, faith, and joy.

Obie: We all need to step back every once in a while to see the forest and not just the trees.

Remember, in this internal work you get to choose your own family beliefs and rules.

Family Meetings

You have seen that one of the ways to empower the connections in your family is to increase the communication between dyads, that is, to have different parts of you talk to each other one at a time. Now we want to look at empowerment through a sense of community, and in particular through your internal family as a unit.

One of the things that the alcoholism and chemical-dependency field has contributed to family-systems work is the idea that families need to have family meetings. The purpose of a family meeting is to establish:

- A forum where everyone can talk and check in with one another and say what's going on for them in the past week as well as in the week ahead
- A place to feel listened to, respected, and valued
- A forum for resolving the problems and conflicts that face any of the family members individually and/or the family as a whole
- A place to establish a sense of unity and common purpose
- A sense of community

The purpose of an internal-family meeting is the same as it is for an external family.

Look at your extended list of family members—the owned and disowned parts of you, the parts of you that you're proud of and the ones you're not so proud of, the beauties and the beasts. Can you imagine having all of these folks in the same room at the same time? That's what a family meeting entails.

Lance pictured his internal-family members sitting at a round table, "kind of like Sir Lancelot and his Round Table in Camelot." Liz had all of her internal family sit around a table in directors' chairs with each member's name on the back. "At first I couldn't even see their faces, just their names on the chairs. But the more I trusted this process, the more they began to come alive."

Now that you have customs and a purpose for your internal meetings, let's look at how, when, and where these family gatherings are going to take place. How will these meetings be run? Will there be an agenda for each meeting? Who will have power? Are your meetings a democracy, an autocracy, a dictatorship (benevolent or not)? How will conflict be resolved? How will you all begin to work together as a team?

These are all questions that you and your (internal) family need to get together to ask and, better yet, to answer. In fact the more we talk about these meetings, the more questions we seem to have about them:

- When is your first meeting going to be?
- Will you all sit around a table?
- Will that table be square, round, or oblong?
- Will there be a head of the table?
- If so, who will sit at the head?
- Who will have the gavel?

Before you have your first family meeting, we suggest that you fill in the following chart:

FAMILY MEETINGS

1. The members who will be attending my family meetings are: _____.
2. The purpose of my family meetings is: _____.
3. The rules that we will use to govern these family meetings include: _____.
4. We will meet once _____ at _____ time,

                  (per day, week, month)   (hour of day)

and our first meeting will be _____.

                         (date, time)

5. We will meet at the following location: _____.
6. We will conduct our first meeting as a _____ and

                      (democracy, autocracy, dictatorship, etc.)

_____ will act as the leader with the gavel in hand

(name of part)

until we decide otherwise.

7. We will resolve conflicts in the following manner:

_____

_____

Andrea did this exercise and came up with the following information:

ANDREA'S FAMILY MEETINGS

1. The members who will be attending my family meetings are: Psyche, Heardt, M. Power, She, Spirit, Soul-be, Lonestar, Vic, Witch, When, Whole, Humbe, and Obie along with Pushy, Critic, Hag, Wimp, Sloth, Down, Boaster, and Decie.
2. The purpose of my family meetings is mainly to help me, Andrea, to act as one whole person and to establish a forum where everyone can talk and check in with one another and say what has been going on for them in the past week. Also, we will have a place to feel listened to, respected, and valued, and to have a forum to resolve problems and conflict that face any of the family members individually and/or the family as a whole and to have a place to establish unity, common purpose, and a sense of community.

3. The rules/customs that we will use to govern these internal family meetings include the following:

- Be open and receptive.
- We are each responsible for our own behavior.
- We all need to have choice.
- Listen intently to one another.
- We are equals.
- Take care of ourselves and one another and be self-nurturing.
- We each have the right to say no and to have no accepted by others in our family.
- It's okay to take time out sometimes to let things be.
- Practice daily letting things go.
- Keep our feet on the ground, one day at a time.
- Listen to the messages that our mind, heart, body, and soul give us.
- Analyze just the right amount. Too much can be bad for us.
- Know that both work and play are important.
- It's okay to moan and groan and complain and okay to gripe and be grumpy if we need to. It's important to be able to express unhappiness.
- All feelings are important to express.
- Remember that our feet are made of clay. But also remember that there is within us hope, faith, and joy.
- Know that we're all in this together. We are all one. Everything is interdependent.

4. We will meet daily for five minutes and once a week at five P.M. on Sundays for half an hour, and our first meeting will be tomorrow, Sunday, Mother's Day.
5. We will meet in our living room.
6. We will conduct our first meeting as a democracy, and Obie will act as the leader until we decide otherwise.
7. We will resolve conflicts in the following manner:

- We will all try to remain nondefensive and nonargumentative.
- We will try not to withdraw, nor to justify and defend our positions.

- We will try not to give in with resentment.
- We will try to problem-solve—to inquire about the others' feelings, to mirror back what we hear, and to listen well.
- We will try to make our points clearly and to express our feelings in a nonblaming way.
- We will be willing to take time out if the going gets too rough.
- We'll keep in mind that we're all aiming for the same goal—to feel whole and integrated.

Our goal in pulling our internal family together and in getting everyone to work cooperatively is about achieving a sense of connection inside ourselves and outside ourselves. We suggest that you have a brief family meeting in whatever form that takes every day. Take a few moments to check in with all your parts to see if they have anything to say to you. It's important to experience the energy of each part each day. Sometimes it helps to allow each part of you to write you a brief note each day in your journal, on your computer, or even to talk into a tape recorder. This may become part of a daily ritual if you choose. It's an excellent means for checking in with yourself before your busy day dominates your mind. It can be a very simple drawing of one large circle representing "I" with several smaller circles in varying sizes within the larger circle. For example the critic might be the largest part of yourself one day, whereas on another day the nurturer or the wounded child may be the largest.

Patricia chose to draw a simple picture of her internal family in a journal each morning. Then she checked in with each part.

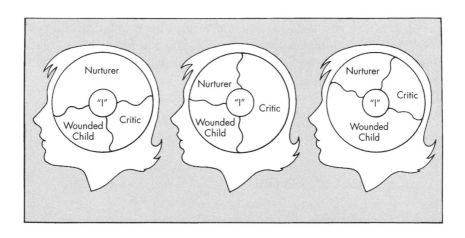

As you can see, Patricia was able to tap into each part on a daily basis even if for just a moment. She was amazed at the results. "After I did this for twenty-eight days in a row, I couldn't believe how much more in control of my life I felt. It was like I got to choose which parts of me were out every day. The biggest difference was in my relationship. I was able to ask to be held from a very adult position when I needed that rather than to whine and snivel like a little child until my partner got it that I needed to be held. I was able to practice what I had preached to my children all of those years: 'Ask for what you want.' "

The purpose of these daily internal family meetings is to practice taking all of you into account in times of nonstress. Then when you have a problem to solve or a crisis to resolve, you can readily gather everyone together to help you problem-solve. You can use all of you to come to a win-win resolution.

Do you remember that one of the two primary tasks of a young child in a family is to be connected, and the other is to find out the answer to the question Who am I? Internal-family work helps you achieve these same two goals as an adult. When the stage is set and it feels safe, when you have compassion for the all of you, and when lines of communication have been opened between the many parts of you, these parts will begin to work together as a team. This is when you'll really feel connected, when you'll be well along the road to knowing who you are.

INTEGRATING THE PARTS OF YOU

The task of pulling all the parts of you together is not as simple as the snap of a finger. It takes work and it takes time, as we're sure you know by now. You'll find that as soon as you think you have a part integrated, you'll hit a crisis in your life and that part will fall out of sync again.

Marie told us about an insight that came to her when she watched her seventy-year-old mother struggling to put a thousand-piece jigsaw puzzle of the world together:

> Mother was at this for days, maybe months. Each time I visited her, I'd see that she'd managed to put a few more pieces together. It went slowly. Sometimes I watched her get really frustrated. Periodically she took time out. I also saw her passionate

fervor, and her sense of accomplishment. She didn't have to finish the puzzle immediately to enjoy herself or what she was creating. I saw her get excited when she would get a corner completed. Or one little piece that pulled two central themes together would suddenly be there. She would take a piece and look at it from every angle. Finally it dawned on me that this was a lot like life—putting together the puzzle pieces one at a time.

Cindy, who is an oncology nurse, told us about a dying cancer patient she was tending. The patient told her, "You know, life is like putting a puzzle together. Sometimes you think you have a piece in place and then something happens and it's out of place again. And sometimes pieces fall into place almost magically. You helped me find my missing pieces, Cindy, by helping me accept who I am and by helping me accept that I am dying. But you know, Cindy, you've spent your life helping people put their puzzle pieces in place, and now it's your turn to find your own missing pieces and to put your puzzle together. It's your turn to experience the power of the puzzle." The patient rolled over, sighed, and breathed her last breath.

We've both watched people over the years struggle to integrate parts of themselves—to put their own puzzles together. Leslie has done this by watching individuals in psychotherapy. Claudia has seen this happen with groups of people in recovery communities and workshops throughout the country. From these two very different vantage points we have noticed that there's a common thread that winds through individual and group integration processes. Integrating the parts of self is very much like weaving a tapestry together one thread at a time. Picture a beautiful tapestry being woven by a master. That's what you are doing for yourself as you weave together the parts of your internal family of selves.

The Process of Integration

In real life the integration of the parts of you is not always so simple. Pieces do not go into place in any particular order nor in any particular manner nor on a particular time schedule. Integration is not always a question of the pattern falling into place one piece at a time. Sometimes pieces overlap. Sometimes there are spaces between the pieces. For the sake of simplicity let's look at how you might put one piece of your puzzle into place. The following are eight identifiable steps in this process of integration, steps that over-lap and crisscross back and forth over each other in a spiraling process.

STEPS TO INTEGRATION

1. The process begins when you don't even know anything is missing. Your thoughts, feelings, and behaviors are incongruent, but you may not even know it. Others around you may see that something is missing, while you don't even have a clue that there's anything wrong in your life.

2. But finally, one day, you wake up, look in the mirror, and re-alize that something is amiss in your life. At this point you prob-ably have no idea that you have the resources within you to fix things.

3. So you begin to look outside yourself to find this missing piece. You look to others to provide what's lacking in your life. You might even slip into believing that someone "owes you something," and you establish a relationship with the someone or something that you think will provide the missing pieces for you.

4. Then something comes up for you in your everyday life and you stop and realize that you don't know how to handle it. You turn to those around you and ask what they'd do in your shoes. It's like taking a survey. At this point you'll probably choose to do whatever the majority suggests. You don't seem to have much of an internal filter to run this through. You do what others tell you, or you do the opposite! In other words you're taking advice from the outside because you feel you don't have much internally to help you decide how to handle this "here and now" situation.

5. The next time you run into a dilemma or a problem in your life, you begin to handle it in a similar manner. Once again, you take a survey, but this time you run the data you collect through an internal filter. You're beginning to move beyond taking other people in "hook, line, and sinker." You're beginning to take only pieces of others in, keeping what fits and leaving the rest behind. You are finding that the all of you is actually beginning to decide what to do.

6. When the next problem comes up, instead of having to call to speak to a friend, a therapist, a sponsor, and/or a mentor di-rectly, you call and listen to their voice on a tape recorder, or you look at something that they wrote to you or gave to you. You

find that this is enough to help you get in touch with what they may have to say about your current situation. When you hear their voice(s) or when you touch something that they gave you, you're able to pull up an image of them, to sense their presence, to hear their advice.

7. When the next situation arises in your life, you simply ask yourself what this friend/therapist/sponsor/mentor would say. You don't need to call them directly and you don't even need to hear their voice. You're well into the process of incorporating this external person or these external persons into you in the form of holograms. You're able to pull up the hologram of them you have inside of you and ask what they would do in the given situation. It's such good news that you run to tell them what it is that you just did. You need to speak to them. You need their pat on the back for a job well done.

8. Once again something in your here-and-now life comes up. This time without really thinking about it, you simply respond to the situation. It's not until someone else compliments you on how well you did it that you even realize you handled things the way your friend, therapist, sponsor, or mentor would have. This time you've added a healthy dose of yourself to the equation. This time you've not only integrated parts of those external people into your internal family. You've blended them in and made them a part of your own special you-ness.

Cindy shared this process with us over a long period of time, and as with most processes like this, it didn't exactly go as the textbook said it would.

> As I look back, I realize that I went for years on end taking care of other people before I woke up and realized—not long after that patient of mine died—that I wasn't taking very good care of myself. I'd like to tell you that this has been an easy look in the mirror, but it wasn't. I was depressed. I was afraid to speak my mind. I couldn't even identify my own needs anymore. All I knew was that I had to be there for everybody, and yet I wasn't important to anybody. It was very painful. When I was able to pick myself up, I turned to some friends, who kindly and firmly told me, "Cindy, you need some help with this."
>
> I began to see a therapist named Betty. I picked her because she was so motherly—just how I wish my mother had

been. My therapist even sat in a rocking chair just like my grandmother who loved me a lot when I was a kid. Over time I found that I began to turn to this therapist to nurture me in the way that I had not been. I actually expected her to do for me what all those others had not done for me in the past. She was able to do this some. It was a rude awakening when I finally got it that no one, not even Betty, could ever make up for the lack of nurturance from when I was so little.

When situations would come up in my life, I would either ask her what to do and do that—or the opposite. Then I began to ask and filter what she said through some sense of me. I mixed Betty's advice with my own. Then I'd call her answering machine or hold a little teddy bear she'd lent me while I tried to figure out what she'd say for me to do. I didn't need to call her directly at this point, but I did need to contact her by connecting with her voice mail or a postcard she'd sent me once when she was on a long vacation.

Much to my surprise one day I found that in the middle of a tough situation at work I spontaneously identified that I needed to take care of myself, and to nurture myself. I stopped and asked myself, "What would Betty say to do if I called?" It felt like she was there. It was strange—in a good way.

Another time I realized, after the fact, that I'd taken care of a situation without even stopping to ask what Betty would suggest. Amazingly enough, when I told her about what I'd done, she said, "I couldn't have done it better myself, Cindy." I was so glad that she was there for me to tell about this. It seemed like I had to tell her, you know.

Weeks later another set of circumstances came up, and I handled it, took care of myself, and was able to pat myself on the back for it. It's only now that I'm telling you about this that I realize that the way I handled this was part Betty and part me. Wow, this stuff works!

Thread by thread Cindy seems to have woven a self-nurturing part into her tapestry of self. She has taken parts of Betty and left other parts behind. She has in turn merged these parts into herself and come up with her own Cindy-blend of self-nurturance. This is not to say that she no longer seeks out friends for nurturance. She does. We all need friends and support—more at some times than at others. The good news is that today Cindy can and does nurture herself better than she ever has before. Cindy said, "Today my friends help nurture me *and* so do I."

Imagine this process of integration for one part and then multiply it by however many parts you have. It's not that one part gets integrated at a time, or even that the parts of you will do each of these steps of integration in order. Sometimes it's one step forward and two steps back. Sometimes you may think that you have a part totally integrated into the whole of you and then a crisis comes along that challenges you.

Let's say that Cindy ends up in a situation in which she feels forced into her old behavior of taking care of others first and herself last. When she does so, she feels drained, as you might expect. At this point she may need a gentle reminder from a friend of hers: "Cindy, you need to take care of you here, okay?!" Or maybe Cindy's friends actually need to take over and nurture her. Cindy may even feel that she's lost the self-nurturing part of her she worked so hard to integrate. In time, with a little bit of the pressure of the moment removed, she'll be able to access her internal nurturer once again. In this instance the nurturer is not a missing piece; it's simply one that has been buried for a little while and that needs some attention paid to it again.

Self-healing takes patience above all. You need to be patient with yourself. Lifetime patterns are not broken overnight, no matter how many missing pieces you find and integrate back into the whole of you. Remember, as you come full circle in this work on integration, the goal is progress, not perfection. It's through your imperfections that your uniqueness and beauty come forth.

CHAPTER 9

Making It Happen

All the inner work you've done so far is only valuable if it facilitates change in your life. We assume that if you've reached this point in the book, you're highly motivated and that you do want to make changes. This chapter is a very practical one. It's designed to help you put this material to work in your everyday life. We help you to look at which portions of each part you want to keep and which to let go of. Then we look at what might get in the way of you working with your internal family of selves. Next we summarize ways to use your internal family both retrospectively and prospectively. And finally we examine the process of constant change and growth among your many parts of self.

WHAT TO KEEP AND WHAT NOT TO KEEP

Do you remember those times when you were growing up that you wanted to be just like someone else? You tried to walk like them, tried to talk like them, even your gestures were like theirs. You consciously, or perhaps unconsciously, took them in "hook, line, and sinker." In your own mind you were them, and you just loved it when someone told you that you reminded them of this person.

Sonny looked, talked, and dressed like his father. He even had the same signature as his father. He remembers, "It was so cool when one day my mom showed me pictures of my dad when he was my age and we couldn't tell the difference between him and me."

But Sonny continues, "Years later when my dad left Mom, Jack, and me to go live with another woman, I didn't like it that I was just like him. I saw the pain in my mother's eyes, and I never, ever wanted to do that to someone I loved. Thank goodness my mom was wise enough to get me into therapy to help me separate this all out. In time I was able to separate out the ways that I was similar to Dad from the ways that I wasn't. I found that I had some choice. I could take the parts of him that fit and leave the rest behind. What a relief! Since then I've begun to realize I can do that with everyone I encounter in my life. I can take the parts of them I choose and leave the rest behind."

Sonny learned an invaluable lesson—one that many of us don't learn until we're much older than he was. As long as you're conscious about it, you have choice in what parts of someone else you emulate and what parts you don't.

We once taught an elementary-school workshop in which we helped third-graders make a list of the positive and negative traits of Mom, Dad, sisters, and brothers. We then had them literally set aside the traits that they didn't like. Each kid role-played the traits of Mom they liked. Then, in the second act of the play, they acted out the aspects of Mom that they didn't like. This was a little rougher, but they amazed us—they did it.

Finally in the third act of the play the children acted out who they would be if they couldn't be who they were in either the first or the second act. Most of them acted out a person in this last act that was strikingly similar to the positive Mom from act 1. Even at such a young age they seemed to have a choice about which parts of Mom they kept and which parts they didn't.

Months later we checked back with them, and several of the children spontaneously told us about how "cool" it had been to do the play with us. One class convinced us that they wanted to do another play, one they themselves had made up without their teacher knowing about it. As we watched the play, tears came to our eyes. It was about a little girl named Sheila. In act 1 she walked, talked, and acted just like her dad. Then, in act 2, Sheila could be seen hitting her doll the same way her daddy had hit her.

But the moment of glory came in act 3, when Sheila got very mad because her brother was teasing her. She picked up her doll, the one that she had pulverized in act 2. She raised her arm to hit it, but then she stopped her hand in midair. After a moment that lasted a decade Sheila gave the doll a hug and tucked her into bed, saying, "I don't want to do to you what Daddy did to me. I can be different from him. I don't want to scare you." Sheila then walked to the other side of the stage. The walk that had been so much like Dad's began to take on a flavor of its own. The audience was breathless. What was Sheila going to do? The answer came quickly.

This little girl, with the wisdom of someone much older than she, picked up the newspaper by the fireplace and began to draw all over it in wild, angry strokes. She then shredded the paper and put it in the wastebasket. You could see this little girl's jaw jut forward in anger. But she was taking her anger at being teased and releasing it in a nondestructive manner. If only her father could learn from his child! Sheila had truly learned that you can take what you choose from significant others in your life and leave the rest behind.

You can do this with your internal family of selves too. Look back at the list of parts of you that you worked with in chapter 7, where you listed the positive and negative aspects as well as the opposite of each part. Your present task is simple and yet so profound, just like Sheila's. Take each part in all of its color and depth. Pretend that each part is like a real person in your life. Let the part walk off the page as you do the following exercise:

A THREE-ACT PLAY[1]

> 1. Pick a part of you. Look at its positive aspects and then look at its negative aspects.
> 2. Come up with a miniplay in which you act out in act 1 this part's positive side. In act 2 you will act out its negative side, its opposite.
> 3. Now, in act 3, take this part and be whichever aspects of it you want to be. Blend the good in with the bad. Most of all blend this part in with who you really are, with your true nature.
> 4. Actually perform the play for a group of friends. Maybe they'll want to do the same with parts of themselves too.

We did this exercise in one of our Missing Piece groups, and amazingly the very thing that had happened with the children in the local elementary school happened with the adults. The impact that a seemingly simple and silly exercise had on their sense of control over parts of themselves left them awestruck. James summed it up well sometime later: "This was unreal. I've never felt that I could be my own man before. But somewhere between acts 1, 2, and 3 I felt I had some real choice. For the first time in my life I could choose to be like my father in some ways and not like him in others. Not only did the father part inside me change, but even more significantly how I father my own son has begun to change."

BLOCKS TO INTEGRATION
AND WHAT TO DO ABOUT THEM
Internal Chaos

The road is not always smooth as you head toward integrating all of the parts of you into an empowered whole. Sometimes along the way as you spiral through your process of integration, parts of you may seem less than cooperative. Sometimes they all speak up at once. It's like a board meeting that's gotten out of control. Sometimes one part hogs the stage. Sometimes it won't listen to other parts. Sometimes parts fail to treat the other parts with respect. Sometimes you may even treat a part that you don't like with very little respect. Sometimes a part gets demanding. Sometimes you get demanding. Sometimes you just can't stand a part. Sometimes the part can't stand you. Some parts may withdraw into a shell and not talk at all. Sometimes you may do that too.

Sometimes parts are scared and sometimes they're confused. Sometimes parts seem to lack the tools for integration, and sometimes you wonder if you have the tools yourself. Sometimes parts of you get stuck in the belief that the answers are outside of you, and then the parts feel helpless. Sometimes parts are incredibly needy, and sometimes they're rageful. Neither is exactly pleasant to be around, especially if all this is going on inside you twenty-four hours a day. Sometimes parts of you need a break, and yet they feel pressured to change fast and join the whole right now—or better yet, yesterday. Sometimes you need the break, and parts of you don't like that.

Remember the inner critic? Sometimes it feels like the critic is the only one home, and you wonder what to do. Whom do you consult? Whom do you turn to when no one's home?

These are the times when it can be incredibly valuable to share your frustrations with others, whether these frustrations are external or internal ones. Getting it all out seems to dissipate the embarrassment and shame you may feel by not having it all together all of the time. Oftentimes others outside you, and perhaps even inside you, may very well be able to offer a different perspective on the situation. They may be able to suggest different resources—both external and internal ones that could help you past a stuck point.

Creating Order

It's our belief that all of us have the answers inside of us and that at times we just need a little help in accessing those answers to get past a stuck point.

Allison, for example, called an internal-family meeting. "We elected a new parliamentarian and bought a new gavel to help me gain some control over the parts of me who kept speaking up all at once."

Wendy was able to bring in her nurturer and her protector to help soothe and appease her very wounded child. Wendy told us,

> It felt better when I found that I was able to hold and comfort myself. Nurturer stood on one side and protector on the other, and together they both embraced little Wendy. It helped so much. When these two caring parts of me held the wounded part of me, I was able to cry and cry and cry at a very deep level. Amazingly some of my neediness diminished. And better yet, since then I've been able to access these parts of me whenever I'm feeling needy. I just touch the ring I wear that my grandmother gave me years ago when she was my external nurturer and protector. It helps me access those parts of me that are so much like her.

Judy found that she wasn't listening to the rebellious part of her. The result was somewhat predictable. "I've found myself rebelling lately, and we're not talking about rebelling against my parents' strict curfew rules. This time I'm rebelling against myself. I've never binged so much on ice cream in my life. I know I shouldn't have it because of my diabetes. But I just can't help myself. It's like I have no control."

The solution for Judy was to listen to what was going on for her. "I had to listen to Reb [the rebel part of her]. He had a lot of valuable things to say. He told me that I need to lighten up on myself.

He told me that my rules about food are too strict for him. He said that because I won't listen to him, he feels the only way he can get my attention is with the old ice-cream trick: 'You know, "I scream, you scream, we all scream for ice cream." Well, I'm screaming for your attention in the only way I know how.' "

Tony told us about an experience with his critic. "One day," Tony said, "I just told my critic to shut up. He'd been ragging on me and ragging on me to the point that I couldn't stand him any longer. And he stopped for a while! I think that's the first time I ever stood up to this awesome critic inside of me. He must have been in shock. I wish I'd gone back to listen to what the critic had to say later that day. But just as I might have predicted, the critic ragged on me even worse the next time I messed up. I wish I'd treated him with respect so that he'd do the same with me. Now I've really got a mess on my hands—the critic has upped the ante."

Billy said that his critic yelled so loudly at him that his protective part of self, called Standup, was "blown away so bad that I couldn't even find him. Critic had leveled standup." Actually this standup part of Billy had wisely retreated until the critic had cooled off. Standup found solace in his shell, and in due time when critic calmed down and it was safe, "All of the parts of me that had headed for shelter when critic came blasting out were now able to show up and have their say. Now I am able to listen to what both standup and critic had to say. It needed to be safe first, though. And when it was safe, these parts of me began to talk."

When our friend Alan's wife, Marlene, was recently diagnosed with ovarian cancer, it didn't look good for her. Alan shared with us, "This is like a flashback. When I was eight, my sister died of a rare lung disease, and when I was twenty-two, my first wife left me for another man. Now I'm scared that Marlene is leaving me just like they did."

But as Alan told us about this, there was a change in his facial expression. A new light came into his eyes as he told us, "You know, I just realized that I'm not eight and I'm not twenty-two. I'm fifty-six. I have different tools today than I did at those ages, and I need to deal with this as who I am today, not from the shoes of yesterday!" And he did. He walked through the horrors of the cancer diagnosis and the subsequent treatment with Marlene in ways he certainly wouldn't have been able to muster as a child, nor even as a young adult.

"I called upon my divider so that I could separate out what

needed to be attended to first. My rager was given a voice, but I always called the nurturer to be there on standby to take care of me as my rager voiced his anger and rage. Joey, my vulnerable child, was able to be seen, and heard as she was surrounded by strength and spirit. Yes, I felt grief and rage, but I did what was needed, and because of it I was able to stay available to my wife. I know that I'll be able to walk through whatever is in front of me from now on."

Yolanda told us about a time in her growth work when she just needed some time out—a vacation of sorts from the parts of herself. And she used a combination of the parts of herself to get that break. "I decided to go to Palm Springs for the weekend. I had a massage, we played tennis, and just rested." The parts supported Yolanda in her time out. "We all needed a time out. It's nice to be able to choose it ourselves rather than having to get sick to get that break."

Judith told us about the time she felt like "no one's home. I can't stand it. I know up in my head that I have an internal family. After all, I've read this book all the way up to this page, so I know about this stuff. I've even connected with and made real some of the parts of me. But it's like there's a black cloud looming over me right now. The sky's gray and it's about ready to rain. I can feel that there's hope somewhere—I've seen the light before. But right now there's no one home inside me."

In working with Judith we were able to get her to be the black cloud for a while. She gave the cloud a voice, and then she wrote the following poem while still in the midst of trying to "turn the lights back on" inside her internal family:

> They say there's a new dawn
> Acomin'.
> I believe that
> In the soul of
> My being.
> Yet
> It is so dark
> When I go
> To open
> My eyes out there.

I stretch with each
Breath into the corners of my soul.
Sometimes I forget to breathe.
The new dawn is there.
Look. Look. Can you see?
The sun's rays are coloring
The room of my body
With a brilliant and vibrant rainbow.
And as I look
And as I turn my eyes inward
I can see a movie of the radiant rays
Emerging from the earth of my being.
From the darkness
Evolves the light.
Look. Look.
Can you see what
I see.
The breath pulses more deeply than yesterday
And the heart still hurts.
And the eyes,
Tear.
Maybe those are dew drops.

It was probably no coincidence at all that Judith wrote this poem a few days after being inspired by Maya Angelou's poem about renewal that was written for the inauguration of President William Jefferson Clinton. Judith internally, and the nation externally, stood at what many hoped was the dawn of a new day.

HOW AND WHEN TO USE YOUR INTERNAL FAMILY

You have a wide range of choices in how you use your parts. You can choose to use your internal family retrospectively (looking back on a situation), or prospectively (looking forward and planning ahead). You can even choose how much of the energy of your parts you want to come forward at any given time. You can choose how and in what way to use your internal family in a crisis in your life. And you can choose how you want to employ all these parts of you when life is going well. And, most profoundly, you can actually choose to have these parts of you help change the patterns in your life.

Calling Forth Parts

First, if you have not already done so, consider looking backward and trying to use parts to explain why you acted the way you did in a certain troubling circumstance. Dan recalled a time when he'd had a tough time making up work in school after he'd been out sick with strep throat for several weeks. "Now that I have the language to explain all of this, I must have called forward the achiever part of me as well as the caretaker. The achiever pushed me to get the work done, and the caretaker made me pace myself so that I wouldn't get sick again."

Lisa shared with us about how she was planning to argue her case in a Small Claims Court action against her landlord. "I'm not going to take my victim with me, or my little wounded child. I'm going to take awesome, my strong, assertive part, as well as the rational and logical parts of me with me. Little kids don't belong in court."

In a situation at work Jill found that a different combination of power and vulnerability was called for when she was being harshly (and, she felt, wrongfully) judged by a supervisor. "After several internal-family meetings I figured out that I needed to blend 80 percent responsibility, assertiveness, and power with 20 percent vulnerability. I've already tried 100 percent power, and that left my supervisor on the defensive, I think. I'm hoping that this eighty-twenty combination will make me seem more human and that we'll be better able to work something out."

Ann found her internal family helpful when her mother died unexpectedly. "My whole external family depended on me. I needed to make all of the decisions and all of the arrangements. Mom had left me in charge of everything, just like when I was a kid. What helped was being able to meet with myself and see that I needed to be responsible the way I'd always been. But I also needed to acknowledge there were some parts of me that were grieving the loss of my mother—parts that needed caring for. I think that if I hadn't had this language about parts of self, I might have ended up overwhelmed and really depressed. I might have passed right by the grief to focus totally on taking care of all the business at hand. This time, with the help of my own internal family, I was able to handle this family crisis in a different way than I had crises in the past."

Trisha said that she first saw the value of her internal family when things were going well in her life. "I've never been able to handle the good stuff in my life. It's like I'm always waiting for the other shoe to fall. But then I had a bunch of internal-family get-togethers. The scared parts of me were able to speak up, and the strong, confident, competent parts were able to reassure them, and subsequently me, that bad did not always have to follow good."

Creating New Patterns

Are there patterns in your life you know you want to change? Do you keep finding unavailable men? Do you always head to the cookie jar when the going gets rough? Or do you space out or run away? Do you withdraw and hide whenever there's conflict? Do you always ask for others' advice without even asking yourself if you have any ideas about how to handle the situation? Do you give gifts to people you're really angry at? Do you intellectualize and analyze everything? Do you find that you end up meeting others' needs before your own?

Patterns are linked to parts of you. Patterns are the result of the ways in which parts of you interact. Therefore one of the ways to change patterns is to get to know and change how the different parts relate to one another. Perhaps there are patterns that you'd like to incorporate into your life—ones that you see others doing but you can't quite do yet. Do you want to take better care of yourself? Or do you want to be more sensitive and feel more? Do you want to be more rational and logical? To be able to keep power for yourself rather than give it away to others? To stand up for yourself more? To be able to stand in another's shoes better? To stop personalizing everything so much? To stop taking on too much to do? To start playing more? To stop being a victim over and over and over again?

These are but a few of the patterns you may want to establish or to eliminate. The choice is yours, although, quite candidly, this isn't easy work. It's not hopeless, though. Your internal family can help you. For starters try this exercise:

CHANGING PATTERNS

- Name and describe the patterns that run your life and the ones that you'd like to have.

- Tracking one pattern at a time, can you remember the first time a particular pattern was present in your life?
- How has the pattern served you? How has it not served you? Be as specific and as honest as you can.
- What parts of you participate in this pattern?
- How might other parts of you help in breaking this pattern?
- What's going to be your cue that this particular pattern is operating in your life?
- Can your internal family come up with a game plan about how to begin to work with changing your patterns? Be as specific about details of your plan as you can.

Sara took a look at a lifetime of being overly responsible. This has always been an extremely socially acceptable pattern. She was the person everyone turned everything over to—the one everyone relied upon. This was a pattern she wanted to let go of. The pattern she wanted to pick up was one of "taking care of me first, not at the expense of others but just so that I get care as good as others have gotten from me."

Sara asked her family members how old she was when they first remembered bragging about how responsible she was. They said that it started the day her brother was born. They'd all been surprised at how helpful she was and how she never seemed jealous of him at all. "There was that time you hugged him around the neck until he was blue, but you were just showing him love, just a zealous hug," they added in Sara's defense. Her family members concurred that you could give Sara anything and she'd do it. In fact sometimes she'd do things for others even before they asked.

In school, as you might guess, Sara turned in every assignment, and her grades were near perfect as well. In her marriage she took care of her husband in a motherly sort of way. She was aghast when he left her for another woman. "After all, he could never get anyone to take care of him like I did." It never even occurred to Sara at the time that maybe her husband didn't want a mother—he wanted a wife.

This pattern of overresponsibility could be seen in Sara's parenting as well. Her children were so well cared for that they had a tough time caring for themselves. "I always did it for them, whatever it was." Sara was overly responsible at work as well. And she did it so well there that she's now out on stress leave after a total burnout. Would it surprise you to hear that Sara had done absolutely all of the exercises in this book, and done them perfectly?

At first it wasn't difficult for Sara to look at how her overresponsibility had served her when she was growing up. After all, everyone likes a responsible person. The tougher area for Sara to take a look at was how being overly responsible was serving her today. She humbly admitted that this pattern had helped her stay safe, keep in control, and keep people at a distance.

"When I'm the one in charge, I don't need to trust others. I can be in control. I know that it'll get done. I don't get hurt, rejected, or disappointed. Actually when I keep this busy, I don't have time to feel anything, let alone the loneliness that's sitting underneath all of this. I'm afraid that if I give up doing everything, I won't know who or what I am.

"In a funny way this overresponsibility keeps me a victim," Sara added.

> I don't like admitting this, but I've been a victim my whole life. And if I overwork, I can still maintain the belief that "Woe is me. It isn't fair that I have to work so hard and others don't." When I feel guilty for things I haven't even done, it's horrible. I feel like a victim of myself. When it gets really bad, I'm immobilized and can't do anything at all. At that point someone else needs to take care of me. I'm in total burnout by that point.
>
> As much as I don't like owning this, at least being a victim is familiar, but it makes me so uncomfortable today that I really want to change this pattern. The problem is that I don't know how.

This part of the process brought up a lot of feelings for Sara. Before moving on to the next question she stayed with and walked through her feelings. As the fog began to clear, she took a look at the parts of her that had been helping her stay stuck in this pattern. She found that the nurturing part she called Cuddles, the perfectionist, and the critic all aided and abetted her overresponsibility. They seemed to feed the victim part that in turn kept her stuck. These parts also seemed to protect her from intimacy. After all, when you're in charge of everything in the world, you are indeed on top. By definition intimacy is between equals. It's not about one person lording it over the other. "Indirectly being overly responsible has been a way for me to stay stuck. But I don't want to be the opposite of responsible. So what can I be?"

Sara then began to wonder what other parts of her she could bring in to help her with this pattern. She decided that the protective part that she called Pro could help out and that the spiritual part that she called Cath (short for the Catholic upbringing she'd had) could help too. Bound, the part of her that helps her establish boundaries, also stepped forward to center stage. The triad of Pro, Cath, and Bound decided they would help out the nurturing part of Sara so that she'd be better able to care for herself without having to spend almost all of her energy taking care of those around her.

Pro and Bound set boundaries so that Sara wouldn't say yes unless she absolutely had to. Bound wouldn't let her take on other people's feelings. Cath helped Sara see that she was enough all by herself—that she could relax and let others help her out—as long as she was connected to her Higher Power.

Sara then added a disciplined part of her to the picture. This part, Disci, helped Sara be self-responsible and stick to a reasonable schedule. You see, the perfectionist part of Sara is scared to death that "If I let go of all of the responsibility, I might become a sloth or a wimp." What a choice in life: overresponsibility and burnout or the doldrums of slothdom and wimpiness, just this side of being catatonic.

Sara made a deal with all of the parts of her internal family to check in with them each day with the specific question How can we take better care of Sara today? Odds are that the answers will change each day as the parts of Sara grow and change.

THE WHOLE PICTURE KEEPS CHANGING

Your sense of self is formed in dynamic interaction with significant others in your life. This is true for your internal family as well. Change in fact is the only known variable in this whole process of finding the missing piece. Each part of you is constantly in motion, and so is the whole of you as well. Our task has been to help you stir things up enough to facilitate change in some of the patterns in your life. You will find that as your parts change, your sense of time will change as well, and vice versa. The goal of this entire change process is to facilitate an internal experience that is powerful enough to make a shift in a pattern that you may very well have lived out for a decade or two or three.

Changing Pieces

As the pieces of the puzzle begin to work together as a team, your Self puzzle will begin to take on a different look. Parts that may once have been negative become positive. Their job functions change. Parts grow up, and yet their essence remains unscathed. Parts get bigger. Parts get smaller. Consequently the dynamics change between parts. The energies that once divided now unite. As the parts work together, they form a new partnership, a new team, and a new internal family that may be very different from the one you grew up in. Furthermore as your Self puzzle becomes whole, it gets increasingly difficult to delineate the differences between parts. It's as if the boxes that the parts were in disappear and the walls between the parts come tumbling down.

Responding to Change

When a child is born, when a young adult goes to college, when an adult child has a baby, when a parent retires, it means a time of transition for each of the individuals in the family as well as for the family as a whole. Rules change; expectations change; family dynamics change; people grieve; people let go; and people take on new responsibilities. Some families respond rigidly to crisis. They become more controlling. Some families don't have enough structure to weather such times, and they become fragmented and chaotic. The healthier ones simply grieve, let go, and move on. We believe that times of transition present opportunities to change patterns, as well as opportunities for individual growth, for growth in a partnership and as a family.

The internal journey you may be experiencing in finding the missing piece may be just such a transition point, just such an opportunity for change—a time to turn both outward and inward. Your internal family may respond rigidly, or it can even fragment just like an external family can. As we have often said, everything is connected. Your internal world is but a mirror reflection of your external world. When you're under stress, do you turn to a special friend? Do you turn to a whole group? Do you just like to be alone? You may very well begin to turn to similar combinations in your internal world for support.

Is there a special member of your external world you turn to for help through the stress at work, or the stress in your relationship with your partner? Is there a similar part that you turn to in your internal world? Are those special someones both inside as well as outside you?

Transformational Change

Change within parts and between parts tends to be evolutionary, not revolutionary. Parts within your internal family slowly evolve over time. Parts are not killed off, they simply transform or change. This kind of change is like a metamorphosis. Any given part can in fact change in form, in nature, and in character. After all, *transformation* means "the change from one thing into another." This is clearly what happens within families, in your external family as well as within your internal family. What remains true in any kind of transformational process is that the essence of what was still is.

There are times within your internal family that a main part of you may even step aside for a while and another part may move to center stage. This may actually be a rehearsal for a transformation of something in your internal-family system. This may be setting the stage for an upcoming transformation of a part or of the whole of you. For example, when Sonya was thirty-five years old and going through a divorce, she was in a tremendous amount of pain. At this time her dominant part—her mother part—stepped aside. What came forward was a part that wrote the following poem:

MOMMY ME
She sits, rocking
tick tocking
Eyes scout
over blanket's edge

Thumb to mouth, sucking
click clucking
Eyes close
under blanket's edge

She weeps, stopping
drip dropping
Eyes blur
into blanket's edge
No mommies in the house today.

Her mommy part wasn't far away, she was just taking a rest. It was the hurting little child part who had moved front and center. The problem was, children do not belong there by themselves. Children require caretakers. They need to be held, rocked, and supported. Interestingly it seems that once Sonya's mommy part had time to rest, she reappeared to hold and nurture this hurt child part. This is what is meant by parenting your inner child. And as you do, that part will be transformed.

Sometimes what may have seemed like a good-bye may actually be a hello. Let's say that a major part of you was once a runner and you have now become permanently or even temporarily disabled. You can no longer run. At first it truly seems as if the runner part of you—a dominant part perhaps—is gone, that it has died. You will begin to grieve. You may become angry at the injustice of it all. You may ask, *Why me?* You may cry and scream, *It's not fair.* This is the victim speaking, and she or he has a right to speak because it really isn't fair. You may begin to blame yourself and anyone who'll listen—and even those who won't. You simply grieve, just as you did years ago when a special someone died. But then, in a brief interlude between the tears and the screams, you may hear a voice inside saying, *I want you to see this from a different perspective.* This might be a wise part of you. You stop dead in your tracks long enough to hear the following dialogue:

> Listen. Listen to me as you have asked me to do for you. Runner is not dying. Runner is still very much within you. She has simply been transformed. I, Spirit, have received much of Runner's power. Many of the parts inside you are here to support you, to empower you, to help you let things just be, and to care for and with you as you heal from this grief.
>
> Hope springs eternal. What we hope for you is that we can be part of your internal sense of community so that you will become even more whole as you grieve the loss of Runner. What we hope you will see is that both you and Runner are disabled, but that as you walk through this, you will come to see that you are also differently-abled. Both are true.
>
> And maybe from this perspective, with all of us supporting you, you will be able to see that good-bye means good-bye, and that good-bye also means hello. Both are true. And tomorrow the sun will rise again.

Parts within your internal family will also change slowly over time. They may be negative and critical at one point but then become very protective as the years go by. Your goal in your growth process may very well be to develop new parts and/or to transform old parts so that the voices of the new parts become louder and stronger than the voices of the older parts.

Let's say that you had a very critical mother who criticized you a lot and that as an adult you have a similar tape that plays inside your head whenever you make a mistake. Your goal may be to have a new tape in your head that plays louder than the old tape when you make a mistake—a tape that plays messages like *It's okay. Sure you made a mistake. We all make mistakes. But what did you learn from your mistake? How could you do it differently next time? Mistakes are human. And you are human. Progress, not perfection is our goal, right?*

Mistakes need to become tools for growth, not weapons for you or others to flog you with.

Thirty-five-year-old Debbie sees her father as Mr. Perfect. In her eyes he's so wonderful, so perfect, that you couldn't even touch him. Debbie took her external father and internalized him as a part she called Star. She then found a photograph that symbolized that part of her. But one day Star symbolically fell off the proverbial pedestal. She found it unbelievable that her father was leaving her mother for a woman Debbie's age after forty-four years of what appeared to be a perfect marriage. At this point Debbie removed his portrait from the fireplace mantel and placed it facedown in her garage.

Soon, with the help of her friends, Debbie was able to grieve the loss of Star, the once-powerful one on the pedestal. And as she did, Star began to change—from sitting on a pedestal to being trashed in her garage to a new place back in her home. Today Star sits among his peers—all the other parts of self. The essence of Star remains the same. He is very powerful. He sets limits. But unlike Debbie's father, Star is consistently self-disciplined. He protects Debbie. He allows her to be her own "wind beneath her wings."

The once-dominant, patriarchal Star has been transformed by blending some of Debbie's own energy into a kind, loving, strong, affectionate protector. "Today Star is some of what my father was to me as a child and some of what he was not." As Debbie has grieved, she has taken on her father's nurturing, protective traits and left the rest behind. She didn't want his patriarchal, dominating arrogance, yet she did want his kind, loving, affectionate strength. He's still Star, but in Debbie's eyes he's very different. Debbie's Star part is now much more open, much more in touch with his feelings, and much better able to protect Debbie. Debbie is better able to accept Star's love for her in the ways that this part is able to show it. It seems as if the healing of the internal family—in this case the transformation of Star—has helped in the healing of Debbie's perceptions of her external family as well.

Changing Times

Time seems to be a key element in any change process. We believe that when you enter a transformational process—like the one you're in now as you work with your own internal family—time enters another dimension, one that is beyond the three dimensions of length, width, and depth we're all so familiar with. When we're talking about healing, time is no longer linear. It spirals across many dimensions.

For centuries Native Americans speak of time as "the long body," of time collapsing over time. They say that in the realm of the healing world there is no yesterday, there is no today, and there is no tomorrow. What you felt yesterday you can feel today, and what you will feel tomorrow you will feel today. They say you can be and are what you were when you were a physically abused child. They say you can be and are today what you will be tomorrow.

To bring this a little closer to home, think about when you last felt sad at the point that a relationship was changing. Do you remember how it felt? Was it as though you were feeling the feelings not only for this current loss, but for all your previous losses as well? Did it seem as though you had typed the word *Loss* on the computer of your mind and up came all your previously unresolved losses? This is what the Native Americans mean by the long body. Feelings are timeless. Feelings do not know time. If you haven't worked through an old feeling, it may very well come back whenever a kissing cousin of it emerges in the here and now. And it will come back in full force, as if it has been waiting for you for years.

Another example of the long body is when you hear a young child speak with the wisdom of an elder. Parts of you—old parts and young parts, male parts and female parts—have been a part of you since birth. It's from the mouths of young children we so often hear: "Why don't adults just tell the truth?" "Why don't you tell him what you feel?" "Is it important to work so hard?" "Why is it important to be right all of the time?"

Experience Leads to Change

Another key element in the change process is experience. Most of us had experiences as children that hurt us to one degree or another, that wounded us, and that left us with some missing pieces. The journey around the Spiral Path is a process of reexperiencing these memories and of feeling the feelings that you might not have felt safe enough to feel when the injury originally occurred. Change can follow the reexperiencing of old wounds. True, lasting change evolves from experience that resonates throughout your being. This kind of change does not occur just in your mind, nor just in your heart, nor just in your body. If it is a change that is more than a lip service to the process, then it involves all three—the mind, the heart, and the body—plus one more, the soul. It involves taking responsibility for your thoughts, your feelings, your physical being, and subsequently your soul. Responsibility is simply the process of increasing your ability to respond. It is when you experience change on all four levels of mind, heart, body, and soul simultaneously that you know the change is here to stay.

Shelly experienced just such a change the day her youngest child left for college. She wept for hours. Her body shook. She couldn't eat. She couldn't even think. It was as though her mind had gone blank. She felt an internal shift as well.

> I've never been through anything like this. Every part of my being was involved. When I opened my eyes, the world had changed. What had been a black-and-white world suddenly became Technicolor. I felt a rainbow emanating from my being. Sure, the kids came home, in and out over the years, but it was never the same again. My role as a mother had changed. I loved it while it was there, but now it's clearly time to move on to another phase of my life. I've always known that in my head. But to experience this internally—in my heart, mind, body, and soul—has been quite a gift. My internal-family members moved too. This was like a birth process—the birth of me by me.[2]

It seems to us that the key to any transformational process is that you stay open and receptive to the process itself. You do the best you can humanly do to stay centered and balanced and open to letting life do you. This doesn't mean letting yourself become a victim of life. This doesn't mean that you need to be a passive nondoer. This doesn't mean becoming a sloth.

It means participating in life. It means doing whatever you do with lots of energy and enthusiasm—in your external world as well as in your internal world. You let life live you as you simultaneously live life. It means do what you do and be what you are with joy and passion.

Conduits for Change

There are many conduits for transformation. Pain is the most familiar one. Music and art can be conduits for change too. Do particular songs on the radio stand out for you? Is there a particular painting or a piece of artwork that calls out to you? Is there some poetry that has touched your soul? How about nature? Is there something there that sings to you—to your body and soul?

Charlotte remembers that as her marriage was ending she listened to a Barbra Streisand song called "Memories" over and over again. She remembers that years before, when she'd returned to law school after years at home raising children, the song and play *I'm Getting My Act Together and Taking It on the Road* moved her. At another transition time in her life Charlotte felt pulled by the poetry of Emily Dickinson. Then there was a time when she belonged to the Sierra Club and that almost every time she went on a nature walk, she saw a butterfly. There was something in the beauty of the butterfly, in the freedom of the butterfly, in the magic of its own transformational process, that pulled her, moved her, changed her. Recently Charlotte felt particularly moved by the sensual artwork of Georgia O'Keeffe.

The exercise that follows may help you remember particular conduits for transformation in your life. You might want to tape-record this exercise and play it back for yourself.

MOVING PIECES

Take yourself to a safe place. Get warm and cozy and close your eyes. Watch your life-giving breath moving in and out, in and out, one breath at a time until your breath and you have become one. Feel the energy of the earth come up through your toes. Feel the warm, tingling energy, the energy of healing, of creation, of change moving up and up through your body, filling all your being.

Now begin to remember a time of major metamorphosis in your life, perhaps a time of much pain or a time of positive change. Can you remember a song, a play, a book, some poetry, a film, or a piece of artwork that inspired you, that carried you, that seemed to draw out something in you? Can you remember what moved you? Put yourself back in the shoes that walked you through the metamorphosis. What kept you moving? Be with that experience. Feel it again, flooding through every part of you.

When it is time, bring this image and these memories back into this room, to this place and this time. Know that you have your feet firmly planted in and on the ground and that you have returned enriched and inspired.

Sometimes you not only create the conduit, the medium for transformation, you can also promote the process of transformation itself. You can do this through the use of ritual. We spoke of the value of ritual in chapter 1 (pages 17–18). Rituals can be another facilitator of change.

Years ago, when Charlotte was letting go of her ex-husband, she participated in a ritual on the eve of the first day of summer, the Summer Solstice, a time ripe for transformation. She and a group of women prepared a ceremony at the beach to honor that time as a group and as individuals. They built a fire to keep warm as the sun set. And as it did, the women as a group went for a swim. They then emerged out of the water. They climbed up the sand dunes and down into a deep valley on the beach, a valley that led to the fire that they had built. They circled around the fire and began to place papers and symbols of things that each one wanted to put into the flames. One grudge at a time, Charlotte tossed in the remnants of her marriage. And as her resentments toward her ex went up in flames, out of the now-raging fire arose a new energy, a new strength, and a new wisdom. The old had given way to the new. Like a phoenix Charlotte rose renewed from the ashes of her old life. A transformation had occurred and was occurring.

Charlotte told us about a time when she created a ceremony to mark the ending of one growth process—the ending of therapy—and the beginning of a new kind of growth. She prepared for weeks for the ceremony, which she did in her therapist's office.

Charlotte put together a collage of songs that represented who she was, where she had come from, as well as where she was going. She prepared an altar of sorts. She brought with her objects that symbolized the changes that she had already gone through and was still going through. She brought poetry and music that set the tone for the transformation that had occurred, was, and still is occurring.

Her therapist did the same. Together they celebrated Charlotte, the changing nature of their relationship, and their connection to other women across time. They grieved the ending of therapy and the birth of a woman that today we call Charlotte. The healer and the healed were both individually and uniquely transformed by the ritual. Their connection to self and others changed.

Dreams can be another conduit for change. If you will listen to your dreams, work with your dreams, honor your dreams, they will transform you. We believe that each image or person in your dreams is symbolic of parts of you. There never seems to be a life transition that passes without dreams to accompany it. Our job is to be aware of these transformative messages. What follows is a brief exercise that will help you remember your dreams:

DREAM PIECES[3]

· As you prepare to go to sleep tonight, as you prepare to move into another world—your sleep world—ask yourself, *Is there anything I would like to ask my unconscious, to ask my dream world?* If there is, make that request in the form of a question.

· Then shorten the phrase to just one word with a question mark at the end. For example, *Why aren't there any men in my life?* becomes *Men?* And *What can I do with my anger?* becomes *Anger?*

· Now repeat your one-word question over and over again as you're falling asleep.

· If you can, hold or tuck under your pillow an object that represents what you're asking your unconscious.

· Holding that dream question and that dream object, allow yourself to fall into a deep, reenergizing, healing sleep.

· Upon awakening write down whatever you remember about your dream(s). It's helpful to have your pen and journal right next to you when you awake so that you can write down what you want to remember. Sometimes it works best to talk into a tape recorder upon awakening.

• Once you've written every little detail about your dream down—especially if it doesn't seem to make sense—then ask yourself, *What's my gut sense about what this dream means?* Giving your dream a title often helps this process.

• The next step is to do some written work with your dream to translate it into a conduit for transformation. Start by listing all of the people, places, and things in your dream. Then begin to free-associate with each and every little thing in your dream. Write down whatever pops into your mind for each word you've listed. Each part of the dream is actually a part of you. Ask yourself, *Which part of my dream is a part of my inner family?*

• Next come up with some wild guesses about what your dream means. What are the messages your dream is bringing you? What changes seem to be in the air?

• Use the Voice Dialogue or Active Imagination techniques you learned in chapter 8 with any particularly puzzling parts of your dream.

• Continue to work with all the parts of your dream until you're satisfied that you understand what your unconscious is trying to tell you.

• Now ask yourself, *How am I going to carry the energy and the message of my dream into my waking hours? How can I enact what the dream is telling me in my conscious world?*

We have found dreams to be invaluable keys to the unconscious. If you want to understand what your dream is truly telling you on all its many levels, you need to work with it using the tools we've suggested or any others you've learned. Maybe you have some other suggestions from within. It is then and only then that you will experience the transformational properties of a dream. You can't simply wish the results of a dream upon yourself. What seems to be true is that in order to grow, to change, and to transform, you have to work the process as well as allowing the process to work you.

Some form of bodywork may be another conduit for change. Kathy remembered a time when she seemed blocked in her growth process. She made an appointment for a massage that involved deep breathing. She was encouraged by the bodyworker to let go, one breath at a time. In so doing she came to feel every cell in her body. Her body became the bridge between her thoughts and her feelings. "I've never felt the same since then. Something shifted with that massage and with that breathwork. I breathe so easily now. And, wow, you should see the feelings that are coming up. I unleashed something here." Regular bodywork can be a helpful addition to therapy.

Hillary, a therapist and professor, found that the victim part of her had come front and center when her car was smashed up by an ex-patient in the parking lot at her office. To top it all off, the police couldn't find the perpetrator. Hillary was so upset that she could hardly move for quite a while. And then, in a bioenergetic-therapy session, her own therapist had her jut her jaw forward and urged her to begin to growl and snarl and eventually to yell about what had happened. It seemed so simple. The movement of a body part brought forward so much emotion, in this case anger. By the end of the day Hillary had her energy back enough to get out of the draining victim part of her and go to the gym to exercise. At her next internal-family meeting Hillary found out that "the victim part of me had been literally sitting on the angry and assertive parts of me." The bodywork had been a conduit for change within Hillary's internal family.

What kinds of things keep you moving externally and internally? What moves you? What might promote the changing of lifelong patterns for you?

Make a list of some of the things that move you to the point of change. Think of at least one thing that will move your mind, one thing that will move your feelings, and one thing that will move your body.

CONDUITS FOR CHANGE IN MY LIFE

- One of the things I can do that keeps things moving forward in my own growth process is _____.
- Something I can do to keep things moving forward in my mind is _____.
- Something I can do to keep things moving forward in my feelings is _____.
- Something I can do to keep things moving forward in my body is _____.

THE NEED FOR BALANCE

Change merely for the sake of change is not what you're after. Your goal is to have balance in both your external, daily living world and your internal world. We spoke earlier about the Hopi Indian concept of *Koyaannisqatsi*—life out of balance. We believe it's important for us to be aware of when we're out of balance, because that's when the natural healing process gets blocked.

We all know our own cues and signals that help us recognize when we're out of balance internally as well as externally. Try completing the following sentences in your journal to remind yourself of your signals:

- I know that I'm not taking care of myself and I'm out of balance when _____.
- I know that I'm not taking care of myself and I'm out of balance when _____.
- I know that I'm not taking care of myself and I'm out of balance when _____.
- I know that I'm not taking care of myself and I'm out of balance when _____.
- I know that I'm not taking care of myself and I'm out of balance when _____.

List the physical, emotional, and mental cues that signal you're out of balance. The goal is to find the early warning signs so that you can short-circuit any energy drains before they take hold. Connie discovered that she was out of balance when she began to work too hard, when she scrimped on her meals, when she "forgot" to take a long bath, and when she did something other than follow her exercise plan. Once Connie had identified the problem, she could begin to solve it. She held an internal-family meeting and all the parts of Connie and herself as a whole unanimously put into action a twenty-eight-day plan that helped her get back in balance.

In doing this, Connie not only began to feel better internally, she felt better externally as well. In meeting daily to enforce the get-in-balance plan, Connie's internal family got rebalanced as well. The rebellious part of Connie didn't like the plan at first, but the compulsive parts did. The critical part wanted her to do it perfectly, but the nurturing part was simply pleased that Connie was taking care of herself. All in all, everyone got heard. The family got in balance, and so did Connie. She had changed a pattern both internally and externally. People around her could tell and, most important of all, so could Connie.

We all change over time. But there are times when change is more profound. One of those times may very well be while you're doing internal-family work. As you have found, your internal family is deeply embedded in your unconscious, and if you can facilitate any change at all in the unconscious, then it will ripple up to the surface and most definitely affect your external world as well. There's no doubt that when you make changes in your external world, they affect you internally as well. Remember that what goes on inside affects us outside and what goes on outside us affects us internally. Everything is interconnected. The avenues and means that you can use to facilitate a change in your life in the here and now are infinite.

PART FIVE

THE
FAMILY
GATHERING

CHAPTER 10

The Empowered Self

Can you remember the last time you felt one thing on the inside and yet showed something different on the outside? Say you felt afraid on the inside but seemed cool and in control on the outside. That's what we call speaking with an incongruent self—when what you say, feel, and do don't match. We've found as we traveled throughout the pages of this book that one of the ways to realign that self is to have you get to know all of the parts of you and to give them each a voice. This is what we have called speaking with a fragmented voice. It is when many parts of you speak up, hopefully one at a time. For example, when your critic speaks, you sound very hard on yourself; when your wounded child speaks, you sound very young and hurt; when your nurturing parent speaks, you sound very caring and loving.

While these many voices all have something to say, they often ignore one another, seldom listening. Sometimes it may sound like a chatterbox in your head. It is important to give each part a voice. It may feel fragmenting at first, but once you have the parts dialogue with each other you will begin to feel more whole.

When you opened up the lines of communication between the different parts of your internal family, you'll feel more empowered and more in control of your life. You're able to be strong *and* vulnerable. You're able to recognize and embrace each part in its uniqueness and specialness and you're also able to sense each part's place in the overall whole of you.

When you can do all of this, you're on the road to speaking with the empowered voice. This is the voice that speaks from the core of you, from the all of you. This is the voice that has the ability to influence self and others. It is both powerful and empowering.

The empowered voice is an integration and blending of your many parts, coupled with the finely tuned ability to listen and draw from the strengths of any and all of the parts at will. When you're empowered, you're able to recognize your vulnerabilities for what they are. You are open to them. You embrace them. When you speak from an empowered self, your power is enhanced by your vulnerabilities.

SUPPORTING VULNERABLE PARTS

It's very common for people with painful family histories to experience only helplessness when they're feeling vulnerable and in pain. This is because when we step into the shoes of the wounded child, we often leave behind the support of the nurturer and the strength of the protector parts of self. When we do this, we unrealistically expect someone outside ourselves in our life today to come and heal us. The person we turn to may be our life partner, a friend, a mentor, a Twelve Step sponsor, or a therapist. The burden is too great when we expect another human being to heal years and years of pain for us. It's inevitable that we will be disappointed, since we're the only ones who can heal ourselves. People outside of us can be of tremendous help. They can hold our hand as we walk down the path to self-empowerment. They can offer support and guidance, but that's it. They cannot do our healing for us. Still, that's a great deal. Most of us feel honored when someone stands by us and holds our hand when we're in pain or guides us when we're confused. We all need people like this to support and guide us. But fortunately or unfortunately, depending on how you're looking at it, they cannot take away our pain.

When Helen, fifty-five, a family-law attorney, received notice that she was being sued by a former client because her services had allegedly been substandard, her reaction was extreme. She seesawed from the all-or-nothing position of being fiercely angry and insisting that her work was more than adequate (with documentation to substantiate that belief), to feelings of incredible despair that would last for hours, even days. In the moments of intense despair, she could only access feelings of total helplessness, futility, and hopelessness. And when she shifted to anger, it was as if her rage was blinding in nature. She kept seesawing back and forth from despair to rage, and from rage back to despair.

What aggravated this situation even more was that Helen was in the process of completing inner work on having had loss issues in her childhood. As a result she was no longer able to compartmentalize her feelings. She was open and vulnerable and not very well defended at the time this crisis hit. Because of this the charges in the lawsuit brought up the intensely profound feelings of helplessness, loneliness, and futility. From one moment to the next she seemed to go from Power Woman to Helpless Toddler. It took a while for Helen to reaccess the strengths that had made her the powerful woman she is today. It took a while for her to separate out the feelings of yesterday from the feelings of today. It was the vulnerable self she wanted to stay connected to, not the helplessness of the wounded child. Helen held many, many voice-dialogue sessions and family meetings between her parts, and as she did so, her moods began to swing less and less. The difference between yesterday and today is that now Helen has access to all the parts of herself, including those that represent her intellect and reasoning ability, those that are mostly feeling oriented, those that are more physical in nature, and those that are vulnerable.

In retrospect Helen shared with us,

> Anyone I know would have been leveled by this lawsuit. I most certainly was. I felt, and feel, everything today so much more intensely than even a few months ago. There's good news and bad news. The good news is that I feel the joy and ecstasy of being human. The bad news is that I feel the pain, the despair, the helplessness, and the futility more than ever before as well. The difference—and this is wonderful news—is that today I have the tools to deal with it. Rather than be immobilized forever as I previously would have been, when I 'got it together,' I could feel my strength and vulnerability and was able to confront this lawsuit. I have access to a whole family inside me to help me through tough times like this. Of course I have relied on friends and other professionals, but they're just part of my team. The old me would have relied on them totally. Today my internal family is a part of the team as well. We all—both those inside me and those outside me—operate in partnership. It still hurts. In fact it actually hurts more. But I guess that's all part of living, and that's what I want to do—live life to the fullest.

Recognizing, getting in touch with, and becoming aware of our vulnerabilities is very different from acting them out. At thirty-six, when Deb visits her childhood home for Christmas, she becomes passive and pouting when her feelings are hurt by her siblings. Deb is acting out her vulnerabilities in a manner that keeps her in a childlike state. When Jon has an affair with a woman that he himself describes as needy and dependent, even though he himself is married to a very powerful woman, he's acting out his vulnerabilities. And as a third example, when Gloria's partner criticizes her, Gloria acts out her vulnerability by withdrawing and not talking.

The goal for us all as we grow is to be aware of our feelings—to know when we're scared, hurt, disappointed, terrified, angry, sad. And to be able to be with those feelings without having to create more dire consequences. Being with our feelings doesn't mean giving up other parts while we're busy feeling. In fact it means the opposite. It means feeling the vulnerability without exaggerating the moment, without catastrophizing it, and without searching for magical answers and solutions. It's one thing to let a feeling pass through you and quite another to let a feeling take over your entire being and to act it out. It's the difference between "being with" and "becoming."

Karen talked about hearing the news that her best friend's mother was dying:

> I felt so sad. I knew how close my friend and her mother were, and I could feel the depth of loss for my friend. It touched my own loss of my mother, who died six years previously. While I certainly grieved that loss, I still love my mom, and once again I became aware of my own pain around my mother's death. For the next couple of weeks I was aware of my own vulnerability. It was hard for some people to understand or be empathetic. They would look at me quizzically and say, "Your friend's mother died, why are you in all this pain? I hear what you say about your own mother, but she died six years ago." And off they go, shaking their heads.
>
> I found myself not being as focused as I wanted to be at work and with my own kids, but I still went to work. I felt really vulnerable. I just tried to stay with my feelings—easier said than done. I was feeling sad, but it didn't interfere with my ability to attend to my responsibilities. However, I did not take on any additional responsibilities for a few weeks because I was aware I needed some time for myself to reflect, to just be, and to be

nurtured. I set boundaries. I acknowledged my limits. I built in some nurturing time for myself.

Karen was certainly in touch with her vulnerable self. But she was also in touch with her adult caretaker, her nurturer, her spiritual self, and her business self. Karen had access to many parts, and in getting them all to work together she felt empowered. When you can own your vulnerabilities and not be overpowered by them, and when you can simultaneously access your strong parts, you will truly feel whole, and be speaking with what we call an empowered "I" voice.

WHO IS THE EMPOWERED SELF?

As humans we naturally seek wholeness. Thousands and thousands of years ago Plato put it so well when he said that the soul is a circle and that the human journey is about making the circle whole. Could it be that this process of seeking the missing pieces is as natural as the process of breathing in and out? Could it be that speaking with an empowered voice is also a natural process, one that many of us have been seeking for a while?

Let's describe what it's like to speak with this voice. Here's a list of the characteristics of the empowered voice that are present when you are operating from a whole and integrated self:

CHARACTERISTICS OF THE EMPOWERED SELF
- You are able to find additional resources and wisdom inside your own self and rely less on external authority.
- You become more and more real.
- You have more and more choice over which part is out and when it is out.
- You have the ability both to be in relationship and to be in solitude.
- You are able to hold the energy of opposites.
- You are able to see and live the shades of gray in your life.
- You find room for differences in your life.
- You feel lighter and have more energy. You feel with more intensity and depth.
- You have the ability to get distance from situations, from others, and from yourself. You have the ability to step out of yourself to get a broader perspective.

- You know what it's like to live your life in balance, and you have the tools to get back in balance when you are off track.
- You have the ability to see and experience the context in which you live.
- You have the ability to enjoy life responsibly.

You are able to find additional resources and wisdom inside your own self and rely less on external authority. We all have the resources within us for healing ourselves, but some resources are more deeply buried than others. The task in healing is to reconnect with these sources for healing inside us, sources that connect all the parts of us. For some of us connecting with these resources is a matter of having both the support available to change and of learning new skills.

When Patrick began his own family as an adult, he was surprised to hear himself scream at his children the way his parents had screamed at him. He had not given a lot of thought to raising children and had been launched unprepared for parenthood through the unplanned pregnancy of a young woman he'd only been dating. He loved his girlfriend, and at a young twenty-three wanted to "do right" by marrying her. One day he was a bachelor and the next he had an instant family. Patrick's only thought about being a parent at the time was to swear, "I'll never do to my kids what was done to me. I won't be so critical, I won't yell. I won't have absurd expectations of them. I know what that's like from the other side."

Patrick's oldest child was six when he sought help. He came into therapy saying, "I couldn't believe it when I heard myself telling my three-year-old she was stupid. When she wouldn't do what I wanted, I used derogatory language with her. I would feel such remorse, but then to my own horror I'd do it again. I lost control spanking my oldest with a belt when she was six, and that's when I decided to get help."

In therapy Patrick worked through a lot of the pain associated with his growing-up years. But to become the parent he wanted to be and the husband he wanted to be, he had to reach inside himself and connect to the nurturer. He had to learn how to support himself as well as others. He had to learn how not to immediately call on his own judge when he was frightened, and to call out his nurturer instead. The major focus of his therapy was to learn to connect with his own inner nurturer/protector. He also discovered how to listen to and embrace his judge so that he could learn from it yet not have it take over. Patrick found that life is a family affair that involved both his external and his internal families.

We develop the empowered self as we find that we need to rely less and less on an external authority for answers and more and more on our own internal experience and wisdom. This takes time. Patrick has a lot of defenses he needs to let go of as he becomes more comfortable with his vulnerable side. He'll need a lot of support as he practices new skills. As he embarks on his journey to find the missing piece, Patrick will need to develop better listening, conflict-resolution, and negotiating skills. He'll need to learn when and how to ask for help. He'll need to learn how to "be with his feelings" rather than rejecting that part of himself.

The empowered self is a voice that embraces all the experiences that gender, ethnicity, religion, culture, and life afford us. It is a voice that embraces our need for community. It is a voice that finds the quality of human relationships more and more important over time.

You become more and more real. As you travel on your journey toward wholeness—finding, owning, and embracing your missing pieces—you will be able to speak with this empowered voice more and more. You will find that your mimic, false, or protective self will be out less and less. The you that you project to the world will become more and more real. It will become more and more your true self—a confident, secure, and empowered self. Your many masks, the false mimic self and the protective parts of self have served you well. They protected you when you had no other way of protecting yourself. And they aren't going to disappear either. They will remain a part of you. As you move on in your growth process, other parts will continue to emerge. You will then have more choice about when you call forth the protective parts of you.

Before Patrick began to address his personal issues, people who met him would describe him as "a tough guy, a man's man." Yet as he began to recognize his own woundedness and his own vulnerabilities, he became softer and gentler. The hard lines in his face softened because the mask was being set aside, and the real Patrick, which was a combination of vulnerability and strength, was emerging. He was becoming more real every day.

You have more and more choice over which part is out and when it is out. As you become more whole, as your self becomes more integrated, and as members of your internal family become more of a unit that works together, you'll feel more and more empowered. You'll still have access to your mimic or protective self, but you'll have other choices too. Having choices seems to be the key here—the choice to pick which part of you is out there to the world, the choice to feel whole.

In the grief-work process, in recovery from sexual abuse, in recovery from alcohol and food addictions, in sexuality, in relationships, in parenting, and in a spiritual search, finding your empowered voice will offer you a better connection with yourself and with others. For the first time you'll truly feel that you're not alone. And the reality is that in fact you are not alone—not when you have access to this rich community inside you.

Patrick put it well when he said, "Now I get to choose when the wall protects me rather than having to accept its being up all the time. I seem to have other parts of me that can protect me as well. The wall is basically a last resort now. It doesn't have to carry the burden of being my only way of protecting myself."

You have the ability both to be in relationship and to be in solitude. Having a sense of community is the essence of any growth process. You have a community within you, and you are a part of a community outside you. The more connected you feel within yourself, the more connected you will feel with others. Years ago Freud said that the definition of good mental health is the ability to be in relationship. We would like to extend that thought to include the following:

SIX COMPONENTS OF GOOD MENTAL HEALTH
- The ability to be in solitude
- The ability to soothe oneself
- The ability to modulate feelings
- The ability to manage self-criticism
- The ability to respond instead of react
- The ability to be in nurturing relationships

All six of these components of good mental health are related to the inner family you've been working with. Which parts help you be alone without feeling lonely? Which parts help you soothe yourself? And which parts help you calm yourself and bring yourself back into balance, back to being centered, when you're off track? Which parts help you manage your self-criticism? Which parts help you be responsive instead of reactive? And which parts help you be in relationship with others?

The ability to be in a mostly nurturing relationship and to be in solitude are related to each other. When you have a sense of connection with your inner family, you can be alone without feeling lonely. This close relationship with all your parts makes it easier for you to feel connected to others in your outer life. What is outside is mirrored inside and what is inside is mirrored outside. Once again it seems clear that the entire journey of finding the missing piece seems to be both an inside and an outside job.

Patrick's wife was the first to notice the biggest difference in him: "He never used to be able to stand being alone. He hung around me like a forlorn puppy dog. And when I did pay attention to him, I felt like I was connecting to a little boy, not a grown man. Nowadays he has a healthy balance between his alone time with his work projects in the garage and with his buddies who he rides bikes with, *and* we have real quality family time and couples time. I used to dread being with him because it felt like I had another child to take care of. Today I look forward to being with him."

You are able to hold the energy of opposites. As you've transformed the fragmented voice to the empowered voice, you may have found that you're more and more comfortable holding apparent opposites within you. It's in this process of integrating the "I" of you that you become empowered. Change and transformation seem to occur when you're able to contain the tension of opposites. Empowerment comes through realizing that you are both powerful and powerless, that you can be both oppressed and an oppressor, destructive and creative, dependent and independent. The absolute beauty of self is that we are all of these things.

For a moment have your observer part imagine that you're holding the energy of chaos in one hand and the energy of control in the other. Can you do this? How does it make you feel? Can you keep your balance? How?

Try the visualization again, only this time feel the energy that allowed you to create and build a tall building with Legos as a child and then the energy that had you knock it down and destroy it in one fell swoop. Can you hold your building-up energy in one hand and your knocking-down energy in the other? How does it feel? Are you maintaining your balance? How can you use this technique in your outer life?

How deep do you have to dig to become big enough to hold such opposites? Do you have to go into the heart of you, into the soul of your being? Can you expand enough to be aware of both the creative and the destructive sides of you so that you can realize that it's possible to both love and hate the same person?

Danielle said that it took a lot for her to own that she wasn't always the caring person she thought she was.

> I had always perceived myself to be very kind, generous, and caring toward others. That was my image, and I liked it. I was the sweet, kind person that everyone strives to be. So it was with great terror and ultimately anger that I recognized that while a part of me is that kind, generous, and caring person, there's also another part of me that flat out doesn't like being around people. And when I'm in that energy, I don't want to be kind, caring, and generous at all. The funniest part of all this is that I like who I am today. I like not being all one way. I'm actually more comfortable knowing the all of me. It is okay to have opposites when you quit judging yourself. Today I can grin at my opposites.

It's really scary to own the fact that there may be opposites to certain parts of you. You may fight this knowledge, especially if the opposite is a negative part. It's understandable that you might even become angry about it. Yet there's a wonderful sense of freedom that emerges when you stop denying a disowned part. All this energy is freed up—energy that can now be used in other more productive and creative areas of your life. For example, Danielle found that when she acknowledged the part of her that couldn't stand being around other people, it was like a breath of spring. She even found herself breathing more easily and naturally—until the day her inner critic got wind of this new freedom and began to flood her with guilt for being so selfish as to want time on her own. She realized that she needed to work with this critic to help it see that having a part that doesn't like people is a natural balance to a part that likes people too much, that opposites are to be welcomed, not scorned. When Danielle was able to accept this paradoxical behavior in herself, she was once again able to breathe naturally.

You are able to see and live shades of gray in your life. Not only does this principle of opposites apply internally, it applies externally as well. When you feel empowered internally, you're able to see that life is not an all-or-nothing, black-or-white experience, but that it is full of shades of gray. The notion of something's being right or wrong, good or bad, better or worse disappears. The empowered person is able to see that we all view things from different perspectives.

The notion of seeing things as all black or all white is childlike. A young child does indeed see the world through all-or-nothing lenses. "Mommy loves me, or she hates me. I love Mommy, or I hate her." A slightly more grown-up version of the same thing is espoused by the liberal political activist who says, "Either you agree with my stand on this or you don't. There's no gray area here. There's no compromise and no other perspective." Similarly the conservative activist on the other side of the same issue is also into all-or-nothing thinking: "If you're not with me, you're against me." In fact all of us get rigid in our views at times. There must be an occasion or two when you righteously believed that you were right and that the other person was absolutely wrong, and you were not willing to budge on your position. That's all-or-nothing thinking. We've all done it.

We see this kind of uncompromising all-or-nothing thinking on an international level as well. Many countries take extremely rigid, nonnegotiable stands that are reflective of all-or-nothing decisions.

Whether the issue is personal, within the community, or on an international level, the ability to move out of an all-or-nothing position lies in the ability to put oneself in the other person's shoes. So often individuals, families, systems, countries, and international powers get stuck in being able to see things from only one perspective — their own. For them "it's my way or no way at all. I'm right and you're wrong. It's just that simple." All-or-nothing thinking inevitably leads to conflict, whether it's between you and a friend, between you and your boss, between Congress and the president, or between one country and another.

Patrick once thought that children were meant to be seen, not heard. He believed, "These kids need to respect me. And I mean right now. There are no two ways about this. They will mind me." But then, as a result of therapy, he was able to find the gray areas in the issue of discipline. He found a way to have some control over his children without demanding that they practically stand at attention when he came home from work. Today Patrick is enjoying his new, more flexible way of being. "This feels good. The kids are less scared of me. And they seem to respect me more. I certainly respect me more."

Those who are able to see the grays instead of just the all-or-nothing perspective of a situation feel secure in themselves, and they feel good about themselves. They have a strong sense that is capable of maintaining its balance when facing the challenges in both their internal and external lives.

You find room for differences in your life. People who speak with an empowered voice have room in their lives for people, places, and things that are different. They're able to accept and even welcome differences of opinions, values, and beliefs. They may not agree with the person who thinks, feels, or does something differently. They may choose not to be around such a person, but they do not make them wrong, bad, or less than. The person with the empowered voice has learned to accept differences. They may not change their own opinions, but for those with an empowered voice, different doesn't mean wrong.

An example of this is the older person who sees that teenagers have good ideas and that they, too, possess wisdom. In turn those that are younger who speak with empowerment would be able to see that older people are not all fuddy-duddies or boring advice givers. Both age groups would be able to respect the other's different experiences, perspectives, and wisdom.

From a cultural perspective if people were able to speak with this empowered voice, they would not need to see others as wrong or in some way inferior. On a more global level, if those in the industrial world spoke with an empowered self, they would be able to accept and understand that those in less technologically advanced countries simply have different experiences and perspectives in life, and consequently they would not push their ways of doing things on them.

Patrick put it well when he said, "You know, I'd never looked at it from my kids' shoes before. Now I see how scared they were when I'd yell at them or when I actually shook or hit them. Today I truly believe that they have some really worthwhile ideas and ways of seeing things. I'm starting to learn from them. Now I see that kids are not only here to be seen but to be heard from as well."

Janey, whose eighteen-year-old son was in the process of leaving home, was able to respect at a very deep level how different her son was from her. She was able to see where he was coming from with his long hair and idealistic political views. She was able to see the value of his laid-back style of life. She enjoyed the poetry that he wrote. She didn't necessarily share his worldview, but she believed that his way of doing things had as much value and merit as hers. "I used to fight him so much. Now I truly see where he's coming from. He's not right and me wrong, or me right and him wrong. It's just all okay. In fact it's more than okay. I see what he means when he says that 'we in this world need to embrace, not scorn, our differences.' He's really wise, you know."

You feel lighter and have more energy. You feel with more intensity and depth. You may even find that the more you speak with this empowered voice, the lighter you will feel. After all, this whole process of finding the missing piece is one of bringing light to matter. Is it not true that when one lets light in, things become lighter?

The empowered voice speaks with a lot of energy. After all, once you can accept the all of you, you need to use less energy to defend against resentments about the past and fears of the future. Energy that was once used to hold the disowned parts out of awareness can now be rechanneled into new endeavors. As you work through the past and as you gain access to the all of you, you will have more energy to spend on just being you. The more times you have circled around the Spiral Path, the more energy there will be available to you.

Patrick noticed that "for the first time ever in my life, I was able to enjoy the sun as it set over the mountain. It was so luscious that you just wanted to reach out and touch it. Another plus in my life is that last week I got another promotion at work. My boss said that my work efficiency and productivity has increased tenfold in the past year." Energy that was once used to hold back the childhood feelings and to fend off his own internal rage at his children was now available for mastering the responsibilities in life, such as work, and for enjoying the beauties of life, such as the sunset.

Marie was in the midst of this process of integration when her sixteen-year-old daughter, Ann, won a major student state political office. "If I'd been into my fragmented self, I would have been too into myself to appreciate and celebrate Ann's accomplishment with her in the way that I did. But from this empowered place I could bask in my daughter's glory, revel in her pride, and go crazy with joy with and for her. This was her 'one moment in time,' and I treasured the opportunity to share it with her."

When you speak from the empowered voice, you may very well feel what you feel with much more intensity and much more depth. You'll find that you have a full and vast range of feelings. You will come to know yourself as the being that many different energies pass through. You will probably find that you take things less personally. You will be able to sense and be with a part of you without having to become that part. You may even be able to laugh at and with yourself at times. When you can do this, the parts of you will be like well-oiled parts of a machine that runs with maximum energy efficiency.

You have the ability to get distance from situations, from others, and from yourself. You have the ability to step out of yourself to get a broader perspective. As you feel more whole, you'll be able to get some distance from situations, from others, and from yourself and the process as well. Teenagers remind us of this all the time, "Oh, Mom, not everything is an *issue!* Give us a break. There's no hidden meaning here; sometimes a cigar is just a cigar. It's just not a big deal. Chill!" And they're right. You don't have to work on yourself all the time. We all need people in our lives who help us to lighten up, to laugh, to see how funny this "healing stuff" can be some of the time.

Think about it for a minute. Can you get enough distance from all of your "processing" to put together a comedy routine about all of this? Can you begin to imagine how funny it would be to picture all the parts of your partner wandering around in his or her head? In fact there was a television comedy show called *Herman's Head* that mocks this entire process. Herman, a single advertising executive, has five selves—the passionate one, the intellectual, the anxious or worried one, the addicted one, and the creative one. If you have a strong sense of self in place, you may even be able to laugh at your own process without discounting it. Try it.

The more empowered you feel, the more you'll be able to step out of yourself. The early process of finding your missing pieces is very self-focused. It needs to be. During this intense healing part of the process of finding your missing pieces, others may experience you as self-centered, even self-obsessed. It's okay. It's just part of the journey, although you don't want to get stuck there.

But once you've healed some of your wounds, you'll have freed up some excess energy you can use elsewhere. Much to his own surprise, Patrick became the local Scout master in his son's Cub Scout den. "It feels great to give away some of what I've learned. You know how the saying goes, 'What you give away, you get to keep.'"

As you feel healed and more empowered, you, too, will find that you have more energy—energy that you can utilize to connect with others in your external world, in your friendships, in your family, and in your community.

You know what it's like to live your life in balance, and you have the tools to get back in balance when you are off track. As you feel more whole, you'll find that you cherish the moments when your life is in sync and in balance. You'll have a model for what it feels like to have everything going smoothly, and you'll do what you can to keep things that way. When you speak from this empowered position, you're less likely to sabotage yourself or pull yourself back into the chaos, stress, and tension of your old life. By this stage of the game you have the tools to notice when you're out of sorts, out of balance, off track. And you have the skill to utilize these tools to get back on track.

Do you feel in balance in your life as you read this line? What does it feel like? If you're not balanced at this moment, how do you know? What does this imbalance feel like? Jill said she felt she'd been in a work mode for too many days in a row, that the pusher part of her had been out too long. She knew that the way to get back on track was to bring forward the nurturer, and to let her do what she knows best how to do.

James just felt funny and out of sorts. He was grumpy and didn't know why. His wife teased him that "it must be that time of the month for you." It took many days of journaling and using Active Imagination and internal-family meetings for James to sort through what was going on for him. "No, it isn't hormonal," he said defensively, "but it is a time of growth and change for me. I can see, after all the work I've been doing with my internal family, I need to make some changes in my life. I need to have more fun time. Life has become such a grind—work, eat, sleep, work, eat, sleep. The only breaks I have are when I sleep, and I just seem to sleep so that I can work. Something's wrong with this picture. Where's the enjoyment in life that I've worked for?"

Getting back in balance was a simple task for Jill, and a slightly more complex one for James. Both needed to do some work with their internal families and some shifting around of various parts. It seems that the road to balance in one's external life may be an inside job first.

You have the ability to see and experience the context in which you live. As you become increasingly whole, you'll be able to see more readily that you exist in a context, that you're part of a larger whole—the community in which you live. You may also begin to see that you're simply one part in a universe in which all things are interconnected and interdependent. Joseph Campbell described this well in his book *The Inner Reaches of Outer Space:*

In outer space there is a universe of unimaginable magnitude and inconceivable violence. Billions upon billions, literally, of roaring thermonuclear furnaces scattering from each other. Each thermonuclear furnace being a star and our sun among them. Many of them actually blowing themselves to pieces littering the outermost reaches of space with dust and gas out of which new stars with circling planets are being born right now. And then, from still even more remote distances beyond these there come murmurs. Microwaves, which are echoes of the greatest cataclysmic explosion of all, namely of the Big Bang of creation, which according to recent reckoning must have occurred some 18 billion years ago.[1]

Is the Big Bang of creation still going on inside of you? Have you found that once again what goes on inside you is simply a mirror of your external world? That what goes on outside seems to be mirrored in your internal world as well? Could it be that we are only one little microbit in this great magnitude? In some sense we are all one. And it all begins here in this moment in time.

You may see yourself as a speck of sand in the vast expanse of beaches that stretch along all the coastlines of the world. You may come to see that you can make a difference as you join with all the other specks of sand. Just as you are a piece of the larger whole, so the parts of you are simply pieces of the larger puzzle called Self. The more the pieces of you begin to work together and the more your puzzle comes together, the more empowered you will feel.

You have the ability to enjoy life responsibly. You may already consider yourself a responsible person, and perhaps you also enjoy life. But you may be wondering how in the world these two things come together. They do. When you speak from the empowered self, you are able to be responsible—to show up at work on time, to pay the rent or the mortgage, and to keep promises. And you are simultaneously able to enjoy life. Work doesn't have to be tedious. You can enjoy it. Household chores and errands need not be a burden. They, too, can become part of life if you can adopt the "whistle while you work" philosophy.

From this position in life you can balance your ability to analyze things with your capacity just to let things be, to see the whole picture. You can not only get your work done, you can also have fun for fun's sake. You're able to make a distinction between the things that you're able to control and those that you can't. You have a great appreciation for both your past experience and all that you've been through to get where you are today. You hold the past in one hand with respect, not reverence—and you hold the future in the other hand with awe, not fear. And in so doing you're able to be in the moment and to observe it with perspective.

You are able to embrace your humanness—to learn from your past mistakes and to forgive yourself as well as others. You're even able to laugh at yourself. You're much less demanding and critical of yourself. It's as if your inner critic has been given a much-needed vacation.

You're able to speak from a point of vulnerability with strength. And you get to choose the blend. If you feel it works best for you to have one part present with 20 percent intensity while you have another part present with 80 percent intensity, it's your choice. Sara, for example, chose to have 20 percent of the strong, protective part of her (which she called Steel) present when she tapped into the 80 percent of the more vulnerable, sensual part of her (which she called Magnolia). This twenty/eighty combination worked well for her—a mix between protection and vulnerability that she controlled, a mix that became her version of a Steel Magnolia.

Once you're in this empowered position, no one can permanently take it away from you. You can step back and lose your footing at times, but you will not lose all of the ground that you gained. It may feel like it at times, but those times are temporary, not permanent. Do you remember the example of Helen, the attorney who was being sued, whom we discussed earlier in this chapter? She was in this process of integration of her internal family when she got the summons indicating that a client was suing her.

> I felt devastated. I was scared that I was going to lose all that I had gained, and I don't mean anything to do with my law practice. I mean all of this internal work. As the pendulum swung back and forth between my Power Woman and my Helpless Toddler, I have to admit that I wondered if I was ever going to be able to open up lines of communication again between all of the parts of me. I felt like I needed to call in the internal American Red Cross disaster unit to soothe the wounded and to set up phone lines to help communication. But once the shock had subsided, and once the pendulum had stopped its wild swings, I was able to hold internal-family meetings. As you might imagine, both my Power Woman part and my Helpless

Toddler part had things to say about what was going on. But other parts of me were able to help me get perspective not only on the lawsuit but on the rest of my life as well. In time I got back in balance.

The way that I feel about this today is that if this internal-family stuff works in a crisis like this, it'll work under any circumstances. I'd hate to think of where I'd be right now if I hadn't had access to all of those parts of me. Life's good today. From where I sit today, the lawsuit is just one of life's many challenges.

INCONGRUENT SELF TO FRAGMENTED SELF TO EMPOWERED SELF

Let us follow Phyllis as she describes her process of finding her missing piece from beginning to end:

How It Was

I believe that I was whole as a young child. There was depth, intensity, and color in both my external and internal worlds. I felt safe at home. I remember a lot of activity around the house with the entire family. I had two sisters. I can remember loving to go to visit my grandparents. But then one of my sisters was killed in front of school by a runaway car while she was waiting for my dad to pick her up, while I stood by watching.

Suddenly everything changed. Home didn't feel safe anymore. My parents were like zombies. I felt lost and scared. I thought I was going to die. Sometimes I even wished that I would die. My grandparents were sad, and we didn't see them as much. I used to turn to them when I had problems as well as when I just wanted to have fun, but now it was like no one was home.

My mom was always getting angry with my other sister and me. To cope, to just survive, I created a protective self and I cut off and split off parts of me. I tried to contain the pain. I tried to assuage the pain. And in so doing I became many me's all operating within one me. The comic was my strongest voice. But there was also Rover, who roamed around like a dog to different friends' houses, looking for comfort and safety. I could never let anyone know of my pain, so they only saw my comic. I walled off my scared self. I spent a lot of time by myself and wrote poems that I never showed to anyone else. This was my creative self, which along with my vulnerable self, were my more hidden parts.

By my young adult years the protective self had become flat. We had lost some of our depth, intensity, and color. We weren't so funny, nor were the once-hidden parts able to remain hidden. I had parts of me I didn't know were there. My vulnerable self started to pop out when I least expected it. I call her Crybaby. I have a runner self too. It kept busy and focused on everyone else so that I didn't have to be with my pain. Oh, I still had what others called a great sense of humor, and I was quick, and there was a lot of reinforcement for that. But with each passing day I felt more and more distant from myself and others.

WHAT CHANGED?

Obviously the self that I put out to the world was not the self who lived inside me. My way of coping worked for a while. It helped me be me in the world. But then it stopped working. I can even tell you when. I just knew one morning when I was in that never-never land between sleeping and waking. I knew that something had to change, and that change needed to occur now. By now I was twenty-eight, and while I was the life of most every party, I couldn't allow myself to get close to anyone. After my sister died, my family never really came back together again. My mother never forgave my dad for not being at school on time to pick up my sister and always blamed him. Mom said that if Dad had been there, my sister would still be alive today. And Dad was carrying his own guilt.

I couldn't do enough to get their attention. I thought this sister who had died must really have been so special that my parents simply forgot they had two more kids. I wanted to be noticed. This is clearly where the comic came in, but I never believed anyone would ever find value in me, so I couldn't let them get too close. But maybe because I never really believed that I was that bad, I could finally give in to my loneliness. I'd been trying to medicate my pain by always being busy and having lots of people around me all the time.

I hunted for my missing piece the way a child seeks a treasure—with fervor and curiosity. I followed the string in the ball of yarn, one hand over the other, looking for the beginning of the string. I sought and sought and sought the missing piece. But all of the time I kept thinking that it was really something outside of myself that would be the answer. And so the answer kept eluding me.

Finally I began to look at myself. I began to travel the Spiral Path. The journey was—and still is—a painful one. Like the missing piece in the Shel Silverstein story called *The Missing Piece*,[2] I ran into many stone walls along the way. And each time I felt the pain. Sometimes I fought it. Sometimes I surrendered to it. Sometimes I walked through it.

When I did look inside, it was not surprising to find that in essence I had done a lot of what my parents had done. They were my models for shutting down, for creating a self that protected myself in a tightly compartmentalized way. Today I go about searching for and getting to know the missing parts of me—my creative self, my vulnerable self, and my nurturer. My playful self is now genuine, no longer simply a protector and part of my mask. And my joker is my playful nurturer and no longer my defensive anger.

A sense of understanding and a sense of compassion are part of the picture today. It seems as if I have reconnected—with the missing pieces, with the all of me. And it seems now that I am better able to truly and deeply connect with all of you.

This journey to find the missing piece has often been one of solitude, and yet I knew that I was not alone—not alone inside as I discovered all the richness in my internal family, and not alone outside as I began to connect at an even deeper level with friends—some new, some old.

How It Is Today

I feel a sense of compassion at a level that is deeper than I could ever imagine. I have an acceptance of myself that I have never had before. I am able to appreciate my differences, not just someone else's. I appreciate my humanness. That was once so hard to admit. I wanted to be invulnerable. I didn't want ever to have to hurt. Well, now when I hurt, I don't succumb to a never-ending hole of darkness. Today I have the tools to help myself not slip into that place. I seem to have a perspective over all the parts of my life. I continue to use the skills that I learned in this process.

At least once a day I find myself having some sort of internal dialogue with myself. "Okay, Ms. Super Woman, do you really need to have the answer to this decision today?" I found compassionate one reminding me, "You know you are competent. You know you will handle the situation whatever the outcome will be. But there are other parts of you, such as Ms. Body, and she needs some exercise and some good food. Take a break and go attend to the other parts of your life for the rest of the day."

Not too long ago I was feeling very sad about something, and my vulnerable self simply asked, "What do you need?" The good news is that I listened to myself and I was able to respond. This sense of connectedness feels enlivening. It is empowering. It feels as if a new energy, a new power has been unleashed. I can sense every part of me and the whole of me simultaneously. I feel that I am pulsing with the universe and the universe is pulsing with me.

As I reflect on my journey, I feel both profound sadness and equally profound joy—opposite and intense feelings all in the same moment. I simply want just to let it be. I don't want to analyze, to possess, or to criticize. What I do want is to hold and to embrace these feelings in a state of respect, humbleness, reverence, and awe.

The Personal Is Political

The more you work with those in your own internal community, the more you will feel you are a part of the larger community in which you live. And as you work together with others in your community, you will find you can make a difference in the world as a whole.[3] You will do so with great humility, for remember that you are but a speck of sand on the coastlines of the world. You know that to be powerful, you will need to join other specks of sand within your community, both within your internal family and within your external communities—all the groups that you're a part of.

Look around you. Look at the context in which you live. Do you feel a sense of connectedness in your family and in your communities? The larger whole that we once knew as the Soviet Union a few years ago became a commonwealth of separate and independent nations. The question that remains to be answered is whether or not the nation will one day become an integrated commonwealth, a country that speaks with an empowered voice—a voice that embodies that country's wholeness as well as the separateness and uniqueness of all its parts.

Look around you even closer to home. Look at the United States of America. It may very well be that the reason this country has lasted as long as it has is that there is embodied in our Constitution a respect for individual pieces (states) as well as for the whole (the nation). The question this country faces is whether this sense of respect can and will be offered at even deeper levels. Will the other pieces of this puzzle that we call the USA be treated equally and given equal power?

Will all people, regardless of their ability to pay, be provided with health care? Will other communities have as much of a voice as the dominant, patriarchal community? Will women, racial groups, the poor, lesbians and gays, and others who have less power be given status and power equal to the group of white males who dominate the power centers in this country? Will the three arms of our government (the executive, the legislative, and the judicial), established over two hundred years ago "to ensure domestic tranquillity," be able to embrace, respect, and work with one another? If all the levels of this puzzle are not treated with equanimity and respect, there is always the fear that the puzzle itself will fall apart.

It seems as if the plight of each one of us not only as individuals, but as a family, a community, a state, a nation, and a world that is part of a universe, is directly related to our ability to honor, embrace, and respect individual pieces as well as the whole. Each of us has a place in the puzzle, a place that is unique and important, and an integral part of the whole. From this perspective the climb around the Spiral Path and this journey of finding the missing piece seem to be both individual and universal.

There have been times in history when we as humans have possessed a hunger for recognition, when our desire for uniqueness has outweighed our yearning for connectedness. There have also been times when the opposite has been true. What seems to be the case now is that as a collective—in both our external worlds and our internal worlds—we hunger for both uniqueness and connectedness. Yet so much of what we have lost in our society is our sense of relatedness.

As a person you are unique and special, someone who needs and deserves to be honored and celebrated. No one has the same internal family of selves as you do. Your puzzle is yours and only yours, and no one can ever take it away, unless of course you give it to them. Yet it's also true that we all seem to be deeply related in one way or another to one another. So why do we so often fail to recognize these important connections?

Is it possible that in times of crisis—whether we're talking about an individual crisis, a community crisis, a national crisis, or a global crisis—there are choices to make? Is not the ability to choose the true hallmark of well-being? So what do we do, as a part of the human race, when we are in crisis, when our current resources and patterns no longer work? What do we do when we ask ourselves over and over again, Which way do we turn? Do we turn inward and dig deeper into our own internal resources, into our strengths, into the core of our being, into our internal community, and into the spiritual peace within us? Or do we turn to others in our support system, in our external community?

Perhaps the answer to this question is that we need to do both. It could be that our external world is simply a reflection of our collective internal world and vice versa. Perhaps our true task is to find enough silence—both external and internal—to access the spiritual peace that connects our internal world with an energy source much greater than each of us, or even all of us. Perhaps the missing piece of your Self puzzle is not only a part of you that you have disowned or has been unknown to you, but maybe what has been missing for you has been the spiritual piece of your puzzle.

CREATING YOUR OWN METAPHOR

In this book we have offered you the metaphor of finding the missing piece of a puzzle called Self. We've described this puzzle as an onion, a multidimensional internal family portrait that forms layer after layer, from the earliest self out to the surface of today's reality. This metaphor was created to serve as a guide to help you get to know yourself better.

Metaphors are symbols or multidimensional images that have depth, intensity, and color, as well as movement in time and space. Can you now create a metaphor or symbol of your own that describes your own journey of getting to know yourself? How would you describe your process as you have read and worked with this book? Perhaps it was like building a bridge, or climbing a mountain, or diving into the depths of the ocean, or even painting a picture? Perhaps your process has been like making a tapestry or a quilt, one thread, one piece, at a time. Creating your own family portrait is just one metaphor and one image for the healing process. Stop for a moment to write or draw your own personal symbol for your journey.

THE SYMBOL FOR MY JOURNEY

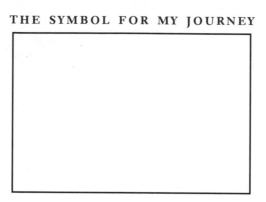

It seems that images are an integral part of any healing process. It's not until we can imagine in our mind's eye how we would like things to be that change can actually occur. Try it. Imagine a change. See if it is true. See if, when you picture how you would like things to be, you feel an energy shift. Does this image open up your resources for a quantum change, a change in perspective, a change at a soul level? Metaphors and images literally create a bridge across the corpus callosum—the membrane that connects the hemispheres of your brain—a bridge between your left or analytical brain, and your right or creative brain. Metaphors and images seem to speak to the soul, where the deep healing of self occurs.

Do you remember the snapshot you came up with in the beginning of this book, the picture that best represents your experience of your childhood? Can you see that picture from a different perspective today? Do you remember the story you wrote about your life in the beginning of this book? Would you tell that story the same way or differently today? When you look at your portrait and your story from yesterday and compare it to your portrait and story from today, it may lead you to your own special and unique metaphor. If you choose, share your story, your image, your metaphor with a friend.

Remember that there's no one metaphor for your personal journey that is "right." Any metaphor or symbol you choose is okay. This book provided some guidelines and tools for your journey. But our way is not the only way. The journey is yours.

Embrace and enjoy your metaphor. Now that you have created it from inside you, let it do you, let it be with you and work you. It represents your strength and richness—your community of parts. And as you continue in your journey, you will find that your ability to speak with an empowered voice will become stronger and stronger. You will find yourself experiencing a natural rhythm. Speaking with an empowered self is like having a peak experience—an experience of connection with the harmony of simply being. You are able to be both in and with the process and detached from it all at the same time. When you speak with this empowered self, there is a radiance that lights up the room wherever you are and a warmth that sets hearts on fire.

CHAPTER 11

The Spiritual Peace

This search for your missing piece has taken time and a great deal of effort on your part. Your patience has most likely been tested more than once along the way. The journey along the Spiral Path has helped you strengthen the container of self that houses all the parts of you, at all levels—body, mind, emotions, and spirit. Along the way you may have found that the things you once saw as character defects were actually key pieces of your Self puzzle. The things you once thought were wrong with you have now become the very qualities that ground you. Your past has illuminated the way to your present. One step at a time, you have discovered that as T. S. Eliot said "so the darkness shall be the light, and the stillness the dancing." Sometimes it's not until we get quiet, until we step into the silence, that we discover the treasures it contains.

As you've continued on your journey, have you found a sense of spirituality—that powerful inner piece of self that gives us our sense of connection with the universe? Is that what's been missing? Perhaps this spiritual piece can be found in the moments between breaths, in the pause between heartbeats, in the spaces between sentences.

WHAT IS SPIRITUALITY?

Spirituality is defined as "the quality or state of being spiritual," and *spiritual* as "the principle of conscious life; the vital principle in man, animating the body or mediating between body and soul; an attitude or principle that inspires, animates, or pervades thought, feeling, or action; the divine influence as an agency working in the heart of man."[1]

Spirituality, however, is a process, not a goal. We can all seek it, but are we likely to attain it perfectly? Perhaps the paradox is that the very thing that makes us perfect is that we are imperfect. Our spiritual essence is both the gift we receive as we move through the process of change and the deep beat that carries us through the storms of life. This is what the anonymous poem "Footprints" tells us:

One night I had a dream.
I dreamed I was walking along the beach with God, and across the sky
  flashed scenes from my life.
For each I noticed two sets of footprints in the sand,
One belonged to me, and the other to God.
When the last scene of my life flashed before me,
I looked back at the footprints in the sand.
I noticed that many times along the path of life,
There was only one set of footprints,
I also noticed that it happened at the very lowest and saddest times of
  my life.
This really bothered me and I questioned God about it.
"God, you said that once I decided to follow You, You would walk with
  me all the way.
But I noticed that during the most troublesome times in my life there
  was only one set of footprints.
I don't understand why in the times I needed You most, You would
  leave me."
God replied, "My precious, precious child, I love you and I would
  never, never leave you during your times of trials and suffering.
  When you see only one set of footprints, it was then that I carried
  you."

The spiritual piece we all seek is that which integrates the light with the dark, that which allows us to hold the light within. It is the part that helps us see that we can't have light without dark and that we can't have dark without light. It is that which integrates the mind with the heart and the body. It is the energy that brings together the dynamic, the rational, in-the-world parts of us with the parts that just are, whose magnetic pull draws the things we need toward us.[2] The spiritual piece is the core part of us that holds us as we walk through life.

Our sense of spirituality is hidden deep within self. Some believe that spirit *is* Self. So often in life we look outside ourselves for the answers, even for our inner sense of the spiritual. We attend church. We do the proper, socially acceptable things and hope to be saved, yet as you've come to learn as you followed the processes in this book, the answers lie within. Jeffrey Moses said it well in his book, *Oneness:*[3]

> Life is structured so that the finest, most meaningful aspects are often hidden from outer exposure. The sweetness of an orange is hidden within a bitter skin. The seed of a tree, from which life will spring, is protected within a hard shell, and a man may walk the earth, not knowing that a vast depository of riches lies hidden deep within the ground beneath his feet. From earliest childhood our senses respond to outward sensations. Without guidance and understanding, we could spend a lifetime appreciating the world only in an outward direction. But the true riches of life lie within. Through appreciation of the wisdom of the past, through prayer, and, most of all, through deep meditation, we can become one with the inner silence that is part of God.

The false self with which you may have masked your vulnerability is like that bitter skin of the orange or the hard shell of the seed. We hope that as you have traveled throughout the pages of this book, you've found some of your own true sweetness deep within. We hope that you've now begun to appreciate your inner world as well as your outer worlds. As Jeffrey Moses suggested, perhaps it is through prayer and deep meditation that you will be able to get in touch with the spiritual piece of yourself.

> When that silence is reached, it begins to radiate throughout all of one's activities. When a large number of individuals radiate this inner silence, heaven will begin to be seen on earth.

While we're deeply interested in helping you find your inner sense of peace, please keep in mind that one of the guiding principles of this work is that what is outside is inside, and what is inside is outside. We can only begin to imagine what our world would be like if we all accepted one another in ways that we have urged you to accept your own parts of self—a world where diversity is not only acknowledged but celebrated. We can only begin to imagine an entire world where there is both inner peace and outer peace. That's what spirituality is about—a sense of connection that begins within each of us and spreads throughout the world.

FINDING THE SPIRITUAL PEACE

For most of us the spiritual journey is a lifelong process. No sooner do we have it in our grasp and embrace it than we find we've lost it again. Sometimes we lose it for a moment, sometimes for quite a while. Spiritual peace may show up in a moment in nature, or while you're being quiet and meditating. It can be there when you connect with a friend, while you're doing the dishes, or when you look in the mirror. For some of us our spiritual piece peeks out when we first awaken in the morning. For others it comes through our dreams.

Sometimes you feel the presence of this spiritual peace when you're alone. Sometimes you feel it when you're with special others. Spirit also works through the power of a group—the group within you (your internal family of selves) or a group outside you (friends, co-workers, teammates, or through those in a support or therapy group).

Wherever and whenever this spiritual peace appears, it brings an experience of connection with the harmony of being—an unforgettable moment, a moment of awe that is indeed worth waiting for. One's spiritual being is always present. The question seems to be When are you present enough to feel it? When are you present enough to sense that in the stillness is the dancing? Finding and experiencing spiritual peace is individual and unique. Stop for just a moment, find a safe place, and sense the stillness. Sometimes we can become very quiet, but the sense of spirit may not move in that particular moment. The goal is to create the right atmosphere and wait.

Your spiritual piece is the glue that holds together your entire puzzle of Self. It is the piece that holds your strengths with humility as you feel your vulnerabilities. It allows you not to shatter. It is larger than any individual piece. It is the center of the puzzle. It is the very essence of Self.

While the spiritual peace in you is the piece that you may have felt was missing, perhaps the truth is that the missing peace you've been looking for has never really been missing. It was simply waiting to be revealed.

Now that you've made your peace, you will discover what we've learned—that we learn best what we teach. Sometimes it's difficult to tell the difference between the teacher and the student, between the healer and the healed. For that which you have taught us, we thank you. For your courage and strength and persistence, we thank you. And we wish you all the best on your continuing adventure along the Spiral Path.

Adjectives to Describe You

absentminded
active
adaptable
adventurous
affected
affectionate
aggressive
alert
aloof
ambitious
analytical
anxious
apathetic
appreciative
argumentative
arrogant
artistic
assertive
athletic
attractive
autocratic
awkward
bitter
blustery
boastful
bossy
calm

capable
careless
cautious
changeable
charming
cheerful
childlike
children-loving
civilized
clear-thinking
clever
coarse
cold
committed
commonplace
compassionate
competitive
complaining
complicated
conceited
conciliatory
confident
confused
conscientious
conservative
considerate
contented

conventional
cool
cooperative
courageous
cowardly
cruel
curious
cynical
daring
deceitful
decisive
defensive
deliberate
demanding
dependable
dependent
despondent
determined
dignified
diplomatic
discreet
disorderly
dissatisfied
distractible
distrustful
dominant
dreamy

dull
easygoing
effeminate
efficient
egotistical
emotional
energetic
enterprising
enthusiastic
evasive
excitable
fair-minded
faultfinding
fearful
feminine
fickle
flirtatious
foolish
forceful
foresighted
forgetful
forgiving
formal
frank
friendly
frivolous
fussy
generous
gentle
gloomy
good-looking
good-natured
greedy
gullible
handsome
happy
hard-headed
hasty
headstrong
healthy
helpful
high-strung
honest
hostile

humorous
hurried
idealistic
imaginative
immature
impatient
impulsive
independent
indifferent
individualistic
industrious
inefficient
infantile
informal
ingenious
inhibited
initiating
insightful
intelligent
interests narrow
interests wide
intolerant
inventive
irresponsible
irritable
jealous
jolly
kind
lazy
leader
leisurely
likable
logical
loud
loyal
mannerly
masculine
mature
meek
methodical
mild
mischievous
moderate
modest

moody
nagging
natural
nervous
noisy
obliging
obnoxious
opinionated
opportunistic
optimistic
organized
original
outgoing
outspoken
painstaking
patient
peaceable
peculiar
persevering
persistent
pessimistic
playful
pleasant
pleasure-seeking
poised
polished
practical
praising
precise
prejudiced
preoccupied
progressive
prudish
quarrelsome
queer
quick
quiet
quitting
rational
rattlebrained
realistic
reasonable
rebellious
reckless

reflective
relaxed
reliable
resentful
reserved
resourceful
responsible
restless
retiring
rigid
risk-taking
robust
rude
sarcastic
secretive
self-centered
self-confident
self-controlled
self-denying
selfish
self-pitying
self-punishing
self-reliant
self-seeking
self-sufficient
sensitive
sentimental
serious
severe
sexy
shallow
sharp-witted
shiftless
show-off
shrewd
shy
silent
simple

sincere
slipshod
slow
sly
smug
snobbish
sociable
soft-hearted
soft-spoken
solemn
sophisticated
spendthrift
spineless
spontaneous
spunky
stable
steady
stern
stingy
stolid
strong
stubborn
submissive
suggestible
sulky
superstitious
suspicious
sympathetic
tactful
tactless
talkative
temperamental
tender
tense
thankless
theatrical
thorough
thoughtful

thrifty
timid
tolerant
touchy
tough
trusting
truthful
unaffected
unambitious
unassuming
unconventional
undependable
understanding
unemotional
unexcitable
unfriendly
uninhibited
unsystematic
unintelligent
unkind
unpredictable
unrealistic
unscrupulous
unselfish
unstable
vindictive
versatile
warm
wary
weak
whiny
wholesome
wise
withdrawn
witty
worrying
yielding
zany

APPENDIX 2

External-Family Scorecard

Questions	Responses
YOUR BEGINNINGS What is your name? Who named you? What do you like to be called? Were you named after anyone in particular? Do you carry a legacy in your name? Do you or did you have a nickname (and at what ages)? What does it mean or stand for? What do you know about the circumstances in your family and the world surrounding your conception? And what do you know about the circumstances and the world around your birth?	

Questions	Responses
YOUR CARETAKERS Who are the members of your family? What was your father's most common advice to you? What is the best thing your father said to you? What did you feel? When, or in what kind of situation, did you feel closest to your father? What is the worst thing your father ever said to you? What did you feel? What was it that your father, way down deep, really did not want you to do? What was your mother's most common advice to you? What is the best thing your mother said to you? What did you feel? When, or in what kind of situation, did you feel closest to her? What is the worst thing your mother said to you? What did you feel?	

Questions	Responses
What was it that your mother, way down deep inside her, really did not want you to do?	
SIBLINGS AND OTHER SIGNIFICANT PERSONS Describe your sister(s), brother(s), or others. Fill in the following questions for each sibling or significant other. Their common advice to you. Best thing he or she said to you. When did you feel closest to this person? Worst thing this person said to you. What did he or she not want you to do?	
FAMILY RULES AND ROLES What were the rules in your family? What are the rules you operate by today? Are they helpful or hurtful? Would you like to change any of them? As a child what roles did you play in your family?	

Questions	Responses
POWER, SURVIVAL, AND SAFETY Who had power in your family? How was power wielded in your family? How did you survive some of the hurt and pain in your family—no matter what kind, how little, or how much you were wounded? Where did you go to feel safe? To whom did you go to feel safe?	
HAPPY MEMORIES What are your fondest memories of growing up?	
THE MAGIC WAND If you had a magic wand, what would you keep and what would you change about the family in which you grew up? **STORIES** What's your favorite childhood story? How old were you when you read it? How does the story go? What's the most important part of it for you? What is your family story? Where are you in this story? What's the most important part of your family story?	

Family Tree

To better understand your family system, it is often helpful to have a mental picture of your family. Fill in the names of your family members.

MOTHER'S SIDE	FATHER'S SIDE

MOTHER'S SIDE

Maternal Grandparents
Grandmother / Grandfather

_____   _____

Name Aunts with Partners

_____   _____

        Name children

        _____
        _____
        _____
        _____

_____   _____
        _____
        _____

_____   _____
        _____

Name Uncles with Partners

_____   _____

        Name children

        _____
        _____
        _____
        _____

_____   _____
        _____
        _____

_____   _____
        _____
        _____

FATHER'S SIDE

Paternal Grandparents
Grandmother / Grandfather

_____   _____

Name Aunts with Partners

_____   _____

        Name children

        _____
        _____
        _____
        _____

_____   _____
        _____
        _____

_____   _____
        _____

Name Uncles with Partners

_____   _____

        Name children

        _____
        _____
        _____
        _____

_____   _____
        _____
        _____

_____   _____
        _____
        _____

You may also fill in the information you know regarding extended family in your grand-parents' generations and prior, and in the generations younger than yourself.

To develop a picture of your relationship with different family members or your relation-ships to another you may use the following signs:

Very Close ≡

Conflictual ⊗

Estranged − − − − −

Distant ⇒⇐

YOUR PARENTS

2nd Husband (Stepfather)	Mother	Father	2nd Wife (Stepmother)
_____	_____	_____	_____
_____			_____

Sisters and Brothers, Lastly Yourself	Partner	Children	
_____	_____	_____	_____
_____	_____	_____	_____
_____	_____	_____	_____
_____	_____	_____	_____
_____	_____	_____	_____
_____	_____	_____	_____
_____	_____	_____	_____
		_____	_____
		_____	_____
_____	_____	_____	_____

As well, indicate with a circle (○) the names of people whom you know who have ex-perienced alcohol and other drug problems.

Check (✓) the names of people whom you know have experienced eating disorders.

Mark with an x the names of people whom you know were physical abusers and/or were abused.

Indicate with a square symbol (□) the names of people whom you know were incest abusers and/or incest victims.

Note (C) the names of people you know experienced chronic illness.

Indicate with a star (★) the names of people whom you know experienced other iden-tifiable dysfunctions, and name the problem.

APPENDIX 4

Resources

Following is a list of names, addresses, and phone numbers of professional organizations and self-help groups that can make referrals in your area:

Adult Children of Alcoholics
   (ACA)
2225 Sepulveda Blvd., #200
Torrance, CA 90505
(310) 534-1815

AIDS Packet
P.O. Box 6063
Rockville, MD 20849

Al-Anon Family Group
   Headquarters, Inc.
P.O. Box 862
Midtown Station
New York, NY 10018-0862
(212) 302-7240
(800) 356-9996

Alcoholics Anonymous (AA)
Box 459
Grand Central Station
New York, NY 10163
(212) 686-1100

Alzheimer's Association
919 N. Michigan Ave., Ste. 1000
Chicago, IL 60611
(800) 272-3900

American Association of Marriage
   and Family Therapists
1100 17th St. NW, 10th Floor
Washington, D.C. 20036
(202) 452-0109

American Medical Association
   (AMA)
515 N. State St.
Chicago, IL 60610
(312) 464-5000

American Psychological
   Association
750 1st St. NE
Washington, D.C. 20002-4242
(800) 374-2721

Anxiety Disorders Association
6000 Executive Blvd., Ste. 513
Rockville, MD 20852-4004
(301) 231-9350

Autism Society of America
7910 Woodmont Ave., Ste. 650
Bethesda, MD 20814
(301) 657-0881
(800) 328-8476

Cancer Information Service
(800) 422-6237

Child Find of America
P.O. Box 277
New Paltz, NY 12561
(800) 426-5678

Childhelp USA
(800) 422-4453

Cocaine Anonymous (CA)
International Office
P.O. Box 2000
Los Angeles, CA 90049-8000
(310) 559-5833
(800) 347-8998

Cocaine Hotline
(800) 262-2463

Depression After Delivery Support
    Network
P.O. Box 1282
Morrisville, PA 19067
(215) 295-3994

Epilepsy Foundation of America
4351 Garden City Dr.
Landover, MD 20785
(301) 459-3700
(800) 332-1000

Gamblers Anonymous
International Office
P.O. Box 17173
Los Angeles, CA 90017
(213) 386-8789

March of Dimes Birth Defects
    Foundation
1275 Mamaroneck Ave.
White Plains, NY 10605
(914) 428-7100

Narcotics Anonymous (NA)
World Service Office
P.O. Box 9999
Van Nuys, CA 91409
(818) 780-3951

National AIDS Hotline
(800) 342-2437

National Association of Children
    of Alcoholics (NACOA)
11426 Rockville Pike, Ste. 301
Rockville, MD 20852
(301) 468-0985

National Association of Social
    Workers
750 1st St. NE, Ste. 700
Washington, D.C. 20002
(800) 638-8799

National Center for Missing or
    Exploited Children
2101 Wilson Blvd., Ste. 550
Arlington, VA 22201
(800) 843-5678

National Child Abuse Hotline
(800) 422-4453

National Council on Alcoholism
and Drug Dependence
American Society of Addiction
Medicine
12 W. 21st St.
New York, NY 10010
(212) 206-6770

National Foundation for
Depressive Illness, Inc.
P.O. Box 2257
New York, NY 10016
(212) 620-7637
(800) 248-4344

National Runaway Switchboard
(800) 621-4000

Overeaters Anonymous (OA)
P.O. Box 44020
Rio Rancho, NM 87174
(505) 891-2664

Sex Addicts Anonymous
National Service Organization
P.O. Box 70949
Houston, TX 77270
(713) 869-4902

Sex and Love Addicts Anonymous
(SLAA)
P.O. Box 119
New Town Branch
Boston, MA 02258
(617) 332-1845

The National Easter Seal Society,
Inc.
230 W. Monroe St., Ste. 1800
Chicago, IL 60606-4802
(312) 726-6200

The Orton Dyslexia Society
724 York Rd.
Baltimore, MD 21204
(301) 296-0232
(800) 222-2123

United Cerebral Palsy Association,
Inc.
1522 K St. NW, Ste. 1112
Washington, D.C. 20005-1202
(202) 842-1266
(800) USA-5UCP

Women for Sobriety
Box 618
Quakertown, PA 18951
(215) 536-8026

NOTES

Acknowledgments

1. "Missing Piece Groups" are short-term educational/therapy groups that Leslie has conducted since 1984. Guidelines for running such groups are available from Leslie Drozd at 1001 Dove Street, Suite 140, Newport Beach, Calif. 92660.

2. In addition to those acknowledged in the beginning of the book we would both like to individually thank the following people:

    Claudia thanks: my dear friends and colleagues Sheila Fields, Victoria Danzig, Lynn Sanford, Jack Fahey, Susan Burden, Faith Sheehan, Drauzin Kern, Leslie Cuva-Wayne—all of whom have been a significant part of my life as *The Missing Piece* was created. Individually and collectively you've been my teachers.

    Leslie acknowledges with much appreciation, gratitude, and respect: Sheila Kelly, Doris DeHardt, the late Lu Blecher, and Francie Latimore for being an intimate part of her outer and inner circle of mentors. Thank yous also go to many others who have been a part of her circle of teachers: Betty Bosdell, Carolyn Conger, Brugh Joy, Richard Hycner, Margot Robinson, Sheila Benjamin, Marion Woodman, and Helen Watkins. A special thanks goes to Stephanie Covington, the first teacher to introduce Leslie to the idea of a "missing piece."

    And finally as part of Leslie's circle of professional connections she offers genuine gratitude to two highly acclaimed and respected attorneys, Brad Bunnin and Brandt Caudill.

    Leslie's circle of friends and colleagues over the past few years, many of whom have listened to her for hours about this book, some of whom have read, re-read, and given her feedback about portions of this book, and all of whom have supported her through this process include: Jean Angle, Jim Berry, Sandy Berry, Belle Chalmers, Gail Dickenson, Barbara Farran, Jean Fromm, Jeanne Harris, Anne Holman, Cathy Joseph, Tricia Kelly, Alyce LaViolette, John Land, Robin Lynterra, Linda McGee, Karen Rhyne, Laurie Roades, Patricia Rozee, Susan Shallit, Ruth Stafford, Liane Toal, Debbie Traves, Charlotte Winters, and Nancy Young.

None of this would have been possible without the love and support of Leslie's family—her mother, the original "puzzle-maker," for teaching the patience that it takes to put puzzles together one piece at a time, her father, who helped mold the determination and perseverance pieces of her Self puzzle, and Nana, who provided the glue that holds the puzzle together—unconditional love. Leslie's family today to whom this book is dedicated includes her children, Dan and Jaime, who themselves are in the midst of their own rite of passage into adulthood. "It's been a privilege, kids!"

"Thank you *all* for being a part of my circle of support—my 'external family.' Know that today you are all part of my 'internal family' as well."

CHAPTER 1: *Tools for the Journey*

1.   Ingri D'Aulaire, and Edgar Parin D'Aulaire, *D'Aulaire's Book of Greek Myths* (New York: Doubleday & Co., 1962), pp. 74–75.

2.   The specific material mentioned in this section about resiliency and children of divorce comes from a seminar called "Everything You Want to Know About Divorce," which Leslie teaches at the University of California Irvine Women's Opportunity Center with Karen A. Rhyne, Esq., certified family law specialist, and Victoria Felton-Collins, Ph.D., author and financial planner. Some of the material in this section was influenced by the works of Cantor and Bernay, Clair and Genest, Dugan and Coles, Garmezy, Sanford, and Werner and Smith. See Suggested Readings, Resiliency.

3.   The Twelve Step groups referred to here are those that operate under the steps, principles, and traditions of Alcoholics Anonymous. For more information about these and other support groups, see Suggested Readings, Twelve Step and Other Related Recovery Programs.

4.   The concept of a "safe environment" is delineated in Laura Davis and Ellen Bass's work *Courage to Heal: A Guide for Women Survivors of Child Sexual Abuse* (New York: Harper & Row, 1988). The concept of a "safe person" is an extrapolation from analytic works on "good enough" parenting.

5.   The "observer self" concept is based in part on the work of Hal and Sidra Stone. They call this concept "Awareness." See Suggested Readings, Voice Dialogue.

CHAPTER 2: *How Pieces End Up Missing*

1. The "sense of self" concept is rooted in analytic literature on self psychology by authors such as Kernberg, Kohut, and Masterson and from numerous cognitive psychologists as well. Much of our work on the dimensions of self has been influenced by:

N. Cantor and J. F. Kihlstrom, *Personality and Social Intelligence* (Englewood Cliffs, N.J.: Prentice-Hall, Inc., 1987).

Leslie M. Drozd and Constance J. Dalenberg, "Self as a Mediator in the Psychopathology of Children of Alcoholics," *International Journal of Addictions* 29, no. 14, December 1994.

V. G. Guidano, *Complexity of the Self: A Developmental Approach to Psychopathology and Therapy* (New York: The Guilford Press, 1987).

V. G. Guidano and G. Liotti, *Cognitive Processes and Emotional Disorders: A Structural Approach to Psychotherapy* (New York: The Guilford Press, 1983).

Otto F. Kernberg, *Borderline Conditions and Pathological Narcissism* (New York: Jason Aronson, 1976).

——. *Object Relations Theory and Clinical Psychoanalysis* (New York: Jason Aronson, 1976).

Heinz Kohut, *The Analysis of Self* (New York: International Universities Press, 1971).

——. *The Restoration of the Self* (New York: International Universities Press, 1977).

——. "The Search for the Self," in P. H. Ornstein, ed., *Selected Writings of Heinz Kohut: 1950–1978* (New York: International Universities Press, 1978).

——. Summarizing Reflections at UCLA Conference on "Progress in Self Psychology," October 5, 1981.

——. *How Does Analysis Cure?* (Chicago: University of Chicago Press, 1984).

Hazel Markus, "Self-Schemata and Processing Information about Self," *Journal of Personality and Social Psychology* 35, no. 2 (1977): 63–78.

——. "The Self in Thought and Memory," in D. M. Wegner and R. R. Vallacher, eds., *The Self in Social Psychology* (New York: Oxford University Press, 1980), pp. 102–30.

Hazel Markus et al., "Self Schemas and Gender," *Journal of Personality and Social Psychology* 42, no. 1 (1982): 38–50.

Hazel Markus, R. Hamill, and R. Sentis, "Thinking Fat: Self-Schemas for Body Weight and the Processing of Weight Relevant Information," unpublished manuscript, University of Michigan, 1979.

Hazel Markus and R. Sentis, "The Self in Social Information Processing," in J. Suls, ed., *Psychological Perspectives on the Self* (Hillsdale, N.J.: Lawrence Erlbaum Associates, Publishers, 1982), 1: 41–70.

James F. Masterson, *The Real Self* (New York: Brunner/Mazel, 1985).

James Masterson and Ralph Klein, eds., *Psychotherapy of the Disorders of the Self: The Masterson Approach* (New York: Brunner/Mazel, 1989).

R. B. Rogers, N. A. Kuiper, and W. S. Kirker, "Self-reference and the Encoding of Personal Information," *Journal of Personality and Social Psychology* 35 (1977): 677–88.

2. Erik Erikson, *Childhood and Society*, 2nd ed (New York: W. W. Norton, 1963).

3. The tasks of children to connect and to learn who they are are described in the psychoanalytic literature. See:

Lawrence E. Hedges, *Listening Perspectives in Psychotherapy* (Northdale, N. J.: Jason Aronson, Inc., 1991).

———. *Interpreting the Counter-Transference* (Northdale, N. J.: Jason Aronson, Inc., 1992).

———. *In Search of the Lost Mother of Infancy* (Northdale, N. J.: Jason Aronson, Inc., 1995).

———. *Working the Organizing Experience: Transforming Psychotic, Schizoid, and Autistic States* (Northdale, N. J.: Jason Aronson, Inc. 1995).

Daniel N. Stern, *Diary of a Baby: What Your Child Sees, Feels, and Experiences* (San Francisco: HarperCollins, 1990).

4. Laurie A. Roades, Ph.D., of Veterans Administration Hospital, Long Beach, Va., has made a tremendous contribution to the sections on power, gender, and cultural variables that affect self-development.

Much of what we have written about power and the development of one's sense of self in this chapter has been influenced by feminist writings. See:

Nancy Chodorow, *The Reproduction of Mothering* (Berkeley, Calif.: University of California Press, 1978).

Susan Faludi, *Backlash: The Undeclared War Against American Women* (New York: Crown Publishing, 1991).

Thelma Jean Goodrich, Cheryl Rampage, Barbara Ellman, Cheryl Halstrad, *Feminist Family Therapy: A Casebook* (New York: W. W. Norton & Company, 1988).

T. J. Goodrich, ed., *Women and Power: Perspectives in Family Therapy* (New York: W. W. Norton & Company, 1991).

Jean Baker Miller, *Toward a New Psychology of Women* (Boston: Beacon Press, 1976).

———. *Women and Power* (Wellesley, Mass.: Stone Center for Development Services and Studies, 1981).

Starhawk, *Truth or Dare: Encounters with Power, Authority, and Mystery* (San Francisco: Harper & Row, 1987).

5. This section on gender has been influenced by some of the following work:

R. W. Connell, *Gender and Power* (Palo Alto, Calif.: Stanford University Press, 1987).

Cynthia Fuchs Epstein, *Deceptive Distinctions: Sex, Gender, and the Social Order* (New York: Russell Sage Foundation, 1988).

R. T. Hare-Mustin, and J. Marecek, eds., *Making a Difference: Psychology and the Construction of Gender* (New Haven: Yale University Press, 1990).

6. The work that is being done on women's development is being done out of the Stone Center for Developmental Services and Studies, at Wellesley College in Massachusetts. The leading person known for her work in this area is Carol Gilligan:

Carol Gilligan, *In a Different Voice* (Cambridge, Mass.: Harvard University Press, 1982).

Her work, though, has been criticized by many, including:

S. D. Cochran and L. A. Peplau, "Value Orientations in Heterosexual Relationships," *Psychology of Women Quarterly* 9 (1985): 477–88.

C. Benton et al., "Is Hostility Linked with Affiliation Among Males with Achievement Among Females? A Critique of Pollak and Gilligan," *Journal of Personality and Social Psychology* 45 (1983): 1167–71.

7. This section has been very much influenced by the growing body of research on trauma. Researchers such as John Briere, Ph.D., at the University of Southern California, have major theoretical and research studies in progress. For this and other works on trauma, see Suggested Readings, Sexual Abuse.

8. These dimensions of self come from research studies by Markus and Drozd and Dalenberg. See Footnote 1.

CHAPTER 3: *Naming the Pieces*

1. This section on the multiplicity of selves has been influenced by the work of Watkins and Watkins, Stone and Stone, and Joy and Conger. See Suggested Readings, Healing and Spirituality; Multiplicity of Self; Voice Dialogue.

2. "Ego-state disorder" is a concept explored by Helen Watkins and John Watkins. See Suggested Readings, Multiplicity of Self.

3. American Psychiatric Association, *Diagnostic and Statistical Manual, Fourth Edition* (Washington, D.C.: APA Publishing, 1994), pp. 484–87.

4. The band analogy comes from a friend and colleague, Nancy Young, Ph.D., a clinical psychologist in Costa Mesa, California.

5. This exercise is adapted from a list of personality styles written about by

Aaron Beck, Ph.D., and associates. Christine Padesky, Ph.D., actively works with this model at the Center for Cognitive Therapy in Newport Beach, Calif. See:

Aaron Beck, Arthur Freeman and Associates, *Cognitive Therapy of Personality Disorders* (New York: Guilford Press, 1990).

Frank M. Dattilio and Christine Padesky, *Cognitive Therapy with Couples* (Sarasota, Fla.: Professional Resources Exchange, Inc., 1990).

6. Many of the "Common Parts" of self that are listed in "Stepping Stone 6" have been written about by Hal and Sidra Stone. See Suggested Readings, Voice Dialogue.

7. The section on gender has been influenced by Carol Tavris's work:
Carol Tavris, *The Mismeasure of Woman: Why Women Are Not the Better Sex, the Inferior Sex, or the Opposite Sex* (New York: Simon & Schuster, 1992).

8. The "I" or core part of self is similar to "ego" written about by the Stones. See Suggested Readings, Voice Dialogue.

9. *Schindler's List*, dir. and prod. Steven Spielberg, screenwrit. Steven Zaillian, Universal City Studios, Inc. Universal City, Calif. 1993.

CHAPTER 4: *Your Family Portrait*

1. The terms *family of choice* and *family of chance* are used by Sharon Wegscheider-Cruse, whose work was greatly influenced by Virginia Satir. In addition, Satir, Wegscheider-Cruse, and Claudia Black discuss the roles that children play in families. See Suggested Readings, Troubled Families.

2. Many of the questions about the "external family" are adapted from Bader and Pearson. See:
Ellyn Bader and Peter T. Pearson, *In Quest of the Mythical Mate: A Developmental Approach to Diagnosis and Treatment in Couples Therapy* (New York: Brunner/Mazel, 1988).
———. The Couples Institute, Menlo Park, Calif.

3. Wally Piper, *The Little Engine That Could* (New York: Platt & Munk, 1930).

4. Holly Near's autobiographical one-woman play, *Fire in the Rain*, has toured nationwide. It inspired this section about your family portrait coming alive in Technicolor. Holly Near's work is available through Redwood Cultural Work, 1-800-888-SONG.

CHAPTER 5: *The Spiral Path*

1. Janis Joplin, "Me and Bobby McGee," *Pearl* (New York: Master Sound/ Legacy, Columbia Records).

2. The concept of surrender in the therapeutic process was most clearly described by Harry M. Tiebout, M.D., nearly half a century ago:
Harry Tiebout, "The Act of Surrender in the Therapeutic Process: With Special Reference to Alcoholism," *Quarterly Journal of Studies on Alcohol* 14 (1949): 58–68.
————. "Surrender Versus Compliance in Therapy: With Special Reference to Alcoholism," *Quarterly Journal of Studies on Alcohol* 14 (1953): 58–68.

3. The original concept for the Spiral Path of recovery was presented in a lecture by Cathleen Brooks at California School of Professional Psychology, San Diego, 1983.
In addition the Spiral Path that we developed was influenced by the work of:
Julie Bowden and Herbert Gravitz, *Guide to Recovery: A Book for Adult Children of Alcoholics* (Holmes Beach, Fla.: Learning Publication, Inc., 1986).
Stephanie Brown, *Treating the Alcoholic: A Developmental Model of Recovery* (New York: Wiley & Sons, 1985).
————. *Treating Adult Children of Alcoholics: A Developmental Perspective* (New York: Wiley & Sons, 1988).
Trina Paulus, *Hope for the Flowers* (New York: Paulist Press, 1972).

4. The stories mentioned in this section—*The Velveteen Rabbit, The Little Prince,* Dorothy in *The Wizard of Oz,* and Johnny in *Finding the Green Stone*—can be found in the following books:
L. Frank Baum, *The Wizard of Oz* (Indianapolis: Bobbs-Merrill Company, 1900).
Antoine de Saint-Exupéry, *The Little Prince* (San Diego, Calif.: Harcourt Brace & World, 1943).
Alice Walker, *Finding the Green Stone* (Orlando, Fla.: Harcourt Brace Jovanovich, 1991).
Margery Williams, *The Velveteen Rabbit* (New York: Alfred A. Knopf, 1985).

5. Lenore Walker, *The Battered Woman* (New York: Harper & Row, 1979).

6. The American Psychological Association has studied this issue of repressed memory. A task force issued a preliminary report press release November 1994 and a preliminary report in February 1995. For more information please call or write A.P.A., Washington, D.C.

7. The Serenity Prayer was originally adapted from the words of Friedrich Otinger, an evangelical Pietist of the eighteenth century. The more recent adaptation has been traced to Richard Niebuhr, *The Serenity Prayer*, 1932.

8. Chuck C., *A New Pair of Glasses* (Irvine, Calif.: New-Look Publishing Company, 1984).

9. This term has been popularized by Susan Faludi. (See footnote 4, Chapter 2).

10. This T. S. Eliot poem, which can be found in the following reference, is one that was first heard by us at a workshop by Marion Woodman:
T. S. Eliot, *Collected Poems, 1909–1962: The Centenary Edition, Four Quartets, East Coker* (San Diego, Calif.: Harcourt Brace Jovanovich, 1988), lines 123–28, p. 186.

CHAPTER 6: *The First Look Inside*

1. Voice Dialogue and Active Imagination, which are both briefly introduced here, are referenced in Chapter 8 Notes.

2. Libby Roderick, "How Could Anyone Ever Tell You," *If You See a Dream* (Alaska: Turtle Island Records, 1990).

3. This quote is from a poster by Sister M. Madeliva, 1987, in which she has referenced Picasso.

4. The idea of changing the volume of a part came from Betty Bosdell, Vista, Calif.

CHAPTER 7: *Getting to Know You*

1. The "family of selves" referred to here comes from the clinical and theoretical literature on sense of self, and is referenced in chapter 2.

2. The movie *Koyaanisqatsi* is available on video:
Koyaanisqatsi: Life Out of Balance, Pacific Arts Video Records, Carmel, Calif., 1983.

3. The reference to *Truth or Dare* refers to a book by Starhawk previously referenced in chapter 2.

4. The "wild" part of self is modeled after the idea of the "wild woman" as delineated in Clarrisa Pinkola Estes's work:
Clarissa Pinkola Estés, *Women Who Run With the Wolves* (New York: Ballantine Books, 1992).

CHAPTER 8: *Coming Full Circle*

1. C. L. Barnhart and J. Stein, eds., *The American College Dictionary* (New York: Random House, 1968).

2. In her national best-seller, *You Just Don't Understand: Women and Men in Conversation*, Deborah Tannen, Ph.D., addresses the communication patterns between men and women. Underneath these problems are disowned parts of self, which "hook" the partner into a never-ending cycle of poor communication. See:

Deborah Tannen, *You Just Don't Understand: Women and Men in Conversation* (New York: Ballantine Books, 1990).

3. Sidra and Hal Stone in their seminal work on Voice Dialogue speak about dialogue between a facilitator and the person.

Hal Stone and Sidra Winkelman, *Embracing Ourselves: Voice Dialogue Manual* (Marina del Rey, Calif.: Devorss & Co., 1985).

We have extended this work to teaching readers to dialogue between not only themselves and a friend but between parts of self and the core of them, the "I", and between parts and other parts. See Suggested Readings, Voice Dialogue.

4. The idea of an "angel mother" comes from work done by Clarrisa Pinkola Estés in *Women Who Run With the Wolves*, which is referenced in chapter 7.

5. The concept of Active Imagination was developed by Robert Johnson. See:

Robert Johnson, *Inner Work: Using Dreams and Active Imagination for Personal Growth* (San Francisco: Hazelden, 1989).

CHAPTER 9: *Making It Happen*

1. The ideas for this three-act play came from a series of questions asked to children in a clinical setting: "If you could be any animal, what animal would you be—and what would you do if you were that animal? Then, if you had to be the animal that you'd hate to be, what animal would you have to be—and what would you have to do if you were that animal that you never ever wanted to be? And finally, if you couldn't be the animal you most want to be and you couldn't be the animal you hate, what animal would you be?" The original ideas for this projective technique came from the Menninger Foundation in Kansas.

2. The "birth of a woman" idea comes from the birth chant from Ellen's Story which is on a poster by Marca Scolo Rizzi of the It's All Right to Be a Woman Theatre. The saying on the poster is "I am a Woman Giving Birth to Myself."

3. This format of doing dreams has evolved from the following people's ideas and work: Stephanie Covington, Christine Downing, and Tricia Kelly.

CHAPTER 10: *The Empowered Self*

1. Joseph Campbell, *The Inner Reaches of Outer Space* (New York: Harper & Row, 1986).

2. Shel Silverstein, *The Missing Piece* (New York: Harper & Row, 1985).

3. This chapter has been influenced by Fritjof Capra, *The Turning Point: Science, Society, and the Rising Culture* (New York: Simon & Schuster, 1982).

CHAPTER 11: *The Spiritual Peace*

1. C. L. Barnhart and Jess Stein, eds., *The American College Dictionary* (New York: Random House, 1968).

2. This chapter has been influenced through an exchange of letters and tapes between Leslie Drozd (author) and Barbara Farran of Greensboro, N.C., 1991–1992.

3. Jeffrey Moses, *Oneness: Great Principles Shared By All Religions* (New York: Ballantine Books, 1989).

SUGGESTED READING

ANGER

LERNER, HARRIET G. *The Dance of Anger: A Woman's Guide to Changing the Patterns of Intimate Relationships.* New York: Harper & Row, 1986.

TAVRIS, CAROL. *Anger: The Misunderstood Emotion,* 2nd ed. New York: Simon & Schuster/Touchstone, 1989.

WEISINGER, HENDRIE. *Dr. Weisinger's Anger Work-out Book.* New York: Quill, 1985.

EATING DISORDERS

FALLON, P., S. KATZMAN, and C. WOOLEY, eds. *Feminist Perspectives on Eating Disorders.* New York: The Guilford Press, 1994.

HOLLIS, JUDI. *Fat and Furious.* New York: Ballantine Books, 1994.

———. *Fat Is a Family Affair.* New York: Harper & Row, 1988.

KANO, SUSAN. *Making Peace with Food: Freeing Yourself from the Diet/Weight Obsession.* New York: Harper & Row, 1989.

ORBACH, SUSAN. *Fat Is a Feminist Issue I, II.* New York: Berkley Publishing Group, 1987.

ROTH, GENEEN. *Feeding the Hungry Heart.* New York: New American Library, 1982.

———. *Breaking Free from Compulsive Eating.* New York: New American Library, 1985.

———. *Why Weight? A Guide to Ending Compulsive Eating.* New York: New American Library, 1989.

———. *When Food Is Love: Exploring the Relationship Between Eating and Intimacy.* New York: Dutton, 1991.

WOODMAN, MARION. *The Owl Was a Baker's Daughter: Obesity, Anorexia Nervosa, and the Repressed Feminine*. Toronto: Inner City Books, 1980.

GRIEF AND LOSS

BLOOMFIELD, HAROLD H., and PETER MCWILLIAMS. *How to Heal Depression*. Los Angeles: Prelude Press, 1994.

BUSCAGLIA, LEO. *The Fall of Freddie The Leaf: A Story for All Ages*. New York: Slack, Inc. 1982.

COLGROVE, MELBA, HAROLD H. BLOOMFIELD, and PETER MCWILLIAMS. *How to Survive the Loss of a Love*. Los Angeles: Prelude Press, 1976, 1991.

———. *Surviving, Healing, & Growth: How to Survive the Loss of a Love: The Workbook*. Los Angeles, Prelude Press, 1991.

FERGUSON, DON. *The Lion King*. New York: The Walt Disney Company, 1994.

KINGMA, DAPHNE ROSE. *Coming Apart: Why Relationships End and How to Live Through the Ending of Yours*. New York: Ballantine Books, 1987.

KÜBLER-ROSS, ELISABETH. *On Death and Dying*. New York: Macmillan, 1969.

MIDDLETON-MOZ, JANE, and LORIE DWINELL. *After the Tears*. Deerfield Beach, Fla.: Health Communications, 1986.

OSHERSON, SAMUEL. *Finding Our Fathers: How a Man's Life Is Shaped by His Relationship with His Father*. New York: Ballantine Books, 1986.

VIORST, JUDITH. *Necessary Losses: The Loves, Illusions, Dependencies and Impossible Expectations That All of Us Have to Give Up in Order to Grow*. New York: Ballantine Books, 1986.

HEALING AND SPIRITUALITY

CARLSON, RICHARD and BENJAMIN SHIELD, eds., *Healers on Healing*. Los Angeles: Jeremy Tarcher, 1989.

CHRIST, CAROL P., and JUDITH PLASKOW, eds. *Woman Spirit Rising: A Feminist Reader in Religion*. San Francisco: HarperCollins, 1992.

CONGER, CAROLYN, with music by Michael Sterns. *Sacred Pool*. Marina del Rey, Calif.: M'Ocean Studio, 1985. (800-833-0611).

———. with music by Michael Sterns. *Vision Quest*. Marina del Rey, Calif.: M'Ocean Studio, 1990. (800-833-0611).

DREHER, DIANE. *The Tao of Inner Peace* (formerly titled *The Tao of Peace: A Guide to Inner and Outer Peace*). New York: HarperCollins, 1990.

DUREK, JUDITH. *Circle of Stones: Woman's Journey to Herself*. San Diego: LuraMedia, 1989.

HAMPLE, STUART, and ERIC MARSHALL. *Children's Letters to God: The New Collection*. New York: Workman Publishing, 1991.

JOY, BRUGH W. *Joy's Way: A Map for the Transformational Journey.* Los Angeles: Jeremy Tarcher, 1979.

——. *Avalanche: Heretical Reflections on the Dark and the Light.* New York: Ballantine Books, 1990.

KARPINSKI, GLORIA D. *Where Two Worlds Touch: Spiritual Rites of Passage.* New York: Ballantine Books, 1990.

MOORE, THOMAS. *Care of the Soul.* New York: HarperCollins, 1992.

MOSES, JOSEPH. *Oneness: Great Principles Shared by All Religions.* New York: Ballantine Books, 1989.

NEAR, HOLLY. *The Great Peace March.* New York: Henry Holt & Company, 1993.

PECK, M. SCOTT. *The Road Less Traveled.* New York: Simon & Schuster, 1978.

REDFIELD, JAMES. *The Celestine Prophecy: An Adventure.* New York: Warner Books, 1993.

SULLIVAN, DEIDRE, ed. *What Do We Mean When We Say God?* New York: Doubleday, 1990.

TOOR, DJOHARIAH. *The Road by the River: A Healing Journey for Women.* San Francisco: Harper & Row, 1987.

WOODMAN, MARION. *The Pregnant Virgin: A Process of Psychological Transformation.* Toronto: Inner City Books, 1985.

INNER CHILD

ABRAMS, JEREMIAH, ed. *Reclaiming the Inner Child.* Los Angeles: Jeremy Tarcher, 1990.

CAPACCHIONE, LAURA. *The Power of Your Other Hand.* North Hollywood, Calif.: Newcastle Publishing, 1988.

——. *Recovery of Your Inner Child: The Highly Acclaimed Method for Liberating Your Inner Self.* New York: Simon & Schuster, 1991.

TAYLOR, CATHRYN L. *The Inner Child Workbook.* Los Angeles, Calif.: Jeremy Tarcher, 1991.

WHITFIELD, CHARLES, M.D. *Healing the Child Within.* Deerfield Beach, Fla.: Health Communications, 1987.

——. *A Gift to Myself: A Workbook and Guide to Healing My Child Within.* Deerfield Beach, Fla.: Health Communications, 1989.

MULTIPLICITY OF SELF

WATKINS, JOHN G., and HELEN H. WATKINS. "The Theory and Practice of Ego-State Therapy." In H. Grayson, ed., *Short-Term Approaches to Psychotherapy.* New York: Human Sciences Press, 1979, pp. 176–220.

——. "The Management of Malevolent Ego States in Multiple Personality

Disorder." *Dissociation: Progress in Disassociative Order*, vol. 1 (1988): 67–72.

——. "Hypnosis and Ego-State Therapy." In P. A. Keller and S. R. Heyman, eds., *Innovations in Clinical Practice*. Sarasota, Fla.: Professional Resource Exchange, pp. 23–37.

WATKINS, H. "Ego-State Therapy: An Overview." *American Journal of Clinical Hypnosis*. 35: 232–40.

WATKINS, HELEN H. "Ego-State Therapy." Chapter 22 in Watkins, J. G., *The Therapeutic Self*. New York: Human Sciences Press, 1978.

RECOVERY BOOKS

BLACK, CLAUDIA. *Repeat After Me*. Denver, Colo.: MAC Publishing, 1985.

——. *It Will Never Happen To Me*. New York: Ballantine Books, 1987.

——. *Double Duty: Dual Dynamics Within the Chemically Dependent Home*. New York: Ballantine Books, 1990.

——. *It's Never Too Late to Have a Happy Childhood*. New York: Ballantine Books, 1990.

——. *Changing Course: Turning Points to Recovery*. Denver, Colo.: MAC Publishing, 1993.

BRADSHAW, JOHN. *Healing the Shame That Binds You*. Deerfield Beach, Fla.: Health Communications, 1988.

——. *Bradshaw on The Family: A Revolutionary Way of Self-Discovery*. Deerfield Beach, Fla.: Health Communications, 1988.

FARMER, STEVEN. *Adult Children of Abusive Parents*. New York: Ballantine Books, 1989.

FOSSUM, MERLE A., and MARILYN J. MASON. *Facing Shame: Families in Recovery*. New York: W. W. Norton, 1986.

MOONEY, AL J., ARLENE EISENBERG, and HOWARD EISENBERG. *The Recovery Book*. New York: Workman Publishing, 1992.

SATIR, VIRGINIA. *People-Making*. Mountain View, Calif.: Science and Behavior Books, 1972.

WEGSCHEIDER, SHARON. *Another Chance*. Palo Alto, Calif.: Science and Behavior Books, 1981.

RESILIENCY

CANTOR, DOROTHY, and TONI BERNAY with JEAN STOESS. *Women in Power: The Secrets of Leadership*. New York: Houghton Mifflin Company, 1992.

CLAIR, D., and M. GENEST. "Variables Associated with the Adjustment of Offspring of Alcoholic Fathers." *Journal of Studies on Alcohol*. 48, no. 4 (1987): 345–55.

DUGAN, TIMOTHY F., and ROBERT COLES, ed. *The Child in Our Times:*

Studies in the Development of Resiliency. New York: Brunner/Mazel, 1989.

GARMEZY, N. "Stress-Resilient Children: The Search for Protective Factors," in J. E. Stevenson, ed. *Recent Research in Developmental Psychopathology: Journal of Child Psychology and Psychology and Psychiatry Book Supplements No. 4.* Tarrytown, N.Y.: Pergamon Press, 1984, pp. 213–33.

SANFORD, LINDA T. *Strong at the Broken Places.* New York: Avon Books, 1992.

WERNER, E. E. and R. S. SMITH. *Vulnerable but Invincible: A Study of Resilient Children.* New York: McGraw-Hill, 1982.

WOLIN, STEVEN J., M.D., and SYBIL WOLIN. *The Resilient Self.* New York: Villard Books, 1993.

RITUALS

ARDINGER, BARBARA. *A Woman's Book of Rituals & Celebrations.* San Rafael, Calif.: New World Library, 1992.

COLES, ROBERT. *The Spiritual Life of Children.* Boston: Houghton Mifflin Company, 1990.

FEINSTEIN, DAVID, and PEG ELLIOT MAYO. *Rituals for Living and Dying: How We Can Turn Loss and the Fear of Death into an Affirmation of Life.* San Francisco: HarperCollins, 1990.

IMBER-BLACK, EVAN, and JANINE ROBERTS. *Ritual for Our Times.* New York: HarperCollins, 1992.

SELF-PARENTING

PAUL, MARGARET. *Inner Bonding.* San Francisco: HarperCollins, 1992.

POLLARD, JOHN K. *Self Parenting: The Complete Guide to Your Inner Conversations.* Malibu, Calif.: Generic Human Studies Publishing, 1987.

SEX ABUSE

American Psychological Association. *Interim Report of the Working Group On Investigation of Memories of Childhood Abuse.* Washington, D.C.: Public Affairs Office, November 11, 1994.

BASS, ELLEN, and LAURA DAVIS. *Courage to Heal: A Guide for Women Survivors of Child Sexual Abuse.* New York: Harper & Row, 1988.

BLUME, E. SUE. *Secret Survivors: Uncovering Incest and Its Aftereffects in Women.* New York: John Wiley & Sons, 1990.

BRIERE, JOHN. *Therapy for Adults Molested as Children: Beyond Survival.* New York: Springer, 1989.

COURTOIS, CHRISTINE. *Healing the Incest Wound: Adult Survivors in Therapy*. New York: W. W. Norton, 1988.

CREWDSON, JOHN. *By Silence Betrayed: Sexual Abuse of Children in America*. New York: Harper & Row, 1988.

DAVIS, LAURA. *Courage to Heal Workbook*. New York: Harper & Row, 1988.

DOLAN, YVONNE M. *Resolving Sexual Abuse: Solution-Focused Therapy and Ericksonian Hypnosis for Adult Survivors*. New York: W. W. Norton, Inc., 1991.

ENGEL, BEVERLY. *The Right to Innocence: Healing the Trauma of Childhood Sexual Abuse*. New York: Ballantine Books, 1989.

FINKELHOR, DAVID. *New Theory and Research*. New York: Free Press, 1984.

——. ed. *A Sourcebook on Child Sexual Abuse*. Beverly Hills, Calif.: Sage Publications, 1986.

GIL, ELIANA. *Outgrowing The Pain: A Book For and About Adults Abused as Children*. Walnut Creek, Calif.: Launch Press, 1983.

HEDGES, LAWRENCE E. *Remembering, Repeating, and Working Through Childhood Trauma: The Psychodynamics of Recovered Memories, Multiple Personality, Ritual Abuse, Incest, Molestation, and Abduction*. Northdale, N. J.: Jason Aronson, Inc., 1994.

LEW, MICHAEL. *Victims No Longer*. New York: Harper & Row, 1990.

LOFTUS, ELIZABETH L. "The Reality of Repressed Memories." *American Psychologist*. 48 (1993): 518–37.

MALTZ, WENDY. *The Sexual Healing Journey: A Guide For Survivors of Sexual Abuse*. San Francisco: HarperCollins, 1991.

National Committee for Prevention of Child Abuse. *NCPCA Fact Sheet 14: Substance Abuse and Child Abuse*. Chicago, Ill., 1989.

ROTH, NICKI. *Integrating the Shattered Self: Psychotherapy with Adult Incest Survivors*. N. J.: Jason Aronson, Inc., 1993.

SCHARFF, JILL SAVEGE, and DAVID E. SCHARFF. *Object Relations Therapy of Physical and Sexual Trauma*. N. J.: Jason Aronson, Inc., 1994.

SGORI, S., ed. *Vulnerable Populations: Evaluation and Treatment of Sexually Abused Children and Adult Survivors*. Lexington, Mass.: Lexington, 1988.

SHENGOLD, LEONARD L. *Soul Murder: The Effects of Childhood Abuse and Deprivation*. New York: Ballantine Books, 1989.

YAPKO, MICHAEL D. *Suggestions of Abuse: True and False Memories of Childhood Sexual Trauma*. New York: Simon & Schuster, 1994.

TRAUMA

BARNETT, OLA W. and ALYCE D. LAVIOLETTE. *It Could Happen to Anyone: Why Battered Women Stay*. Newbury Park, Calif.: Sage Publications, 1993.

GROVE, DAVID J., and B. I. PANZER. *Resolving Traumatic Memories: Meta-*

phors and Symbols in Psychotherapy. New York: Irvington Publishers, Inc., 1989.

HERMAN, JUDITH. *Trauma and Recovery.* New York: Basic Books, 1992.

JANOFF-BULMAN, RONNIE. *Shattered Assumptions: Towards a New Psychology of Trauma.* New York: The Free Press, Inc., 1992.

MILLER, ALICE. *The Drama of the Gifted Child: The Search for the True Self.* (Formerly called *Prisoners of Childhood*). New York: Basic Books, 1981.

Some of the most exciting and ground-breaking work in the field of trauma and anxiety disorders has been pioneered by Francine Shapiro, Ph.D., from the Mental Research Institute in Palo Alto, California.

SHAPIRO, FRANCINE. *Eye Movement Desensitization on Reprocessing Basic Principles, Protocols, and Procedures.* New York: Guilford Press, 1995.

TWELVE STEP AND OTHER RELATED RECOVERY PROGRAMS

Al-Anon Family Groups. *From Survival to Recovery.* New York: World Services Organization, 1994.

Alcoholics Anonymous. *The Big Book of Alcoholics Anonymous, 3rd Edition.* New York: World Services Organization, 1976.

Alcoholics Anonymous. *Twelve Steps and Twelve Traditions.* New York: World Services Organization, 1981.

COVINGTON, STEPHANIE. *A Woman's Way Through the Twelve Steps.* Center City, Minnesota: Hazelden, 1994.

KASL, CHARLOTTE D. *One Road, Many Journeys.* New York: HarperCollins, 1992.

Recovery Publications. *Twelve Steps: A Way Out.* San Diego: Recovery Publications, 1987.

SWAN, BONITA. *The Thirteen Steps: An Empowerment Process for Women.* San Francisco: Spinsters/Aunt Lute Book Company, 1989.

KILPATRICK, JEAN. *Women for Sobriety.* Box 618, Quakertown, Pa. 18951 (215-536-8026).

VOICE DIALOGUE

STAMBOLIEV, ROBERT. *The Energetics of Voice Dialogue: An In-Depth Exploration of the Energetic Aspects of Transformational Psychology.* Mendocino, Calif.: LifeRhythm, 1992.

STONE, HAL, and SIDRA WINKELMAN. *Embracing Ourselves: Voice Dialogue Manual.* Marina del Rey, Calif.: Devorss and Co., 1985.

———. *Embracing Each Other: Relationship as Teacher, Healer & Guide.* San Rafael, Calif.: New World Library, 1989.

———. *Embracing the Inner Critic: Turning Self-criticism into a Creative Asset.* San Francisco: HarperCollins, 1993.

INDEX